The **XSL** companion

Second Edition

Neil Bradley

ADDISON-WESLEY

An imprint of Pearson Education
London • Boston • Indianapolis • New York • Mexico City • Toronto • Sydney • Tokyo • Singapore
Hong Kong • Cape Town • New Delhi • Madrid • Paris • Amsterdam • Munich • Milan

PEARSON EDUCATION LIMITED

Head Office:
Edinburgh Gate
Harlow CM20 2JE
Tel: +44 (0)1279 623623
Fax: +44 (0)1279 431059

London Office:
128 Long Acre
London WC2E 9AN
Tel: +44 (0)20 7447 2000
Fax: +44 (0)20 7447 2170
Websites: www.it-minds.com
www.aw.com/cseng

First published in Great Britain in 2002

© Pearson Education Limited 2002

The right of Neil Bradley to be identified as the Author of this work has been asserted by him in
accordance with the Copyright, Designs and Patents Act 1988.

ISBN 0 201 77083 0

British Library Cataloguing in Publication Data
A CIP catalogue record for this book can be obtained from the British Library.

Library of Congress Cataloging in Publication Data
Bradley, Neil.
    The XSL Companion / Neil Bradley.-- 2nd ed.
      p. cm.
    Includes bibliographical references and index.
    ISBN 0-201-77083-0 (pbk.)
      1. XML (Document Markup Language) I. Title.

    QA76.76.H94 B773 2002
    005.7'2--dc21

                                                                                    2002025588

10 9 8 7 6 5 4 3 2 1

Typeset by the Author
Printed and bound in Great Britain by Biddles Ltd of Guildford and King's Lynn

The Publishers' policy is to use paper manufactured from sustainable forests.

Preface

This book covers a family of standards developed by the W3C (*World Wide Web Consortium*). These standards emerged out of a proposal for a stylesheet language, submitted in 1997, which was to be called **XSL** (*eXtensible Stylesheet Language*). However, during its gestation this proposal was pulled apart and became three separate standards. **XPath** defines a mechanism for locating information in XML documents, and has many other uses beyond its role in formatting documents. **XSLT** (*XSL Transformations*) provides a means for transforming XML documents into other data formats, including (but not limited to) formatting-focussed markup languages. Finally, the term 'XSL' is now properly used only to name a standard for embedding XML-based formatting information in documents.

Due to their shared history, these three standards are still related and are used together to provide a means to format XML documents, especially in preparation for the particular demands of presentation on print media. The XSLT standard includes XPath constructs in a number of places, and can be used to convert an XML document that conforms to an arbitrary document model into an XSL document. But each standard can also be used alone or with alternative technologies. Because the XSL formatting language is less mature than XSLT, and not yet well supported, XSLT is initially being used primarily to convert XML documents in to **HTML** (or XHTML) documents, possibly enhanced with **CSS** (*Cascading Style Sheets*) styling instructions. Both of these formats are therefore explained in depth.

When formatted documents have to be edited before they can be presented or printed, it is necessary to use a word processor or DTP package, but none of these packages yet support XSL as an import format. Two popular import formats existing today are **RTF** (Rich Text Format) and **Quark Tags**. Issues concerned with the use of XSLT to convert XML documents into these two formats are discussed.

Second edition

Since the release of the first edition of this book, almost two years ago, much has happened to warrant the creation of a second edition.

The XSLT standard is now firmly established as a companion to XML for all manner of transformation needs, and experience of using this standard to solve serious practical problems has resulted in more explanatory material and suggestions on how to exploit it to the full.

Because XSLT makes heavy use of XPath, its popularity has also helped establish XPath as *the* way to navigate through XML documents. XPath is now being incorporated into XML databases as a query language. It therefore deserves more prominence and now has a section of the book to itself.

The XSL standard has now progressed to Recommendation status. This edition covers the final release.

Acknowledgements

Thanks to Rubus (www.rubus.com) for support in developing this book, and to Katherin Ekstrom at Pearson Education. The many individuals who have worked together to develop the standards covered in this book richly deserve acknowledgement. Finally, thanks once again to Adobe for *FrameMaker+SGML* (which was used both in the preparation and publication of this book).

Feedback

Comments and suggestions for a possible future edition are welcomed. They should be sent to the author at ***neil@bradley.co.uk***. Updates, additions and corrections can be obtained from the author's Web page at ***http://www.bradley.co.uk***.

Neil Bradley
April 2002

Contents

1. Using this book

Assumptions

Some familiarity with XML markup concepts is assumed. The reader should at least be comfortable with the syntax, scope and purpose of XML elements and attributes, with comments and processing instructions, and to a lesser extent with entities and document type definitions (DTDs).

Book structure

After Chapter 2, this book is divided into four major parts. The first three of these are each devoted to one of the standards that arose out of the original proposal for XSL.

The first part, *Transformations using XSLT*, covers the features of the XSLT language. These chapters should be read in the order presented, because they each build on examples from previous chapters. In particular, Chapter 3 and Chapter 4 should be read first.

The second part, *XPath expressions*, covers the XPath standard in detail. All of the chapters in this part should be read in the order given.

The third part, *Formatting with XSL*, describes the XSL standard in depth, with chapters that work down from page templates to individual characters.

Finally, the *References* part includes information on other formatting and style-sheet languages, explains how to analyze XML DTDs and lists the characters in the popular ISO 8859/1 character set.

Style conventions

A name or term that appears in **bold style** has specific meaning in XSL, XPath, XSLT or a related technology, and is emphasized in this way on each significant occurrence in the text (but not necessarily on its first occurrence). Note that the highlighted occurrences are referenced in the *Index*.

Words displayed in *italic style* are either quotations or just used for emphasis.

Quoted text appearing in a mono spaced font, '`like this`', represents example data (usually an XSL or XML fragment). Substantial examples are separated from the text thus:

```
This is a sample line of text.
```

Three dots ('...') are used to denote omitted material, such as missing attributes and element content:

```
<template ...>...</template>
```

When italic styling is used in a code fragment, this indicates that the text never appears as seen, but is replaced by something more concrete (the word 'expression' below is a substitute for any real XPath expression):

```
<template match="expression">...</template>
```

Although bold typeface is often used to emphasize part of an example, it does not have the significance described above. Emphasis is used in this context to highlight any part of the example of particular interest:

```
The only part of this sentence of particular significance
is this part, the remainder is only here to give some con-
text.
```

Many examples consist of three parts, including a fragment of an XSLT stylesheet, preceded by source data and followed by the output that would result from processing this data according to the instructions in the template. The source and result are indented to highlight this arrangement:

```
    <source>original data</source>


<template match="source">
  <text>output from stylesheet</text>
</template>


    output from stylesheet
```

Examples of presented material (printed or displayed output) appear as follows:

    This is presented material.

For the sake of clarity, element and attribute names are capitalized in the text ('the Name element contains a name'), but are usually lower-case in XML fragment examples, ('`<name>Smith</name>`'), despite the fact that names are case-sensitive in the XML standard. When elements and attributes defined in a specific DTD or schema are shown, the letter-case used in examples strictly follows the requirements of that document model.

Note that mid-Atlantic spelling conventions are used in the text (due to the nationality of the author), but some terms and keywords appear with US spelling when consistency with a standard described in this book is important. For example, 'centre' is used in the text but 'center' is a parameter value in the HTML table-formatting model.

2. Background concepts

XML markup divides a document into identifiable fragments that can be located, analysed, extracted, manipulated for software consumption, and formatted and re-formatted for human consumption. But XML cannot achieve any of these things alone; other technologies are required to unleash this potential. This chapter introduces a set of related technologies that are used to locate, transform and format XML document structures.

Transformation languages

XML is not a scripting or programming language; as a markup language it is essentially a very passive technology. XML markup creates intelligent documents that are ready to be exploited, but the XML standard says nothing about how this can happen. When XML is used as a software configuration file format, or as a data exchange format, then exploitation simply takes the form of parsing the data. But almost all other applications of XML require XML document structures to be **transformed** in some way.

Consider the following XML document, which contains information about a book. This document includes the title of the book, the name of the author and the name of the publisher:

```
<book>
  <title>My Life</title>
  <author>J. Smith</author>
  <publisher>ACME Publishing</publisher>
  . . .
  . . .
</book>
```

The owner of this document may send it to somebody else who intends to import the data into an application that is sensitive to a different document model. This application might, for example, expect XML data that takes the following form, where both the names of the elements and the order in which they occur are different to that shown in the example above:

```
<BOOK-ENTRY>
  <PUB>ACME Publishing</PUB>
  <BOOK-TITLE>My Life</BOOK-TITLE>
  <BOOK-AUTHOR>J. Smith</BOOK-AUTHOR>
</BOOK-ENTRY>
```

Clearly, the recipient of the original XML document needs to be able to **transform** the document into this other format. Theoretically, this could be done by loading the original document into memory and directly manipulating the element and text structures, but in practice it is far more practical to create a process that takes the source document as input and creates the new document as output.

XML data can be converted into other formats using a **transformation language**. Transformation languages have existed for many years, and tools originally developed to transform **SGML** (Standard Generalized Markup Language) documents have been adapted to work with XML too. Some of these languages are essentially cut-down programming languages that have particular strengths in reading, analysing, manipulating and outputting XML data. Other transformation languages are more passive, consisting of a set of templates that react to (or are 'triggered' by) the existence of specific elements in the source XML as they are encountered during parsing of the document. Each template then specifies the output that should be generated. (This second approach is more relevant to the subject of this book.)

The one thing that all of these transformation languages have in common is that they are proprietory (though some general purpose scripting languages, such as Perl, have recently gained XML-sensitive extensions that allow them to act as transformation languages). It would be more desirable to standardize on a single language, supported by many vendors, thus allowing maximum flexibility in the choice of tools and greatly increasing the ability of experts to transfer their skills to new products. It would also be desirable for such a language to be usable by non-programmers (the standards described in this book achieve this goal).

Formatting languages

XML is a markup language with a distinguished heritage. It is essentially a subset of the more complex SGML language, an ISO standard that was itself based on the earlier **GML** language, and the key feature they have in common is that they focus on the task of describing the content of a document. But most markup languages specify how the content is to be presented, rather than describe the document content.

Originally, the majority of these **formatting languages** were developed by the creators of typesetting machines, and were therefore closely tied to the capabilities of specific devices. When general purpose computers became capable of preparing documents for print, more open languages began to appear, including **TROFF** (Text Run OFF) and T_EX. More recently, DTP applications and word processors have acquired the ability to import and export document text, complete with formatting information, of which **RTF** (Rich Text Format) is perhaps the most widely known today. The following fragment is formatted using RTF **markup** tags:

```
This is a paragraph in an \bRTF\b0 document.\par
```

At RTF-sensitive word processor can read this text and interpret the embedded commands, so detecting the bold word and the end of the paragraph:

This is a paragraph in an **RTF** document.

Yet the most widely known markup language today serves a different purpose entirely. The **HTML** (HyperText Markup Language) format emerged as a practical method for including formatting information in hypertext-linked documents that are to be presented in Web browsers:

```
<P>This is a paragraph in an <B>HTML</B> document.</P>
```

A Web browser would interpret the tags in the example above, finding both a paragraph and a bold word, and render the text accordingly:

This is a paragraph in an **HTML** document.

HTML is remakably similar to the old-fashioned typesetting machine languages. Perhaps more surprisingly, HTML document markup resembles XML document markup. Indeed, the latest version of HTML is called **XHTML** and is a true application of XML (while HTML itself is an SGML application, which breaks some of the stricter XML syntax and grammar rules).

Stylesheets

Most XML documents do *not* conform to a document model that could be described as a formatting language. XML tags do not, as a general rule, specify the formatting to be applied to the text they contain (though some applications of XML, such as XHTML, deliberately break this convention). While the following example clearly identifies the title, author and publisher of a book, it contains no clues as to how these items should be presented:

```
<book>
  <title>My Life</title>
  <author>J. Smith</author>
  <publisher>ACME Publishing</publisher>
</book>
```

Formatting details therefore need to be obtained from another source. This source could be a data file, called a **stylesheet**, that contains a set of rules, each one specifying how a specific element in the document is to be presented.

Stylesheets have been around for many years and differ widely in capability. A typical stylesheet is able to specify the font to use, the size of the text, any styles to be applied to the text (such as bold emphasis), and the size of gaps between paragraphs. Some stylesheets are also able to automatically number items in a list, add prefix text (such as 'Warning:' before the content of a Warning element), and divide a page into header, body and footer regions. Advanced stylesheets are even able to resequence and reuse information (typically in order to build content lists and indexes).

Using a stylesheet, the XML fragment above could be formatted in the following way:

Even if stylesheets were not really needed to format XML documents, they would still be very useful. An important benefit of using stylesheets is that one can be substituted for another, in order to present the material in a different way. This may be done to take advantage of the features of a different publishing medium, or to attract a new audience with special requirements:

Proof that this is a desirable concept can be demonstrated by the fact that style-sheets are widely used with HTML documents, which can also be presented reasonably well without one. The **CSS** (*Cascading Style Sheets*) standard is a popular companion to HTML (see Chapter 29).

Most stylesheets are quite complex. But even simple stylesheets need a mechanism for specifying where each new rule begins, and for matching an element name to an output style. Stylesheets must therefore conform to a syntax specification that is defined in a **stylesheet language**. For example, the syntax of the CSS stylesheet language involves the use of curly brackets, colons and semi-colons. The following CSS rule defines a font size for paragraphs and maps the HTML Emphasis element to bold styling:

```
P    { font-size: 10pt; }
EM   { font-weight: bold; }
```

The 'official' stylesheet language for use with SGML (the precursor of XML) is **DSSSL** (Document Style and Semantics Specification Language). DSSSL is based on the SCHEME computer language, which is powerful but difficult to read.

Some older stylesheet languages adopted an SGML-based syntax. An application-specific SGML-based stylesheet language was used to format this book, which was created using Adobe *FrameMaker+SGML*. The paragraphs in this book (including this one) were formatted by the following template, which specifies that all paragraphs are to be spaced consistently and presented in Times 10pt:

```
<Element>
  <Tag>Para</Tag>
  <Container>
    ...
    <TextFormatRules>
      <AllContextRules>
        <ParagraphFormatting>
          <PropertiesBasic>
            <ParagraphSpacing>
              <SpaceAbove>9pt</SpaceAbove>
            </ParagraphSpacing>
            <LineSpacing>
              <Height>12.5pt</Height>
            </LineSpacing>
          </PropertiesBasic>
          <PropertiesFont>
            <Family>Times</Family>
            <Size>10pt</Size>
          </PropertiesFont>
          ...
        </ParagraphFormatting>
      </AllContextRules>
    </TextFormatRules>
  </Container>
</Element>
```

Most of the SGML element names in the example above are clearly self-describing. For example, the value of the SpaceAbove element within the ParagraphSpacing element specifies the amount of space to create above each paragraph.

It should not be surprising to find that XML is now being used as the base syntax for newer stylesheet languages. It is at least as suitable as SGML for this task. A stylesheet language based on XML can be created, validated, displayed and manipulated using XML tools.

The XSL standards

The title of this book refers to the acronym 'XSL', which is short for eXtensible Stylesheet Language. This name was originally chosen as the title of a single W3C specification that covered all of the major technologies discussed in this book. But things became a little more complicated during the development of these technologies, and the final specification was divided into three separate standards: XSL, XSLT and XPath. The respective roles of these standards can be explained in isolation, before showing how they work together to perform the task of formatting XML documents.

XSL

The XSL standard describes a new XML-based formatting language. Conceptually, this makes XSL similar to XHTML. However, XSL element and attribute names are very different, and this language is much more powerful. In the following example, the Block element contains a text block, such as a paragraph, and the Inline element contains a range of text to be styled in a specific way (in this case, to add bold emphasis):

```
<block>This is an <inline font-weight="bold">XSL</inline>
document.</block>
```

This is an **XSL** document.

It was never intended that users would create an XSL document directly. The real purpose of this language is to serve as a delivery format, to a typesetting engine or an advanced Web browser, for data that originates in another, more generalized XML format. However, it could also become a popular export and interchange format for DTP software.

XSLT

XSLT (*XSL Transformations*) is, as its full name suggests, a transformation language. Using XSLT, XML documents can be transformed into new XML documents with a different structure, perhaps conforming to a different DTD or XML Schema model. Element content can be reused, suppressed, repositioned, sorted, split or merged with other content, and even transformed into attribute values.

As before, the letters 'SL' in XSLT stand for 'Stylesheet Language'. XSLT therefore claims to be both a transformation language and a stylesheet language. This is not as odd as it first appears. A transformation language can be considered to be a stylesheet language as well, when that it is being used to create documents that conform to a formatting language. The only difference between XSLT and most other stylesheet languages is that the result of applying a stylesheet is a new document that contains the information needed for it to be presented. The task of presenting the document simply occurs later.

XSLT is an example of the second kind of transformation language (it is not a programming language), and therefore consists of templates that are triggered by the presence of specific elements in the source document. The templates may contain replacement element tags and 'boilerplate' text (text that is always wanted, so does not need to explicitly included in the source file).

At the time of writing, the most popular use of XSLT is to convert XML documents into XHTML documents, or less strictly tagged HTML documents (discussed in Chapter 28). The XSLT stylesheet fragment below formats an XML fragment, containing a paragraph with an emphasized term, into equivalent XHTML constructs:

```
<paragraph>A <emphasis>Highlighted</emphasis>
term</paragraph>


<template match="paragraph">
  <html:P>
    <apply-templates/>
  </html:P>
</template>

<template match="emphasis">
  <html:B>
    <apply-templates/>
  </html:B>
</template>


  <P>A <B>Highlighted</B> term</P>
```

XSLT can also convert XML documents into arbitrary text-based data formats, including such formatting languages as TROFF, T$_E$X and RTF (see Chapter 30), but also into other data formats that have nothing to do with document presentation.

XPath

The **XPath** standard defines a general purpose **expression language** for interrogating XML document structures. It is used as a searching/query language (in the XPointer standard) and for advanced hypertext linking schemes (in the XQL proposal). It is even used for validating XML documents (in the proposed Schematron standard).

Unlike XSL and XSLT, this language is not XML-based. It has a compact syntax that has been designed to be suitable in a number of different circumstances. For example, expressions can be found in attribute values, and on the end of URLs. The following expression identifies Paragraph elements within Chapter elements that have a Type attribute value of 'important':

```
chapter//paragraph[@type='important']
```

Combining XSL, XSLT and XPath

The XSLT standard makes reference to the XPath standard. It does this because it needs the expression language that XPath defines to provide much of its more advanced functionality. Most significantly, expressions are needed to determine which template is most suitable for processing a particular element in the source document. Expressions are also used to copy material from elsewhere in the document, to automatically number items in a list, and to do many other things.

XSLT, with the assistance of XPath expressions, offers an ideal way to transform arbitrary XML documents into XSL documents ready to be formatted for presentation. The following example shows an XSLT rule that maps a Paragraph element in the source document to a bold paragraph in XSL format, but only when the paragraph is inside a Chapter element and has a Type attribute value of 'important':

```
<template match="chapter//paragraph[@type='important']">
  <fo:block font-weight='bold'>
    <apply-templates/>
  </fo:block>
</template>
```

This book describes these three standards. Chapters 3 to 18 cover XSLT, Chapters 19 to 23 cover XPath, and Chapters 24 to 27 cover XSL.

Naming confusion

The term 'XSL' has been used to describe three different things. First, it is still correctly used to name the XSL standard itself. Second, more commonly but far less accurately, it has been used to refer to the XSLT standard, though this usage has become less widespread as awareness of XSLT has increased. Third, for historical reasons, it continues to be used to describe the combination of XSLT (including XPath) and XSL, where an XSLT stylesheet is used to create XSL documents. In this book, the third definition is used as well as the first because no other term has emerged to describe the whole package (the context of the discussion should indicate which meaning applies). Some people use the term 'XSL-FO' (XSL Formatting Objects) to describe the actual XSL standard (for reasons discussed in Chapter 23) in order to clarify things a little:

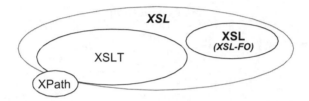

Software support

Software modules and applications are emerging to support each of the standards described above.

XSLT processors

An **XSLT processor** works with in-memory XML document tree structures. The processor gathers material from this **source tree**, which it uses to drive the creation of a **result tree**, driven by rules provided in the XSLT stylesheet:

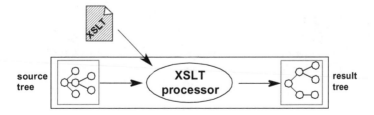

These trees may, in some cases, be accessed and created using the DOM (Document Object Model) interface. This approach allows users of XML parsers that support this standard to create the source document in memory, and to interrogate or modify the result tree before sending it on to a data file or output stream.

XSLT applications

An XSLT processor may be embedded within an **XSLT application** that has the single purpose of reading an input file (to create the source tree) and creating an output file (from the result tree):

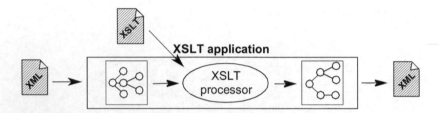

Non-XML output

The output of the XSLT application may not have to be an XML document. Some features of the XSLT language are targetted at the use of stylesheets to create non-XML data formats, but these features can only be exploited when the XSLT processor being used is part of an XSLT application that can directly output the result of the transformation. Such an application could, for example, create an HTML file that exploits element tag minimization techniques not allowed in XML documents.

Multiple stylesheets

XSLT may be used in several different ways: to create an XSL-styled document or a formatting file of another kind (such as HTML), or to create a new XML document. Usually, a separate XSLT stylesheet is employed for each of these purposes:

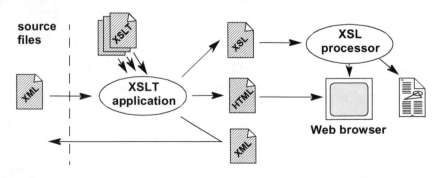

XSL processors

As shown above, an **XSL processor** takes the output of the stylesheet and creates a visual representation of the document. It may simply display the document, or it may be able to create a **PostScript** file or **PDF** (*Portable Document Format*) rendition.

Applications may soon arise that will include both an XSLT processor and an XSL processor. Such an application will be tightly integrated into a publishing application of some kind, such as a Web browser or a DTP package, and the output from the processors will therefore be rendered immediately. This application will appear to treat the XSLT stylesheet much like a traditional stylesheet that directly drives the display of the document.

Why XSL?

Some have argued that XSL (comprising XSLT, XPath and XSL) is an unwanted intruder in an already crowded market. There were many formatting, stylesheet and transformation languages in existence before XSL. Yet there were several valid reasons for the development of this technology.

XSL has an obvious advantage over product-specific stylesheet languages. As a set of industry standards, it is already supported by a wide range of tools from competing vendors, deployed on all of the major computer platforms. These are, of course, benefits complementary to the use of XML itself. However, this still leaves a small number of existing standards to discuss.

The **CSS** language was initially introduced to give Web page authors more control over format; it was simply a way to override the browser's default formatting settings in order to extend the formatting power of HTML. In its simplest form, the formatting instructions are not even stored in a separate stylesheet at all, but in an HTML attribute called 'Style'. CSS can be used with XML, and some have argued that CSS is all that is needed for this task. But XSL is far more powerful than CSS, and the task of learning both has been simplified by the adoption of CSS-style property names in XSL.

The **DSSSL** (*Document Style Semantics and Specification Language*) standard has been a major influence on the development of XSL, despite a dramatic difference in syntax. The initial impetus for the development of XSL came from a desire to replicate the power of DSSSL in a language that had a simpler, XML-based syntax. Although DSSSL includes both transformation and formatting characteristics, they are not separated (as they are with XSLT and XSL) so DSSSL cannot be used for anything other than the preparation of a document for presentation by a DSSSL-sensitive formatter.

XML was introduced to fill a gap between the simple but limited HTML format and the powerful but complex SGML format. Likewise, XSL is intended to sit between the simple but limited CSS format and the powerful but complex DSSSL format.

Example stylesheet

For those keen to get started with XSLT, the following stylesheet is a simple but working example that can be modified and extended to test the concepts described in the following chapters:

```
<xsl:stylesheet
        xmlns:xsl="http://www.w3.org/1999/XSL/Transform"
        xmlns="http://www.w3.org/TR/xhtml1/strict">
  <xsl:template match="book">
    <HTML><BODY><xsl:apply-templates/></BODY></HTML>
  </xsl:template>
  <xsl:template match="title">
    <H1><xsl:apply-templates/></H1>
  </xsl:template>
  <xsl:template match="author">
    <H3><xsl:apply-templates/></H3>
  </xsl:template>
  <xsl:template match="publisher">
    <P><I><xsl:apply-templates/></I></P>
  </xsl:template>
</xsl:stylesheet>
```

This stylesheet can be used to process XML source documents such as the following:

```
<book>
  <title>My Life</title>
  <author>J. Smith</author>
  <publisher>ACME Publishing</publisher>
</book>
```

It converts these documents into HTML documents that can be viewed in any Web browser:

```
<HTML>
  <BODY>
    <H1>My Life</H1>
    <H3>J. Smith</H3>
    <P><I>ACME Publishing</I></P>
  </BODY>
</HTML>
```

3. Templates

Every XSLT stylesheet will contain at least one template, and most stylesheets will contain many templates. They lie at the heart of the standard, and are very flexible and powerful. Unfortunately, they can therefore be quite complex, and a number of concepts needs to be understood in order to use them effectively.

Templates

An XSLT processor matches a node in the source tree to the most suitable **template** it can find in a stylesheet. The node type, name and location in the tree may all contribute to deciding which template should be selected to process it. This template generates the desired output for the node. The template may contain static text that is simply copied to the result tree, and it may contain instructions that generate different, context-specific text, each time is is used.

Template element

Each template is represented by the **Template** element:

```
<template...>
  ...
</template>
```

When there are multiple templates, the order in which they are placed in the stylesheet is not usually significant, though in some special circumstances the order can be important.

Template output

A template specifies the output to be generated to create part of the result tree. The following template adds the text 'HELLO WORLD' to the result tree:

```
<template ...>
  HELLO WORLD
</template>
```

Depending on the exact requirement, this text may include markup, including XML elements tags. However, XML tags could be easily confused with XSLT elements that can also occur in the template, so namespaces are used to distinguish between them (see Chapter 17).

But the real flexibility of templates comes from their ability to dynamically generate some or all of their contents. Embedded XSLT instructions are replaced by the content they generate or select from the source document. The template is built by adding the results of these instructions to any static text in the template. This is done each time the template is selected because some of the instructions may produce different output each time they are processed. The template finally contains a result tree fragment that is then added to the result tree.

Template selection

The templates defined in a stylesheet lie dormant waiting to be activated, or 'triggered', by the XSLT processor. Only one template can be activated at any one time. The XSLT processor only triggers a template when it finds material in the source document that is suitable for processing by that template.

Matching templates to contexts

Each template 'advertises' its own purpose so that the XSLT processor will know when it is appropriate to use it. The **Match** attribute is used in the Template element to specify which element, or other document component, the template applies to. In the following example the template is targetted at Para elements, and is *not* used to process the Title and Note elements:

```
<title>The Title</title>
<para>A source paragraph.</para>
<note>A note.</note>
<para>Another source paragraph.</para>
```

```
<template match="para">...</template>
```

To be more precise, when an element name appears in the Match attribute it is actually an example of a very simple **expression**, and an abbreviation of a more verbose XPath instruction. The content of this attribute can be much more complex (later chapters explore the XPath expression language in depth).

Nodes

Although elements are very important, it must be recognized that XML documents often contain other document components such as attributes, comments and processing instructions. Most importantly of all, XML documents often include text within and between the elements. The generic term '**node**' is used to refer to any significant item in an XML document.

Warning: it may be tempting to ignore or skim the following discussion on nodes and trees because it appears to be not directly relevant to understanding or building XSLT stylesheets. But the investment made in understanding these concepts is worthwhile. The behaviour of XSLT instructions is much easier to understand once these concepts have been grasped.

There is a subtle but important difference between the text content of an element, and the element itself. Two nodes are required to model this structure. A node for the entire element, which includes such information as the element name, refers to another 'child' node that holds the text content:

```
<para>This is a TEXT node in a PARA node.</para>
```

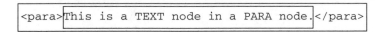

In terms of XML markup, the distinction is best made by imagining that the start-tag and end-tag are within the element node, but outside the text node:

```
<para>This is a TEXT node in a PARA node.</para>
```

It is necessary to make this distinction because an element that may contain text is often able to contain embedded elements as well. Such elements are represented by further element nodes, and these nodes are situated between specific characters in the text content. This circumstance requires at least two child nodes. In the following example the Paragraph element node contains three child nodes representing the embedded Emphasis element node, and the text that precedes and follows this element. But the Emphasis element node contains only a single child node representing all of the text content of this element:

```
<para>This <emph>paragraph</emph> is emphasized.</para>
```

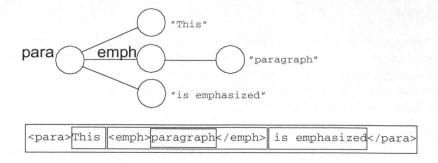

Trees

As the examples above demonstrate, nodes are organized into hierarchical structures. A hierarchy is really nothing more than a tree. A tree trunk divides into a number of major branches, then into minor branches, then into twigs, and then finally into leaves. This explains the terms 'source *tree*' and 'result *tree*'. Of course, the tree metaphor has long been adopted to illustrate ancestral family relationships. For example, a particular 'branch' of a family tree may be discussed, and individuals can search for their 'roots'. It should not be surprising that XML document components are usually discussed using terminology derived from familiar descriptions of real trees and family trees. For example, each node has a 'parent' node except for one, which is known as the 'root' node.

By default, an XSLT processor works through the source tree landing on each node, as if it were a stepping-stone, in what is termed a **tree-walking** process:

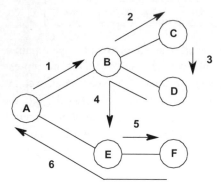

Regardless of which node is the **current node**, the next step to be taken in the walking process is decided on using a simple algorithm. First, if the current node has children, then the first child is chosen (as in the steps from A to B, from B to C and from E to F in the diagram above). Otherwise, if the current node has following siblings then the next sibling is chosen (as in the step from C to D). Otherwise, the following sibling of the nearest ancestor with following siblings is chosen (as in the step from D to E). If no such ancestor exists, then the process is complete (as in the step from F to the end of the document).

Root node

A single node, called the **root node**, sits at the base of the tree (or at the top or side, depending on how the tree is oriented). It is a common mistake to assume that the root node is the root element node (or the 'document element' as it is officially named), but this not the case. The root node has the root element node as one of its children, but it may also contain other nodes representing any comments or processing instructions surrounding the root element:

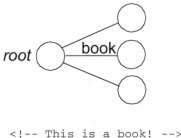

```
<!-- This is a book! -->
<book>...</book>
<?ACME process-me?>
```

Tree nodes and non-tree nodes

Not all of the nodes that represent significant components of an XML document are present in the tree structure. The components that form a hierarchical structure are the required root node and the root element node, plus any embedded element nodes, text nodes, comment nodes and processing instruction nodes. But attribute nodes are not part of the tree structure. They are directly attached to element nodes. Each attribute has an element parent, but strictly speaking they are not children of the element (as odd as this statement sounds). In the following illustration two attributes have element A as a parent, and two attributes have element B as a parent, but A has only its two element children, and B has no children at all.

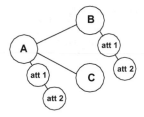

Similarly, namespace nodes are not part of the tree.

Document processing

A template is activated after each step taken. However, this procedure is not totally automatic. Instead, the stylesheet developer must insert an instruction that tells the XSLT processor to process children of the current node. This is done using the **Apply Templates** element.

In its simplest form, the Apply Templates element is empty and has no attributes. In this form, it indicates that children of the node that triggered the template need to be processed (which may in turn activate more templates):

```
<template match="chapter">
  <apply-templates/>
</template>

<template match="title">
  <apply-templates/>
</template>

<template match="para">
  <apply-templates/>
</template>
```

Note that the Apply Templates instruction is added even to the templates for elements that do not contain child elements. This instruction is needed in these templates because the text node children of the element nodes need to be processed too (in order to trigger a template that is dedicated to dealing with text, and which typically just pushes this text through to the result tree).

Multiple 'active' templates

A template is triggered for each node in the source tree, and is only released after the XSLT processor has processed all of its descendent nodes. This means that several templates may be 'open' at the same time (though only one is ever active at any given moment):

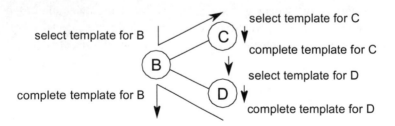

Consider the following source document fragment:

```
<chapter>
  <title>The Title</title>
  <para>A paragraph.</para>
  <para>Another paragraph.</para>
</chapter>
```

To process this sample, it may be appropriate to create three templates: one for the Chapter element, one for the Title element and one for the Paragraph elements:

```
<template match="chapter">...</template>
<template match="title">...</template>
<template match="para">...</template>
```

The first of these templates will be triggered when the processor reaches the Chapter element, but will not be released until after the other templates have been triggered and completed:

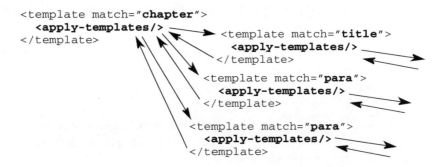

Adding boilerplate text

A template may contain text that is to be copied to the result tree. Traditionally, this has been called 'boilerplate text'.

Replacement text

In the simplest case, text is output in place of an element or other object in the source document. In the following example, each PageBreak element in the source document is replaced by the text '[PAGE BREAK]' in the output document:

```
<pagebreak/>
```

```
<template match="pagebreak">[PAGE BREAK]</template>
```

```
[PAGE BREAK]
```

Note that the Apply Templates element is not present. It is not needed here.

Prefixes and suffixes

Text can be added both before and after the original content of an element. The location of the Apply Templates element within the template is critical to the distinction between preceding and following material. The first example below adds a prefix to the content of the Note element, and the second encloses the content of the Quote element in quotation marks:

```
<template match="note">NOTE:<apply-templates/></template>
```

```
<template match="quote">"<apply-templates/>"</template>
```

Text element

Boilerplate text may be enclosed in the **Text** element. In some circumstances, it does not make any difference whether this element is used or not, and the following two examples are equivalent:

```
<template match="note">NOTE:<apply-templates/></template>
```

```
<template match="note">
  <text>NOTE:</text><apply-templates/>
</template>
```

But this element can be used to distinguish between whitespace that is used to format the stylesheet and whitespace that needs to be copied to output. It also provides other benefits that are explained later.

Default element template

If a template contains nothing but the Apply Templates element, then the distinction between preceding and following output becomes irrelevant. In the following example, the template for the Paragraph element simply states that children of this element should be processed:

```
<template match="para">
  <apply-templates/>
</template>
```

However, this very simple and common requirement is so fundamental that it is not even necessary to create an explicit template to perform this operation. The template for the Paragraph element above is just a more specific example of the following template, which is built-in to every XSLT processor, and so does not need to be physically present in the stylesheet:

```
<template match="*|/">
  <apply-templates/>
</template>
```

The value of the Match attribute is more complex than examples above, but for the moment it is only necessary to know that the '*' symbol is a wildcard character that represents any element. This template would therefore be activated for 'para' elements if there was no explicit template for this element type.

This implied template plays an important role in the tree-walking process. Typically, some elements in the source document have no direct role in creating the output, and it is therefore not necessary to create templates for these element types. Yet it is also possible that such an element will contain other elements for which templates *are* needed. An obvious question that arises is how these templates will ever be triggered.

Consider the following example, where there appears to be no template for the Intro element that could trigger the paragraph templates:

```
<book>
  <intro>
    <para>Embedded paragraph.</para>
    <para>Second embedded paragraph.</para>
  </intro>
  ...
</book>
```

```
<template match="book"><apply-templates/></template>

<!-- MISSING TEMPLATE FOR INTRO -->

<template match="para"><apply-templates/></template>
```

In fact, the paragraphs in this example *will* be selected and processed as normal, because of the implied template. This template is only selected when a more specific template cannot be found for the given element node in the source tree.

Recall that the value of the Match attribute in the implied template is '*|/'. The implied template actually matches two circumstances – the vertical bar symbol '|' is used to separate them. The '/' symbol represents the root node and is needed so that the tree-walking process can get started if there is no explicit template to process this node.

Hiding content

Some of the content of an XML document can be ignored, or suppressed, so that it will not play any role in creating the output document. The content of a specific element can be excluded simply by creating a template for it that does not contain the Apply Templates element. In the following example, the template for the Comment element does not contain the Apply Templates element. Even though there is a template for paragraphs, this template is never triggered for paragraphs within a Comment element:

```
<comment><para>...</para><para>...</para></comment>
```

```
<template match="comment"><!-- SUPPRESS --></template>
```

```
<template match="para"><apply-templates/></template>
```

Similarly, omitting the Apply Templates element in the template for an element that contains text means that the text will not appear:

```
<secret>This is secret text, do not show</secret>
```

```
<template match="secret"></template>
```

Flexible tree-walking

The tree-walking process does not have to involve traversal over every node in the entire tree. It is possible to ignore certain branches, thereby preventing the content of nodes in these branches from contributing to the result tree. Conversely, it is also possible to walk over the same branches several times, thereby reprocessing the content of the nodes in these branches.

Selective processing

It may be desirable to suppress the processing of some of the child elements of the current node. The **Select** attribute can be used to indicate which children to process. In the following example, only the Title elements within Chapter elements are processed (all of the other children are ignored):

```
<template match="chapter">
  <apply-templates select="title"/>
</template>
```

It would be tempting to think that the default value for the Select attribute must be '*' indicating that all child elements will be selected. However, this instruction also needs to select text, comments and processing instructions. Its real default value is therefore '**node**()', which represents all child nodes rather than just element nodes (but not any namespace and attribute nodes that may be present because they are not considered to be children of element nodes). The following examples are therefore equivalent:

```
<apply-templates/>

<apply-templates select="node()"/>
```

Repeated processing

The Apply Templates element can occur more than once in a template. One reason to do this would be to ensure that the child elements are processed in a particular order. In the example below, the title would be output before the paragraphs, even if it were not the first element in the chapter:

```
<template match="chapter">
   <apply-templates select="title"/>
   <apply-templates select="para"/>
</template>
```

Another reason for using multiple Apply Templates elements is to process the same child or children more than once. In the following example, the title is output twice; the first time explicitly and the second time as part of general child processing:

```
<template match="chapter">
   <apply-templates select="title"/>
   <apply-templates/> <!-- ALSO PROCESSES TITLE -->
</template>
```

Note that the elements selected do not have to be children of the current element. Chapter 12 explains how this feature can be employed to reuse information from elsewhere in a document.

It is possible to place text and markup between multiple Apply Templates element. For example:

```
<template>The author of <apply-template select="title"/>
is <apply-template select="author"/>.</template>
```

Processing source text

The default behaviour of a stylesheet is to output any text that is present as element content in the source tree. In other words, the content of all text nodes encountered during the tree-walking process is automatically copied to the output tree.

For this to work there must be a template to process text nodes, but once again there is an implied template that simply passes-through the content of the node. If made explicit, this template would appear as follows:

```
<template match="text()|@*">
  <value-of select="."/>
</template>
```

Text nodes are represented by the **text**() keyword (if the brackets were omitted,the template would be triggered by an element called 'text' instead).

The Value Of element is discussed in detail later. For now, it is sufficient to know that this instruction is replaced by the text content of the node, in the same way that Apply Template elements are replaced by the content of triggered templates. But the Apply Templates element is not used here because a text node does not contain any further nodes (it is always a 'leaf' node) so there are no templates waiting to be triggered.

Unlike the default template for text nodes, the default template for element nodes does not add anything to the ouput. The standard behaviour of a stylesheet is therefore to output only the text content of a document:

```
Book Title
Chapter One Title
Paragraph one.
Paragraph two.
...
```

Note that this implied template is also used to handle attribute values, though attributes are not processed by default. The '@*' part of the Match attribute intercepts attributes, and is described later.

The only reason to make this template explicit would be to change the default behaviour (Chapter 8 discusses a technique for performing string replacements in order to 'escape' significant characters when outputting text in a data format other than XML). The following template would suppress the text output because the Value Of element is absent (in this case, the implied template continues to be used for attribute values):

```
<template match="text()"></template>
```

Processing instructions and comments

The source tree may contain nodes that represent comments and processing instructions. These nodes will trigger templates, just as element and text nodes do. Again, there is an implied template for these node types. By default, it is assumed that neither comments nor processing instructions in the source document will be relevant to the output document, and so the implied template does nothing. The **comment**() keyword and the **processing-instruction**() keyword are used in the Match attribute:

```
<template match="comment()|processing-instruction()">
</template>
```

The lack of either an Apply Templates element or a Value Of element ensures that these markup constructs are not passed-through to the result tree (just as element content can be suppressed by the lack of the first of these instructions).

Comments or processing instructions can be processed by making this template explicit. In the following example, only comments are processed by the explicit template, and in this case are simply replaced by the words 'COMMENT HERE':

```
<template match="comment()">
   COMMENT HERE
</template>
```

Tag replacement

The main purpose of XSLT is to convert an XML document into another XML document. In the simplest case, this could mean just replacing one set of tags with another, while duplicating the document structure. Fortunately, the start-tag and end-tag of the element in the source document that triggers a template are automatically discarded as the source document is parsed into its in-memory tree form, and the XSLT processor does not attempt to reconstitute them. Replacement tags are included in the template, surrounding the content of the element, in place of the prefix and suffix text discussed earlier. The following example transforms the element 'title' into another one called 'H1' (an HTML heading element):

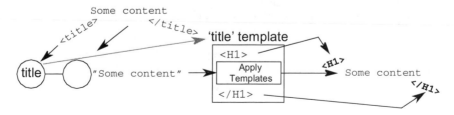

The names of the new tags usually conform to definitions in an appropriate DTD or schema. They may, for example, conform to the XSL standard model (see Chapters 24 to 27). Other options include HTML tags, as shown above. Because HTML is such a well-known standard, it is used in most of the examples in this chapter and throughout the rest of the book (see Chapter 28 for details).

Adding output elements to the template can be done in two very different ways. First, it is possible to simply add the output element tags to the content of the template as **literal** elements (the element tags are 'literally' present in the stylesheet). The Namespaces standard is used to distinguish XSLT elements from output elements. In the following example, the XSLT elements have the prefix 'xsl:' and the HTML elements have no prefix (they use the default namespace):

```
<xsl:template match="title">
  <H1><xsl:apply-templates/></H1>
</xsl:template>
```

Complex templates are relatively easy to read and understand with this approach. The following example should be immediately intelligible to anybody familiar with HTML document markup:

```
<xsl:template match="book">
  <HTML>
    <HEAD><TITLE>The Title</TITLE></HEAD>
    <BODY>
      <xsl:apply-templates/>
    </BODY>
  </HTML>
</xsl:template>
```

When using a guided XML authoring package, a DTD or XML Schema model must be created that contains both sets of elements, with content models that permit a mixture of these two sets. While creation of such a model is not a trivial exercise, it can be expected that models for some of the most common requirements will become freely available (certainly for XSLT/HTML and XSLT/XSL).

Note that it is possible to pass-through an element from the source document to the output document by recreating the source element in the template, as the following example demonstrates. However, the presence of attributes in the source element causes complications that are not catered for by this simple technique:

```
<xsl:template match="book">
  <book><xsl:apply-templates/></book>
</xsl:template>
```

The second technique for creating output elements is discussed in Chapter 5. That technique avoids namespaces and stylesheet DTD complications, and has other advantages. But it also has some disadvantages and the technique described above seems to be the more popular approach.

Identity transformations

There may be a need to create a slightly modified version of an XML document. For example, consider a document that contains many Secret elements, and the need to create a variant of the document that does not contain these elements (in order to send it to somebody who should not read the sensitive material these elements contain). In this scenario, there is clearly a need for a template that prevents all of the Secret elements from reaching the result tree, and the technique for hiding source elements has already been discussed:

```
<template match="secret"><!-- SUPPRESS --></template>
```

But this is the easy part. It is also necessary to copy all the other elements in the source document through to the result tree without change, and to copy any comments and processing instructions in the document. This can be achieved by creating templates for each element type, such as in the following examples, and making explicit templates for comments and processing instructions that push-through rather than suppress these constructs:

```
<xsl:template match="book">
<book><xsl:apply-templates/></book>
</xsl:template>

<xsl:template match="para">
<para><xsl:apply-templates/></para>
</xsl:template>
```

But this is hardly a convenient approach. Indeed, if the source document is complex this would be both a tedious and error-prone activity. It does not even allow for the possible presence of attributes in the source elements.

Fortunately, the root node and all of the element, attribute, text, comment and processing instruction nodes can be processed by a single template that also recreates them for insertion into the result tree. The following template would achieve this:

```
<template match="@*|node()">
<copy><apply-templates select="@*|node()"/></copy>
</template>
```

This is called the **identity transformation** template because it transforms the document without losing its original identity. If this were the only template in a stylesheet then the XSLT processor would create a document identical to the source document (which would be rather pointless).

It is too early to discuss the exact details of the workings of this template, but it should be apparent that it is intended to be triggered both by nodes of any kind that exist in the source tree, and by the attribute nodes that may be attached to some of the element nodes. The embedded Apply Templates element also specifically selects attributes as well as all child nodes, so that this same template can be triggered to add attributes to their parent elements. The Copy element is discussed later (in Chapter 6).

The only occasion this template is not selected is when a more specific template, such as the one designed to handle the Secret element shown above, is present (the concept of some templates being more specific than others is discussed at length in Chapter 9).

Including spaces

Spaces are often used in the construction of stylesheets to make them more legible. The following templates produce identical output:

```
<xsl:template match="para">
  <P><xsl:apply-templates/></P>
</xsl:template>
```

```
<xsl:template match="para">
  <P>
    <xsl:apply-templates/>
  </P>
</xsl:template>
```

In both cases, the output generated should be something like the following:

```
<P>The content.</P>
```

In the second template above, there is a line-feed and four spaces before the Apply Templates element, but none of this whitespace appears in the output. If leading spaces *are* required, the **Text** element must be used to make this explicit. In the following example, a single space is required at this position:

```
<xsl:template match="para">
  <P>
    <xsl:text> </xsl:text><xsl:apply-templates/>
  </P>
</xsl:template>
```

```
<P> The content.</P>
```

Values of elements and attributes

Sometimes it is useful to be able to access the content of an element as a string, regardless of whether the element contains sub-elements or not. Instead of activating templates on the content of the current element, the content can be converted into a string and inserted into the template using the **Value Of** element. This element has a **Select** attribute, which in the simplest case is used to select the current element. The expression '.' refers to the current node. Embedded element markup is ignored by this instruction:

```
<para>All the <emph>text</emph> here is the value</para>
```

```
<value-of select="."/>
```

```
All the text here is the value
```

The value of a sub-element can be 'dragged up' and inserted into the template. This approach to selecting specific content for formatting does not require other templates to be created in order to process the content of the sub-elements. The name of the child element is simply entered into the Select attribute:

```
<name>
  <firstName>John</firstName>
  <lastName>Smith</lastName>
</name>
```

```
<template match="name">
  First: <value-of select="firstName"/>
  Last: <value-of select="lastName"/>
</template>
```

Note that if there were two first names in the example above, only the first would be output (the Apply Templates instruction would select both). The expression 'firstName[2]' (see Chapter 22) would be needed to select the second one.

This element can also be used to select the value of an attribute. Attribute names are distinguished from element names by adding the '@' symbol as a prefix; so '@type' would refer to an attribute called 'type':

```
<para type="secret">This is a secret.</para>
```

```
<xsl:template match="para">
  <P>[<xsl:value-of select="@type"/>]
  <xsl:apply-templates/>
  </P>
</xsl:template>
```

```
<P>[TYPE: secret] This is a secret.</P>
```

Direct processing

Transformations that rely on use of the Template element can be described as 'event-driven' processes. Individual templates in the stylesheet are triggered by events that are caused by the presence of specific nodes that are encountered during the tree-walking process. The source document therefore controls the order in which the templates are triggered. With the direct approach described here, processing is controlled by the stylesheet instead. This approach is applicable when the output format is totally independent of the source document structure. In this case, the stylesheet may even consist of a single template.

The **For Each** element is used for this purpose. It selects other elements and applies an embedded template to each occurrence. Consider the following example, where information about a number of customers is present:

```
<customers>

<customer>
  <name>J Smith</name>
  <order>123</order>
  <order>456</order>
</customer>

<customer>
  <name>P Jones</name>
  <order>987</order>
  <order>654</order>
</customer>

</customers>
```

To create an HTML table from this structure, with one row for each customer, four templates would normally be required:

```
<xsl:template match="customers">
  <TABLE><TBODY><xsl:apply-templates/></TBODY></TABLE>
</xsl:template>

<xsl:template match="customer">
  <TR><xsl:apply-templates/></TR> <!-- ROW -->
</xsl:template>

<xsl:template match="name">
  <TH><xsl:apply-templates/></TH> <!-- HEADER CELL -->
</xsl:template/>

<xsl:template match="order">
  <TD><xsl:apply-templates/></TD> <!-- DATA CELL -->
</xsl:template/>
```

These four rules can be replaced by a single rule that is both shorter and clearer in its intent. A template is created for the Customers element and the table structure is built within it. Each Customer element is selected using the For Each instruction with each match building one row of the table, creating a header cell and placing the Name element content within it, and then activating a further For Each command that adds a table data cell for each Order element:

```
<xsl:template match="Customers">
  <TABLE>
    <TBODY>

      <xsl:for-each select="Customer">
        <TR>
          <TH>
            <xsl:apply-templates="Name"/>
          </TH>

          <xsl:for-each select="Order">
            <TD>
              <xsl:apply-templates/>
            </TD>
          </xsl:for-each>

        </TR>
      </xsl:for-each>

    </TBODY>
  </TABLE>
</xsl:template/>
```

Many examples of this feature (including the one above) show its use in looping through child elements. However, the Select attribute can actually hold any expression. Consider the example of a complex document that contains a number of Name elements – some holding the names of people, others holding company names. When the requirement is simply to output all the personal names, and then all the company names, in both cases as a list, then the direct processing approach is appropriate:

```
<xsl:template match="Document">
  <HTML><BODY>
  <H1>Individual Names</H1>
  <OL>
    <xsl:for-each select="//Name[@type='personal']">
      <LI><xsl:value-of select="."/></LI>
    </xsl:for-each>
  </OL>
  <H1>Company Names</H1>
  <OL>
    <xsl:for-each select="//Name[@type='company']">
      <LI><xsl:value-of select="."/></LI>
    </xsl:for-each>
  </OL>
  </BODY></HTML>
</xsl:template>
```

The value of the Select attribute above is a complex XPath expression that finds all the Name elements in the document that have specific Type attribute values.

Named templates

Software developers will usually be familiar with languages that include procedures, used to avoid repeating a number of instructions needed in various places in
the program. A similar concept is provided in XSLT. A **named template** is identical to a normal template, except that it does not have a Match attribute. Instead,
the **Name** attribute is used to name the template, and this template is explicitly activated from instructions in other templates.

For example, a dividing line may need to be output above a number of different
output structures:

```
<xsl:template name="divideLine">
  <BR/><HR/><BR/> <!-- break line, rule, break line -->
</xsl:template>
```

This template can be referenced from within other templates using the **Call Template** element. This element also has a **Name** attribute, which is used to name the
template to use:

```
<xsl:template name="chapter">
  <xsl:call-template name="divideLine"/>
  <H1>NEW CHAPTER</H1>
  <xsl:apply-templates/>
</xsl:template>

<xsl:template name="section">
  <xsl:call-template name="divideLine"/>
  <H2>NEW SECTION</H2>
  <xsl:apply-templates/>
</xsl:template>
```

The named template does not change the current node, and if it contains Match,
Priority or Mode attributes they have no effect. It is simply a convenient wrapper
for material needed in several places.

Parameters

As described above, named templates appear to be of limited value. It is not very
common for identical material to be needed in a number of different circumstances. For example, it is unlikely that a dividing line between chapters will be the
same as that between sections (it may be thicker or wider). Therefore, just as procedures in programming languages can use passed parameters, it is also possible
to pass parameters to a named template (parameters are discussed in Chapter 13).

Messages

Many software developers will be familiar with the (now primitive) technique of adding 'print' statments to their programs in order to track down bugs. A similar technique is available to XSLT stylesheet developers using the **Message** element. This element can be placed in a template holding an appropriate message for display when the template is activated:

```
<template match="warning">
  <message>Template Warning has been activated</message>
  <apply-templates/>
</template>
```

This element has no effect on normal output from the stylesheet. Instead, the text content of the Message element is somehow presented to the user of the XSLT processor software. In a windows-based system, a pop-up window may appear. On a command-line system, the messages would appear as standard output:

```
D:\xslt> xsltProcessor In.xml Out.htm
D:\xslt> MESSAGE: Template Warning has been activated
D:\xslt> FINISHED
D:\xslt>
```

The **Terminate** attribute, which has a default value of 'no', may be set to 'yes' in order to terminate document processing immediately:

```
<template match="problem">
  <message terminate="yes">Problem element detected
  correct the error and restart</message>
</template>
```

The Message element may be used within other elements that a Template element can contain:

```
<template match="para">
  <if test="@secret='yes'">
    ...
    <message>Secret paragraph found.</message>
  </if>
  ...
</template>
```

The Message element may in turn contain all these other elements, including the Value Of element, which is particularly useful for reporting on the current context. For example, the name of the current element can be reported (the name() function represents the name of the current node):

```
<template match="warning|caution|note">
  <message>A <value-of select="name()" /> has
          been detected</message>
  ...
</template>
```

This functionality could be added to a named template:

```
<template name="elementName">
  <message>
    ELEMENT: <value-of select="name()" />
    ID: <value-of select="@id" />
  </message>
</template>

<template match="chapter">
  <call-template name="elementName" />
  ...
</template>

<template match="para">
  <call-template name="elementName" />
  ...
</template>

<template match="warning">
  <call-template name="elementName" />
  ...
</template>
```

4. Stylesheets

An XSLT stylesheet contains instructions that an XSLT processor uses to transform an XML document into another format. Typical stylesheets consist of little more than a set of templates. However, there are a number of other instructions a stylesheet can hold to influence the way that the source tree is used to construct the result tree.

Stylesheets can be linked to XML documents in a number of different ways and may be constructed from instructions in several separate data files.

XML-based stylesheet documents

An XSLT stylesheet is an XML document that conforms to the XSLT DTD, perhaps enhanced to include literal output elements. This DTD is described in an appendix to the XSLT standard. The term 'XSLT element' is used here to identify any element that is defined in this DTD.

A number of interesting benefits arise from the fact that XSLT stylesheets are XML documents. First, it is possible to use a DTD both to validate a stylesheet and, along with an XML-sensitive editor, to guide stylesheet authors. Second, a stylesheet can be stored in an XML repository, where it can be manipulated and versioned down to the element level. Third, because XSLT stylesheets process XML documents, it is possible to write stylesheets that convert other XML/SGML-based stylesheets into XSLT format, and even to create XSLT stylesheet variants from another XSLT stylesheet. Finally, a stylesheet can be produced to format other stylesheets for presentation or printout.

Using stylesheets

In order for an XSLT processor to be able to produce a result tree it needs to be supplied with both a source tree and a stylesheet. A number of different techniques are available for providing these two resources. A stylesheets can be embedded in the source tree, be referenced from the XML document this tree represents, or be separately selected by the XSLT processor.

Embedded stylesheets

A stylesheet can be embedded in the document to be processed. This is only possible because both the stylesheet and the document containing it are XML structures, and the Namespaces standard describes how fragments from different kinds of XML document can be combined into a single document:

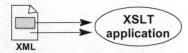

The main problem with this approach is that the same stylesheet could be embedded in a large number of similar source documents. This is inefficient and makes stylesheet maintenance very difficult.

Referenced stylesheets

It is common practice for a document to include a reference to a stylesheet. This reference is detected by the XSLT processor. The stylesheet is immediately accessed and interpreted, then applied to the content of the document. In this way, the same stylesheet can be easily applied to a number of XML documents:

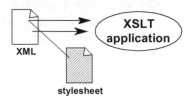

This is done using an XML processing instruction with the name '**xml-stylesheet**', a **Type** parameter that indicates the data format used to hold the stylesheet instructions ('text/xml'), and a parameter called **Href** that holds a URL reference to the stylesheet:

```
<?xml-stylesheet type="text/xml"
                 href="styles/format1.xsl"?>
<book>...</book>
```

The obvious weakness of this approach is that it is necessary to edit the XML declaration whenever a different stylesheet is going to be applied to the document (a weakness that is shared with the previously described 'embedding' technique).

Runtime stylesheet selection

One possible approach, which avoids any issues with applying different stylesheets at different times, is to pass the document and the stylesheet to the processor separately:

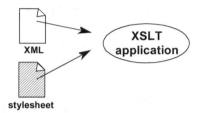

The following example shows a typical invocation of an XSLT application. The first parameter is the name of the stylesheet ('MyStylesheet.XSL'). The second parameter is the name of the source XML document ('MyDoc.XML'). The third parameter names the output file to be created from the result tree:

```
C:\xsl> XSLTApp  MyStylesheet.XSL  MyDoc.XML  MyDoc.HTM
```

The Stylesheet element

The root element of a stylesheet document is the **Stylesheet** element:

```
<stylesheet ...>
  ...
</stylesheet>
```

However, there is an alternative root element. To emphasize the fact that a stylesheet can be used to transform one XML document structure into another XML document structure, the **Transform** element may be used instead:

```
<transform ...>
  ...
</transform>
```

These two elements are interchangeable; they take the same attributes and have the same content model. In practice, however, the Stylesheet element seems to be much more popular than the Transform element (and all following examples that include the root element follow this lead).

XSLT version number

Every stylesheet must declare which version of XSLT it conforms to. At the time of writing, only version 1.0 exists. The version number *should* appear in the **Version** attribute, but in practice some XSLT processors will accept the omission of this attribute and assume a default value of '1.0' when it is not present:

```
<stylesheet version="1.0" ...>
  ...
</stylesheet>
```

The XSLT standard incorporates a mechanism that allows an XSLT processor to work with stylesheets that include features it does not understand. A processor written to support the 1.0 specification, if asked to interpret a stylesheet with a Version attribute value of '1.1' or higher, would simply ignore any element directly embedded within the Stylesheet element that it does not recognize, and would also ignore any unknown attributes on remaining elements:

```
<stylesheet version="1.3" ...>
  ...
  <ignorable-1.3-feature>...</ignorable-1.3-feature>
  <template ignorable-1.3-feature="...">...</template>
  ...
</stylesheet>
```

Namespace declarations

An XSLT stylesheet document may contain elements that do not belong to the XSLT DTD. The main reason for this is to allow elements to be included as literal elements within templates. The problem of how to mix elements from different DTDs in the same document has been addressed by a separate standard called **Namespaces in XML** (see Chapter 17). Each set of elements is a **namespace**, identified by a URL. The namespace for XSLT is identified by the URL http://www.w3.org/1999/XSL/Transform. An XSLT processor is not expected to follow this link; it is simply a unique, universally known identifying string. In principle, this identifier should be added as a prefix to each element from this namespace, but this would be both unwieldy and invalid (URLs usually contain characters that are not legal in XML element names). The namespaces standard therefore maps the URL to a shorter, legal substitute string, such as 'xslt'.

An attribute named '**xmlns:**...' is used to identify the namespace URL and map it to a substitute string. The value of the attribute is the URL for the namespace. The rest of the attribute name is the substitute string. The example below identifies the Stylesheet element as belonging to the XSLT namespace, and the attribute declares the prefix string to be 'X'. The 'X' prefix must appear on all the XSLT elements, including the Stylesheet element itself:

```
<X:stylesheet
    xmlns:X="http://www.w3.org/1999/XSL/Transform" ...>
  ...
</X:stylesheet>
```

The namespaces standard includes the concept of a default namespace. Any element with no prefix is deemed to belong to this namespace. The attribute name '**xmlns**' identifies the default:

```
<stylesheet xmlns="http://www.w3.org/1999/XSL/Transform" >
  ...
</stylesheet>
```

It is possible to put namespace declarations on embedded elements. Using this technique, it is also possible to override a wider definition, just by reusing the same prefix for a different namespace. Indeed, using this technique the default namespace could also be used for elements from different namespaces.

Of course, it is not possible for two namespaces with global scope to both use the default namespace. The stylesheet author is usually left with the choice of whether to use the default for XSLT elements or for literal elements (assuming that the override mechanism is not employed). For the benefit of clarity, examples of XSLT elements in this book use the default namespace, except when literal output elements also appear in the example. The prefix 'xsl:' is used when this happens:

```
<template>
  NO LITERAL OUTPUT ELEMENTS (namespaces not needed)
</template>


<xsl:template>
  <P>
    <!-- LITERAL OUTPUT ELEMENT (namespace for XSLT
         elements) -->
  </P>
</xsl:template>
```

But it is not unknown for an explicit namespace to be used for the literal elements:

```
<template>
  <HTML:P>...</HTML:P>
</template>
```

Stylesheet contents

Elements that may be inserted directly into the Stylesheet element are known as **top-level** elements. These elements may not be used anywhere else, and other XSLT elements may not be inserted at this location.

The Template element is a top-level element. Other top-level elements are used to import material from other stylesheets, to specify space preservation rules for output elements, to specify the output format, and to define global variables, stylesheet parameters, linking schemes, the format of decimal numbers, and sets of attributes for use in templates:

```
<stylesheet ...>
    <import...>
    <include...>
    <strip-space...>
    <preserve-space...>
    <output...>
    <key...>
    <decimal-format...>
    <attribute-set...>
    <variable...>
    <param...>
    <namespace-alias...>
    ...
    ...
</stylesheet>
```

These elements may repeat, and may appear in any order (apart from the Import element, which must occur first). Most of these instructions are explained in later chapters; others are introduced or are fully described below.

Single template short-cut

The Template element is not required when only a single template is needed, and it happens to be matched to the root node of the source document. Even the Stylesheet element is redundant in this circumstance. Instead, the root element of the 'stylesheet document' can be the root output element.

However, namespaces are needed to support this feature. The root element needs to hold the XSLT version and namespace declarations:

```
<book xsl:version="1.0" xslns:xsl="...">
  ...
</book>
```

Elements normally appearing within templates can be used freely, except for the Apply Templates element (because there are no other templates to apply):

```
<book ...>
  ... <xsl:if...> ... <xsl:value-of.../></xsl:if> ...
</book>
```

Embedded stylesheets

The Stylesheet (or Transform) element can be embedded in other XML structures, allowing a document to contain the stylesheet that needs to be applied to it. This is not a popular technique because in practice it is common for a single stylesheet to be applicable to many documents (and for many stylesheets to be applied to each document too), and it would be inefficient for each document to contain a copy of the same stylesheet. However, a document and an applicable stylesheet could reasonably be packaged for delivery to a publishing system using this approach.

It is not sufficient simply to embed a Stylesheet element in a larger document because the XSLT processor still needs to be able to find it. When this is done using a stylesheet processing instruction, the URL reference in the Href parameter needs to point to the Stylesheet element. Using HTML linking conventions, a link can be made to an embedded element instead of a remote data file by giving the element a unique identifier. The '#' symbol precedes a reference to this identifier:

```
<?xml-stylesheet type="text/xml" href="#myStylesheet" ?>
<book>
  ...
</book>
```

The Stylesheet element has an **Id** attribute to hold the unique element identifier. In theory, this will only be recognized as an element identifier if it is defined as such in an XML DTD, but in practice some software will just assume it is a unique identifier in any case:

```
<?xml-stylesheet type="text/xml" href="#myStylesheet"?>
<!DOCTYPE book SYSTEM="..."> <!-- INCLUDES ID DEF -->
<book xmlns="...">
  ...
  <xsl:stylesheet xmlns:xsl="..."
                  version="1.0"
                  id="myStylesheet" >
  ...
  </xsl:stylesheet>
</book>
```

In most circumstances, the stylesheet itself should not be considered to be part of the document to be formatted because its purpose is complete once the formatting it specifies has been applied to the rest of the document. Yet it is physically part of the document, and by default will be formatted along with the rest. Although there will not be any templates present to explicitly format any of the XSLT elements, any text in the templates will still be output. This is avoided by creating a template for the Stylesheet element that does not include the Apply Templates element:

```
<xsl:template match="xsl:stylesheet">
    <!-- SUPPRESS STYLESHEET FORMATTING -->
</xsl:template>
```

Fragmented stylesheets

The term 'stylesheet' implies a continuous 'sheet', represented by a single data file containing the Stylesheet or Transform element, along with all the templates and other instructions required. Indeed, this will often be the case, particularly for simple stylesheets. However, it is possible for a stylesheet to be pulled apart and divided into a number of separate data files. One reason for doing this would be to make a huge stylesheet easier to manage and edit. A much better reason, though, would be to make it possible to share parts of a stylesheet with other stylesheets, and to create libraries of commonly used templates.

For example, an organization may begin to create three stylesheets in order to format the same series of books in three different ways (for different audiences or publishing media) but discover that some typical components, such as tables and lists, are to be styled in the same way in all three circumstances. It makes sense to extract these common components into separate files in order to avoid unnecessary repetition, and to simplify the task of updating these items:

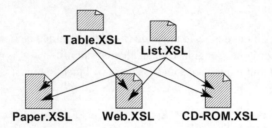

XSLT includes two features to support this concept. Files containing common templates and other instructions can be either 'included' or 'imported' into a stylesheet. These terms are not interchangeable because in this standard they have subtly different meanings.

The term 'main stylesheet' is used in the following discussion to refer to the stylesheet that is initially processed by the XSLT processor. This stylesheet contains instruction elements to include and import other 'subsidiary' stylesheets.

Including external definitions

Definitions in one stylesheet can be referenced and used in another stylesheet using the **Include** element. The **Href** attribute is used to identify the stylesheet to be included and contains a URL reference to locate the file:

```
<include href="file:///D:/xsl/tables.xsl" />
```

The base location for a relative URL reference is the location of the main style-sheet. For example, if the subsidiary file is in the same directory as the main style-sheet, then only the file name is needed:

```
<include href="tables.xsl" />
```

Conceptually, this element is replaced by the content of the stylesheet referenced as soon as it is encountered by the XSLT processor. The inserted templates are then treated exactly the same as templates originating in the main stylesheet.

A subsidiary stylesheet may also contain Include elements, but when this feature is used extensively, care must be taken to avoid the possibility that the same file will be included more than once, because this would introduce duplicate templates. In addition, it is not legal for a file to either directly or indirectly include itself:

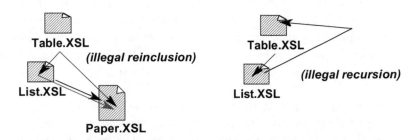

Importing external definitions

Material from another stylesheet can be 'imported' rather than included. The mechanism is identical, except that the element name is **Import**. The **Href** attribute has the same purpose, and again contains a URL reference:

```
<import href="tables.xsl" />
```

However, the Import element must, if present, appear before all other elements in the Stylesheet or Transform element:

```
<stylesheet ...>
  <import .../>
  <import .../>
  ...
</stylesheet>
```

The XSLT processor must move any Import elements it finds in an included docu-ment to a position just after the native ones:

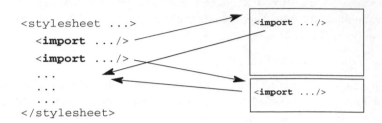

```
<stylesheet ...>                        <import .../>
  <import .../>
  <import .../>
  ...
  ...
  ...                                   <import .../>
</stylesheet>
```

When imported templates and other instructions conflict with templates and instructions in the main stylesheet, a mechanism is needed to decide, in each case, which to use and which to ignore. One instruction can be more 'important' than another. Each instruction is assigned a level of importance, which depends on the order in which files are imported. When a template occurs in two or more files, only the one in the file with the highest importance is considered; all the others are ignored. This means that, after importing a set of templates, some of these templates can be overridden by the main stylesheet. However, the exact nature of importance levels varies, depending on the type of instruction.

The overriding of imported templates can be done in a more subtle way than simply masking the imported template. Instead, the imported template can be 'extended'. In essence, the main template becomes a wrapper around the imported template, adding surrounding output text and literal tags. The **Apply Imports** element is used to invoke the imported template:

```
<para>This is a paragraph.</para>
```

```
<!-- IMPORTED TEMPLATE -->
<xsl:template match="para">
  <P><apply-templates/></P>
</xsl:template>

<!-- MAIN TEMPLATE -->
<xsl:template match="para">
  <DIV CLASS="P"><xsl:apply-imports/></DIV>
</xsl:template>
```

```
<DIV CLASS="P"><P>This is a paragraph.</P></DIV>
```

In complex cases, where imported documents contain further Import elements, the final importance levels are calculated as follows, with (1) being the highest priority and (5) being the lowest. The importance level decreases as each file is imported, with the first one imported having the highest priority of all:

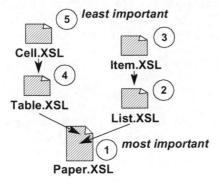

It is not an error if the same file happens to be imported twice. The following example is acceptable, though the higher level version will be ignored (but a stylesheet still cannot import itself):

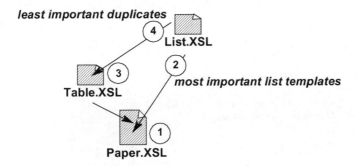

Output formats

Output generated by an XSLT processor can be customized in a number of ways. The **Output** element is an empty element but has attributes that specify various requirements for formatting of the output:

```
<output ... />
```

Output method

The **Method** attribute controls fundamental formatting characteristics that are required for XML, HTML and text output. It holds the value '**xml**', '**html**' or '**text**' accordingly. The implications of these settings are explained in later chapters.

By default, the setting is 'xml', except when an HTML document is recognized by its root element name ('<HTML>'). The **Version** attribute supports this feature and is used, for example, to indicate which version of HTML to output:

```
<output ... method="html" version="3.2" />
```

Encoding

The **Encoding** attribute specifies the character set to use for output, such as 'UTF-8' (the default) or 'ISO-8859-1' (the usual set used on the Web for English pages):

```
<output ... encoding="ISO-8859-1" />
```

Output indentation

The **Indent** attribute can be used to format XML output by indenting embedded element structures. It takes the value 'yes' or 'no' (the default). When set to 'yes' whitespace is added to make the document easier to read:

```
<output ... indent="yes" />


<book>
  <title>The Book Title</title>
  <chapter>
    <title>The Chapter Title</title>
    <para>A paragraph.</para>
  </chapter>
</book>
```

But there is a danger with this kind of formatting. For elements that have mixed content, unwanted space may be added as in the following example:

```
<para>Do
  <emph>NOT</emph>
  add whitespace.</para>
```

Do   **NOT**   add whitespace.

Media types

The **Media Type** attribute specifies the type of data output required. For XML, this would be **text/xml** or **application/xml**. Use of this attribute has no effect on the output document itself, and it is only of interest if the XSLT processor is able to transmit the output data directly over a network that uses the MIME scheme to indicate the data type of the information transferred (such as over the Internet):

```
<output ... media-type="text/xml" />
```

With HTML documents it has more widespread application, as explained later.

Merging Output element attributes

The attributes from multiple Output elements (possibly from parts of a stylesheet that have been imported) are merged, with the highest-importance definitions for each attribute used (except for the CDATA Section Elements attribute (explained later), which combines values from all of the separate definitions).

Space preservation

The XML standard defines the term '**whitespace**' to represent the invisible characters that separate words and end lines of text. These include the space character, the tab character, and the line-feed and carriage-return control characters (used to start a new line in a text file).

Source document formatting

Some whitespace characters may be included in an XML document in order to make the markup easier to read. The following examples are considered to be equivalent in terms of the information they contain, but the second is more legible:

```
<chapter><title>The Chapter Title</title><para>A para-
graph.</para></chapter>


<chapter>
  <title>The Chapter Title</title>
  <para>A paragraph.</para>
</chapter>
```

In both examples, the Chapter element appears to contain two children, namely the Title element and the Para element. However, the way that the second fragment is arranged means that whitespace characters appear between the child elements to create new lines and indentation. Additional text nodes are required to hold these characters:

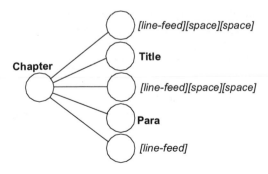

Note that even if the indents were to be removed, the same number of child nodes would be present because there would still be a text node for each line-feed:

```
<chapter>[LF]
<title>The Chapter Title</title>[LF]
<para>A paragraph.</para>[LF]
</chapter>
```

By default, an XSLT processor does *not* treat text nodes containing only whitespace characters differently from other nodes. It would retain all five child nodes of the Chapter element in the example above.

Space stripping

The fact that the two XML fragments shown above are considered identical means that it should not matter that the XSLT processor will preserve this whitespace. However, it is possible to instruct the processor to remove text nodes that contain only whitespace characters. The **Strip Space** element is used to indicate which elements to strip whitespace from. A space-separated list of element names is placed in the **Elements** attribute:

```
<strip-space elements="book chapter section" />
```

If the Elements attribute contains just '*' this indicates that all elements are affected, so all elements are stripped of insignificant whitespace:

```
<strip-space elements="*" />
```

This feature is particularly useful when outputting a text file, rather than an XML document, because most text file formats treat all whitespace as significant. In such circumstances, it is necessary to remove all whitespace only intended to make the source file easier to read. But even when outputting an XML document, there are occasions when it is useful to remove whitespace, if only to reduce the size of the output file.

Space preservation

Stripping whitespace from elements that have mixed content (a mixture of elements and text) can be dangerous. Consider the following example:

```
<para>Another <emph>great</emph> <name>ACME</name>
product</para>
```

In this example, there is a whitespace-only text node between the emphasized word and the company name. Stripping this space would cause these terms to be merged on output:

Another **great**ACME product

Even when the Strip Space element specifies the removal of whitespace from all elements, it is still possible to make exceptions for such cases. The **Preserve Space** element also uses an **Elements** attribute to list elements that are not to be trimmed in this way:

```
<preserve-space elements="para" />
```

Recall that by default all elements are preserved. The following rule is therefore implied:

```
<preserve-space elements="*" />
```

When both the Strip Space and Preserve Space elements are used, any conflicts are resolved. For example, when one element contains '*' and the other contains an element name, the element name is deemed to be more explicit than '*' and so overrules the general case. The Elements attribute is allowed to contain either '*' or a space-separated list of element names (which can be qualified with a name-space, such as 'html:pre html:code').

Stylesheet whitespace

Spaces are often used in stylesheets to make them easier to read, for the same reasons as they are in other XML documents. But in this case, all insignificant whitespace is removed by the XSLT processor automatically. The two examples below would produce identical output:

```
<xsl:stylesheet match="para"><P><xsl:apply-templates/></
P></xsl:stylesheet>
```

```
<xsl:stylesheet match="para">
<P>
  <xsl:apply-templates/>
</P>
</xsl:stylesheet>
```

This is why the **Text** element is so important – it preserves whitespace belonging to the actual document that would otherwise be removed.

5. Outputting elements

Most stylesheets output element tags, whether they are being used to transform an XML document into another XML document, or to create an HTML rendition for viewing in a Web browser. There are a number of issues to consider and XSLT features targetted at this need.

Element output

It has previously been shown that literal result elements can be embedded in a template. This approach can be used to create XHTML, XSL and arbitrary XML documents.

XSL format output

The XSLT standard was initially developed primarily to support the XSL formatting language. In this case, it is necessary to create a file that contains formatting instructions, and the output must be an XML document that contains elements and attributes that hold this formatting information. The **Formatting Objects** namespace defines these elements and attributes. In the specification, and in all the examples in this book, these elements have a namespace prefix of **fo** (formatting object). For example, to format a Note element as a bold paragraph block, the Block element is required with a Font Weight attribute that indicates bold styling:

```
<template match="note">
  <fo:block font-weight="bold">
    <apply-templates/>
  </fo:block>
</template>
```

This template would match the following XML document fragment:

```
<note>This is a note</note>
```

When encountering this fragment, the output from the XSL processor would be:

```
<fo:block font-weight="bold">This is a note</fo:block>
```

XHTML format output

The XHTML standard is an XML compliant standard. Like XSL, the XHTML formatting elements are defined by an XML DTD. XHTML documents can be output using exactly the same teachniques:

```
<xsl:template ...>
  <DIV><B><xsl:apply-templates/></B></DIV>
</xsl:template>
```

But the older HTML standard is not fully compliant with XML syntax requirements, despite looking very similar.

XML transformation output

It is not obligatory for an XSLT processor to produce an XML document that conforms to the Formatting Object namespace, the XHTML namespace, or indeed to a formatting language of any kind. The output can instead be another generic XML document. The pattern-matching and resequencing capabilities described in later chapters can be used to manipulate the document into other forms, perhaps omitting or repositioning information.

The output can be a document that conforms to a different document model. In the following source document, the name precedes the employee number:

```
<employee>
  <name>J Smith</name>
  <number>123</number>
</employee>
```

A single template can rearrange the embedded elements and give these elements new names:

```
<xsl:template match="employee">
  <PERSON>
  <NUM><xsl:apply-templates select="number"/></NUM>
  <NM><xsl:apply-templates select="name"/></NM>
  </PERSON>
</xsl:template>
```

The result would be as follows:

```
<PERSON><NUM>123</NUM><NM>J Smith</NM></PERSON>
```

In this context, the name 'stylesheet' is a little misleading, because no actual styling is involved in the process.

Element generation

The use of literal element tags is not the only way to add elements to the result tree. Another technique can be used that has some advantages (and disadvantages).

The Element element

The **Element** element can be used to generate element tags. The name of the element to output is specified in the **Name** attribute:

```
<element name="OL">
  ...
  <!-- CONTENT OF OL ELEMENT -->
  ...
</element>


   <OL>...</OL>
```

Comparison with literal element tags

At first sight, this appears to be a less elegant alternative to simply embedding literal element tags within the stylesheet. Indeed, most people would agree that the stylesheet is less readable when using this technique. The contrast can be demonstrated by the following examples, which are functionally identical:

```
<xsl:template match="book">
  <DOC>
    <TITLE>Test</TITLE>
    <MAIN>
      <xsl:apply-templates/>
    </MAIN>
  </DOC>
</xsl:template>


<template match="book">
  <element name="DOC">
    <element name="TITLE">Test</element>
    <element name="MAIN">
      <apply-templates/>
    </element>
  </element>
</template>
```

However, one good reason for using this technique is that an element can be created with a name that is derived from the result of a computation. This is because the Name attribute contains an XPath expression. This expression could be a variable reference (see Chapter 13), or used to calculate the name of the element to output in some other way.

Another good reason for using this element is to avoid the problem that arises when attempting to use a DTD-sensitive XML editor to create the stylesheet. Incorporating output elements into the document requires that the DTD be updated to allow them to occur (and it is not suffcient simply to copy the original element and attribute declarations into the XSLT DTD because element content models must also be changed to allow embedded XSLT elements). When formatting the stylesheet on-screen to assist with stylesheet authoring, it would also be necessary to create display formats for each of the elements. But the Element element is already part of the XSLT DTD and a capable XML document editor will allow the Name attribute value to be presented at all times, at least partly overcoming the legibility issue:

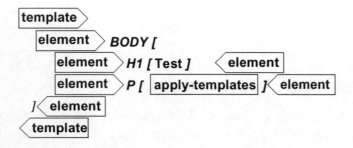

Finally, as the comparative examples above demonstrate, there is no real need for namespaces when using this technique, which simplifies and therefore clarifies the stylesheet document markup.

Attributes

Just as there are two methods for creating an element in the result tree, there is also a second way to create an attribute and attach it to an element.

The Attribute element

The **Attribute** element represents a single output attribute. The **Name** attribute specifies the name of the attribute, and the content of this element represents the attribute value:

```
<attribute name="author">J. Smith</attribute>
```

This example would create the following attribute, within an element start-tag:

```
author="J. Smith"
```

Usage with element definitions

The primary need for this element is to add attributes to output elements defined using the Element element described above. The Attribute element is placed within the Element element:

```
<template match="book">
  <element name="doc">
    <attribute name="author">J. Smith</attribute>
    <apply-templates/>
  </element>
</template>
```

```
    <doc author="J. Smith">...</doc>
```

The attribute is attached to the nearest ancestor element definition (the nearest element that encloses it). In the following example, the first attribute is attached to the Doc element, but the second is associated with the Para element:

```
<element name="doc">
  <attribute name="author">J. Smith</attribute>
  <element name="para">
    <attribute name="type">SECRET</attribute>
    <apply-templates/>
  <element>
</element>
```

```
    <doc author="J. Smith">
      <para type="SECRET">...</para>
      ...
    </doc>
```

Usage with output elements

The Attribute element can also be used when the element is a literal element:

```
<xsl:template match="book">
  <doc>
    <xsl:attribute name="author">J. Smith</xsl:attribute>
    <xsl:apply-templates/>
  </doc>
</xsl:template>
```

In most cases, this would be a clumsy way to add an attribute to a literal element when it can be more easily entered directly in the start-tag. The following example generates output identical to the one above:

```
<xsl:template match="book">
  <doc author='J. Smith'>
    <xsl:apply-templates/>
  </doc>
</xsl:template>
```

But usage of the Attribute element in this scenario cannot be totally dismissed. This element may hold a wide range of other instruction elements, which can be useful when the attribute value needed depends upon some complex contextual circumstance. For example, a paragraph could be designated 'secret' if it contains an embedded Secret element (and 'normal' otherwise):

```
<xsl:template match"para">
  <Para>
    <xsl:attribute name="type">
      <xsl:choose>
        <xsl:when test=".//secret">SECRET</xsl:when>
        <xsl:otherwise>NORMAL</xsl:otherwise>
      </xsl:choose>
    </xsl:attribute>
    <xsl:apply-templates/>
  </Para>
</xsl:template>
```

Note that, by placing multiple attribute definitions within a Choose element, the previous example could be reformulated to avoid the need for instructions within the Attribute element. The XSLT processor will not attempt to add the attribute to the enclosing Choose element because it is able to distinguish between XSLT elements and output elements.

Multiple definitions

When there are multiple definitions for an attribute with the same attribute name, only the last is used. In the following example, the author name becomes 'J. Smith', not 'M. Moore' or 'K. Jones':

```
<xsl:template match"book">
  <doc author="M. Moore">
    <xsl:attribute name="author">K. Jones</xsl:attribute>
    <xsl:attribute name="author">J. Smith</xsl:attribute>
    <xsl:apply-templates/>
  </doc>
</xsl:template>


    <doc author="J. Smith">...</doc>
```

Attribute sets

Consider the possibility that Note, Warning and Danger elements are to be formatted in the same way, using XSL formatting attributes. If the specification were to change, all three of the templates below would need to be edited:

```
<template match="note">
  <fo:block color="blue" font-weight="bold">
    <apply-templates/>
  </fo:block>
</template>

<template match="warning">
  <fo:block color="blue" font-weight="bold">
    <apply-templates/>
  </fo:block>
</template>

<template match="danger">
  <fo:block color="blue" font-weight="bold">
    <apply-templates/>
  </fo:block>
</template>
```

When the same attributes need to be attached to a number of output elements, they can be defined in a single place and referenced each time they are needed. The group of attributes concerned are defined using **Attribute** elements, but these elements are enclosed in the **Attribute Set** element. This set of elements is referenced by name, which is given by the **Name** attribute:

```
<attribute-set name="attention">
  <attribute name="color">blue</attribute>
  <attribute name="font-weight">bold</attribute>
</attribute-set>
```

The 'attention' set defined above can then be inserted by reference into the three templates using the **Use Attribute Sets** attribute. This attribute can be used in the Element element:

```
<template match="note">
  <element name="block" use-attribute-sets="attention">
    <apply-templates/>
  </element>
</template>

<template match="warning">
  <element name="block" use-attribute-sets="attention">
    <apply-templates/>
  </element>
</template>

<template match="danger">
  <element name="block" use-attribute-sets="attention">
    <apply-templates/>
  </element>
</template>
```

This attribute can also be added to output elements, but the namespaces scheme requires a prefix that maps to the XSLT namespace:

```
<xsl:template match="note">
  <block xsl:use-attribute-sets="attention">
    <xsl:apply-templates/>
  </block>
</xsl:template>
```

Conveniently, it is possible to override one or more of the attributes defined in the set simply by specifying a new value in the output element:

```
<xsl:attribute-set name="attention">
  <xsl:attribute name="color">blue</attribute>
  <xsl:attribute name="font-weight">bold</attribute>
</xsl:attribute-set>
```

```
    <block xsl:use-attribute-set="attention" color="red">...
```

Expressions can be used in the attributes defined in an attribute set, and expressions that take into consideration the current context of the node being processed will work correctly. Variables may also be included, but only variables that are defined at the top level will be 'visible' within the attribute set definition.

When an imported stylesheet contains an Attribute Set element of the same name as one in the main stylesheet, importance rules dictate that an attribute with the same name, but of lower importance, will be ignored.

Breaking well-formed constraints

Because an XSLT document must be a valid XML document, it follows that it must be well-formed. This means that the XSLT instruction elements must be properly nested, that any literal XML or HTML output elements must also be properly nested, and finally that the mixture of both sets of elements must also be properly nested. On occasions, this requirement can cause difficulties. For example, a list of alternating names and employee numbers may need to be converted into a number of paragraphs, each containing a name and following number:

```
<name>J Smith</name>
<number>123</number>
<name>P Jones</name>
<number>321</number>
```

The obvious way to do this is to create a new Paragraph element at the start of each name and end it after the following number, but this would make the stylesheet itself invalid because the Paragraph element would then start in one Template element and end in another, therefore crossing other element boundaries:

```
<xsl:template match="name">
  <P>
  <xsl:apply-templates/>
</xsl:template>
<xsl:template match="number">
  <xsl:apply-templates/>
  </P>
</xsl:template>
```

illegal overlapping structure

Ineffective 'solutions'

It is not possible to overcome this limitation by 'hiding' the markup with the use of entity references, or even character entity references. The following does not work because the '<' and '>' references are output in this form, not as actual '<' and '>' characters, and so no application (not even a Web browser) will ever 'see' them as markup delimiters:

```
<xsl:template match="name">
  &lt;P&gt;    <!-- DOES NOT WORK -->
  <xsl:apply-templates/>
</xsl:template>

<xsl:template match="number">
  <xsl:text> </xsl:text>
  <xsl:apply-templates/>
  &lt;/P&gt;    <!-- DOES NOT WORK -->
</xsl:template>
```

```
  &lt;P&gt;J Smith 123&lt;/P&gt;
  &lt;P&gt;P Jones 321&lt;/P&gt;
```

Note that this *is* a good way to demonstrate XML or HTML markup in a Web page. The example above would appear to the audience as follows:

```
<P>J Smith 123</P><P>P Jones 321</P>
```

Neither would it help to use CDATA sections, as in the next example. Again, the processor would either preserve the CDATA section in the output file or convert the characters into references:

```
<xsl:template match="number">
  <xsl:apply-templates/>
  <![CDATA[</P>]]>    <!-- DOES NOT WORK -->
</xsl:template>
```

Disable output escaping

This problem can be overcome by using the **Disable Output Escaping** attribute, setting its value to 'yes'. This attribute can be applied to the Text element and the Value Of element, and ensures that entity references representing significant XML markup delimiters are replaced by the characters they represent in the result tree:

```
<template match="name">
  <text disable-output-escaping="yes">&lt;P&gt;</text>
  <apply-templates/>
</template>

<template match="Number">
  <text> </text>
  <apply-templates/>
  <text disable-output-escaping="yes">&lt;/P&gt;</text>
</template>
```

```
<P>J Smith 123</P><P>P Jones 321</P>
```

J Smith 123

P Jones 321

The problem can also be overcome in a more efficient way if the XSLT processor supports the text output mode (see Chapter 8).

6. XML output

One of the most significant transformation tasks that XSLT can achieve involves the creation of a new XML document that conforms to a different model to the source document. Conversion to the XSL document model is just one example of this capability. XSLT therefore includes a number of features for outputting XML structures including the XML declaration and the document type definition, comments and processing instructions, character data sections, and whole branches of the source tree.

The material in this chapter is directly relevant to those interested in creating XHTML documents from arbitrary XML documents, but Chapter 7 contains more relevant material on the creation of HTML documents (which do not fully conform to the XML standard).

XML output format

By default, an XSLT processor usually expects to output a new XML-format document. Just to be certain, however, an XSLT processor can be explicitly told that the transformation will create another XML document. The **Method** attribute in the **Output** element contains the value '**xml**'. This is a top-level element, so is directly placed within the Stylesheet element:

```
<stylesheet ...>
  <output method="xml" />
  ...
</stylesheet>
```

The XSLT processor then does its best to ensure that the output conforms to the XML standard.

Note that by default an XSLT processor will assume that the output mode is not XML in the single case that the result tree root element is '<html>' (or '<HTML>'). In this one case, it assumes that the ouput will be an HTML document.

XML declaration

The **Omit XML Declaration** attribute specifies whether or not an XML declaration is to be included in the output document and has the value 'yes' or 'no'.

When set to 'no', the declaration is created (it may appear confusing that 'no' means *do* include the declaration, but the trick is to focus on the word 'omit' in the name of this attribute):

```
<output ... omit-xml-declaration="yes" />


   <book>
   ...
   </book>


<output ... omit-xml-declaration="no" />


   <?xml ...?>
   <book>
   ...
   </book>
```

When this attribute is set to 'no' (the declaration is to be created) the **Standalone** attribute can be used to specify whether or not the output document is a standalone XML document (one that does not require a DTD to be accessed for accurate interpretation). This attribute also takes a value of 'yes' or 'no'. If the **Encoding** attribute is used, its content will also be copied into the XML declaration:

```
<output ... omit-xml-declaration="no"
            version="1.0"
            encoding="ISO-8859-1"
            standalone="yes"  />


   <?xml version="1.0" encoding="ISO-8859-1"
                       standalone="yes" ?>
```

At this time, it is not strictly necessary to include the **Version** attribute in the Output element, because a version value of '1.0' will be assumed. When future versions of XML exist, it will become more useful (it is already relevant when outputting HTML documents).

Document type declaration

The **Doctype System** attribute specifies that the output document should have an XML document type declaration, with the system identifier provided by the value of this attribute:

```
<output ... doctype-system="dtds/book.dtd" />


   <!DOCTYPE book SYSTEM="dtds/book.dtd" >
   <book>...</book>
```

The **Doctype Public** attribute specifies the public identifier to supply. The Doctype System attribute must be given as well, in order to conform to XML rules, even if it contains only an empty string:

```
<output ... doctype-public="myBookDef" doctype-system=""/>


   <!DOCTYPE book PUBLIC="myBookDef" "" >
   <book>
     ...
   </book>
```

Comments

An XML comment can be created using the **Comment** element. When output, the start-tag is replaced with '<!--' and the end-tag with '-->':

```
<comment>This is a comment</comment>


   <!--This is a comment-->
```

Content limitations

Because the '-' symbol is significant in the resulting comment markup, there are some constraints on its use in the text of the comment. An error may be reported if '--' appears in the text because it would signify early temination of the comment. An error may also be reported if a single '-' symbol ends the comment:

```
<comment>The -- sequence is illegal, as is -</comment>


   <!--The -- sequence is illegal, as is --->
```

Sophisticated XSLT processors may recover from such problems on the user's behalf by inserting spaces at significant points:

```
<!--The - - sequence is illegal, as is - -->
```

Copying-through comments

Comments in the source document can be copied-through to the output by creating a template to match **comment**() nodes. Both examples below will work equally well (the Copy Of element is discussed later):

```
<template match="comment()">
  <comment><value-of select="."/></comment>
</template>

<template match="comment()">
  <copy-of select="."/>
</template>
```

But this will only work if the parser and application reading the source file on behalf of the XSLT processor have not already discarded source comments. A better method is described below (when discussing the Copy element).

Constructing comment text

The first example above shows the use of the Value Of element within a comment. This element can be used to do far more than simply copy an existing comment through to the output. In addition, a number of other instruction elements may be used within the Comment element. Although the final content of any comment must be a simple text string, this string can be constructed using advanced XSLT features. For example, the Apply Templates element can be used. This is useful for transforming an element in the source document into a comment in the output:

```
<author-note>Edit the following text</author-note>
```

```
<template match="author-note">
  <comment><apply-templates/></comment>
</template>
```

```
<!--Edit the following text-->
```

As another example, it is possible to insert the value of an attribute into a comment, and to generate content depending upon a condition such as the presence of this attribute (the '@' prefix identifies an attribute name):

```
<book author="J. Smith">...</book>
```

```
<template match="book">
  <comment><text>This is a book</text>
    <if test="@author"/>
      <text>, the author is </text>
      <value-of select="@author">
    </if>
  </comment>
</template>
```

```
<!--This is a book, the author is J. Smith-->
```

The elements that may be used in Comment elements (including several not yet introduced) include Apply Templates, Call Template, Apply Imports, For Each, Value Of, Copy Of, Number, Choose, If, Text, Copy, Variable and Message (as well as the Fallback element).

Processing instructions

An XML processing instruction can be created using the **Processing Instruction** element. It has a **Name** attribute to hold the name of the target application (which becomes the first word in the processing instruction). The content of the element becomes the actual instruction:

```
<page-break/>
```

```
<template match="page-break">
  <processing-instruction name="ACME">
    {new page}
  </processing-instruction>
</template>
```

```
<?ACME {new page}?>
```

Because a processing instruction ends with the characters '?>', it is illegal for the text in the instruction to contain this sequence of characters. An error may be reported if such a sequence occurs.

Copying-through

Processing instructions in the source document can be copied through to the output by creating a template to match **processing-instruction**() nodes:

```
<?ACME {new page}?>
```

```
<template match="processing-instruction()">
  <processing-instruction name="ACME">
    <copy-of select="."/>
  </processing-instruction>
</template>
```

```
<?ACME {new page}?>
```

But this will only work if the parser and application that read the source file and build the source tree have preserved such markup. Also note that the alternative method shown to copy-through comments (using the Value Of element) will not work for processing instructions because it is also necessary here to copy-through the target application name. However, a better method is described below when discussing the Copy element.

Construction

A number of instruction elements may be used within the Processing Instruction element, allowing an embedded instruction to be generated in a variety of ways. For example, the instruction may need to vary depending on the value of a variable in the enclosing element:

```
<entry type="major">...</entry>
```

```
<entry type="minor">...</entry>
```

```
<template match="entry">
  <processing-instruction name="ACME">
    <if test="@type='major'"/>
      {new page}
    </if>
    <if test="@type='minor'"/>
      {new column}
    </if>
  </processing-instruction>
</template>
```

```
<?ACME {new page}?>
```

```
<?ACME {new column}?>
```

A large number of instruction elements may be used here (see the list at the end of the Comments section above).

Copying source structures

There may be times when some source document constructs need to be copied to the result tree without modification. Two instructions are available for specifying the copy-through of source document fragments.

Copying document fragments

The **Copy Of** element can be used to copy such structures directly to output. The **Select** attribute contains an expression that locates the fragment (or fragments) to copy-through. To copy the current element and all of its descendants, the expression needs to refer to the current element ('.'). For example, a source document that contains tabular structures that are already coded according to the XHTML table standard could be converted into an XHTML document, in which case the table could be copied through untouched:

```
<template match="table"><copy-of select="."/></template>
```

It is important to reiterate that all the content of the given element is copied to output including descendent elements and their attributes, the text content of elements, as well as processing instructions and comments.

Other expressions copy-through elements from elsewhere in the source document. The following example copies all of the Title elements in the source tree to output as a single block, but at the beginning of a book:

```
<template match="book">
  <copy-of select="//title" />
  ...
</template>
```

The meaning of the '//' in the Select attribute is explained in Chapter 9.

The fragment copied does not have to be an element. The examples below show how this instruction can be used to copy-through other markup such as comments and processing instructions.

Copying nodes

A more limited variant of copying-through is available – it copies the current node, but not its descendent nodes. The **Copy** element represents the current node. For example, the templates to copy-through comments and processing instructions can be made much simpler than in the techniques shown previously:

```
<template match="comment()">
  <copy/>
</template>
```

```
<template match="processing-instruction()">
  <copy/>
</template>
```

This works reliably because these node types have no child nodes, unlike elements. However, even element nodes can be usefully processed in this way.

Although element nodes can be copied using this technique, their attributes and children (text and sub-elements) are *not* copied. This problem can be overcome by selectively re-adding attributes and copying through the attribute values. But if the stylesheet author cannot be sure which attributes an element may contain, then a simple and effective method is to apply templates to all attached attributes, as in the following example:

```
<template match="*">
  <!-- copy-through original start-tag -->
  <copy>
    <!-- add original attributes to new start-tag -->
    <apply-templates select="@*" />
    <!-- now process child elements -->
    <apply-templates />
  <!-- output original end-tag
  </copy>
</template>
```

The fact that the original node type is inferred means that some of the templates shown above can be combined into a single template. When the template matches a comment, it is a comment that is created; when it matches a processing instruction, it is a processing instruction that is created:

```
<template match="comment()|processing-instruction()">
  <copy/>
</template>
```

But the following example demonstrates the ultimate single template for all document nodes:

```
<template match="node()|@*">
  <copy>
    <apply-templates select="node()|@*" />
  </copy>
</template>
```

This is the identify transformation template that was first introduced in Chapter 3.

Note that this does not work reliably if any text is added to the template around the Copy element.

CDATA sections

The text content of selected elements can be output as character data sections (CDATA sections), '<![CDATA[...]]>'. These structures are used to avoid the need for '<', '&' and other entity references to represent significant markup characters when they appear in the text. The **Cdata Section Elements** attribute holds the names of the *output* elements concerned (*not* the source elements). In the following example, it is the generated Code element that is mentioned in this attribute, rather than the source Software element:

```
<software>if (6 &lt; 9) then ...</software>
```

```
<xsl:output cdata-section-elements="code ... ..." />
...
<xsl:template match="software">
  <code><xsl:apply-templates/></code>
</xsl:template>
```

```
<code><![CDATA[if (6 < 9) then ...]]></code>
```

Note that if the text happens to contain the characters ']]>' then this must be broken into two parts to avoid indication of an early end to the CDATA section. Two CDATA sections are created with the ']]' sequence between them and the '>' in the second:

```
<![CDATA[ ... ]]>]]<![CDATA[> ...]]>
```

7. HTML output

The first important use of XSLT has been to convert XML documents into HTML Web pages for display in browsers. This can be done either by treating the HTML output as just another XML document, with some complications, or by use of a special HTML output mode. Readers not intending to use XSLT for this purpose can safely ignore this chapter (but note that Chapter 28 provides an overview of HTML that may assist with understanding the HTML examples throughout this book).

Pseudo HTML output

The HTML data format used to tag Web pages for presentation in browsers is, like XML, based on SGML concepts and syntax. The format of start-tags, end-tags, attributes and entity references is essentially the same. For this reason, there is enough similarity between HTML documents and well-formed XML documents that it is possible to output an XML file that will be accepted as an HTML document by existing Web browsers. For example, the HTML tag '<P>' (Paragraph) can also be considered to be a valid XML tag. The following example replaces a Note element with HTML P and B (Bold) elements:

```
<xsl:template match="note">
  <P CLASS="notepara1"><B><xsl:apply-templates/></B></P>
</xsl:template>
```

Minimization issues

It is important to note here that none of the markup minimization techniques allowed in HTML documents are permitted in XML. For example, the following template is not legal for two reasons: the Paragraph end-tag is missing, and the attribute value is not quoted. The stylesheet itself is therefore an invalid XML document instance:

```
<xsl:template match="note">
  <P CLASS=notepara1><!-- MISSING QUOTES -->
    <B><xsl:apply-templates/></B>
  <!-- MISSING END PARA -->
</xsl:template>
```

But this is only of minor inconvenience. These problems are easily avoided by ensuring that no minimization techniques are used. The following example is a valid version of the one above, and the HTML output is recognized and rendered by a Web browser in the same way:

```
<xsl:template match="note">
  <P CLASS="notepara1">
    <B><xsl:apply-templates/></B>
  </P>
</xsl:template>
```

Empty element issues

Much more serious than the minimization issues raised above, there is a discrepancy between HTML and XML concerning the format of empty elements. The XML specification allows empty elements to be represented by a single tag, ending with '/>'. HTML does not use this form but does allow the end-tag to be omitted. In some cases a browser may even insist on the end-tag being omitted. The next section describes a clean way to generate true HTML output; but that option may not be supported by the chosen XSLT processor, in which case the more primitive techniques described here must be used.

In HTML 4.0, the empty elements are:

- AREA (a clickable area of an image)
- BASE (a specified new base 'home' directory)
- BASEFONT (a specified font to use as the default)
- BR (break – start a new line)
- COL (definitions of various attributes for one column of a table)
- FRAME (specification for a single independent region of the browser window)
- HR (horizonal rule – a line across the page)
- IMG (image identifier)
- ISINDEX (query allowed)
- LINK (linked resources, including stylesheets)
- META (meta data)
- PARAM (applet parameter).

The most commonly needed are IMG and BR. Some current browsers object to the '/>' empty element markup, even if a preceding space is inserted (and retained by the XSLT processor on output). Using end-tags is preferable, though some XSLT processors may automatically reduce tags with no content to the single tag form. It may therefore be necessary to ensure that this does not happen by enclosing a preserved single space in a text element:

```
<xsl:stylesheet match="newline">
  <BR><xsl:text> </xsl:text></BR>
</xsl:stylesheet>
```

Current browsers accept this approach, but in the example above interpret this as two line-break instructions instead of one.

Attribute name and value issues

HTML exploits one of the minimization features of SGML that allows an attribute name, equals symbol and quotation marks to be omitted, leaving only the attribute value present in the start-tag. The presence of this value is sufficient to 'switch-on' the feature it describes. For example, the word 'COMPACT' in the start-tag of a list-describing element instructs the browser to close up the list items:

```
<OL COMPACT>...</OL>

<SELECT NAME="colour">
  <OPTION>red</OPTION>
  <OPTION SELECTED>green</OPTION>
  <OPTION>blue</OPTION>
</SELECT>
```

This minimization feature is not permitted in XML documents. The attribute name, equals symbol and quotation marks must all be present. The attribute name is simply the same word as the attribute value:

```
<OL COMPACT="COMPACT">...</OL>

<SELECT NAME="colour">
  <OPTION>red</OPTION>
  <OPTION SELECTED="SELECTED">green</OPTION>
  <OPTION>blue</OPTION>
</SELECT>
```

True HTML output

The previous section outlined a number of issues that are raised when attempting to output an HTML document that conforms to the XML standard. To avoid these problems, the XSLT standard includes a mechanism for outputting documents that conform to the HTML standard. The **Output** element is used to specify the output format required. When the value '**html**' is entered in the **Method** element, HTML tags are recognized and processed intelligently:

```
<stylesheet ...>
  <output method="html" ... />
  ...
</stylesheet>
```

Note that the default value will be 'html' (rather than 'xml') if the root element to be output is named 'html' or 'HTML' (or any other variant on letter-case such as 'Html'), has no namespace prefix, and is preceded by nothing more than whitespace characters.

HTML output characteristics

Perhaps the most significant change when outputting in HTML mode is that empty elements adopt HTML syntax conventions. For example, the empty element BR is output as a normal start-tag, and the end-tag is omitted:

```
... first line<breakline/>second line ...
```

```
<xsl:template match="breakline">
  <BR/>
</xsl:template>
```

```
... first line<BR>second line ...
```

Special markup characters are the same in HTML as in XML and serve the same purposes. In HTML, '&' is used to represent '&', '<' is used to represent '<' and '>' is used to represent '>' wherever usage of the actual character could confuse the browser as it attempts to identify entity references and element tags. However, an HTML document does not use the escape sequences in some special cases, and so the XSLT processor must output original characters in these circumstances. Specifically, the content of the SCRIPT and STYLE elements conform to formats other than HTML (typically JavaScript and CSS respectively):

```
<SCRIPT> ...  ( A < B ) ... </SCRIPT>
```

In HTML, an attribute is allowed to contain the '<' character. The entity reference '<' should therefore be transformed in to '<':

```
<xsl:template ...>
  <IMG ... ALT="figure showing that 6 &lt; 7"></IMG>
</xsl:template>
```

```
... <IMG ... ALT="figure showing that 6 < 7"> ...
```

Recognizing HTML elements

Even when HTML mode has been set using the Output element, this mode is only used for elements that have no namespace mapping to a URL. To distinguish HTML elements from XSLT elements, it is therefore usual to map the XSLT elements to a prefix instead of the HTML elements:

```
<xsl:stylesheet ... xmlns:xsl="...">
  <xsl:template...>
    <HTML>
      <HEAD><TITLE>The Page Title</TITLE></HEAD>
      <xsl:apply-templates/>
    </HTML>
  </xsl:template>
</xsl:stylesheet>
```

There have been a number of HTML versions released since the introduction of this language in 1995. The number of tags differs between versions. New tag names have been introduced as old ones have been first discouraged, and then made obsolete. The **Version** attribute specifies the version of HTML to use for the output. A value of '4.0' (the default) specifies HTML 4.0 output (where other valid options include '3.2' and '2.0'):

```
<output ... version="4.0" />
```

In future, this attribute value may be used to warn an XSLT processor that it is being asked to create a version of HTML that was released after the program was created, and which it therefore does not understand. In this case, it may warn the user, or even refuse to continue.

Elements that are deemed to be HTML elements by their namespace designation (using the default namespace), but are not recognized as elements belonging to the specified version of HTML, are nevertheless treated as HTML elements. But, because they are unknown, they cannot be processed intelligently. The fallback behaviour is to treat such elements as in-line, non-empty elements:

```
<P>This paragaph contains an <UNKNOWN>unknown</UNKNOWN>
element.</P>
```

HTML element tag names are not case sensitive. A tag in the stylesheet will be recognized as an HTML tag if the name matches, regardless of the letter-case used. The following examples both produce BR elements:

```
<xsl:template...>
  <BR></BR>broken text<br></br>
  <xsl:apply-templates/>
</xsl:template>
```

```
    ... <BR>broken text<br> ...
```

Processing instructions

HTML processing instructions differ slightly from XML processing instructions. The question mark delimiter character is not needed at the end of the tag (the Processing Instruction element is discussed in Chapter 6):

```
<template...>
  <processing-instruction name="SPECIAL">some-
    instruction</processing-instruction>
  <apply-templates/>
</template>
```

```
    ... <?SPECIAL some-instruction> ...
```

Minimized attributes

When an HTML attribute can have only one value, and the presence or absence of the value acts as a simple switch, the convention is to include only the value in the element start-tag (omitting the attribute name, equals symbol and enclosing quotes). For example, the OL element (ordered list) may take the 'COMPACT' attribute to close up items in the list:

```
<xsl:template...>
  <OL COMPACT="compact"><xsl:apply-templates/></OL>
</xsl:template>
```

```
    <OL compact> ... </OL>
```

DOCTYPE declaration

The HTML file produced can be given a document type declaration by specifying the **Doctype Public** and/or the **Doctype System** attributes:

```
<output ... doctype-system="html4.0.dtd" />
```

```
    <!DOCTYPE HTML SYSTEM "html4.0.dtd">
    <HTML>...</HTML>
```

```
<output ... doctype-public="-//html..."
            doctype-system="html4.0.dtd" />
```

```
    <!DOCTYPE HTML PUBLIC "-//html..." "html4.0.dtd">
    <HTML>...</HTML>
```

Characters

The **Encoding** attribute in the Output element specifies the output character scheme. Its value should be copied to the **charset** attribute of a suitable META element in the HEAD element (if the HEAD element has been created):

```
<output ... media-type="text/html"
             encoding="ISO-8859-1" />


  <HEAD>
    <META http-equiv="Content-Type"
          content="text/html" charset="ISO-8859" >
  </HEAD>
  ...
```

Note that the **Media Type** attribute is also used, but in this case to populate the **content** attribute.

The HTML format allows for the possible use of entity references for many extended characters. The reference names are taken from sets defined by the ISO and so are often the same as those defined in XML source documents. For example, 'é' is almost universally used to represent the e-acute character 'é' (see Chapter 34).

8. Text output

XML data often needs to be processed for delivery to tools that are not XML-compliant. For example, there are many text-based formatting languages including RTF, XPress Tags, TROFF and T$_E$X. It is necessary to suppress formatting spaces and XML markup constructs, and to gain precise control over the location of line-end codes. It is often also necessary to 'escape' characters in the text that are significant in the tagging language concerned.

Non-XML output

It may seem obvious that it is not necessary for the output of an XSLT transformation process to be an XML document. After all, there is no requirement to include output element tags in the templates. For example, the following template outputs RTF tags instead of XML element tags:

```
<template match="para">
  <text>\pard\fs24</text>
  <apply-templates/>
  <text>\par</text>
</template>
```

Yet there are some issues that need to be addressed. It is necessary to avoid outputting all XML-specific markup, while catering for any special requirements that the replacement data format imposes.

There are two ways of outputting text documents. The first uses various techniques to avoid the generation of XML markup constructs, such as the XML declaration. The second involves telling the XSLT processor to output data in a special 'text mode'.

Regardless of which method is used, it must be recognised that many text-based data formats place particular significance on line-endings. For example, the CSV (Comma Separated Values) format uses line-end codes to indicate the end of each record. So it is often also necessary to suppress any line-end codes in the source XML document and in the stylesheet that might inadvertently be copied to output, while inserting new line-end codes at appropriate locations.

Pseudo text output

The first technique for outputting non-XML documents uses a combination of techniques to suppress XML markup. This includes entity references that represent significant XML delimiter characters, the presence of an XML declaration, and the generation of namespace prefixes on text that resembles XML element tags. Although the alternative technique described later is preferable, it relies upon an optional feature of the XSLT standard, so may not be supported by every XSLT processor. The techniques described here must be employed instead when this is the case.

Avoiding XML character escaping

Due to the default assumption that the output file will be read by an XML parser, special XML markup delimiter characters are represented by XML entity references when appearing as normal data characters. In particular, if the characters '<', '>' or '&' appear in the replacement text, they will be output as '<', '>' and '&' respectively. But only XML parsers will recognize these as codes that represent single characters. These codes must be avoided if the output file is not going to be read by an XML parser. Earlier, it was shown that the Disable Output Escaping attribute may be used to overcome this problem. Consider the following example, which attempts to output data that contains many '&' characters:

```
<template select="names">
  <value-of select="name1">
  <text disable-output-escaping="yes"> &amp; </text>
  <value-of select="name2">
  <text disable-output-escaping="yes"> &amp; </text>
  <value-of select="name3">
  <text disable-output-escaping="yes"> &amp; </text>
</template>


    Smith & Jones & Peterson
```

It is also necessary to deal with special characters that occur in the source text. By default, when the Apply Templates instruction is applied to a text node, the characters '&', '<' and '>' are output as '&', '<' and '>'. To avoid this happening, it is necessary to override the default processing of text nodes as follows. The value of the current text node is output, with escaping disabled:

```
    <company>Smith &amp; Son</company>


<template match="text()">
  <value-of select="." disable-output-escaping="yes" />
</template>


    ... Smith & Son ...
```

Avoiding the XML declaration

Clearly, there should be no XML declaration at the top of anything but an XML data file. The **Omit XML Declaration** attribute can be set to 'yes' in the Output element in order to suppress it:

```
<output ... omit-xml-declaration="yes" />
```

Avoiding namespaces

Only the XML data format uses the namespaces scheme, yet stylesheet processors are only too keen to add namespace declaration to the output. By default, all output files have the namespace attached to the root output element. Of course, there should not be an issue here because elements are not being output. But if something that merely resembles an element tag is output, the namespace attribute will be attached to it. One way to avoid this is to use the default namespace, and to set the **Exclude Result Prefixes** attribute value in the Stylesheet element to '#default' (to omit the declaration for the default namespace), or simply to not use any namespace for output elements at all:

```
<stylesheet ... exclude-result-prefixes="#default">
  ...
</stylesheet>
```

Text output mode

The techniques described above are complex and untidy. Fortunately, the XSLT standard includes a mechanism that makes output of non-XML data much simpler. However, this is an optional mechanism so an XSLT processor is not guaranteed to support it. In this circumstance, the techniques described above must be used.

Most XSLT processors support the **text mode** output option. In this mode, none of the reserved escape characters are converted into their entity reference form ('&', '<' or '>'). This makes the Disable Output Escaping attribute redundant. The main reason why this mode may not be supported is if an XSLT processor does not have control over the outputting of the result tree.

The **Output** element is used to specify text format output. The **Method** attribute is given the value '**text**':

```
<stylesheet ...>
  <output method="text"/>
  ...
<stylesheet>
```

It is important to note that text that resembles an element start-tag or end-tag is not copied to output. The first example below does not add any prefix or suffix 'tags' to the output, but the second example works as expected:

```
<xsl:template match="title">
  <!-- DOES NOT WORK -->
  <TITLE><xsl:apply-templates/></TITLE>
</xsl:template>

<xsl:template match="title">
  &lt;TITLE&gt;<xsl:apply-templates/>&lt;/TITLE&gt;
</xsl:template>
```

The **Media Type** attribute can be used in this scenario. The default value is '**text/ plain**':

```
<output method="text" media-type="text/xyz" />
```

The **Encoding** attribute can be used to specify how to represent special characters. If one or more characters in the source data cannot be represented by the format specified, the XSLT processor should then report an error:

```
<output method="text" encoding="ISO-8859-1/" />
```

Extended characters can be specified in the template using the '&#...;' mechanism. This same mechanism is very useful in the following discussion concerning line-endings.

Line-ending issues

Line-endings in text files have no relevance when the data format is XML, but in many other formats they are very important. For example, in the TROFF format, each formatting command must appear at the start of a new text line.

Adding line-endings to output

Line-end characters can be inserted into the output using XML character entity references. On Macintosh systems, the Carriage Return character (ASCII value 13) is used. On Unix sytems, it is the Line Feed character (ASCII value 10). On MS-DOS-based systems (Microsoft Windows) both characters are used, in the sequence Carriage Return followed by Line Feed. But, depending on the parser underlying the stylesheet processor, either character alone may produce the platform-specific outcome required (so this needs to be tested in the local environment). The following example outputs TROFF commands with each command beginning a new line on a UNIX system ('.PP' specifies a new paragraph):

```
<template match="warning">
.PP&#10;
WARNING:&#10;
.PP&#10;
<apply-templates/>
</template>


    .PP
    WARNING:
    .PP
    ......
```

Stylesheet whitespace

Whitespace in the stylesheet can cause problems here. As previously described, nodes that consist only of whitespace characters, including the line-feed and carriage-return characters, are removed from the stylesheet when it is processed. The following example therefore does not work as intended:

```
    <name>John Smith</name>
    <name>Peter Jones</name>


  <template match="name"><apply-templates/>&#10;</template>


    John SmithhPeter Jones
```

The obvious solution is to use the Text element to enclose the codes. This preserves them as required:

```
<template match="name">
  <apply-templates/><text>&#10;</text>
</template>
```

It is even possible to omit the entity references but include a 'hard' line-feed within the stylesheet instead, though this technique offers less control over exactly which line-feed characters are generated and spoils the formatting of the stylesheet:

```
<template match="name">
  <apply-templates/><text>
</text>
</template>
```

Source document line-endings

Whitespace in the source document can also cause problems. Specifically, a line-feed or carriage-return character in an element is normally just copied-through to the output:

```
    <code>10 PRINT "HELLO"</code>
    <code>20 GOTO
10</code>
```

```
<template match="code">
CODE LINE: <xsl:apply-templates/>
</template>
```

```
    CODE LINE: 10 PRINT "HELLO"
    CODE LINE: 20 GOTO
    10
```

This problem can be solved by replacing the Apply Templates instruction with the Value Of instruction, ensuring that the string it selects (the content of the current element) is normalized before it is inserted into the output:

```
<template match="code">
CODE LINE: <value-of select="normalize-space(.)" />
</template>
```

```
    CODE LINE: 10 PRINT "HELLO"
    CODE LINE: 20 GOTO 10
```

Whitespace issues

Whitespace characters inserted into the source XML document, to make the document easier to read, could have unfortunate consequences if included in the output. Using the **Strip Space** instruction (in the Stylesheet element) ensures that this whitespace is removed from all elements prior to template processing:

```
<strip-space elements="*" />
```

However, this instruction must be used with caution (as described in Chapter 4).

Escaping significant characters

When outputting in text mode, and creating a file that conforms to a data format other than XML, it is often the case that the file format will include markup of some kind and will have an escaping mechanism for document text characters that are also used as significant markup delimiter characters. For example, in the RTF format the character '{' is a significant markup character, and when this character is used in the text of a document it must be escaped using a '\' character, giving '\{'. This is of course similar to the XML escaping mechanism, where '<' stands-in for the '<' character.

Normally, a stylesheet will not be aware of this need. The default template for text nodes simply passes-through every character without modification. As a reminder, the following example is an explicit version of this template:

```
<template match="text()"><value-of select="."/></template>
```

Intercepting significant characters

Clearly, there is a need to intercept each text node and replace significant characters with their escaped forms. This can be done but it is not straightforward because
XSLT and XPath do not include any string replacement features, beyond a simple
function that replaces every instance of one character with a different character.
This function is inadequate because escaping strings almost inevitably consist of
multiple characters. A method is needed to replace a single character with a character string, such as '{' with '\{'.

String replacement template

The following template will perform string replacements (see Chapter 10 for
details on the decision-making instructions, Chapter 13 for details on how this template uses variables and parameters, and Chapter 22 for information on the XPath
functions used):

```
<template name="recursiveStringReplace">
  <param name="subString"/>
  <param name="findString"/>
  <param name="replacementString"/>

  <choose>
    <when test="contains($subString, $findString)">
      <value-of select="substring-before($subString,
                                          $findString)"/>
      <value-of select="$replacementString" />
      <variable name="restOfString"
                select="substring-after($subString,
                                        $findString)"/>
      <choose>
        <when test="contains($restOfString,
                             $findString)">
          <call-template name="recursiveStringReplace">
            <with-param name="subString"
                        select="$restOfString"/>
            <with-param name="findString"
                        select="$findString"/>
            <with-param name="replacementString"
                        select="$replacementString"/>
          </call-template>
        </when>
        <otherwise>
         <value-of select="$restOfString" />
        </otherwise>
      </choose>
    </when>
    <otherwise>
      <value-of select="$subString" />
    </otherwise>
  </choose>
</template>
```

Modified text template

The template above is called, perhaps multiple times, from within an explicit version of the text template. In the following example, the character '\' is replaced by the string '\\', the character '{' is replaced by the string '\{', and the character '}' is replaced by the string '\}' (line-feeds are also first converted into spaces). Variables are used to hold the intermediate strings:

```
<template match="text()">

  <!-- CONVERT LINE-FEED CHARACTERS INTO SPACES -->
  <variable name="string"
            select="translate(., '&#10;&#13;', '  ')" />

  <!-- CONVERT '\' INTO '\\' -->
  <variable name="slashesDone">
    <call-template name="recursiveStringReplace">
      <with-param name="subString" select="$string"/>
      <with-param name="findString">\</with-param>
      <with-param name="replacementString">\\</with-param>
    </call-template>
  </variable>

  <!-- CONVERT '{' INTO '\{' -->
  <variable name="leftBracketDone">
    <call-template name="recursiveStringReplace">
     <with-param name="subString" select="$slashesDone" />
      <with-param name="findStringv>{</with-param>
      <with-param name="replacementString">\{</with-param>
    </call-template>
  </variable>

  <!-- CONVERT '}' INTO '\}' -->
  <variable name="rightBracketDone">
    <call-template name="recursiveStringReplace">
      <with-param name="subString"
                  select="$leftBracketDone"/>
      <with-param name="findString">}</with-param>
      <with-param name="replacementString">\}</with-param>
    </call-template>
  </variable>

  <!-- OUTPUT 'the \\, the \{ and the \} characters
       are escaped!' (or similar!) -->
  <value-of select="$rightBracketDone"/>

</template>
```

9. Contextual formatting

The precise meaning of a particular element type may depend on where that instance of the element occurs within the document structure, and the processing of that element instance may need to be customized accordingly. XSLT is therefore able to identify the context and to apply different templates accordingly.

This chapter introduces XPath expressions, which are described more fully in Chapters 19 to 23.

Context considerations

Good design practice exploits the hierarchical nature of XML documents to minimize the number of different elements needed. For example, it should not be necessary to invent separate elements such as BookTitle, ChapterTitle, TableTitle and FigureTitle when a single Title element can play all of these roles. The precise meaning of any instance of this element can always be determined simply by looking to see what its parent element type is. If the parent element is a Chapter element, then this is a chapter title. There are also other contextual circumstances that may influence how the content of an element should be treated, including the exact nature of its contents, the value of one of its attributes, or what the preceding element is.

Due to widespread adoption of this design policy, effective transformation of XML documents can rarely be achieved simply by assigning one output style to each element type. For example, the title of a book would normally look very different from the title of a chapter or table. The stylesheet must be able to distinguish between each usage in order to apply appropriate formatting in each case. This is known as **contextual formatting**.

XML structures

Contextual formatting often involves the selection of elements that occur in specific locations in a document's structure. It is therefore necessary to first understand what XML element structures are, and to appreciate the terminology commonly used to describe relationships between parts of an XML document.

Note that not all of the concepts described in this section are relevant to contextual formatting, but they are important for later discussions on locating elements for reuse.

Children

An element may contain a number of embedded elements. These are termed **child** elements. These child elements share the same **parent** element. In the following example, the Title element and the Para element are both children of the Chapter element, and it follows that the parent of both of these elements is the Chapter element:

```
<chapter>
  <title>Embedded Title</title>
  <para>Embedded paragraph.</para>
</chapter>
```

Siblings

The Title and Para elements in the example above are **sibling** elements, because they share the same parent. An individual sibling can be identified by its sequential position. The first sibling in the example above is the Title element because it occurs first in the data stream (making it the 'oldest' sibling). The Para element follows the Title element, and it also happens to be the last sibling (making it the 'youngest'). The terms **preceding sibling** and **following sibling** are used to describe such ordering relationships.

Ancestors and descendants

The family tree analogy can be taken further. The term **ancestor** is used to describe any element that contains the one under discussion, no matter how many levels may separate the two. The parent element is also an ancestor element. In the following example, the Para element has three ancestors, including its parent Warning element:

```
<book>
  <chapter>
    <warning>
      <para>Embedded paragraph.</para>
```

Similarly, the term **descendant** is used to describe all embedded elements, including children. In the example above, the Book element has at least three descendants, including its child Chapter element.

Root element

All XML documents must contain a single element that has no parent, as in the Book element above. This is known as the **root** element because it is similar to the root of a tree (the ultimate source of all the branches). Formally, however, this is known as the **document element** (because it contains the entire document). It should be recalled that this element is *not* the root node of the source tree, but is in fact one of the children of this node.

Expressions

Context-specific formatting is provided by using several templates for the same source element. Only one of these templates is activated, and the selection is made by detecting which Match attribute holds the most accurate, context-specific description of the element being processed. Clearly, this means that the Match attributes cannot simply hold the name of the element in question. Each Match attribute must hold the additional information needed to decide which template is most relevant.

The value of the **Match** attribute in the Template element is actually an **expression** (as defined in the XPath specification). The Match attribute in the example below contains a simple expression:

```
match="warning/para"
```

To be more precise, the Match attribute actually holds a particular type of expression, known as a **pattern**. A pattern is a context specification against which the current node is compared. Only some parts of the complete expression language are relevant to this need.

When context is introduced, it is often possible for two or more templates to contain expressions that match the current element. In this case, a mechanism is needed to decide which template has 'priority'. A later section in this chapter discusses the prioritization of templates.

Most of the concepts described below involve analysis of the structure of the XML document within which the element resides, but the expression language syntax is not immediately easy to interpret. Illustrations are therefore used to show the conditions under which a test matches a particular element. The document hierarchy is shown as embedded boxes, representing each element, with the element names appearing within the respective boxes. An element that will be selected by the expression is shown in a highlighted box, as in the X element in the example below:

Alternative elements

When identical formatting has to be applied to the content of a number of different elements, it is not necessary to create a separate template for each one. Instead, a pattern can be used that specifies a list of alternatives. The 'I' symbol is used for this purpose and is placed between the element names:

```
match="X | Y | Z"
```

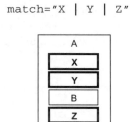

This technique could be used to format names and foreign terms in the same way:

```
match="name | foreign"
```

```
<para>The <foreign>de facto</foreign> stylesheet
language is <name>XSLT</name>.</para>
```

The *de facto* stylesheet language is *XSLT*.

Simple location contexts

Typically, an element that has a significant context is identified simply by its location within the document structure. The name of the parent element, or some other ancestor element, determines the context.

Specific parent

In many cases, it is sufficient to specify what the parent element must be for the template to be applicable. In the following example, an X element is only to be selected when it is directly within a P element. The '/' symbol separates the two element names:

```
match="P/X"
```

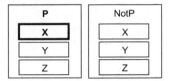

The '/' symbol does not itself indicate that X must be a child of P. This symbol is simply used to separate steps in a **location path**. When a particular step consists of only an element name, this is an abbreviation for the explicit statement 'child::X'. The following example is equivalent to the one above:

child::P/**child::**X

Note that the first occurrence of 'child::' above is redundant, because there is no requirement for P to be the child of some other element (it could be the document's root element).

Using this technique, specific formatting could be applied to paragraphs in a Warning element:

```
<para>A normal paragraph.</para>
<warning>
  <para>Warning paragraph one.</para>
  <para>Warning paragraph two.</para>
</warning>
<para>Another normal paragraph.</para>
```

```
match="warning/para"
```

A normal paragraph.
  WARNING:
  Warning paragraph one.
  Warning paragraph two.
Another normal paragraph.

Specific ancestors

Knowledge of the parent of an element is not always enough. The element containing the parent element may be significant, or an element at an even higher level in the hierarchy. To select an element that is the descendant of specific ancestors, more elements are named in the expression:

```
match="A/P/X"
```

This example makes it clear or that the pattern is read from left to right, and also that the verbose equivalent is in fact *very* verbose in comparison:

```
match="child::A/child::P/child::X"
```

Using this technique, specific formatting could be applied to a warning paragraph that appears in the introduction of a book:

```
<intro>
   <para>An introduction paragraph.</para>
   <warning>
      <para>Introduction Warning.</para>
   </warning>
</intro>
```

```
match="intro/warning/para"
```

An introduction paragraph.

> *Introduction Warning.*

Unknown ancestry

When several different elements could appear at a specific level in the document hierarchy, it would seem necessary to use several patterns, as in the following example – paragraphs are to be formatted in a distinctive way within warnings, notes and errors when these constructs appear in the Intro element:

```
match="intro/warning/para"
```

```
match="intro/note/para"
```

```
match="intro/error/para"
```

The need for three patterns can be avoided using a wildcard that represents any element. The previous three expressions can be replaced by a single expression using the asterisk character '*' as the wildcard:

```
match="intro/*/para"
```

However, although the wildcard can be used repeatedly in the same pattern, this technique is still quite limited because it is necessary to know exactly how many levels deep the target element is. It would not be possible to identify a target element that appears at any point below another element without using a large number of expressions:

```
match="intro/para"

match="intro/*/para"

match="intro/*/*/para"

match="intro/*/*/*/para"
```

But it is possible to specify an unknown number of intermediate elements (including none). This is done using two forward slash characters in sequence, '//'. The following example replaces all four expressions above:

```
match="intro//para"
```

Advanced context

Context need not depend only on the location of the target element in the document hierarchy. The content of the element itself may need to influence the formatting to be applied. For example, an automatically generated prefix of either 'Warning:' or 'Warnings:' may be needed, depending on whether the Warning element contains a single paragraph (one warning) or a list (several warnings).

Specific children

It is possible to select an element that is the parent of another specific element by placing the name of the sub-element in square brackets:

```
match="X[C]"
```

The square brackets actually enclose a **predicate filter**. A filter consists of a test to be made on the node to which it is attached. In this simple case, the test made is that the X element (the current element) contains the C element as a child.

Specific siblings

Predicate filters can be added to any element named in the pattern. For example, a filter can be added to the parent of the target element, where it can be used to determine whether or not another element exists within the parent. It is therefore possible to select an element only when another specified element is present as its sibling.

In the following example, the X element matches the pattern only if its parent, the P element, also contains an S element (and note that it does not matter how many times the S element occurs):

```
match="P[S]/X"
```

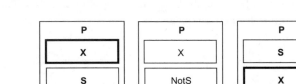

Attribute context

It is possible to select elements that contain a particular attribute, or contain an attribute with a specific value. Attribute names are distinguished from element names using the '@' symbol prefix. This makes it possible for the same name to be used for both an element and an attribute (XML rules allow this to happen). The element X could not be confused with the attribute @X.

To specify that a particular attribute must be present, it is necessary to include the attribute name in the predicate filter:

```
match="X[@A]"
```

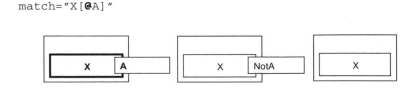

There is one complication that may arise when a DTD is referenced by the XML document being processed. The DTD defines the attributes which may be used with each element, and in some cases it provides a default value to be used when an explicit value is not given. Many parsers cannot distinguish between explicit and default attribute usage. The second example below would match a test for the presence of the Status attribute when the parser validates the document against the DTD, and the parser would be unable to distinguish between explicit and defaulted attribute usage:

```
<!ATTLIST para status (normal|secret) "normal">


    <para status="normal">...</para>

    <para>...</para> <!-- ALSO A NORMAL PARAGRAPH -->
```

It is more common for processing to depend on the value of a given attribute value, rather than just on the presence of the attribute. To select an element that has a specific attribute value, the required value is added between quotes following an equals symbol. Note that different quotation marks must be used from those that enclose the entire attribute value:

```
match="X[@A='abc']"
```

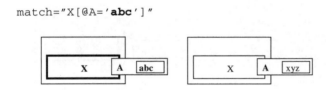

In the following example, the template is activated by secret paragraphs:

```
match="para[@status='secret']"
```

XML is case sensitive and so the value in the expression must exactly match the value in the attribute.

Negative context

Instead of testing for the presence of an element, an attribute or an attribute value, it is possible to test for the absence of any of these items. The **not()** function can be used in XPath expressions, but only within the predicate filter parts of a pattern. This function contains the normal test and reverses the result. A test that succeeds bcomes 'false', and a test that fails becomes 'true'. For example, it is possible to test for the absence of a child element:

```
match="X[not(C)]"
```

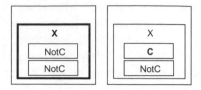

It is also possible to test for the absence of a sibling element:

```
match="P[not(S)]/X"
```

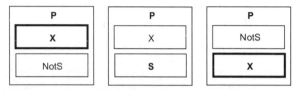

It is also possible to test for the absence of an attribute (or of a specific attribute value):

```
match="X[not(@A)]"
```

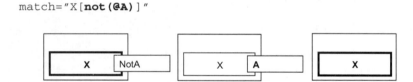

Priorities

The presence of context-specific templates means that a number of templates will often be eligible to format a specific instance of an element. But only one template can actually be selected by the XSLT processor. The following two templates both apply to a Para element. The first matches paragraphs in the introduction of a book. The second matches paragraphs in a Warning element. It is not immediately clear which should be chosen if the paragraph is inside a warning within the introduction, because both templates would be applicable:

```
<template match="intro//para">...</template>

<template match="warning//para">...</template>
```

When this possibility occurs, it is often necessary to explicitly specify which of the candidate templates is to be chosen. This is done using the **Priority** attribute:

```
<template ... priority="2">...</template>
```

Priority values

One template is given precedence over another by assigning a higher priority value to it. In the following example, the warning paragraph takes priority over the introduction paragraph. The paragraph will therefore look the same in all warnings, regardless of whether or not they are also in the introduction section of the document:

```
<template match="intro//para" priority="1">...

<template match="warning//para" priority="2">...
```

Default priorities

It is not always necessary to use the Priority attribute. When it is not included, a default priority value is assigned by the XSLT processor. But the default value varies, depending on the content of the Match attribute.

Simple expressions that refer only to an element name, qualified with a namespace prefix, whether it includes the 'child::' prefix or not, have a default value of '0':

```
<!-- PRIORITY '0' -->
<template match="x:para">...</template>

<!-- PRIORITY '0' -->
<template match="child::x:para">...</template>
```

Almost all other defaults are even less specific so have values below zero.

An element name with no prefix has a default value of '-0.25'. This means that qualified names are more specific than unqualified names:

```
<!-- HIGHER PRIORITY '0' -->
<template match="x:para">...</template>

<!-- LOWER PRIORITY '-0.25' -->
<template match="para">...</template>
```

Finally, the least specific form of all is a simple node test:

```
<!-- PRIORITY '-0.5' -->

<template match="*">...</template>

<template match="comment()">...</template>

<template match="text()">...</template>

<template match="processing-instruction()">...</template>

<template match="node()">...</template>
```

There is therefore a distinction between any element ('*') and any element with a specific namespace qualifier ('x:*'), which overrides the more general case:

```
<!-- LOWER PRIORITY (-0.5) -->
<template match="*">...</template>

<!-- HIGHER PRIORITY (-0.25) -->
<template match="x:*">...</template>
```

All other cases default to a value of '0.5' and so a contextual template automatically overrides a simple element-matching template. It is not necessary to introduce the Priority attribute to distinguish between the general and special cases in the example below:

```
<!-- LOWER PRIORITY (0) -->
<template match="para">...</template>

<!-- HIGHER PRIORITY (0.5) -->
<template match="warning/para">...</template>
```

It would be a mistake to think that the length of an expression has any effect on default priority values. The two examples below both default to a priority level of '0.5':

```
<template match="warning//para">...</template>

<template match="book/warning/para[@type='secret']">...
```

When there is more than one contextual match, the Priority attribute is needed and values should start from '1' to ensure that all of the default cases are overridden.

Conflict resolution

When two or more templates remain applicable after filtering out lower priority matches (regardless of whether or not the Priority attribute has been used in some or all templates), this may be considered to be an error by the XSLT processor. The processor may report the problem and cease to function. But most processors will recover and, if they follow the standard, will simply select the template closest to the end of the stylesheet. If a processor that behaves in this latter way is chosen, then the order in which templates are placed in the file becomes a very important stylesheet design consideration:

```
<template match="book//para">...</template>

<!-- MORE SPECIFIC - APPEARS LAST -->
<template match="warning//para">...</template>
```

10. Choices

Templates can be much more intelligent than previous examples have implied. The output generated by templates may be varied, through the definition of segments that can be enabled or disabled depending on a test condition. This ability greatly increases the power of templates and can reduce the number needed.

Introduction

Unlike programming and scripting languages, XSLT is a declarative language. A stylesheet consists of a static set of formatting instructions. Yet XSLT includes some instructions that will be familiar to software developers. If-then and choose-from features are included in most programming languages. However, they are not used in XSLT to control the flow of processing but to select from optional or alternative portions of templates.

An 'if' statement isolates part of a template and only allows its content to become part of the template when some condition is met. A 'choose' statement is similar but more sophisticated, being more efficient when the template output depends on a characteristic with a wide number of options, and allowing a default value to be chosen when none of the explicit circumstances tested is applicable.

If conditions

An **If** element encloses any fragment of a template that should only be added to the output of the template under special circumstances. The condition is defined using the **Test** attribute, which holds an expression:

```
<if test="...">
  ...
  <!-- OPTIONAL FRAGMENT OF TEMPLATE -->
  ...
</if>
```

The expression in the Test attribute must return a boolean result. A value of 'true' unlocks the content of the If element. A value of 'false' indicates a failed test and the content of this element is then ignored.

Disabling and enabling template fragments

A template fragment can be marked, and then explicitly included or excluded using the 'true()' and 'false()' expressions:

```
<if test="true()">
  ...
  <!-- REQUIRED FRAGMENT OF TEMPLATE -->
  ...
</if>

<if test="false()">
  ...
  <!-- IGNORED FRAGMENT OF TEMPLATE -->
  ...
</if>
```

This simple technique could be used during stylesheet debugging to temporarily enable generation of output intended only to provide assistance with this task.

Expression context

The expression appearing in the Test attribute takes the current element, and the current element list, as its context. This attribute is typically used to make decisions based on attribute values of the current element, or the presence (or absence) of specified sub-elements, as in the following examples.

Well-formed markup constraints

XSLT commands and literal output elements in the template must, as always, be well-formed. The If elements must therefore be placed with great care, both to fit into the well-formed structure of the template and to avoid causing problems regardless of whether or not their content is enabled or disabled. Fortunately, the first requirement automatically takes care of the second. The following example is invalid, according to XML rules, regardless of whether or not the test would succeed:

```
<xsl:template ...>
  <P>
    <xsl:if test="...)"><B>...</xsl:if>
    <xsl:apply-templates/>
    </B>
  </P>
</xsl:template>
```

Note that If elements can be nested within other If elements to any number of levels.

Examples

This first example shows how different prefix text may be generated depending on the value of an attribute:

```
<note>Normal note</note>
<note type="secret">Secret note</note>
```

```
<xsl:template match="note">
  <P>
    <xsl:if test="@type='secret'">SECRET </xsl:if>
    <xsl:text>NOTE: </xsl:text>
    <xsl:apply-templates/>
  </P>
</xsl:template>
```

```
<P>NOTE: Normal note</P>
<P>SECRET NOTE: Secret note</P>
```

This example shows how a default title can be generated if there is no explicit title within a note:

```
<xsl:template match="note">
  <xsl:if test="not(title)"><P>NOTE:</P></xsl:if>
  <xsl:apply-templates/>
</xsl:template>
```

A good example of the use of this element is included in the XSLT standard. When formatting a list of names, the punctuation following each name depends on its location in the list. Commas are appropriate after each name, except for after the last one. In the following example, the test is only true when the name is not the last one in the list:

```
<name>John</name>
<name>Peter</name>
<name>Lucy</name>
```

```
<if test="not(position() = last)"><text>, </text></if>
```

John, Peter, Lucy

Avoiding If

The If element can be avoided by creating an additional template. The expression in the Test attribute is simply moved to both of the Match attributes, and in one of them is enclosed by the not() function. The following example eliminates the If statement by testing for names at the ends of lists in a separate template:

```
<template match="name[not(position() = last())]">
  <apply-templates/><text>, </text>
</template>

<template match="name[position() = last()]">
  <apply-templates/>
</template>
```

However, it can be argued that one of the main purposes of the If command is precisely to avoid the need for additional templates.

Multiple choices

When one option has to be selected from a number of possible options, the If element can, of course, be used repeatedly to test each possibility. But the fact that each If element is independent of the others can be inconvenient in some circumstances. First, it may not be possible to prevent more than one of the tests from succeeding (if this constraint is desired). It is also not possible to take specific action if none of these tests happen to succeed. Both constraints could be overcome if a set of tests could be treated as a group. This concept is the basis of the following technique.

Basic structure

The **Choose** element encloses a number of alternative fragments of the template that can apply under different circumstances.

Each alternative is defined using the **When** element, which works in exactly the same way as the If element described previously. Again, the condition is defined using the **Test** attribute.

At least one When element must be present in the Choose element:

```
<choose>
  <when test="...">
    <!-- OPTIONAL FRAGMENT OF TEMPLATE -->
    ...
  </when>
  <when test="...">
    <!-- OPTIONAL FRAGMENT OF TEMPLATE -->
    ...
  </when>
</choose>
```

An easy way to remember this construct is to learn the phrase '*choose* to include this content *when* this *test* is true'.

If and When

It is possible for there to be only one When element present in a Choose element. However, this is never very useful because a single If element could always achieve the same goal more concisely. The following examples are equivalent:

```
<choose>
  <when test="@secret='true'">
    ...
  </when>
</choose>


<if test="@secret='true'">
  ...
</if>
```

There would also be little point in using this construct if there was nothing more to it than the creation of a list of tests. But grouping the When elements in this way makes it feasible for them to be considered as a whole, which provides the two benefits discussed below.

First successful test only

The order in which the When elements are placed within the Choose element is very important because only the first successful test is obeyed; all remaining When elements are ignored.

In the following example, the two tests on the Colour attribute are only reached for elements that do not have a Type attribute value of 'secret':

```
<choose>
  <when test="@type='secret'">
    <!-- ADD NOTHING - COLOUR NOT SIGNIFICANT -->
  </when>
  <when test="@color='blue'">
    <text>BLUE TEXT - NOT SECRET</text>
  </when>
  <when test="@color='green'">
    <text>GREEN TEXT - NOT SECRET</text>
  </when>
</choose>
```

This feature therefore simulates the 'if-then/else-if' feature of many programming languages, except that here it could be called the 'choose-when-when' feature.

Default action

It may be desirable to take some specific 'default' action when none of the tests succeeds. The optional **Otherwise** element has no qualifying attribute, because its content is always selected when none of the When elements happen to be relevant. It is never activated when a test succeeds:

```
<choose>
  <when test="@color='blue'">
    <text>BLUE TEXT</text>
  </when>
  <when test="@color='green'">
    <text>GREEN TEXT</text>
  </when>
  <otherwise>
    <text>DEFAULT TEXT - ALL COLOURS
    EXCEPT BLUE AND GREEN</text>
  </otherwise>
</choose>
```

The Otherwise element must appear after the list of When elements, immediately before the end-tag of the Choose element.

If only one When element is used, this feature emulates the 'if-then-else' feature of many programming languages.

Naturally, this element could be simulated using a final When element that had, as its test condition, the expression 'not(test1) and not(test2) and not(test3) ...', though the fact that this element could only be triggered if all previous ones had failed means that it would work equally well if it just held the expression 'true()' instead (thus guaranteeing that it would be triggered if all previous tests had failed).

11. Expressions in attributes

XSLT includes a feature for populating the value of an attribute in a literal output element with text returned by an expression, so avoiding the need to use the Attribute element.

Attribute value templates

The XSLT standard has a feature for inserting expressions into attributes in output elements called **attribute value templates**. These expressions are used to generate context-specific values to insert into the attributes. Without this feature, it would be necessary to use the Attribute element instead.

Syntax

Before discussing the various ways in which attribute templates can be of benefit, it is necessary to establish how they are recognized and identify some repercussions of their presence.

When an output element includes an attribute, the attribute is coded according to XML rules – it has a name, and a value enclosed by quotation marks. The value may be any text string allowed in attributes of the given type, assuming the use of a DTD or XML Schema model to validate the output. When a DTD is not relevant, it can be any text string at all. The issue here is how to indicate to the XSLT processor that there is an expression embedded in the string value. The expression is actually delimited by curly brackets. The left curly bracket '{' begins the template, and the right curly bracket '}' ends it. The text between these brackets is interpreted as an expression:

```
MyAttr = "...{expression}..."
```

A single attribute can contain any number of templates:

```
MyAttr = "...{expression}...{expression}..."
```

With the curly brackets taking this special role, the obvious question that arises is how to represent these symbols as normal characters. For example, the value 'a{b}c' may need to appear in an attribute, without the letter 'b' being interpreted as an expression. To solve this problem, the single character '{' is represented by the sequence '{{', and the single character '}' is represented by the sequence '}}'. For example:

```
MyAttr = "This is {{NOT}} an expression"
```

The XSLT processor removes the second bracket in both cases when outputting the string:

```
This is {NOT} an expression
```

String expressions

An expression may result in an object of any type allowed by the XPath expression language. But the need here is for a string value that can be inserted into an attribute value. Therefore, the expression result is converted to a string, as if embedded in the XPath string() function. This function is implied, and so the following two examples are equivalent:

```
="...{true()}..."
```

```
="...{string(true())}..."
```

In both cases, the function true() resolves to the string 'true'. In the latter example, it is first explicitly converted to the string 'true', but this string is then also converted to a string again (without further effect). For the sake of brevity alone, the string function should not be included.

In order to avoid surprises, the XPath **string()** function needs to be fully understood. Software developers familiar with DOM can be easily misled by this function because it does not necessarily return the string value of the object concerned. The string value of an element, for example, is a combination (in document order) of the string values of all the text nodes within that element. An expression that refers to the current element ('.') actually returns all the text in the descendants of that element. The string value of an attribute is the normalized value of the attribute with all whitespace converted to space characters, entity references replaced and, in some circumstances, the removal of multiple and surrounding spaces.

Copy-through attributes

One of the most beneficial ways that expressions can be used is to copy a value from a source attribute into the output attribute. Although the element and attribute names are usually different in the output and input documents, the attribute values often remain the same. A typical example of this is the need to copy an image file name and the dimensions of the image. In this example, the source Image element uses Name, Y and X attributes for the purpose:

```
<image name="boat.gif" y="40mm" x="60mm" />
```

This element needs to be converted to the HTML IMG element as follows:

```
<IMG SRC="boat.gif" HEIGHT="40mm" WIDTH="60mm">
```

To do this, the three values 'boat.gif', '40mm' and '60mm' need to be copied from the source attributes to the output attributes. The current element (the Image element) is the context for each expression, so it is possible to refer directly to the source attributes names:

```
<xsl:template match="image">
  <IMG SRC="{@name}" HEIGHT="{@y}" WIDTH="{@x}" />
</xsl:template>
```

Element to attribute

Almost as common as attribute value copy-through is the need to convert an element value into an attribute value. This could be the direct text content of the current element or the content of sub-elements (or even the content of elements elsewhere in the document).

Current element content

Text content of the current element can be copied into an attribute. For example, in the source document the text to display if the image cannot be presented may be stored in the Image element as element content:

```
<image name="boat.gif" y="60mm" x="40mm">
Picture of a boat.
</image>
```

In the HTML IMG element, this text needs to be placed in the ALT attribute:

```
<IMG SRC="boat.gif" ... ALT="Picture of a boat.">
```

The expression language makes this transformation almost as simple as copying-through attribute values. The text node in the current element is represented by the **text**() function:

```
<xsl:template match="image">
  <IMG ALT="{text()}" ... />
</xsl:template>
```

However, this approach is not infallible. The source element may contain child elements instead of (or as well as) directly containing text. The method shown above finds the first text block contained directly within the source element (if there is one) and ignores everything else. On the other hand, with a technique that found all descendant nodes it would not be appropriate to copy child elements into the output attribute. The solution is to return the value of the current element ('.') (which means the concatenated values of all embedded text nodes):

```
<image ...>Picture of a <bold>BIG</bold> boat.</image>
```

```
<xsl:template match="image">
  <IMG ALT="{.}" ... />
</xsl:template>
```

```
<IMG ... ALT="Picture of a BIG boat.">
```

Child element content

An input structure may include child elements to hold discrete parts of a compound value. Each part may need to be converted into an attribute in the output document. For example:

```
<image>
  <name>boat.gif</name>
  <y>40mm</y>
  <x>60mm</x>
</image>
```

Again, patterns can be used to extract each part of the value into an attribute:

```
<xsl:template match="image">
  <IMG SRC="{name}" HEIGHT="{y}" WIDTH="{x}" />
</xsl:template>
```

This is safe, because the string value of the named element is inserted, including the values of any sub-elements.

Other element content

Using XPath location paths, elements and attributes from elsewhere in the document can be easily copied to the attribute:

```
<author>
  <title>Mr</title>
  <name>Smith</name>
</author>
```

```
<xsl:template match="name">
  <author title="{../title} name="{.}" />
</xsl:template>
```

Static text and multiple expressions

Expressions can be mixed with static text in the attribute value, and there may also be two or more expressions present in the same value.

The expression does not have to comprise the totality of the attribute. For example, if the XML version of the Image element example above assumed a measure of millimetres, so did not include 'mm' in the attributes, then the template would need to be amended as follows:

```
<image name="boat.gif" y="40" x="60" />
```

```
<xsl:template match="image">
  <IMG SRC="{@name}" HEIGHT="{@y}mm" WIDTH="{@x}mm" />
</xsl:template>
```

Also, a single output attribute could contain multiple expression templates. This allows for several source values to be merged into a single value, as in the following example:

```
<widget size = "{@x} across, {@y} down">...</widget>
```

Limitations

XPath expressions are very powerful, but still have their limitations. Another approach is required for complex situations that involve decision logic, or to generate values that are defined in the stylesheet rather than in the source document tree.

The **Attribute** element can be used to assign values to attributes, and it is not necessary to use the Element element to specify the element to which the attribute should be attached. The following is valid (the markup in the Attribute element is explained in Chapter 5):

```
<color>
  <xsl:attribute name="code">
    <xsl:choose>
      <xsl:when test="@color='red'">R</xsl:when>
      <xsl:when test="@color='green'">G</xsl:when>
      <xsl:when test="@color='blue'">B</xsl:when>
      <xsl:otherwise>NONE</xsl:otherwise>
    </xsl:choose>
  </xsl:attribute>
  ...
</color>


  <color code="G">
```

12. Reorganizing material

XML documents have a linear structure and all material has a specific sequential location within a document. In addition, the philosophy of good XML document design promotes data normalization (information should not be duplicated unnecessarily). When preparing material for publication, however, the original ordering may be inappropriate, and for end-user convenience some material may need to be duplicated elsewhere in the document. Information may also be needed from other documents.

Information reuse

There are a number of reasons why information may need to be copied to another location in the output document. One typical example is the need to create a table of contents for a book. In this case, all the chapter titles must be copied to the beginning of the document.

Previous examples have shown how the Apply Templates element can be used to select the children of the current element, so that the entire document can be processed in the correct order (in a tree-walking manner). However, this element can also select material from elsewhere in the document. It has already been shown that the **Select** attribute can be used to select specific children of the current element, but because it can hold any XPath expression it can also be used to select material from other locations. In the following example, all the chapter titles are selected:

```
<apply-templates select="/book/chapter/title" />
```

Each chapter is selected in turn and the title is sought. Templates are applied to each matching Title element, and the output from these templates appears at the current location (a table of contents is created).

Note that the ability to trigger templates to process material beyond the scope of the current element is potentially dangerous. It is possible to select the parent, or indeed any ancestor, of the current element. This can lead to a processing loop that never ends. Some XSLT processors may detect and escape from this condition but others may not.

It should be recalled that a template can hold more than one Apply Templates element. A single template may therefore process the children of the current element, as well as grabbing material from elsewhere. The template below processes the content of a book and also 'drags up' the titles from each chapter to build the table of contents:

```
<xsl:template match="book">
  <HTML>
    <HEAD><TITLE>A book</TITLE></HEAD>
    <BODY>
      <DIV>
        <xsl:apply-templates select="chapter/title" />
      </DIV>
      <xsl:apply-templates/>
    </BODY>
  </HTML>
</xsl:template>
```

When the structure and element names in the information to be copied does not alter on output, the **Copy Of** element can be used instead. The following example copies the chapter Title elements directly to output (and does not change the names of the Title elements, or any of the other elements that they might contain):

```
<book>
  <chapter>
    <title>title one</title>
    ...
  </chapter>

  <chapter>
    <title>title <emph>two</emph></title>
    ...
  </chapter>
</book>


<xsl:template match="book">
  <out-book>
    <table-of-contents>
      <xsl:copy-of select="/chapter/title" />
    </table-of-contents>
    <xsl:apply-templates />
  </out-book>
</xsl:template>


  <out-book>
    <table-of-contents>
      <title>title one</title>
      <title>title <emph>two</emph></title>
    </table-of-contents>
    ...
  </out-book>
```

Context-specific formatting (modes)

The problem with all the examples above is that the formatting of the copied material is not affected by its move to a new location. But in many scenarios, including the building of a table of contents, there is a need to apply different formatting to the material at its new location. For example, chapter titles should be larger than the respective table-of-contents entries (as they are in this book), so the font size needs to be smaller when the table-of-contents is built.

An ideal solution would be to have alternative sets of templates, containing different formatting instructions, and to have one or other set of templates enabled depending on the need at the time. XSLT therefore includes the concept of **modes**. Groups of templates can be assigned to specific modes, and the whole stylesheet can be switched between these modes to enable and disable alternative templates for the same elements. The **Mode** attribute is added to the Template element to assign the template to a specific mode. In the following example, there are two templates that match the Title element, but one of these belongs to the 'contents' mode:

```
<template match="title">...</template>


<template match="title" mode="contents">...</template>
```

The title may be formatted in different ways depending on which mode (in this case the default mode or the 'contents' mode) is in effect at the time. Normally, the current mode is the default mode and all templates that have a Mode attribute are ignored. In the example above, the first template for the Title element is active and the second is inactive. To enable a specific mode, the Mode attribute is also added to the Apply Templates element. The nodes processed as a result of this instruction are matched against templates in the given mode:

```
<apply-templates mode="contents" />
```

In the following example, H1 (header one) elements are used to format the Title element within the chapter, and H4 (header four) elements are used to format the Title element in the table of contents:

```
<xsl:template match="book">
  <HTML><HEAD><TITLE>A book</TITLE></HEAD>
  <BODY>
    <DIV>
      <xsl:apply-templates select="chapter/title"
                           mode="contents" />
    </DIV>
    <xsl:apply-templates/>
  </BODY>
</xsl:template>
```

```
<xsl:template match="chapter">
  <xsl:apply-templates/>
</xsl:template>


<xsl:template match="title">
  <H1><xsl:apply-templates/></H1>
</xsl:template>


<xsl:template match="title" mode="contents">
  <H4><xsl:apply-templates/></H4>
</xsl:template>
```

Note that there are built-in, mode-specific versions of the template that match elements with no explicit template definition. It is not necessary to create such templates as the following:

```
<!-- NOT NECESSARY (default behaviour) -->
<template match="*" mode="contents">
  <apply-templates/>
</template>
```

But this can be done if the intention is to override the default behaviour (such as to avoid processing the descendants of unspecified elements):

```
<template match="*" mode="contents">
  <!-- DO NOT PROCESS ELEMENT CHILDREN OF UNSPECIFIED
       ELEMENTS WHEN IN CONTENTS MODE-->
</template>
```

Moving information

Moving information to a different location in the result tree can be achieved by first copying it, using the technique described above, and then suppressing it at the original location. Again, the Mode attribute is used. The essential difference is that the default template does not contain the Apply Templates element, and so the information is simply not output in its original location:

```
<xsl:template match="title">
  <!-- SUPPRESSED OUTPUT AT ORIGINAL LOCATION -->
</xsl:template>

<xsl:template match="title" mode="new-location">
  <P><xsl:apply-templates/></P>
</xsl:template>
```

However, this technique is quite complex and should only be considered when the new location is far removed from the source. Reordering within a smaller structure can usually be achieved more simply by selective child processing. Consider the following example, where the Name element first contains the title, then the first name, and then the last name:

```
<name>
    <title>Mr</title>
    <first>John</first>
    <last>Smith</last>
</name>
```

Assuming that the final order needs to be last name, first name then title, this can be achieved in either of the following ways:

```
<template match="name">
  <apply-templates select="last" />
  <apply-templates select="first" />
  <apply-templates select="title" />
</template>


<xsl:template match="name">
  <P><xsl:value-of select="last" /></P>
  <P><xsl:value-of select="first" /></P>
  <P><xsl:value-of select="title" /></P>
</xsl:template>
```

The For Each element may also play a significant role in reorganizing material (it is discussed in detail in Chapter 3).

Accessing other documents

It is possible to access information stored in other XML documents using the **document**() function. This function takes at least one parameter. The first may be a string that consists of the URL reference that locates the document file. The XSLT processor finds the document file and then parses it to create an in-memory tree that can be accessed using XPath expressions. For example, consider the following document:

remote.XML

```
<book>
  <title>The Remote Book Title</title>
  <para>Remote paragraph.</para>
</book>
```

If this document is stored in the same directory as the stylesheet, it can be referenced using the function 'document('remote.XML')'. This function could be used as the first part of an XPath location path. For example, the title of the book could be retrieved and inserted into the result tree:

```
... and see <remotebookref/> for details...
```

```
<xsl:template match="remotebookref">
  <I>
    <xsl:value-of
        select="document('remote.XML')/book/title" />
  </I>
</xsl:template>
```

```
...and see <I>The Remote Book Title</I> for details...
```

Using this technique, a change to the document title is automatically reflected in all referencing documents the next time that they are processed.

A node can be passed to this function instead of a string. In this case, the string value of the node is considered to be the URL reference. Perhaps the most obvious use of this feature is to open a document that is named in an attribute:

```
... and see <bookref name="remote.XML"/> for details...
```

```
<xsl:value-of select="document(@name)/book/title" />
```

```
...and see <I>The Remote Book Title</I> for details...
```

Base location paths

Note that relative paths are relative to the location of the stylesheet rather than the source XML document. It is possible to supply a different base-URL address by including a second parameter. For example, if 'remoteXML' is actually to be found in '/D:/remotedocs', then this base path can be included:

```
/D:/remotedocs/remote.XML
```

```
select="document(@name, '/D:/remotedocs')/book/title"
```

Multiple documents

It is possible to access information that could be in one of several documents. Instead of passing a single attribute value (or element content value) to the function, a number of nodes can be passed instead. Each node represents a different document. In the following example, a number of documents are referenced using DocRef elements. Using the expression '/doc/doc-ref', the document function receives all of these elements and therefore reads all the documents into memory. The title of the document that has an attribute value of 'secret' is accessed:

```
<doc>
  <doc-ref>remote1.xml</doc-ref>
  <doc-ref>remote2.xml</doc-ref> <!-- SECRET DOC -->
  <doc-ref>remote3.xml</doc-ref>
  ...
  <find-secret-title/>
</doc>
```

```
<xsl:template match="find-secret-title">
  <P>
    <xsl:value-of
           select="document(/doc/doc-ref)
                       /doc[@type='secret']/title"/>
  </P>
</xsl:template>
```

Reaccessing a document

If the same remote document is likely to be accessed a number of times, it is inefficient to read the whole document into memory each time. It is much more efficient to read it only once, and anchor it to a (typically global) variable (see Chapter 13):

```
<variable name="remote" select="document('remote.xml')" />
```

Fragments of this file can then be accessed from any template:

```
<message>Remote 1, Chapter 2 Title =
  <value-of select="$remote/doc/chapter[2]/title"/>
<message>

<message>Remote 1, Chapter 3 Title =
  <value-of select="$remote1/doc/chapter[3]/title"/>
<message>
```

13. Variables and parameters

Variables and parameters are used to avoid needless repetition, to simplify and clarify the stylesheet, and to pass configuration details to the stylesheet. Parameters also play a significant role in the practical use of named templates.

Variables

A **variable** is a named container for a value that can be referenced, by name, wherever that value is needed. A reference to a variable is replaced by the value it contains when the reference is encountered by the XSLT processor. Software developers will be familiar with this concept because all serious programming languages include the concept of variables. A **variable definition** is used to create a variable. In doing so, it gives the variable a name and a value:

variable definition

name	value

For example, if warning text is always presented in red, and there are a number of places where, for this purpose, the colour red is specified in the stylesheet, then the CSS instruction 'color:red' could be placed in a variable named 'danger':

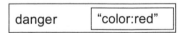

danger	"color:red"

There are two clear benefits to this approach. First, the value is represented by a meaningful name (such as 'danger') which clarifies its purpose. This improves legibility generally, and helps to create a self-documenting stylesheet. Second, if the value needs to be changed the edit is made in a single place (where the variable is defined), which is easier than editing a value in all its occurrences, and eliminates the possibility of introducing inconsistencies (such as forgetting to change one of the values, or making an error while updating one of the values).

Variable types

There are five types of value that a variable can hold:

- boolean
- number
- string
- node-set
- result tree fragment

Every variable value must conform to the characteristics and constraints of one of these data types. A variable is said to 'hold' a value of a particular type. For example, it can be said that a particular variable 'holds a boolean value', and that another 'holds a string value'.

XPath data types

The first four data types listed above are XPath expression data types (see Chapter 22). This is not a coincidence. A variable can be used within an expression, and an expression can also be used to determine the value of a variable. In the first case, it is very important that the value of the variable can become part of the expression. In the second case, it is important that the value resulting from evaluating the expression can become a legal variable value.

When a variable holds a **boolean** value, it has a value of 'true' or 'false'. These are the only two options available, but in practice these two states could represent 'yes'/'no' or 'on'/'off' answers depending on the exact nature of a question that the variable addresses:

When a variable holds a **number**, it is amenable to numerical calculations and comparisons (within an expression):

When a variable holds a **string**, the value can be searched for significant characters or sequences of characters and can be added to existing text:

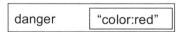

When a variable holds a **node-set**, it actually contains references to one or more nodes in the source tree, and can be used in an XPath location path as a context location, or to copy source tree fragments to the result tree:

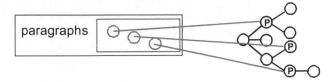

Result tree fragments

In addition to the XPath data types described above, a variable can also hold a **result tree fragment**. This kind of variable holds text and markup that is normally intended to be output to the result tree. A tree structure is created by adding a single, invisible root node to a set of nodes represented by any combination of tags and text. This structure can be said to be held in the variable because it has no independent existence (unlike nodes in a node-set, which are in the source tree) so cannot be 'seen' by other variables and is *not* amenable to interrogation using XPath location paths:

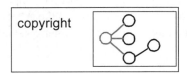

However, it should be noted that this is now considered by many to be a weak option compared with node-sets, which can be interrogated much more effectively, and later versions of the XSLT standard may omit it while widening the use of node-sets.

Converting between types

A variable can often be referenced and used without knowledge of the data type the value happens to conform to. Values are converted from one type to another by the XSLT processor whenever this is desirable for such purposes as comparison with other values. For example, a string that consists of digits and other characters used in numbers, such as '2' and '.', is easily converted to a number whenever it needs to be used in a calculation:

But it is not always immediately obvious how a value can be represented in a different form. For example, it is not clear what it means for a boolean value to be represented as a string. In other cases, it is clear that it is not possible to convert a value into a different form. For example, there is no sensible numeric representation of the string 'ABC'. Conversions between particular data types, and the issues raised by each scenario, are discussed in detail later.

Variable definitions

The **Variable** element is used to create a variable, and the **Name** attribute holds the name of the new variable. In the following example, a variable called 'age' is being defined:

```
<variable name="age" ... />
```

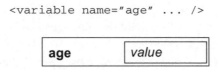

The **Select** attribute is used to evaluate an XPath expression. The result of evaluating the expression becomes the value of the variable. One of the simplest possible XPath expressions is a number. For example, the number '42' can be stored in a variable called 'age'. The 'age' variable therefore holds a numeric value:

```
<variable name="age" select="42" />
```

```
age        42
```

The Select attribute is used in this way to create all values that conform to XPath expression data types. The result of evaluating the expression becomes the value of the variable. The number '42' is a valid expression that (unsurprisingly) evaluates to the numerical value '42'.

A different technique is used to create result tree fragments. In this case the Variable element encloses the value. This approach permits literal element tags to be placed in the value:

```
<xsl:variable name="copyright">
  <P>Copyright Acme Corp. 2001</P>
</xsl:variable>
```

A variable can only have one value, so it is not legal for a Variable element to have both a Select attribute and element content. If this occurs, an XSLT processor may either ignore the error, in which case it will use the Select attribute and discard the element content, or will report the error and refuse to process the stylesheet (the standard does not indicate which behaviour to expect, and XSLT processors do behave differently in this respect):

```
<xsl:variable name="age" select="42">
  <P>FORTY TWO</P>  <!-- ERROR -->
</xsl:variable>
```

A Variable element with no content, and with no Select attribute present, is considered to hold an empty string value.

Variables can be defined within a template, or directly within the root Stylesheet or Transform elements. A variable defined outside of a template is known as a **global variable** because its value can be accessed from all the templates in the stylesheet.

References

For each defined variable there may be any number of **variable references**, including none (although a variable is not worth defining at all if there are going to be no references to it). A variable is accessed by referring to its name. The reference consists of the name of the variable with a '$' prefix that unambiguously identifies it as a reference. For example, '$age' refers to the 'age' variable:

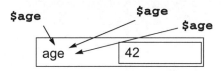

When the stylesheet is processed, the reference is replaced by the value of the variable :

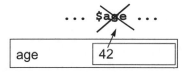

The **Value Of** element can be used to insert a variable value inside a text string. The variable reference is placed in the Select attribute:

```
Age: '<value-of select="$age"/>'.
```

```
Age: '42'.
```

Variables can be referenced from most instruction elements, but cannot be used in the Match attribute of the Template element and the Use attribute of the Key element.

Boolean values

A variable is assigned to the **boolean** data type using the XPath **true**() and **false**() functions (see Chapter 22):

```
<!-- YES, APPROVED -->
<variable name="approved" select="true()" />

<!-- POWER IS OFF -->
<variable name="power" select="false()" />
```

Debugging example

One use for this type of value is to set flags that switch on and switch off parts of a stylesheet as desired. For example, consider a variable called 'debug'. When this variable is given the value 'true', all the debugging messages are to be output; when set to false, they are to be suppressed:

```
<variable name="debug" select="true()"/>

<template match="para">
  <if test="$debug">SOURCE WAS 'para' ELEMENT</if>
  <apply-templates/>
</template>
```

Comparison and output

When boolean variables are output using the Value Of element, these values are automatically converted to the strings 'true' and 'false'. When used in a calculation, they are automatically converted to the numerical values '1' (representing true) and '0' (representing false):

```
<variable name="debug" select="true()" />
<value-of select="$debug" />,
<value-of select="$debug + 1" />
```

```
true, 2
```

Numbers

An expression can be a simple **number** or a calculation that results in a number:

```
<variable name="age" select="42" />
<variable name="age" select="21 + 21" />
```

Calculations

A numeric variable can be used in calculations and comparisons. In the following example, the literal number '19' is compared with the value in the variable. The test succeeds if the value of the variable value is greater than 19:

```
<if test="$age > 19">NO LONGER A TEENAGER!</if>
```

Output as a string

A number can also be output as text using the Value Of element:

```
Age: '<value-of select="$age"/>'.
```

> Age: '**42**'.

This works because a variable reference within the Select attribute has an implied string() function around it (see Chapter 22), so the example below is equivalent (though more verbose, and so rarely used in practice):

```
Age: '<value-of select="string($age)"/>'.
```

Converting to boolean

A numeric value can be used as a boolean test. If the value is zero, this is interpreted as 'false'; any other value is interpreted as 'true'. The following tests are therefore equivalent:

```
<if test="$age">HAD AT LEAST ONE BIRTHDAY</if>
<if test="$age > 0">HAD AT LEAST ONE BIRTHDAY</if>
```

But note that negative numbers are also considered to be 'true', so the second test above is more explicit about only selecting values that are greater than zero.

Strings

A **string** is identified using quotation marks around the characters that constitute the value. These quotation marks must not be the same kind as those used to enclose the Select attribute value. In the example below, the attribute value is delimited by double quotation mark characters, and the embedded string value by single quotation mark characters:

```
<variable name="danger" select="'color:red'" />
```

The entity references '**'**' and '**"**' can be used to include quotation mark characters in the string value when a conflict would otherwise be unavoidable.

Output

The Value Of element is eminently suitable for outputting string variables because this element always converts any value it targets into a string value.

Convert to number

If a string happens to contain only characters that can legally appear in numbers, then the value can be used in numerical calculations (as indicated earlier). This is because the XSLT processor will wrap the variable in an implied number() function (see Chapter 22) when this is needed. The two tests that follow this variable definition are equivalent:

```
<variable name="age" select="'42'" />
<if test="20 > $age">...</if>
<if test="20 > number($age)">...</if>
```

If the string contains characters that are not used in numbers, a special number is created that can be represented by the term '**NaN**' (**Not A Number**). If this number is ever converted back into a string, perhaps by outputting the value using the Value Of element, then this string will contain the sequence of letters 'NaN':

```
<variable name="age" select="'FORTY TWO'" />
<variable name="ageValue" select="number($age)" />
<value-of select="$ageValue" />
```

```
NaN
```

Convert to boolean

A string value can be used in boolean tests. An empty string contains zero characters and is treated as 'false'. All strings that contain at least one character are 'true':

```
<if test="$age">YES, THE AGE HAS BEEN SUPPLIED</if>
```

Node-sets

When the Select attribute of the Variable element contains a location path, the variable becomes a reference to the node selected by this expression:

```
<book>
  ...
  <author>
    <firstName>John</firstName>
    <lastName>Smith</lastName>
  </author>
  ...
</book>

<variable name="BookAuthorNode" select="/book/author" />
```

This variable can be used at the start of expressions in order to home in on substructures:

```
<value-of select="$BookAuthorNode/lastName" />
```

A variable may also refer to several nodes (a 'set' of nodes), simply by employing an expression that does not target a single node. This example would select multiple Title elements that are scattered throughout the source document:

```
<variable name="TitleNodes" select="//title" />

<book>
  <title>Book Title</title>
  ...
  <chapter>
    <title>Chapter One</title>
    ...
  </chapter>
  <chapter>
    <title>Chapter Two</title>
    ...
  </chapter>
  <chapter>
    <title>Chapter Three</title>
    ...
  </chapter>
</book>
```

All of these nodes are output together when the variable is referenced using the **Copy Of** element:

```
<copy-of select="$TitleNodes" />

<title>Book Title</title><title>Chapter One
</title><title>Chapter Two</title><title>
Chapter Three</title>...
```

Node values

For efficiency reasons, the following technique should be used when analysis of the content structure is not needed and when the Value Of instruction will be used to output the entire variable text. In this example, the targetted element content is converted into a string:

```
<variable name="BookAuthorText"
          select="string(/book/author)" />
```

This technique is useful because the work of finding and gathering together the material to output is done as the variable is being created, and not repeated each time a reference occurs.

Convert to boolean

The presence of one or more nodes in a node-set is treated as 'true':

```
<if test="$TitleNodes">YES, THERE ARE TITLES</if>

<if test="not($TitleNodes)">THERE ARE NO TITLES</if>
```

Convert to number

If the node-set contains only characters found in a single number, after first ignoring any tags before, around or after these characters, then the fragment will be converted to a number as needed:

```
<PERSON>...<AGE>42</AGE>...</PERSON>


<variable name="age" select="/PERSON/AGE" />

<if test="$age > 19">NOT A TEENAGER</if>
```

The example below is valid because the characters combine to form a valid number:

```
<SIZE>
  <HUNDREDS>7</HUNDREDS>
  <TENS>9</TENS>
  <UNITS>4</UNITS>
</SIZE>


<!-- VALUE IS 794 -->
<variable name="size" select="/SIZE" />
```

But this next example is not valid because a number is not allowed to contain two decimal points:

```
    <SIZE>
      <FIRST>9.3</FIRST>
      <SECOND>2.4</SECOND> <!-- SECOND DECIMAL POINT -->
    </SIZE>

<!-- VALUE 9.32.4 IS NOT LEGEL (make value "NaN")-->
<variable name="sizes" select="/SIZE" />
```

Convert to string

When a node-set is converted into a string value, the text value of each node is retained while all XML markup is removed.

The Value Of element automatically converts a node-set into a string. This is why the Copy Of element must be used instead if the intention is to output the node-set as a result tree fragment that includes tags.

Result tree fragments

A variable may contain a **result tree fragment**. These are XML fragments that are usually added to the result tree ultimately (perhaps several times). When the variable definition does not use the Select attribute, but has element content instead, then the value is always considered to be a result tree fragment. For example, a copyright notice in HTML format may be enclosed in a paragraph element and contain bold text:

```
<xsl:variable name="copyright">
  <P>(c) <B>ACME</B> Corp</P>
</xsl:variable>
```

The distinction between fragments and strings is critical because the way in which the value is output differs. When the value is a string, the Value Of element is used to reference it. But when the value is a result tree fragment, the Copy Of element should be used instead in order to preserve the embedded markup:

```
<xsl:template match="book"
  <HTML>
    <xsl:apply-templates/>
    <xsl:copy-of select="$copyright"/>
  </HTML>
</xsl:template>
```

A variable of this type can be analysed using the same features as for string variables. It is not possible to treat this type of variable in the same way as node-set variables, such as to navigate into the value using an XPath expression.

Convert to boolean

The absence of any content implies a 'false' value. An empty result tree fragment is like an empty string or an empty node-set.

Convert to number

The conversion of result tree fragments into numeric values follows the same general rule as for converting node-sets into numeric values. If the result tree fragment contains only characters that would be found in a single number, after first ignoring any tags present before, around or after these characters, then the fragment will be converted to a number as needed:

```
<xsl:variable name="age"><AGE>42</AGE></xsl:variable>

<xsl:if test="$age > 19">NOT A TEENAGER</xsl:if>
```

The first example below is valid because the characters combine to form a valid number, but the second is not because a number is not allowed to contain two decimal points:

```
<xsl:variable name="size">  <!-- VALUE IS 794 -->
   <HUNDREDS>7</HUNDREDS><TENS>9</TENS><UNITS>4</UNITS>
</xsl:variable>

<xsl:variable name="sizes"> <!-- VALUE CANNOT BE 9.32.4 -->
   <FIRST>9.3</FIRST>
   <SECOND>2.4</SECOND> <!-- SECOND DECIMAL POINT -->
</xsl:variable>
```

Convert to string

Conversion of result tree fragments to strings is identical to conversion of node-sets to strings.

No expressions in variables

A variable cannot hold a string or node containing an XPath expression that needs to be interpreted as such by the XSLT processor. While a variable can certianly hold the string '/book/author', this string can never be interpreted as an expression (although some XSLT processor implementations may add extensions that can do this). For example, the following will not work:

```
<variable name="ChapterTitle" select="'chapter/title'"/>

                    <!-- ERROR -->
<template match="$ChapterTitle">...</template>
```

References in output attributes

The approach to outputting the value of a variable described above could be used to insert values into literal element attributes, as in the following example where the 'danger' style definition is inserted into the Style attribute:

```
<xsl:template match="Warning">
  <P>
    <xsl:attribute name="STYLE">
      <xsl:value-of select="$danger"/>
    </xsl:attribute>
    <xsl:apply-templates/>
  </P>
</xsl:template>


  <P STYLE="color:red">...</P>
```

However, there is a simpler way to achieve this effect. Variable values can also be inserted directly into output attributes, using an attribute value template. This is because variable references can be included in XPath expressions, and may even constitute the entirety of the expression:

```
<xsl:template match="Warning">
  <P STYLE='{$danger}'>
    <xsl:apply-templates/>
  </P>
</xsl:template>
```

Complex variable definitions

In all the examples above, values are constructed from literal text in the stylesheet, or by selecting material in the source tree. Compound values can also be created, with part or all of the value dependent on the result of a conditional test.

Compound values

It is very easy to create a single value from multiple components when the variable value is a result tree fragment. XSLT instruction elements can be placed in the Variable element. In the following example, the value is built from two attribute values and some static separating text:

```
<variable name="author">
  <value-of select="/book/author/@LastName"/>
  <text>, </text>
  <value-of select="/book/author/@FirstName"/>
</variable>
```

It is also possible to do something similar for string values, using the XPath concat() function (see Chapter 22):

```
<variable name="author"
    select="concat(/book/author/@LastName,
                   ', ',
                   /book/author/@FirstName) " />
```

Indeed, the same technique also works for numeric and boolean values by wrapping the output of the concat() function in either the number() function or the boolean() function:

```
<pi integer="3" fraction="142" />
```

```
<template match="pi">
  <variable name="pi"
            select="number(
                    concat(@integer, '.', @fraction)
                    )" />

  <value-of select="$pi" />, <value-of select="$pi - 3" />
</template>
```

```
3.142, 0.142
```

Context-specific values

Variables may contain XSLT instructions that help to determine what the value should be. The If and Choose elements can be used to test various conditions and to generate suitable content. In the following example, the letter 'r', 'g' or 'b' in the Colour attribute is converted to 'RED', 'GREEN' or 'BLUE' in the variable:

```
<variable name="colour">
  <if test="@colour='r'">RED</if>
  <if test="@colour='g'">GREEN</if>
  <if test="@colour='b'">BLUE</if>
</variable>
```

But this only works for result tree fragment values because all other data types are specified using the Select attribute, which takes an XPath expression, and this expression language does not include decision logic.

It is even possible to include the Apply Templates element in a variable. All of the output from the templates this instruction triggers is collected by the variable, instead of being sent to the result tree. In the following example, the entire source document is processed and gathered up by the variable, and the entire document is then output by writing-out the value of the variable:

```
<template match="/">

  <!-- PUT ALL OF DOCUMENT IN TO AllDocument VARIABLE -->
  <variable name="AllDocument">
    <apply-templates/>
  </variable>

  <!-- OUTPUT ENTIRE DOCUMENT -->
  <value-of select="$AllDocument"/>
</template>
```

Invariable variables

In most programming languages, the term 'variable' is used to describe a named
container for a value that can be assigned after the variable has been defined, and
thereafter replaced at any time. In the following C or Java program fragment, the
variable 'a' is first created, then given a value, then given a different value:

```
int a;          // variable 'a' is created (an integer)
a = 123;        // 'a' is given value 123
a = 987;        // value has now changed from 123 to 987
```

Many programming languages also include the concept of a 'constant'. A constant
is similar to a variable except that the value it holds cannot be modified once it has
been initialised:

```
const int a = 123 ; // constant 'a' is created
a = 987;            // ERROR, CANNOT REDEFINE A CONSTANT
```

Furthermore, a constant is given a fixed value by the developer and can only be
changed by editing the source code of the program. It does *not* acquire a value that
can differ, depending on the context, each time the program is run.

The reason for exploring this distinction is to clarify the precise nature of XSLT
variables because, in truth, they more closely resemble constants than variables (as
these concepts are normally understood). The stylesheet author can only change
the value of a variable between processing runs. However, there are some techniques that help to overcome this apparent weakness. But note that XSLT variables
are not quite analogous to constants either because they can hold a value calculated
from contextual information gathered from the source tree, and so may have a different value each time the stylesheet is used to process another document.

Overriding within templates

To a very limited extent, it is possible to simulate the capability of variables in programming languages to be given a new value. The way to achieve this is to declare a new variable with the same name as an existing variable, but holding a different value. This can only be done in one special circumstance – a definition made within a template can be made that overrides a global variable:

```
<stylesheet...>
  <variable name="blue" ... />
  <!-- ORIGINAL DEFINITION APPLIES HERE -->
  ...
  <template...>
    <!-- ORIGINAL DEFINITION STILL APPLIES HERE -->
    ...
    <variable name="blue" ... />
    ... <!-- OVERRIDE DEFINITION APPLIES HERE -->
    ...
  </template>
  <!-- ORIGINAL DEFINITION APPLIES HERE -->
  ...
</stylesheet>
```

The overriding variable definition is only applicable to subsequent sibling instructions and their descendants. If a variable is created within an embedded structure, it is only 'visible' in the remainder of that structure. This is why the global variable above reasserts its existence beyond the confines of the template that contains the overriding variable. As another example, a variable created within an If instruction is not applicable beyond this instruction. When there is a global definition, this definition becomes relevant again for the remainder of the template:

```
<template...>
  ...
  <if ...>
    <variable ... />
    ...
    <for-each ...>
      <!-- VARIABLE STILL VISIBLE -->
      ...
    </for-each>
    <!-- VARIABLE STILL VISIBLE -->
    ...
  </if>
  <!-- VARIABLE NOT VISIBLE -->
  ...
</template>
```

The possibility that a variable defined in one template might need to be referenced in another template is addressed by a technique discussed later in this chapter (using parameters).

Intelligent value construction

Because variables cannot be redefined, it is not possible to give a variable one value then, depending on the result of a test, override this with a different value. In the following example, the variable is intended to hold either the name of the author, or the word 'NONE' if there is no author, but it is not legal to redefine a variable within a template (and even if it *were* allowed the example below would still not work correctly because the second definition would only be visible in the If element):

```
<variable name="AuthorName" select="/book/author/" />

<if test="not(/book/Author)">
  <!-- ERROR (cannot redefine variable) -->
  <variable name="AuthorName select="'NONE'" />
</if>
```

However, this limitation can be overcome providing that the test can be made at the same time as the initial definition. This is done by including the test within the variable definition itself:

```
<variable name="AuthorName">
  <if test="/book/Author">
    <value-of select="/book/author/">
  </if>
  <if test="not(/book/Author)">NONE</if>
</variable>
```

This technique only works for result tree fragment variable values, but this is usually not a severe handicap.

For-each loops

Variables can be defined within a for-each loop. In this location, it appears that the variable can be modified during each iteration of the loop. In truth, this only works because the variable is actually being re-created each time, though the effect is identical.

In the following example, the variable holds different values during each iteration of the loop (the Id attribute value of the paragraph being processed):

```
<for-each select="para">
  <!-- get ID of this paragraph -->
  <variable name="paraID" select="@id" />
  ...
  ...
</for-each>
```

Other limitations

Variables are evaluated after the stylesheet instructions, so variables cannot be used in Match attributes:

```
            <!-- ERROR -->
<template match="para[$ParaNumber]">
  ...
</template>
```

But they can be used in tests within an expression, along with other items that are evaluated at run-time, such as attribute values. In the following example, the value of the Id attribute of the current element is compared with the value of the WantedId variable:

```
<for-each select="/book/chapter[@Id=$WantedId]">
  ...
</for-each>
```

The Use attribute of the Key element cannot hold a variable either. Just like the Match attribute, this attribute is evaluated as the stylesheet is interpreted, prior to processing the source tree.

Template parameters

When one template activates another, using the Apply Templates element, it is possible for information to be passed to the triggered template using one or more **parameters**. Again, software developers will be familiar with the concept of passing parameters to procedures and functions. The **Param** element works in the same way as the Variable element. It has the same attributes and is referenced in the same way (one consequence of this being that it is not possible to have a variable and a parameter with the same name). The **Name** attribute is used to define the parameter and the value is given by the **Select** attribute or by the content of the element:

```
<xsl:template match="Paragraph">
  <xsl:param name="colour">white</xsl:param>
  <xsl:param name="prefix">none</xsl:param>

  <DIV STYLE='background-color:{$colour}'>
    <xsl:if test="not($prefix='none')">
      <xsl:value-of select='$prefix' />
      <xsl:text>: </xsl:text>
    </xsl:if>
    <xsl:apply-templates/>
  </DIV>
</xsl:template>
```

The one big difference between parameters and variables is that the value specified in the parameter declaration is merely a default value, to be employed only when a specific value has not been passed to the template.

This feature is particularly useful for passing information to named templates, and is commonly used for this purpose.

Parameter values

In order for a template to receive parameter values that will override the default values, these parameters must first be created. Parameters are created using the **With Parameter** element. This element can be used in the Apply Templates element and has the same attributes and content as the Param element (and the Variable element). As before, the **Name** attribute is used to name the parameter and the value is calculated from an expression in the **Select** attribute, or is a result tree fragment within the element.

In the following example, two parameters are passed to any template that is activated as a result of the Apply Templates instruction, specifying the colour and prefix text to be used in this context:

```
<apply-templates>
  <with-param name="colour" select="@colour"/>
  <with-param name="prefix">Note</with-param>
</apply-templates>
```

The names of these two parameters match the names of the parameters in the template for paragraphs shown above. Values are only passed to parameters with the same name, and even letter-case is significant so 'COLOUR' and 'colour' would not match.

Only templates directly triggered by this Apply Templates instruction will 'catch' the parameter values. However, each triggered template could re-create and pass-down the values, though this would be a clumsy technique. A global variable would be preferable whenever it is practical to use one.

Passing-down variables

As discussed above, a variable defined in a template has a fundamental limitation in that it cannot be 'seen' outside this template. However, when a variable is defined in one template but needs to be referenced in other templates triggered by this template, it is possible to pass-down the variable to the other templates using a parameter:

```
<variable name="Security" select="@securityLevel" />

<apply-templates>
  <with-param name="SecurityParameter"
              select="$Security" />
</apply-templates>
```

Document parameters

It is often useful to be able to modify the exact behaviour of a stylesheet each time it is used. One simple way to do this is to pass parameters to the stylesheet. The whole stylesheet can be treated in a similar way to an individual template, receiving parameters using the **Param** element. But in this case the parameters are not created using the With Param element. The method adopted for creating parameters depends on the nature of the XSLT processor in use (documentation supplied with an XSLT application should provide this information). For example, some XSLT processors can be activated from the command-line, and in the example below the value 'RED' is passed to the stylesheet as a parameter named 'colour' (the exact syntax of the command shown below does not illustrate any specific real-world XSLT processor):

```
C:> style MyDoc.xml MyStylesheet.xsl -params colour=RED
```

The stylesheet collects this value by defining a parameter with the same name, while possibly setting a default value (to be applied if no parameter is actually passed to the stylesheet):

```
<stylesheet ...>
  <param name="colour">BLACK</param>
  ...
</stylesheet>
```

Note that an alternative way to pass more complex details or large quantities of configuration information to a stylesheet is available, through an XML-format 'configuration document' that is accessed using the document() function.

14. Sorting

Information is often presented in alphabetical or numerical order. For example, the index at the end of this book is sorted alphabetically. It can be inconvenient to maintain the source material in the correct order; XSLT is therefore able to sort the data during the transformation process. Information can be sorted alphabetically or numerically, and can be sorted repeatedly to create ordered sub-groups.

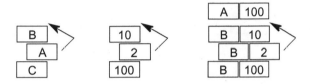

Simple element sorting

One good example of the need to sort elements is the task of creating a glossary. In the following example, the Glossary element contains a number of Item elements, but they have not been arranged in any particular order:

```
<glossary>
  <item>XSL - ...</item>
  <item>XML - ...</item>
  <item>HTML - ...</item>
</glossary>
```

Using techniques described previously, it would be possible to convert this data into an equivalent HTML structure. However, because elements are normally processed in document order, the output shown below is in the same order as the source XML items:

```
<DIV>
  <P>XSL - ...</P>
  <P>XML - ...</P>
  <P>HTML - ...</P>
</DIV>
```

The **Sort** element can be used to override this default ordering. It is placed within the Apply Templates element, where it specifies that the elements selected by this instruction are to be output in sorted order. Strictly speaking, the context list of nodes are sorted before the XSLT processor begins to iterate through them. In the following example, the template for the Glossary element includes the Sort element, indicating that the Item elements embedded in the Glossary element are to be sorted:

```
<xsl:template match="glossary">
  <DIV>
    <xsl:apply-templates><xsl:sort/></xsl:apply-templates>
  </DIV>
</xsl:template>

<xsl:template match="item">
  <P><xsl:apply-templates/></P>
</xsl:template>
```

The Item elements are transformed into Paragraph elements output in the following order:

```
<DIV>
  <P>HTML - ...</P>
  <P>XML - ...</P>
  <P>XSL - ...</P>
</DIV>
```

Note that the Sort element can also be used in the For Each element (see Chapter 3). When it is used there, it must be the first element to appear in the structure:

```
<template match="addresses">
  <for-each ...>
      <sort ...>
      ...
  </for-each>
</template>
```

The example in Chapter 3 (in the section "Direct processing", starting on page 34) can be modified to list names in alphabetical order:

```
<xsl:template match="Document">
  <HTML><BODY>
  <H1>Individual Names</H1>
  <OL>
    <xsl:for-each select="//Name[@type='personal']">
      <xsl:sort/>
      <LI><xsl:value-of select="."/></LI>
    </xsl:for-each>
  </OL>
  <H1>Company Names</H1>
  <OL>
    <xsl:for-each select="//Name[@type='company']">
      <xsl:sort/>
      <LI><xsl:value-of select="."/></LI>
    </xsl:for-each>
  </OL>
  </BODY></HTML>
</xsl:template>
```

Correct ordering

While it is obvious that 'a' should appear before 'z', and that '1' should appear before '9', the sorting process is not always this simple. A number of factors, including language, capitalization and relative string lengths, all contribute to deciding on the correct order.

Language factor

Sorting order will differ for each human language. The Roman alphabet used in English has an obvious order, with 'A' always appearing before 'B', and 'Y' always appearing before 'Z'. But it is far less obvious whether 'e' and 'é' are to be treated as the same or different; and if different which should appear first. This problem is even more marked for other alphabets, such as Greek and Cyrillic. Fortunately, the UNICODE initiative (to create standard ways of storing text electronically for all the world languages) covers sorting issues and the XSLT standard suggests that processors use these recommendations.

For this to work, however, it is important that the language of the text be recognizable by the XSLT processor. The **Lang** attribute is used for this purpose. For example, the value 'EN' represents the English language. The standard states that when this attribute is absent, a default value is derived from the system environment. In practice, this may mean reading the value of an 'xml:lang' attribute in the source document, but when this is also absent English will typically be assumed.

Letter-case factor

The simplest sorting algorithm imaginable would sort using the **ASCII** codes of the characters. This would certainly ensure that words beginning with 'A' (ASCII code 65) would appear before words beginning with 'B' (ASCII code 66), and that terms starting with digits, such as '16-bit', would appear first ('1' has an ASCII value of 49). However, such an algorithm would also place all words beginning with an upper-case letter before the first word containing a lower-case letter, putting 'Zebra' before 'abacus' ('Z' is ASCII code 90, and 'a' is 97), which is rarely desired. XSLT, therefore, requires a more sophisticated approach that ignores capitalization (though not totally, because the order in which 'a' and 'A' must appear may still be important). By default, 'a' precedes 'A', but both 'a' and 'A' appear before 'b' and 'B'.

String length factor

The length of the text string is also significant. A shorter string with the same characters as the first part of a longer string appears first; for example, 'the' appears before 'theory':

```
a
an
and
android
```

Combined factors

A space character is deemed to be more significant than any other symbol. This means that 'a z' appears before 'abc', but the shorter-string rule takes precedence and so 'ab' appears before 'a z' (this needs to be tested with specific XSLT processors because the exact behaviour regarding handling of spaces can differ).

This example of sorted output reflects the various rules described above:

```
<DIV>
   <P>1</P>
   <P>5</P>
   <P>55a</P>
   <P>a</P>
   <P>ab</P>
   <P>Ab</P>
   <P>a z</P>
   <P>abc</P>
</DIV>
```

Identical source strings

When two items have exactly the same content, they must be output in their original order. This may seem a trivial point; if the strings are identical, then the order in which they are output should be irrelevant. However, it is possible to sort an item using only part of its content as the sort key, and in this circumstance the ordering of the remaining part of the value may be significant.

Ordering options

Two options are available for changing the default sorting behaviour in some limited ways. Items can be sorted numerically, and capitals can be placed before lower-case letters. Attributes on the Sort element are used to specify these settings.

Numerical ordering

It is possible to sort by numerical value. This is very different to sorting by characters when the characters happen to be digits. Normal sorting simply ranks digits by their ASCII or UNICODE character code values:

```
<P>1999</P>
<P>299</P>
<P>39</P>
```

In this example, '1999' is the first item because it begins with a '1' character. But the numbers are clearly not ranked by value because '1999' is larger than '29'. Ordering by value can be achieved using the **Data Type** attribute. It has a default value of '**text**' but can be given an explicit value of '**number**'. The values are then ranked in true ascending order:

```
<sort data-type="number"/>
```

```
<P>39</P>
<P>299</P>
<P>1999</P>
```

Although the XSLT standard makes no comment on this point, a value test should not fail if the text string contains letters as well as digits, even if there is no space between leading digits and following non-digit characters. The number should be constructed from the first unbroken series of digits:

```
<P>1xyz</P>
<P>55</P>
<P>333abc99</P>
```

Letter-case ordering

Capital letters can be placed before lower-case letters using the **Case Order** attribute. This attribute can only take two possible values; '**lower-first**' (the default) or '**upper-first**':

```
<sort case-order="upper-first"/>
```

```
<P>Abc - ...</P>
<P>abc - ...</P>
```

This attribute is only relevant when the Data Type attribute has an implied (or explicit) value of 'text'.

Selective sorting

All the examples above assume that the sort order value is the entire content of the elements to be sorted. However, the **Select** attribute can be used to identify a specific portion of the item. The implied value of this attribute is '.' indicating the current element. The following examples are therefore equivalent:

```
<sort/>

<sort select="."/>
```

The current element, in this context, means the element being sorted and it applies to each one of these elements in turn.

This attribute can take any XPath expression, greatly improving the flexibility of the sort feature as the following two scenarios demonstrate.

Child element selection

When elements that contain other elements are being sorted, the sorting criteria can be restricted to the content of one of the sub-elements. In the following example, a list of countries consists of a name and population count (in millions) for each country. One way to organize this list is to sort it by population size:

```
<countries>
  <country>
    <name>USA</name>
    <population>262</population>
  </country>
  <country>
    <name>UK</name>
    <population>58</population>
  </country>
</countries>


<xsl:template match="countries">
  <DIV>
    <xsl:apply-templates>
      <xsl:sort data-type="number"
                select="population"/>
    </xsl:apply-templates>
  </DIV>
</xsl:template>


  <DIV>
    <P>UK  <B>58</B></P>
    ...
    <P>USA  <B>262</B></P>
  </DIV>
```

Attribute selection

Because the Select attribute can take any expression, it can be used to target an attribute instead of an element. For example, if the Country element has a Population attribute instead of a child element, this attribute can be targetted:

```
<countries>
  <country population="262">
    <name>USA</name>
  </country>
  <country population="58">
    <name>UK</name>
  </country>
</countries>
```

```
<sort data-type="number" select="@population" />
```

Again, when deciding on the exact expression needed, it is important to recall that the current element is the element being sorted (in this case, each Country element), not the element from which the sort is specified (Countries).

Multiple sort criteria

The example above raises an interesting problem. Having decided to sort the countries by their population figures, what happens when two countries have the same population value? By default, they are simply output in document order. In the following example, Italy and the UK have the same population and so the order in which they are processed depends entirely on the order in the source file. In this example, a country with a name that begins with 'U' happens to be processed before a country with a name that begins with 'I':

```
<countries>
  <country>
    <name>UK</name>
    <population>58</population>
  </country>
  <country>
    <name>Italy</name>
    <population>58</population>
  </country>
</countries>
```

But it would probably be more desirable to sort countries with the same population count into alphabetical order, thus introducing a secondary sorting requirement. This can be achieved by simply repeating the Sort element in the template:

```
<xsl:template match="countries">
  <DIV>
    <xsl:apply-templates>
      <xsl:sort data-type="number"
                select="population"/>
      <xsl:sort select="name"/>
    </xsl:apply-templates>
  </DIV>
</xsl:template>
```

```
<DIV>
  <P>Italy <B>58</B></P>
  <P>UK  <B>58</B></P>
  ...
  <P>USA <B>262</B></P>
</DIV>
```

The order in which the Sort elements appear is very important. The first occurrence is deemed to be the primary sort field. The secondary Sort element takes effect only on the items within each primary group.

There may, by the same principle, be more than two levels of sorting.

15. Numbering

Numbered lists and sequentially identified document components, such as chapter headings, are common features of many types of document:

1)	A)	i)	1.a.i) ......
2)	B)	ii)	1.a.ii) ......
3)	C)	iii)	......
4)	D)	iv)	55.g.xiii) ......
5)	E)	v)	55.g.xiv) ......

Yet such numbering is often not present in source XML documents, so needs to be added for document presentation. XSLT therefore has an automatic numbering feature.

Automatic numbering

There are good reasons why numbering is rarely present in the source XML document. One reason includes the desire to style and position the numbers in a distinctive way. Another is to facilitate the deletion, insertion and rearrangement of numbered items without creating gaps or duplicated entries that have to be edited. Numbering is therefore commonly left to software that is capable of performing the relatively simple task of counting and generating values for these items. XSLT stylesheets are therefore able to identify the elements to number and to insert appropriate values.

HTML numbering

When transforming XML documents into HTML or XHTML documents, it may not be necessary to use XSLT features at all. The simplest way to number items automatically is to use the OL (Ordered List) and LI (List Item) elements. In this scenario, the stylesheet leaves the numbering task to the Web browser. Take the simple example of a list of procedural steps:

```
<procedure>
  <step>walk to the door</step>
  <step>insert the key in the lock</step>
  <step>turn the key</step>
  <step>turn the handle</step>
  <step>push</step>
</procedure>
```

The following templates would suffice:

```
<xsl:template match="procedure">
  <OL><xsl:apply-templates/></OL>
</xsl:template>

<xsl:template match="step">
  <LI><xsl:apply-templates/></LI>
</xsl:template>
```

These templates would create the following HTML output:

```
<OL>
  <LI>walk to the door</LI>
  <LI>insert the key in the lock</LI>
  <LI>turn the key</LI>
  <LI>turn the handle</LI>
  <LI>push</LI>
</OL>
```

Finally, a Web browser would render this HTML fragment as follows:

1. walk to the door
2. insert the key in the lock
3. turn the key
4. turn the handle
5. push

Advantage can be taken of HTML features for varying the style of the list by adding appropriate attributes to the OL and LI elements (see Chapter 28 for details).

When converting to HTML format, the stylesheet author has the choice of whether to use HTML list elements, as described above, or the XSLT numbering features described below.

Simple numbering

The **Number** element is replaced by a sequential value. In its simplest form, using none of the attributes described below, this element is replaced by a value that represents the position of the element being processed within the context list. The following template numbers each step in a list of procedures. Note that although other elements may occur among the numbered elements, they do not interfere with the numbering process in any way (because they are not in the context list):

```
<procedure>
  <title>Getting Through a Locked Door</title>
  <step>walk to the door</step>
  <para>Make sure you have the key!</para>
  <step>insert the key in the lock</step>
  <step>turn the key</step>
  <step>turn the handle</step>
  <step>push</step>
</procedure>
```

```
<xsl:template match="step">
  <P><xsl:number/>) <xsl:apply-templates/></P>
</xsl:template>
```

```
<H1>Getting Through a Locked Door</H1>
<P>1) walk to the door</P>
<P><B>Make sure you have the key!</B></P>
<P>2) insert the key in the lock</P>
<P>3) turn the key</P>
<P>4) turn the handle</P>
<P>5) push</P>
```

The first occurrence of the target element is given the number '1' and numbering is automatically restarted within each list, as in the following example:

```
<procedure>
  <step>plug in</step>
  <step>switch on</step>
  <step>enter password</step>
</procedure>
...
<procedure>
  <step>shut down</step>
  <step>switch off</step>
  <step>unplug</step>
</procedure>
```

```
<P>1) plug in</P>
<P>2) switch on</P>
<P>3) enter password</P>
...
<P>1) shut down</P>
<P>2) switch off</P>
<P>3) unplug</P>
```

Number format

Lists do not always consist of numerically ordered labels. Some lists are sorted alphabetically, such as 'a. b. c.' or 'A) B) C)', while others are sorted using Roman numbers 'i ii iii iv'.

The **Format** attribute is used to specify the method of numbering desired. When not present, the default value of '1' is used, which has the effect shown above. The letter 'a' specifies lower-case alphabetic numbering, and 'A' indicates the use of upper-case letters. The letter 'i' or 'I' represents Roman numbering (which uses either lower-case or upper-case letters):

```
<xsl:template match="item">
  <P><xsl:number format="a"/>. <xsl:apply-templates/></P>
</xsl:template>
```

```
  <P>a. first item</P>
  <P>b. second item</P>
  <P>c. third item</P>
```

```
<xsl:template match="item">
  <P><xsl:number format="i"/>. <xsl:apply-templates/></P>
</xsl:template>
```

```
  <P>i. first item</P>
  <P>ii. second item</P>
  <P>iii. third item</P>
```

Long alphabetical lists

Unlike digits and Roman numerals which have no upper limit, alphabetically ordered items hit a problem after the letter 'z' or 'Z' has been reached. There are no more letters left to label subsequent items in the list. The solution recommended by the XSLT specification is to use additional letters at this point. After 'z' the next item would be labelled 'aa'. This would be followed by 'ab' and 'ac'. After 'az' comes 'ba' and 'bb'. Presumably, after 'zz' the next item should be 'aaa'.

Surrounding punctuation

The Format attribute can also contain surrounding punctuation and other formatting characters. Typical examples would include '(A)' and '[i.]'.

```
<number format="(A)"/>
```

These characters are output around each generated label giving, for example, '(A)', '(B)' and '(C)'.

There appears to be little advantage in doing this because these characters could just as easily be placed around the entire Number element to achieve the same effect. However, this technique becomes more useful with multipart numbering (discussed later in this chapter).

Expression values

The value to insert into the document can be calculated using an expression that is entered into the **Value** attribute. The expression must return a numeric value because it is to be used as the count value. Expressions are used to count sorted elements and to create interesting effects such as a count-down.

Current location

The most obvious expression that could be used here is the **position()** function, which returns the position of the current element from among the current context list:

```
<number value="position()" format="A"/>
```

However, this function often returns the position of the element among nodes of all kinds, including text nodes, because it refers to the current context list of nodes from which the current template was selected (and the current template may have been activated as the result of an Apply Templates instruction with no Select attribute filtering). The resulting values may not be what is expected. A safer and more flexible solution uses the **count()** function, which can be used to count previous siblings of the required type (or siblings of all element types, using the '*' wildcard). Usually, the expression should include '+1' to include the current element in the count:

```
value="count(preceding-sibling::*)+1"
```

One or more specific element types can be counted:

```
value="count(preceding-sibling::item) +
       count(preceding-sibling::para) + 1"
```

Count in sorted output order

Under most conditions, adopting this approach has no effect on the result, but this technique is the only way to achieve the desired effect when the items are also sorted (see Chapter 14). This is due to the fact that the expression is applied to the final, sorted list and not to the items in their original document order:

```
<list>
  <item>Z</item>
  <item>Y</item>
  <item>X</item>
</list>
```

```
<xsl:template match="list">
  <DIV>
    <xsl:apply-templates><xsl:sort/></xsl:apply-templates>
  </DIV>
</xsl:template>

<xsl:template match="item">
  <P>
    <xsl:number
    value="count(preceding-sibling::item)+1" format="i)"/>
    <xsl:apply-templates/>
  </P>
</xsl:template>
```

```
<DIV>
   <P>i) X</P>
   <P>ii) Y</P>
   <P>iii) Z</P>
</DIV>
```

Reverse numbering

Even when not sorting, this technique raises some interesting possibilities. For example, it is possible to create a reverse list by subtracting the current position from the total number of items:

```
<list>
  <item>first</item>
  <item>second</item>
  <item>third</item>
</list>
```

```
value="count(../item) - count(preceding-sibling::item)"
```

```
<DIV>
  <P>3) first</P>
  <P>2) second</P>
  <P>1) third</P>
</DIV>
```

See the XPath chapters (19 to 23) for more information on expressions.

Elements to count

Previous examples have implicitly counted occurrences of the current element. However, it is possible to override this simple behaviour in various ways: by only counting the element under certain conditions, by adding other elements into the count, or by separately counting other elements.

Selective counting

The **Count** attribute is used in the Number element to control counting. When this attribute is given a value that matches the current element name, this is equivalent to not including the attribute at all. The two examples below are therefore equivalent:

```
<xsl:template match="item">
  <P><xsl:number/>...</P>
</xsl:template>
```

```
<xsl:template match="item">
  <P><xsl:number count="item"/>...</P>
</xsl:template>
```

But the Count attribute actually contains an XPath pattern, and not necessarily just an element name. For example, it would be possible to ignore Item elements that have a Status attribute value of 'ignore':

```
<list>
  <item>first</item>
  <item status="ignore">ignore this</item>
  <item>third</item>
</list>
```

```
count="item[not(@status='ignore')]"
```

```
<DIV>
  <P>1) first</P>
  <P>ignore this</P>
  <P>2) third</P>
</DIV>
```

Including other elements

The 'l' symbol can be used to include other element names. For now, it will be assumed that the current element matches one of the elements named in the pattern (though this need not be the case). In this scenario, the other elements named are included in the count of previous siblings. For example, a step in the procedure that has been removed, but must continue to occupy a place in the sequence, might be represented by a Deleted element. The presence of Deleted elements could then be explicitly included in the calculation for the value of each Item element by including a Count attribute with values of both 'step' and 'deleted':

```
<xsl:template match="step">
  <P><xsl:number count="step|deleted"/>...</P>
</xsl:template>
```

In the following example, as each Step element is processed all previous Step and Deleted elements are included in the count:

```
<procedure>
  <title>Getting Through an Unlocked Door</title>
  <step>walk to the door</step>
  <deleted/>
  <deleted/>
  <step>turn the handle</step>
  <step>push</step>
</procedure>
```

```
<P>1) walk to the door</P>
<P>DELETED ITEM</P>
<P>DELETED ITEM</P>
<P>4) turn the handle</P>
<P>5) push</P>
```

Taking this example further, it is possible to include the same counter in the template for deleted items, thus re-creating the full numbered list:

```
<xsl:template match="deleted">
  <P><xsl:number count="step|deleted"/>) DELETED ITEM</P>
</xsl:template>
```

```
<P>1) walk to the door</P>
<P>2) DELETED ITEM</P>
<P>3) DELETED ITEM</P>
<P>4) turn the handle</P>
<P>5) push</P>
```

Using the value '*' it is possible to include all previous sibling elements in the count without having to list all the possible element names.

Note that when counting elements that share the same parent, as in the examples above, the current element name must be included in the list of elements to count. It is not possible to count only other elements. If the current element type is omitted, this is considered significant and triggers the feature described next.

Counting ancestor elements

It is sometimes useful to count occurrences of an ancestor element. One obvious need for this capability is to add a number to the title of each section of a document (such as the numbered chapter titles in this book). Although it is the Title element that is being processed and styled, it is the Section elements that both precede and finally enclose it that need to be counted.

This effect can be achieved simply by inserting the name of the ancestor element into the Count attribute, instead of the name of the current element.

When an XSLT processor analyses the Count attribute value, it first establishes whether or not the name of the current element appears as a valid match in the pattern. If it does not, then the elements containing the current element (its ancestors) are each analysed until one is found that matches. The counting process then works at *that* level in the document hierarchy, generating a value that represents the number of previous siblings in the usual way.

In the following example, there are two previous sections and one enclosing section, so the generated value for the Title element is '3':

```
<book>
  <section>...</section>          <!-- 1 -->
  <section>...</section>          <!-- 2 -->
  <section>                       <!-- 3 -->
    <title>Section Three</title>
    ...
  </section>
</book>
```

```
<xsl:template match="title">
  <H1>
    <xsl:number count="section"/>) <xsl:apply-templates/>
  </H1>
</xsl:template>
```

```
<H1>3) Section Three</H1>
```

Note that, working up the ancestor list from the current element, it is the first match that is used. If the three sections shown above were all enclosed within another, outer section, the outer Section element would be ignored:

```
<book>
  <section>  <!-- IGNORE THIS ENCLOSING SECTION -->
    <section>...</section>
    <section>...</section>
    <section>
      <title>Section Three</title>
      ...
    </section>
  </section>
</book>
```

The number of levels searched up the ancestor list can be constrained using the **From** attribute. This attribute holds a pattern that names the element or elements beyond which searching should not continue.

For example, a Part element could be specified preventing the inclusion in the count of sections in previous parts:

```
<number count="section" from="part" />
```

```
<book>
  <part> <!-- BLOCK -->
    <section>...</section>    <!-- NOT COUNTED -->
    <section>...</section>    <!-- NOT COUNTED -->
  </part>
  <part> <!-- BLOCK -->
    <section>...</section>    <!-- 1 -->
    <section>...</section>    <!-- 2 -->
    <section>                 <!-- 3 -->
      <title>...</title>      <!-- COUNT TO 3 -->
      ...
    </section>
  </part>
</book>
```

But this would happen in any case, simply because counting is restricted to sibling elements.

The second possible scenario is that the named element prevents access to the element to be counted. But this simply prevents counting, so is equally useless:

```
<book>
  <section>...</section>
  <section>...</section>
  <section>
    <part> <!-- BLOCKED HERE -->
      <title>...</title>
      ...
    </part>
  </section>
</book>
```

The From attribute therefore seems to be irrelevant. However, its use becomes more significant in scenarios introduced later in this chapter.

Multipart numbering

All previous examples have calculated item numbers at a single level – either at the same level as the current element, or at some higher level in the document hierarchy. But there may be a need to create item identifiers that include several counters. Legal and technical documents in particular tend to include such numbers as '1.2.7.3' or 'A–6–iv'. This effect can of course be achieved using multiple Number elements, arranged in sequence:

```
<xsl:template match="title">
  <P><xsl:number count="chapter" .../>.
    <xsl:number count="section" ..."/>
    <xsl:apply-templates/>
  </P>
</xsl:template>
```

However, this approach can be quite clumsy when dealing with several levels. Instead, the **Level** attribute can be used to indicate what type of numbering is required. Previous examples have illustrated the effect of the default setting for this attribute, with numbering being applied at a '**single**' level (the list of siblings, at whatever level in the hierarchy). By including the attribute, and giving it the value '**multiple**', the behaviour of the other attributes are modified to support multipart numbering.

In 'multiple' level mode, the list of ancestors is searched for all occurrences of each of the elements in the pattern. Searching does not cease at the first occurrence found. For example, in a document that contains Section elements within other Section elements, both levels will now be applicable. For each level in the ancestor list for which a match has been made, the previous siblings of that element that also match the pattern are counted:

```
<number level="multiple" count="chapter|section" ... />
```

```
<chapter>...</chapter>          <!-- C 1 -->
<chapter>...</chapter>          <!-- C 2 -->
<chapter>                       <!-- C 3 -->
  <section>...</section>          <!-- S 1 -->
  <section>                       <!-- S 2 -->
    <title>...</title>              <!-- INSERT 3.2 HERE -->
  </section>
</chapter>
```

Each separate count is finally formatted into a single string (see below).

Restricting the search

The **From** element has a more significant role in this scenario. Unlike single-level numbering, searching up the hierarchy of elements does not automatically stop at the first match, and so a blocking mechanism can be useful. For example:

```
<number count="section" from="chapter" />
```

```
<book>
  <section> <!-- NOT INCLUDED -->
    <chapter>
      <section> <!-- INCLUDED -->
```

Note that different XSLT processors give inconsistent results when the From attribute names an element that is not present as an ancestor (or as a prior sibling of an ancestor). In some cases, its absence is ignored. In others, its absence is seen as significant and reason enough to return a null count value.

Compound number formatting

The issue that arises at this point is exactly how a compound value is to be organized and formatted. The separate counts may be just appended to each other, which is rarely desired. Quite apart from lack of visual appeal, a number such as '1234' could be interpreted in various ways from a single value to such combinations as 'section 34 of chapter 12' or 'section 234 of chapter 1'. Typically, multipart numbers contain separating punctuation, such as the full-point as in '12.34' or '123.4'. Some XSLT processors will adopt this convention by default (and actually not allow simple concatenation of numbers). But the **Format** attribute is used to override either default behaviour. Required characters are inserted between tokens that represent each level (from left to right):

```
<number ... format="1.a" />
```

```
1.a
1.b
1.c
...
7.m
7.n
7.o
```

When there are more levels in a generated number than there are tokens in the attribute, the last token (and preceding punctuation) is reused. From the example above, values such as '3.c', '9.f.b' and '12.z.d.m' are all possible.

Document-wide numbering

The hierarchical structure of a document may be irrelevant to the counting scheme required. For example, if there is a requirement to provide each table in a document with a unique, sequential identifier, regardless of where it occurs within the document structure, it is more appropriate to view the document as a simple data stream and to count each table as it occurs in this stream. Setting the value of the **Level** attribute to '**any**' signifies this requirement:

```
<xsl:template match="table/title">
  <TITLE>
    <xsl:number level="any" count="table" ... />
    <xsl:apply-templates />
  </TITLE>
</xsl:template>
```

```
<TITLE>(15) Table Fifteen</TITLE>
```

Restricting the search

In this scenario, it would still be useful to be able to restart numbering from a significant point in the document. For example, tables may need to be numbered separately in appendices. The **From** element can play a very important role here because it does not simply eliminate upper levels in the hierarchy from consideration but instead blocks all elements *before* the named element or elements. For example, a Division element may be used to divide chapters into groups with numbering restarting within each group:

```
<number count="table" level="any" from="division" />
```

```
<book>
  <chapter>
    <table>...</table> <!-- TABLE 1 -->
    <table>...</table> <!-- TABLE 2 -->
  </chapter>
  <chapter>
    <table>...</table> <!-- TABLE 3 -->
  </chapter>
  <division/>
  <chapter>
    <table>...</table> <!-- TABLE 1 -->
  </chapter>
</book>
```

However, the start-tag of an enclosing element is still deemed to occur before the current element:

```
<number count="table" from="appendix" level="any"/>
```

```
<book>
  <chapter>
    <table>...</table> <!-- TABLE 1 -->
    <table>...</table> <!-- TABLE 2 -->
  </chapter>
  <chapter>
    <table>...</table> <!-- TABLE 3 -->
  </chapter>
  <appendix>
    <chapter>
      <table>...</table> <!-- TABLE 1 -->
    </chapter>
  </appendix>
</book>
```

Again, the XSLT processor should be tested to see how it copes with the absence of the element named in the From attribute – some processors may return a null value.

Advanced formatting options

A number of advanced formatting options are provided for padding and punctuating values, and for selecting a language and type of numbering sequence.

Padding

It is possible to make all numbers have the same width by padding shorter numbers with leading zeros. The **Format** attribute contains the number of digits to be presented, with the zero digit used for all but the last, which must be a '1' (as in '0001'):

```
<xsl:template match="item">
  <P>
    <xsl:number format="01"/>. <xsl:apply-templates/>
  </P>
</xsl:template>
```

```
<P>01. first item</P>
<P>02. second item</P>
<P>03. third item</P>
...
<P>09. ninth item</P>
<P>10. tenth item</P>
```

Punctuation

In order to improve legibility, punctuation is often used within values to create groups of digits. Two attributes are available for specifying the mark to use and the number of digits to place in each group. These are the **Grouping Separator** and the **Grouping Size** attributes. For example, in English documents typical values for these attributes would be ',' and '3' respectively:

```
<number ... grouping-separator="," grouping-size="3" />
```

```
<P>1. one</P>
<P>2. two</P>
<P>3. three</P>
...
<P>999. nine hundred and ninety nine</P>
<P>1,000. one thousand</P>
...
<P>1,000,000. one million</P>
```

Language

The **Lang** attribute allows a language to be identified so that an appropriate sequence of characters can be used to label each item. When this attribute is not used, some other method must be employed to determine the language to use. This may be the 'xml:lang' attribute, when it is present in the source document.

Complex alternative numbering schemes

It is widely known, and illustrated above, that in English there are two common ways in which alphabetic characters can be used to create an ordered list. These are the 'abcde' and 'i ii iii iv v' methods. Other languages also have two options, but in some cases both begin with the same character. This means that simply putting the initial character ('a' or 'i' in English) into the Format attribute is not sufficient to identify which method to use. The **Letter Value** attribute is therefore used to identify the method. It has two possible values: '**alphabetic**' and '**traditional**'. The meanings of these two values will vary between languages. There is also no default or preferred value, and so when this attribute is not present an XSLT processor may not behave as predicted.

16. Identifiers and links

Elements can be given unique identifiers. Such identifiers provide a simple, direct and highly efficient way to target a single element, or a group of related elements, for direct formatting in a distinctive fashion. When items are uniquely identified, it is also possible to create links to them, which a user may follow. This chapter describes two mechanisms for identifying elements, then shows how to build hypertext links to uniquely identified items.

XML IDs

The XML language includes the concept of unique element identifiers, allowing a specific instance of an element to be given a name so that it can be located when needed. This information can be used to construct a hypertext linking mechanism, or to identify an important item that needs to be formatted in a distinctive way.

ID attributes

In this scheme, an attribute is used to hold the identifier. There is no restriction on what this attribute can be called because it is recognized by the attribute type assigned to it in a DTD. These attributes are given the type 'ID'. In the following example, the Name attribute of the Item element is assigned this special status. In a conforming document, this attribute must always be present and must always be given a unique value:

```
<!ATTLIST item name ID #REQUIRED>
```

Error detection

An XML parser is able to collect the values of all attributes of this type in the document, and report an error if any values are duplicated. The following fragment is valid because each Name attribute value is different:

```
<item name="a">...</item>
<item name="aardvark">...</item>
...
<item name="zymurgy">...</item>
```

Identifier function

An XPath expression can exploit this feature using the **id**() function. A selection can be made by reference to an ID value. In the following example, the template matches the item with an identifier of 'XSLT':

```
<item name="XML">...</item>
<item name="XSLT">...</item>
<item name="XPath">...</item>
```

```
<template match="id('XSLT')">...</template>
```

Alternatively, this same item can be targetted explicity for immediate processing:

```
<apply-templates select="id('XSLT')"/>
```

The value of this function can be a space-separated list of identifiers. For example, if all items with identifiers consisting of a single letter needed to be formatted in the same way, the following template would be appropriate:

```
<template match="id('a b c d e f g h i j k l m n o p q r s
t u v w x y z')">...</template>
```

Efficiency gains

It can be more efficient to use the id() function rather than refer directly to the attribute value. While the following techniques are functionally equivalent (assuming that it is known in advance that the Name attribute holds the value concerned), the first is typically more appropriate:

```
<value-of select="id('XSLT')"/>
```

```
<value-of select="//*[@name='XSLT']"/>
```

The reason for this is due to the fact that an XSLT processor will often gather-up all the identifiers it finds in a document as the document source tree is being built, and then maintain a list of pointers to the nodes that contain them. The instruction above can then be performed very quickly because there is no need to search the entire document in order to find this node.

Limitations

There are some severe limitations to be aware of with this approach:

- a DTD is required in order to identify the attributes that are assigned to hold unique ID values, and this DTD must be read by the XSLT processor for the attributes to be recognized;
- the identifier must be stored in an attribute value (it cannot be element content);

- a single element can hold only one identifier (regardless of how many sets of relationships that element may participate in);
- only one element can have a particular identifier, so it is not possible to use identifiers to group related items;
- every identified item must have a completely unique identifier value, even when there is no relationship between one set of identifiers and another (perhaps distinguished by different element names);
- the identifier must be a single word that conforms to XML name restrictions.

All of these constraints can be overcome using the XSLT 'key' feature described below.

Keys

A powerful mechanism is included within the XSLT standard that overcomes the limitations of the XML ID scheme described above. This mechanism plays no role in validation, but focusses on the efficiency gains obtained by generating indexes for significant data items.

XSLT can identify elements using a **key**, which is more complex than a mere identifier. A key is actually a combination of three things:

- a specific target element (the purpose of the key is to retrieve this element when required);
- a value by which the element can be identified;
- a name that creates a distinct namespace for the value.

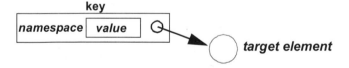

Key namespace

The use of 'namespaces' (not to be confused with the topic of Chapter 17) means that the same value can be used in different contexts without causing any conflicts. For example, the value 'orange' would have one meaning in the 'colour' space and a different meaning in the 'fruit' space. The names 'colour' and 'fruit' make this distinction, and the value 'orange' can be used in both without confusion:

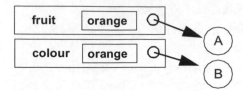

It would not be possible to do this using the DTD mechanism. Only one identifier attribute in an XML document could hold the value 'orange' according to that scheme.

Flexibility

While the key as a whole must be unique, no specific part of it has to be so. A key can have a non-unique namespace, value or target element.

In the case of the name part, this is obvious. It is clear that the name 'fruit' may be used in many keys with the value changing to identify elements that describe different kinds of fruit:

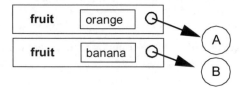

However, it is also true for the value part of the key as well. For example, more than one element may describe an 'orange' fruit. This flexibility allows a group of related elements to be formed and means that when a key is used it may locate more than one element:

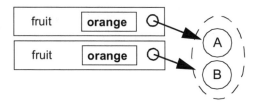

Furthermore, even the third part of the key, the element instance identified, does not have to be unique. A single instance of an element may be involved in more than one key. For example, an element that describes an 'orange' fruit may also be an element that describes an object of a specific colour (in the XML ID scheme, by contrast, only one ID attribute can be defined for an element):

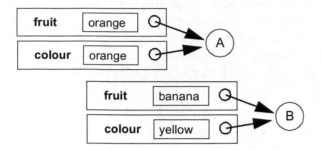

Using these keys, it is possible to apply specific formatting to all elements of a particular colour, or to all elements that describe a particular fruit.

Note that the illustration above also includes an example that demonstrates identical values from different namespaces ('orange' as a colour as well as a fruit).

Generating keys

The **Key** element is used to create keys:

```
<key .../>
```

The **Name** attribute specifies the name to give to each key created by this instruction. For example, it may be useful to create identifiers for all of the terms in a glossary, and this list of identifiers could be called 'Glossary':

```
<key name="Glossary" .../>
```

It is then necessary to identify the element or elements that are to be included in this namespace. This could be just the name of an element, or it could be a more complex XPath pattern. The **Match** attribute is used to do this, and the choice of name for this attribute is particularly appropriate because it has the same purpose and behaviour as when it is used in the Template element. For this example, Item elements will be selected, but only when they appear in a Glossary element:

```
<glossary>
  <item>...</item>
  <item>...</item>
  <item>...</item>
</glossary>

<key match="glossary/item" .../>
```

Finally, it is necessary to identify the text that will provide the unique value within each item. For maximum flexibility, this is done using an XPath expression, contained within the **Use** attribute. It is possible to select an attribute, the text content, or even just the content of a sub-element. Assuming each Item element has the following structure, then the Subject child element is a good candidate for the key value:

```
<item>
  <subject>XSL</subject>
  <description>XML Stylesheet Language</description>
</item>
<item>
  <subject>XSLT</subject>
  <description>XML Stylesheet Language -
  Transformations</description>
</item>
```

```
<key use="subject" .../>
```

By putting these three attributes together in a single Key element, an instruction is created to generate keys for all Item elements within Glossary elements, using the content of the embedded Subject elements for the key values:

```
<key name="Glossary"
     match="glossary/item"
     use="subject" ... />
```

In this case, there is a single Subject element in each Item element, so that the value is simple to determine. However, it is possible that there may be more than one matching element. When this happens, a key is created for each value. In the following example, two keys would be produced for the Item element, each with the same name but with different values ('XSL/XSLT' and 'XSLT/XSL'):

```
<item>
  <subject>XSL/XSLT</subject>
  <subject>XSLT/XSL</subject>
  <description>XML Stylesheet Language and
  Transformations</description>
</item>
```

When keys are present in the main stylesheet, and also in imported stylesheets, the keys defined in imported stylesheets for the same element are *not* ignored if there are multiple definitions at differing importance levels (according to the rules dictated by the import feature).

Using keys

Once generated, the keys can be used in similar fashion to XML identifiers, except that the **key**() function is used instead of the id() function. This function also takes two parameters instead of one. The first parameter specifies which namespace domain to search. The second parameter may be the value to search for, as in the following example – the Item element for 'XSL/XSLT' is located for formatting:

```
<template match="key('Glossary', 'XSL/XSLT')">
  ...
</template>
```

Recall that, because a key with a given name and value is not guaranteed to be unique, it cannot be assumed that such a reference will apply to a single element in the document.

Avoiding keys

A key does not offer anything that cannot be accomplished without this feature. Because a key is constructed using expressions, these expressions could just as easily be used directly. The example above could be expressed as follows:

```
<template match="glossary/item[subject='XSL/XSLT']">
  ...
</template>
```

However, as mentioned earlier, an XSLT processor may include advanced features for indexing elements and may build indexes from the information in the Key element, improving the performance of later searches. This feature also simplifies the expressions in the templates making the meanings clearer.

Hypertext links

Many electronic documents contain **hypertext links**. These are links from references to the objects they reference, which users may follow if they desire. Popular Web browsers have been built around this concept from the start. But for a link to work, the destination object must have a unique identifier of some kind. In some cases, the source document will already have unique identifiers, identified as such within a DTD:

```
<!DOCTYPE book [ ...
<!ELEMENT chapter (para+)>
<!ATTLIST chapter ident ID #REQUIRED>
... ]>
<book>
  <chapter ident="ch1">
  ...
  </chapter>
  <chapter>
    <para>Link to chapter
      <linkto idref="ch1">one</linkto>.
    </para>
  </chapter>
</book>
```

No special effort is needed to convert such a document using XSLT because the attribute values that link the reference to the destination are already in place in the source document and simply need to be copied-through to the output:

```
<BODY>
  <DIV><A NAME="ch1"></A>
  ...
  </DIV>
  <DIV>
    <P>Link to chapter<A HREF="#ch1">one</A>.</P>
  </DIV>
</BODY>
```

A more significant problem is linking to an object that does *not* have a unique identifier in the source document. Using XPath expressions, it is possible to identify such elements but not to assign identifiers to them. However, the **generate-id()** function can be used to create a unique identifier. This function is replaced by a unique value for the element, which is assigned by the XSLT processor. For example, this function can be used to give every paragraph in the output document a unique identifier. The node to assign the identifier to must be passed to it, and in this case the '.' symbol is used to identify the current node:

```
<xsl:template match="para">
  <P ID="{generate-id(.)}">
    <xsl:apply-templates/>
  </P>
</xsl:template>

    <P ID="N123456">...</P>
    <P ID="N123457">...</P>
    <P ID="N123458">...</P>
```

An element will always have the same unique identifier, even if this function is used to refer to the same element from elsewhere. This fact is very important – for example, every paragraph could be given a link to the chapter containing it, acting as a 'back-to-the-top' feature. It would be vital that all the generated identifiers are the same, and as the chapter itself:

```
<xsl:template match="chapter">
  <DIV ID="{generate-id(.)}">
    <xsl:apply-templates/>
  </DIV>
</xsl:template>

<xsl:template match="para">
  <P><A HREF="#{generate-id(ancestor::chapter)}">TOP </A>
    <xsl:apply-templates/>
  </P>
</xsl:template>


    <DIV ID="N987654">
        <P><A HREF="#N987654">TOP </A>...</P>
        <P><A HREF="#N987654">TOP </A>...</P>
        <P><A HREF="#N987654">TOP </A>...</P>
    </DIV>
```

17. Namespaces

Some complex issues arise when using namespaces with XSLT. In particular, complications discussed here are those that arise from the fact that source documents, stylesheets and output documents may all use namespaces, and the stylesheet has to cope with scenarios that involve namespaces, or the lack of namespaces, in any combination of these three locations.

Background

Many of the examples in previous chapters have included a mixture of XSLT elements and HTML, XHTML or other elements, and **namespaces** have been used to distinguish between them. The problem of mixing fragments of XML from different sources within a single data file is widely recognized, and is not limited to XSLT stylesheets. The solution to this problem is the **Namespaces in XML** standard, produced by the W3C and released as a recommendation in 1999. It can be found at http://www.w3.org/TR/REC-xml-names.

When discussing XSLT, the issue of namespaces can arise in three separate places. Namespaces may have been used in the source document. They may also be required in the target document. Finally, namespaces may be needed in the stylesheet document itself (the next section discusses this scenario, while introducing namespace concepts in general).

Namespaces in stylesheets

The concept of namespaces is certainly very important to XSLT when a stylesheet contains a mixture of XSLT rules and literal output elements. It is possible, for example, to imagine the need to create an XML document that contains an element named 'template'. Without namespaces, it would be very difficult for the XSLT processor to interpret the following markup:

```
<template match="...">
  <template>
    <apply-templates/>
  </template>
</template>
```

It is an incidental detail that HTML and XSL formatting elements do not happen to clash with XSLT elements in this way. In other cases, there may well be such a conflict.

Prefixes

At the heart of the namespaces scheme is the concept of an element prefix, which is separated from the element name using a colon, ':'. For example, the HTML element 'H3' could become 'html:H3', and the XSLT element 'template' could become 'XSLT:template'. Using this approach, the example above can be made valid, in this case by assigning the prefix 'XSLT' to all XSLT elements, and 'MyDoc' to all target document elements:

```
<XSLT:template match="...">
  <MyDoc:template>
    <XSLT:apply-templates/>
  <MyDoc:template>
</XSLT:template>
```

Namespace declarations

If prefix names were assigned by the same authorities who created the respective element sets, the same prefix could accidentally be chosen by two or more parties and clashes could then still occur. To avoid this happening, namespaces must be assigned an identifier guaranteed to be unique. A good, ready-made candidate for this is the URL standard. A URL provides a unique, globally recognized address for the description or DTD that defines the elements and attributes that a namespace covers. For example, XSLT is defined at http://www.w3.org/1999/XSL/Transform.

While unique, these text strings would not be ideal as prefix names. They often contain characters that are not allowed in XML element names, and they are too long to be manageable. However, they can be mapped to *locally* defined prefixes that are both short and legal. The namespaces standard provides for this mapping using an attribute that includes the prefix **xmlns** followed by the assigned prefix name. For example:

```
xmlns:html="http://www.w3.org/TR/REC-html40"
```

```
xmlns:xsl="http://www.w3.org/1999/XSL/Transform"
```

In this example, the HTML-4 namespace is mapped, locally, to the prefix name 'html', and the XSLT namespace is mapped to 'xsl'. The document author (the stylesheet author in this case) decides on the prefix names to use, so that conflicts can be avoided simply by choosing different names. Note that for historical, but now confusing, reasons, the convention is to use 'xsl' for XSLT elements, and 'fo' (Formatting Objects) for XSL elements.

The 'xmlns' attribute can be used on the Stylesheet and Template elements:

```
<xsl:stylesheet
        xmlns:xsl="http://www.w3.org/1999/XSL/Transform">
   ...
</xsl:stylesheet>
```

The XSLT standard contains examples that use namespaces for both the XSLT element set and literal output elements:

```
<xsl:stylesheet
        xmlns:xsl="http://www.w3.org/1999/XSL/Transform"
        xmlns:fo="http://www.w3.org/1999/XSL/Format" >
   ...
   <xsl:template...>
     <fo:block><xsl:apply-templates/></fo:block>
   </xsl:template>
   ...
</xsl:stylesheet>
```

At first sight, DTD authors may think that these examples include two instances of the 'xmlns' attribute on the Stylesheet element, which would be illegal according to the rules of the XML specification. However, from the DTD perspective these are considered to be distinct attributes. The names 'xmlns:xsl' and 'xmlns:fo', for instance, are not the same. Creation of a DTD to validate stylesheets (to ensure correct usage of the XSLT elements), or to offer guided authoring of stylesheets, involves consideration of this and other issues.

Default namespaces

Using prefixes for all element sets reduces legibility. Fortunately, one namespace can be assigned to be the **default namespace**. When no prefix is present, the element is assumed to belong to this default namespace. The following is therefore valid:

```
<xsl:stylesheet
        xmlns:xsl="http://www.w3.org/1999/XSL/Transform"
        xmlns="http://www.w3.org/1999/XSL/Format" >
   ...
   <xsl:template match="para">
     <block><xsl:apply-templates/></block>
   </xsl:template>
   ...
</xsl:stylesheet>
```

The alternative approach is to make the XSLT elements the default set:

```
<stylesheet xmlns="http://www.w3.org/1999/XSL/Transform"
            xmlns:fo="http://www.w3.org/1999/XSL/Format">
  ...
  <template match="para">
    <fo:block><apply-templates/></fo:block>
  </template>
  ...
</stylesheet>
```

Theoretically, this method can even be used with HTML output because the XSLT processor could be clever enough to recognize the HTML URL, realize from this that it is dealing with HTML elements, understand that current Web browsers cannot cope with output in the form '<html:HTML>...</html:HTML>', and therefore remove the prefixes on output. But some XSLT processors may not do this so it is worth testing first.

Attributes that have no prefix are assumed to belong to the same namespace as the elements they belong to. They therefore have their own concept of a 'default' namespace. A prefix is always needed on an attribute if it belongs to a namespace other than the one the element belongs to. For example, some XSLT attributes may be used in result elements. The attribute 'use-attribute-sets' may be used in literal elements to attach predefined attribute names and values to the element, but when used here it must include the XSLT namespace prefix:

```
<P xsl:use-attribute-set="common-set" version="1.3">
  ...
</P>
```

Note that this will not work if the XSLT namespace was assigned to be the default namespace because the lack of an explicit prefix on the attribute name would actually imply that the attribute belonged to the same namespace as the element it is in, rather than to the XSLT namespace.

Namespaces in source documents

Documents to be processed using an XSLT processor may already conform to the namespaces standard, usually because they contain elements from more than one namespace. The stylesheet clearly needs to be able to distinguish between elements from different namespaces when selecting templates. This is done by including the prefix in the Match attribute:

```
    <widget>normal widget</widget>
    <acme:widget>an ACME widget</acme:widget>

<template match="widget">
  <!-- PROCESS NORMAL WIDGETS -->
</template>

<template match="acme:widget">
  <!-- PROCESS ACME WIDGETS -->
</template>
```

However, there is one complication that addresses an obvious issue. Because XML
document authors are free to choose any prefix they wish, it is not always possible
for the stylesheet author to anticipate which prefix has been used in any particular
source document. Indeed, stylesheets are typically required to process many documents created by numerous authors each having arbitrarily chosen a prefix name.
A more robust technique matches the URLs to which prefixes are mapped, rather
than matching the prefixes themselves.

Essentially, the example above remains valid but the prefix in the Match attribute
is not directly compared with element tag prefixes in the source document. Instead,
the XSLT processor first looks-up the URL to which the prefix is mapped *in the
stylesheet itself*. It then compares the fully qualified name with input elements that
have been similarly qualified. The actual prefixes are not directly compared, so
possible differences between them is not an issue. This is achieved by adding a
suitable namespace declaration to the stylesheet:

```
<xsl:stylesheet ... xmlns:B = "ACMEnamespace">
  ...
</xsl:stylesheet>
```

The following example, therefore, works as expected despite that fact that the
source document uses the prefix 'acme:' and the stylesheet uses the prefix 'B:':

```
    <widgets xmlns:acme="ACMEnamespace">
      <widget>normal widget</widget>
      <acme:widget>an ACME widget</acme:widget>
      ...
    </widgets>
<xsl:stylesheet xmlns:xsl = "..."
                xmlns:A   = "Widget-namespace"
                xmlns:B   = "ACMEnamespace">
  ...
  <xsl:template match="B:widget">
    <!-- PROCESS ACME WIDGETS -->
  </xsl:template>
  ...
  ...
</xsl:stylesheet>
```

Namespaces in output documents

Namespace details may need to be added to the elements and attributes output by an XSLT processor. Indeed, this is vital when the created document contains elements from more than one namespace.

Multiple namespaces

It is a simple matter to include literal output elements in the stylesheet that have various different prefixes, though it is of course necessary to include namespace declarations for each prefix used.

When the output document contains elements from more than one namespace, the root element of this document usually needs to contain multiple namespace declarations. All namespace declarations in the stylesheet are automatically copied to the output document root element, except for the XSLT namespace declaration and any others that are explicitly excluded (see below).

Avoiding namespaces

It is sometimes useful to be able to create output documents that do not use namespaces. Some simple XML-based applications may not be aware of the namespaces standard and may be 'hardwired' to expect specific element and attribute names. Such applications will not recognize names that include a namespace prefix. Web browsers, for example, will certainly recognize 'br' (as the name of an element that breaks the flow of text by starting a new line after the tag) but may not recognize 'html:br' as a valid equivalent.

The easy way to omit element name prefixes is to avoid using prefixes for these elements in the stylesheet (to make the output element set use the default namespace). But there are complications that concern the use of default namespaces in the stylesheet document, and the possible use of namespaces in the source document.

Previously, it has been suggested that when no prefix is used for output elements, a default namespace declaration is nevertheless used to identify the namespace of these elements. Normally, this declaration would be copied to the output but in this scenario (the creation of 'namespace-dumb' output) the declaration is not wanted. One way to solve this problem is to remove this declaration from the stylesheet because it is not strictly necessary. But there is a better way that also resolves the following issue.

The previous section explained how a namespace declaration is needed in the stylesheet document to deal with source documents that use namespaces. Unfortunately, these namespace declarations will also be copied to the output document, regardless of whether or not this document will contain any elements from the given namespace.

The **Exclude Result Prefixes** attribute can be used to suppress a namespace declaration (whether created for use with default namespace output elements, or to deal with namespaces in source documents). The value of this attribute consists of one or more space-separated prefix names. The following example deals with the 'acme' namespace discussed previously:

```
<stylesheet xmlns:acme="ACMEnamespace"
            exclude-result-prefixes="acme">
  ...
  <template match="acme:widget">
    ...
  </template>
  ...
</stylesheet>
```

Unfortunately, the default namespace in a stylesheet has no prefix name (because it is the default). The keyword **#default** is used as a stand-in identifier for this namespace:

```
<xsl:stylesheet xmlns="OUTnamespace"
                exclude-result-prefixes="#default">
  ...
</xsl:stylesheet>
```

The following example deals with both of the main issues discussed above to create a namespace-free output file:

```
<xsl:stylesheet
        xmlns:xsl="..."
        xmlns="OUTnamespace"
        xmlns:acme="ACMEnamespace"
        exclude-result-prefixes="#default acme">
  ...
  <xsl:template match="acme:widget">
    <OUT-WIDGET><xsl:apply-templates/></OUT-WIDGET>
  </xsl:template>
  ...
  ...
</xsl:stylesheet>

  <OUT>
     <OUT-WIDGET>...</OUT-WIDGET>
  </OUT>
```

Note that, because declarations are otherwise automatically copied to output from the stylesheet itself, attempts to copy-through the namespace declaration on the root element of the source document, using general techniques for copying-through attribute values, are not applicable in this special case.

Embedded namespaces

A large document may contain small fragments that conform to a different namespace, and the namespace declaration can appear on the 'root' element of each fragment instead of on the root element of the entire document. The **Element** element has an optional **Namespace** attribute, which holds the URL of the namespace. An XSLT processor is able to generate a valid prefix to use for the contents, though it is not obliged to create a very meaningful one (prefixes such as 'ns1' (namespace one) are not unusual):

```
<template match="acme:widget">
  <element name="OUT-WIDGET" namespace="OutURL">
    <apply-templates/>
  </element>
</template>
```

```
    <ns1:OUT-WIDGET xmlns:ns1="OutURL">
      <ns1:NAME>...</ns1:NAME>
      ...
    </ns1:OUT-WIDGET>
```

Alternatively, the processor may just assign the output to an overriding default namespace:

```
    <OUT-WIDGET xmlns:="OutURL">
      <NAME>...</NAME>
      ...
    </OUT-WIDGET>
```

The **Attribute** element may also use the **Namespace** attribute. This is a practical option if a document contains only a very small number of attributes from another namespace. Two attributes are created. First, the named attribute is created and given the stated value, as usual, but the name of this attribute includes a generated prefix. Second, a namespace declaration attribute is also created on the element, including the URL given in the Namespace attribute as its value, and the generated prefix as part of its name. For example, the following Namespace attribute would be appropriate if a document occasionally contained a Currency attribute that conformed to the (fictional) 'Registered Currencies' format, and this format were to be assigned the namespace 'currencyURL':

```
<template match="price">
  <element name="PRICE">
    <attribute name="CURRENCY" namespace="currencyURL">
      <value-of select="@WhichCurrency" />
    </attribute>
    <apply-templates/>
  </element>
</template>


  <WIDGET>
    <PRICE ns1:CURRENCY="EN-pounds"
           xmlns:ns1="currencyURL">134</PRICE>
    ...
  </WIDGET>
```

Outputting stylesheets (namespace alias)

Because XSLT documents are XML documents, they can be created using another XSLT stylesheet. This approach might be used to convert other SGML/XML-based stylesheet languages into XSLT equivalents. Consider the following example stylesheet rule (from a fictional language):

```
<rule trigger="warning">
  <style type="block" format="bold">
    <trigger-rules/>
  </style>
</rule>
```

Now consider the need to convert this structure into the following XSLT template, replacing the product-specific formatting information with HTML equivalents (in this case bold and paragraph tags):

```
<!-- <rule trigger='warning'> -->
<xsl:template match="warning">
  <!-- <style type='block' ...> -->
  <P>
    <!-- format='bold' -->
    <B>
      <xsl:apply-templates/> <!-- <trigger-rules/> -->
    </B>
  </P>
</xsl:template>
```

In principle, this is a trivial transformation. The Rule element needs to be converted into an XSLT Template element, the Style element needs to be converted into HTML Paragraph and Emphasis elements, and the Trigger Rules element needs to be converted into an XSLT Apply Template element. An XSLT stylesheet should be able to accomplish this task.

But there is a problem that arises when attempting to use an XSLT stylesheet to create an XSLT stylesheet. The literal output elements 'template' and 'apply-templates' must not get confused with the stylesheet rules. The XSLT namespace cannot be assigned to the literal output elements because this would indicate to the XSLT processor that it should interpret these elements as instructions instead of output elements. Yet the output document must refer to the XSLT namespace or it will not be later recognized as an XSLT stylesheet.

This conflict can be resolved by using an alias for the URL used to identify output elements, and the **Namespace Alias** element to map the alias to the true output namespace. The **Stylesheet Prefix** and **Result Prefix** attributes hold the before-and-after names:

```
<xsl:namespace-alias stylesheet-prefix="alias"
                     result-prefix="xsl" />
```

This ensures that the correct URL is specified in the output document (the URL for 'xsl' in this case):

```
<xsl:stylesheet version="1.0"
        xmlns:xsl="http://www.w3.org/1999/XSL/Transform"
        xmlns:alias="ThisIsAnAlias" >
  ...
  <xsl:namespace-alias stylesheet-prefix="alias"
                     result-prefix="xsl" />
  ...
<!-- CONVERT RULES TO TEMPLATES -->
  <xsl:template match="rule">
    <alias:template match="{@trigger}">
      <xsl:if test="style='block'">
        <P>
          <xsl:if test="format='bold'">
            <B>
              <alias:apply-templates/>
            </B>
          </xsl:if>
          ...
        </P>
      </xsl:if>
      ...
    </alias:template>
  </xsl:template>
  ...
</xsl:stylesheet>
```

The resulting output for the source rule shown above, and for the whole document, might appear as follows:

```
<alias:stylesheet ...
        xmlns:alias="http://www.w3.org/1999/XSL/Transform">
    ...
    <alias:template match="warning">
      <P><B><alias:apply-templates/></B></P>
    </alias:template>
    ...
</alias:stylesheet>
```

However, the standard does not make clear whether the prefix should also be changed to that used in the stylesheet itself giving the following:

```
<xsl:stylesheet ...
        xmlns:xsl="http://www.w3.org/1999/XSL/Transform">
    ...
    <xsl:template match="warning">
      <P><B><xsl:apply-templates/></B></P>
    </xsl:template>
    ...
</xsl:stylesheet>
```

Both behaviours have been observed in disparate XSLT processors. But it does not really matter so long as the prefix output is mapped to the correct namespace declaration (as it is in both examples above).

18. XSLT extensions

Although this book focusses on the inherent capabilities of XSLT version 1.0, this standard includes some features for handling future enhancements and product-specific additions. The purpose of this is to help an XSLT processor to recover gracefully when it is given a stylesheet that has unrecognized enhancements. However, it remains the responsibility of the stylesheet author to be aware of these features and to implement the safeguards they provide.

Extension functions

A vendor may add custom functions to the expression language. As these cannot be XSLT or XPath functions, they must be defined using a different namespace. For example, a vendor may add a function that can reverse the characters in a text string:

```
<alphabet>abcdefghijklmnopqrstuvwxyz</alphabet>
```

```
<xsl:template match="alphabet">
  <P><xsl:value-of select="acme:reverse(.)"/></P>
</xsl:template>
```

```
<P>zyxwvutsrqponmlkjihgfedcba</P>
```

New functions must have a prefix, or they will be assumed to be additions to those defined by XPath or XSLT (in a later version of these standards).

While an XSLT processor that does not understand the new function must raise an error if an attempt is made to use it, the processor will *not* raise the error merely because it is present in the stylesheet. This allows the stylesheet to contain such functions, but also to include a mechanism to avoid them when they will not be understood. The **function-available**() function returns 'false' if the function name passed to it is not supported. It can be used in If and Choose elements to avoid calling unknown functions and to take some other 'fallback' action instead:

```
<xsl:template match="alphabet">
  <P>
    <xsl:if test="function-available(acme:reverse)">
      <xsl:value-of select="acme:reverse(.)"/>
    </xsl:if>
    <xsl:if test="not(function-available(acme:reverse))">
      <xsl:value-of select="."/> (NORMALLY REVERSED)
    </xsl:if>
  </P>
</xsl:template>
```

When the function returns 'false', the following would be output:

```
<P>abcdefghijklmnopqrstuvwxyz (NORMALLY REVERSED)</P>
```

Extension elements

A vendor may add some new instruction elements to those allowed in a template. Because these would not be XSLT instructions, they must be defined using a different namespace. For example, a vendor may add an instruction that can reverse the characters in a text string, called Reverse:

```
<alphabet>abcdefghijklmnopqrstuvwxyz</alphabet>
```

```
<xsl:template match="alphabet">
  <P><acme:reverse select="."/></P>
</xsl:template>
```

```
<P>zyxwvutsrqponmlkjihgfedcba</P>
```

Note that this mechanism only applies within templates. Top-level elements that are not recognized are simply ignored (see below).

Recognizing extension elements

An XSLT processor needs to know which elements are extension elements so that it will not treat these as literal output elements. All XSLT processors can be informed that an element is an extension element, rather than an output element, by registering its namespace as an extension namespace. The **Extension Element Prefixes** attribute may be used on the Stylesheet element, and it holds a space-separated list of namespace prefixes used for extension elements:

```
<xsl:stylesheet ...
                  extension-element-prefixes="acme" >
  ...
  <xsl:template match="reverse">
    <P><acme:reverse select="."/></P>
  </xsl:template>
  ...
</xsl:stylesheet>
```

Note that the keyword '#default' can be entered in this attribute if the extension elements happen to use the default namespace.

Testing for functionality

When an XSLT processor does not support a particular extension element (developed by another vendor), it can detect and avoid it. Unknown instructions can be avoided by first asking the processor if it understands the instruction, then stepping-over the instruction if the processor does not understand it. The **element-available**() function returns 'true' if the element name passed to it is an instruction supported by the XSLT processor. This function can be used in the If and Choose elements:

```
<P>
  <xsl:if test="element-available('acme:reverse')" >
    <acme:reverse select="." />
  </xsl:if>
  <xsl:if test="not(element-available('acme:reverse'))" >
    <apply-templates/> (NORMALLY REVERSED)
  </xsl:if>
</P>
```

When the function returns 'false', the following would be output:

```
<P>abcdefghijklmnopqrstuvwxyz (NORMALLY REVERSED)</P>
```

Fallback processing

An alternative mechanism embeds 'fallback' instructions in the new instruction itself. If the processor does not understand the instruction, it must implement the instructions embedded in the **Fallback** elements instead:

```
<acme:reverse select=".">
  <fallback>
    <apply-templates/> (SHOULD BE REVERSED)
  </fallback>
</acme:reverse>
```

If the processor recognizes the extended instruction, it ignores the Fallback element embedded within it.

Multiple Fallback elements may be used but are normally only needed when extension instructions are also embedded in the main instruction.

Forward compatibility

XSLT processors developed to support XSLT version 1.0 should be able to cope with stylesheets developed to conform to later versions of this standard. When the stylesheet contains a **Version** attribute with a value other than '1.0', the processor should adopt a **forwards-compatible** mode to help it cope with unexpected features. When the processor has adopted this mode, it is given permission to ignore any top-level elements it does not recognize:

```
<stylesheet version="1.3">
  <import.../>
  ...
  <new-feature /> <!-- 1.0 processors IGNORE -->
  ...
  <template>...</template>
  ...
</stylesheet>
```

Also, any unexpected elements appearing in a template do not cause an error. It is possible to step-over such elements by testing the version of XSLT that the processor understands. The **system-property**() function can be used to request the supported version number by passing the parameter value '**xsl:version**' to it (as described in Chapter 23). The return value can then be compared with the version that supports the feature:

```
<template>
  <if test="system-property('xsl:version') >= 1.2">
    <new-template-feature />
  </if>
  ...
</template>
```

Alternatively, the 'fallback' feature described above can be used:

```
<template>
  <new-template-feature>
    <fallback>...</fallback>
  </new-template-feature>
  ...
</template>
```

Finally, unknown attributes are simply ignored.

19. XPath

Earlier chapters in the first part of the book have introduced the expression language used by the XSLT standard to trigger and configure templates, to locate and reuse material in the source tree and to define keys. This expression language is defined in a separate standard called XPath (though XSLT adds some functions and defines a subset of XPath for use in special circumstances). This chapter introduces a thorough examination of the XPath standard and the XSLT enhancements to it.

The XPath standard

Version 1.0 of the **XML Path Language** (**XPath**) was developed by the W3C and released as a recommendation in 1999. This standard can be found at http://www.w3.org/TR/xpath.

Origins

The XPath standard was originally developed as part of an early draft of the XSL standard but (just like XSLT) was eventually extracted into its own standard, giving it an independent existence so that it could be referenced from any other standard that requires the capability to navigate around XML documents. This includes the XPointer hypertext linking standard, and the proposed XQuery database and Schematron document modelling standards.

Patterns, paths and expressions

Some parts of the XPath standard form discrete subsets that are referenced from XSLT and other standards. Following chapters discuss the component parts of the **XPath expression** language and the extended expression language used in XSLT. XSLT adds some functions to the XPath expression language, which includes the concept of **location paths** for navigating around XML documents, and defines a useful subset of location paths named **patterns**. The relationships between these concepts can be illustrated as follows:

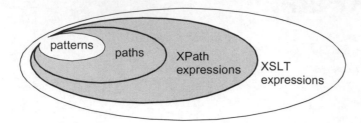

The pattern 'book/chapter/para' could be used to determine whether or not the current element is a Paragraph element, directly contained within a Chapter element, directly contained within a Book element. In XSLT, the Match attribute in the Template element holds a pattern.

The location path 'preceding::title' could be used to locate and select the initial title of the chapter, or other structure, that contains the current element. In XSLT, the Copy Of element holds a location path so that material can be copied from anywhere else in the document structure.

The XPath expression 'count(/book/author) > 5' could be used to identify a document that has more than five authors. In XSLT, complete XPath expressions can be found in predicate filters and the Test attribute of the If element, and this expression could be used in an If element that contains the text 'lots of authors' when there are more than five document authors.

The XSLT function 'format-number(/book/price, '##,##0.00')' could be used to format the price information embedded in a book, creating '3,456.78' from the value '3456.781'.

These concepts are described in detail in the following four chapters, starting with patterns working outward to the full XSLT implementation and extension of the XPath expression language.

Expressions in attributes

The syntax of the XPath expression language was carefully crafted to be applicable in a wide range of circumstances. For example, in some applications of XPath it is useful to be able to add an expression to a URL reference, and so the syntax needs to be both brief and consistent with the characters allowed in such references. Similarly, for its use in XSLT, expressions must be valid attribute values.

Quotation marks often appear in expressions. When an expression is placed within an attribute value, there must be no conflict between these quotation marks and those used to enclose the attribute value. Either single or double quotation marks can be used. When the expression contains only one set of quotation marks, it is therefore a relatively simple matter to avoid using the quotation mark characters acting as attribute value delimiters:

```
match="id('abc123')/..."
```

```
match='id("abc123")/...'
```

However, when the expression contains quotation marks within quotation marks this solution will not work. Fortunately, the entity references **"** and **'** may also be used to represent the embedded quotation marks.

If an expression contains a left chevron character, '<', this must be avoided by using '**<**' because this character is not allowed in attribute values:

```
match="... [position() &lt; 6]"
```

20. Patterns

An XSLT template needs to be matched to applicable nodes in the source document tree, so that it can be triggered only when it is appropriate to use this template. For this purpose, it is only necessary to compare the name and ancestry of a given element, or other markup construct in the document, against a pre-defined 'pattern' that specifies the required name and ancestry.

Introduction

Some XML-sensitive applications, including XSLT processors, traverse a tree-like representation of an XML document, landing on the nodes in the tree that represent the elements, the text content of elements, and the comments and processing instructions that comprise the content of the documents. Each of the document components is represented by a **node** in the tree. These applications usually have to perform different operations, depending on what kind of document component the 'current' node happens to be. In the case of element nodes, it is also usually necessary to establish which element type it is, and sometimes exactly where it is in the document structure too. Context-sensitive processing is especially important when the same element type is used in various places, but has subtly or radically different meanings, depending on the name of its parent element or on the name of some other ancestor element. A simple, compact technique for identifying node types and contextual constraints would therefore be useful. A **pattern** is a limited form of XPath location path (the additional features of which are described in the next chapter) that can fulfil this need.

Partly because the need for patterns is limited to such tasks as matching XSLT templates to nodes in the source tree, but for historical reasons too, the pattern language is actually defined in the XSLT standard, rather than in the XPath standard itself. This is despite the fact that it is a subset of the expression language defined by XPath (other standards that require the same functionality should reference the relevant part of the XSLT standard).

A pattern returns a boolean value of 'true' or 'false'. When the value returned is 'true' this indicates that the pattern does apply to the given node (it is 'true' that the identity and location of the node can be described using this pattern). Conversely, when the value returned is 'false' this indicates that the pattern does not apply to the given node.

In XSLT, patterns are used in the Match attribute of the Key and Template elements, as well as in the Count and From attributes of the Number element:

```
<template match="pattern">...</template>


<key match="pattern">...</key>


<number count="pattern" from="pattern">...</number>
```

In the Template element, the pattern is compared with the current node to decide whether or not the template applies. If it does apply, the template may be triggered (depending on relative priority levels when other templates are also applicable).

In the Key element, the pattern is used in the Match attribute to identify those elements that take part in the key (the Use attribute also holds an XPath expression, but this expression is not limited to the constraints of the pattern subset of this language).

In the Number element, the Count and From attributes hold patterns that specify which elements are to be used to build the count, and which elements restart numbering.

Element names

One of the simplest forms of pattern is a reference to an element name. The pattern applies when the node is an element node and, in addition, is an element of the given type:

```
<template match="para">...</template>


    <title>Non-Matching Title</title>
    <para>Paragraph that matches the pattern.</para>
    <note>Note that notes do not match.</note>
    <para>Another matching paragraph.</para>
```

A simple name such as 'para' is actually an abbreviation of a longer pattern. The equivalent unabbreviated version of the pattern would be 'child::para'. This makes sense when discussing location paths, as will be shown later, but seems odd here. The expression above works because the parent of a paragraph node must (by definition) have this element as one of its children. The parent may be another element or it may be the document root node that holds the root element.

Because element names are case sensitive in XML documents, the pattern will only match if the name given in the pattern is exactly the same as the name of the element in the document. For example, the pattern 'para' will not match an element called 'Para'.

Multiple patterns

A pattern can be divided into several distinct sub-patterns, separated by the vertical bar symbol 'I'. the entire pattern succeeds if any of the sub-patterns are valid. For example, the following template matches Note, Warning and Danger elements. The template is triggered if the current node is an element of any of these types:

```
<template match="note|warning|danger">...</template>
```

```
<para>...</para>
<note>...</note>
<para>...</para>
<danger>...</danger>
<warning>...</warning>
```

Steps and children

Many patterns consist of a number of **steps**. Each step is separated from preceding and following steps using the '/' symbol. The following example has two steps – it matches paragraphs within chapters (the introduction and section paragraphs in the example below are therefore not relevant):

```
match="chapter/para"
```

```
<book>
  <para>This is an introduction paragraph.</para>
  <chapter>
    <para>This is a chapter paragraph.</para>
    <para>This is another chapter paragraph.</para>
    <section>
      <para>This is a section paragraph.</para>
```

Although the expression above is used to find Paragraph elements that are children of Chapter elements, it needs to be made very clear that the '/' symbol itself does not specify the required parent/child relationship between the two nodes. This impression is easily given because there appears to be nothing else in the pattern that could signify this intent. But this symbol is actually just a step separator and when discussing full location paths (in the next chapter) it will be seen that there are many alternatives to specifying a path that 'drills-down' the document structure in this simple way. Any confusion regarding the role of the '/' symbol can be avoided by making the selection of children specific. This is done by adding the 'child::' prefix to the element name:

```
match="child::chapter/child::para"
```

It is now clear that 'child::para' is a sensible construction because the paragraph must be a direct descendant of the Chapter element. However, it still seems odd for this keyword to be used before 'chapter' in the example above, because the chapter does not have to be a child of another element, but it does have to be the child of something.

Root identifier

The step separator has a significant role when it happens to be placed before the first step, and is therefore the first character in the pattern. This implies that the element named in the first step is a child of the root node, and that it is therefore the root element (or 'document element' as it is officially known):

```
match="/book/chapter/para"
```

It is only necessary to include this initial separator when the element named in the first step is allowed to occur elsewhere in the document structure, but these other occurrences are to be ignored. For example, it is not necessary to include this initial separator in the example above if the Book element can only occur as the root element of the document. The following pattern should work just as well:

```
match="book/chapter/para"
```

However, even in this scenario it may be worthwhile including it. There are two reasons for this. First, it makes it clear to anybody reading the expression that it locates an object that has a precise location in the document. Second, it may improve the efficiency of the XSLT processor if it happens to read patterns from left to right instead of right to left (see the next section).

Pattern directions

Patterns can be sensibly read from right to left. Consider the following pattern:

```
<template match="book/chapter/para">...</template>
                      3        2        1
```

In this example, the first part of the pattern (part 1) is compared against the current node. If the current node is a Paragraph element, as required, then the next part of the pattern (part 2) is compared against the parent of this node. Providing that the parent is a Chapter element, the final check made is that this element is in turn enclosed by a Book element.

It is also possible to think of the expression as working in the opposite direction. Indeed, this is the officially approved way to view how a pattern works:

```
<template match="book/chapter/para">...</template>
                      1        2        3
```

In this view, the pattern only succeeds if the current node is to be found in the node set created by evaluating the expression as a location path (explained in the next chapter). All elements of the type required by the first step are found, and each is searched for elements of the type required by the second step, and each one of these is then searched for elements of the type required by the third step. The result is a potentially huge set of elements (in this case probably most of the Paragraph elements in the book) that must finally be searched to see if it includes the current node.

Clearly, the second approach implies an exhaustive process and for that reason alone it may never be implemented in practice. Nevertheless, when the first step is expected to be the root element, making this explicit by placing a '/' character before it (as explained above) could save a lot of processing time because the XSLT processor or would at least know that it does not need to search the entire document for other examples of the Book element that could theoretically occur.

Attribute patterns

A pattern can be used to identify an attribute instead of an element. The last step in a pattern can be the name of the attribute required. However, in order to ensure that an attribute is found, rather than an element with the same name, the prefix '@' is needed:

```
/book/@date
```

```
<book date="...">...</book>
```

For example, an XSLT template could be created to output the values of a given attribute type:

```
<template match="para/@date">
  <value-of select="."/>
</template>
```

Just as 'child::' can be used to indicate a search for a child element, the keyword **attribute::** can be used as the longhand form for '@':

```
/book/attribute::date
```

Intermediate step wildcards

The '*' symbol may be used to represent the name of any element in the document, so 'child::*' is a step that works for any element. Note that '@*' also represents any attribute.

Consider the need to create a single template for paragraphs, wherever they might appear in a book. The pattern 'book/para' will only match paragraphs that are directly within the Book element, so is not suitable. While it would be possible to use multiple patterns to cover each possibility, the resulting compound expression would be ungainly and inefficient. Even using '*' to reduce the number of patterns, it would still be necessary to know how many levels deep the target element could possibly be. The following example only copes with three levels:

```
<template match="book/para |
                 book/*/para |
                 book/*/*/para">
  ...
</template>
```

But this need can be met using a single pattern that includes an **empty step**. When a step is empty, there are two adjacent '/' symbols, '//', indicating any number of intermediate elements of any kind. This example matches all the following paragraphs:

```
match="book//para"
```

```
<book>
  <para>This is a book.</para>
  <chapter>
    <para>This is a chapter paragraph.</para>
    <section>
      <para>This is a section paragraph.</para>
```

There do not need to be *any* intermediate steps between the tests at each side of the empty step. In the example above, the first paragraph is relevant, even though it is directly within the Book element, and could therefore also be selected by the simpler 'book/para' pattern (in this sense, an empty step really can be empty).

Axis specifiers

Each step in a pattern is either a test for children of the nodes selected by the previous step, or is a test for a descendent node of any kind, or is a test for an attribute belonging to an element specified in the previous step. The term '**axis**' is used to describe different directions that can be taken in a path. In patterns there are only the **child axis**, the **attribute axis** and the **descendant-or-self axis** (in location paths, there are many more). The keywords 'child::' and 'attribute::' are therefore revealed to be **axis specifier** keywords. But the third possibility needs further explanation.

Descendant-or-self axis

Although there is a keyword for the third axis mentioned above, this is never seen in patterns. The descendant-or-self axis has been used in some of the examples above, but its role has been hidden. This axis represents a step down to any descendant node that matches the requirement, or a step that goes nowhere at all (if the current node itself matches the requirement). In a pattern, this axis can only be used in an empty step, and the keyword must be absent (an extreme form of abbreviation) in this location. The empty step, '//', is really shorthand for the expression fragment '/descendant-or-self::node()/' but must be used in place of this more verbose equivalent.

Abbreviated axis specifiers

All three axis specifiers allowed in a pattern have an abbreviated form. As just explained, in one case there is no option; the descendant-or-self axis *must* be abbreviated when used in a pattern (and must be used as part of an empty step). In the other two cases, abbreviations are optional. As already discussed, the 'child::' axis specifier may be omitted entirely, and the '@' symbol can be used as an abbreviation for 'attribute::'.

It is an interesting fact that only the three axis specifiers allowed in a pattern can be abbreviated. The additional axis specifiers needed for location paths cannot be abbreviated at all. This is not a coincidence – the steps allowed in a pattern are the most commonly needed steps, so it is these that have a shorthand form of axis specifier.

Node tests

Each step in a pattern is tested against a candidate node in the source document tree in order to see whether the pattern applies or not. Apart from element and attribute node tests, it is also possible to test if the node is a comment, a processing instruction, or the text content of an element.

Element and attribute node tests

A node that represents an element can be tested to determine in a single operation not only if it is an element, but which element type it is too, simply by naming the element. The node test 'para' is a test for an element node, which must also be of type 'para'. Most of the examples above are element node tests.

A node that represents an attribute can be tested to determine not only if it is an attribute, but which attribute type it is too, also in a single operation. But in this case the '@' or 'attribute::' axis specifier must be included too so that the name will not be confused with an element node test. The node test '@author' is a test for an attribute node which must also be of type 'author'.

Comment node tests

The **comment**() node test is used to discover whether or not the node is a comment node. In XSLT, this node test can be used to create an explicit template that processes comments (there is an implicit template that otherwise suppresses comments):

```
<template match="comment()">
  <!-- ALL COMMENTS -->
  ...
</template>
```

This test can be made at the end of a longer pattern, to target comments in particular parts of the document:

```
<template match="/book/comment()">
  <!-- COMMENTS IN THE BOOK ELEMENT -->
  ...
</template>
```

Processing instruction node tests

The **processing-instruction**() node test is used to test whether or not the node is a processing instruction node. In XSLT, this node test can be used to create an explicit template that processes processing instructions (there is an implicit template that otherwise suppresses processing instructions):

```
<template match="processing-instruction()">
  <!-- ALL PIs -->
  ...
</template>
```

This test can be made at the end of a longer pattern, to target processing instructions in particular parts of the document:

```
<template match="/processing-instruction()">
  <!-- PIs AROUND THE ROOT ELEMENT -->
  ...
</template>
```

Text node tests

The **text**() node test is used to discover whether or not the node is a text node. In XSLT, this node test can be used to create an explicit template that processes text (there is an implicit template that would otherwise simply output the text):

```
<template match="text()">
  <!-- ALL ELEMENT CONTENT TEXT -->
  ...
</template>
```

This test can be made at the end of a longer pattern, to target text in particular parts of the document:

```
<template match="para/text()">
  <!-- ALL PARAGRAPH TEXT -->
  ...
</template>
```

General node tests

The **node**() node test is used to test that the node really is a node, though it could hardly be anything else. Surprisingly, this test does have some important uses. For example, in XSLT this node test can be used to create a template that processes elements, comments, processing instructions and the text content of elements:

```
<template match="node()">
  <!-- ALL NODES (except for attribute nodes) -->
  ...
</template>
```

The reason why this template would not match attributes as well is because the 'child::' axis specifier is assumed when no axis specifier is supplied, so the example above is actually short for 'child::node()', and attributes are not considered to be children of element nodes (even though attributes have a parent element). However, a pattern can consist of multiple patterns, separated by a 'I' symbol, so a single template could process attributes too, using the pattern 'node()|@*'.

The node() test can also represent attributes in other circumstances (this is covered in the next chapter).

Node tests are not functions

The XPath language includes several functions, such as position() (see Chapter 22), that resemble node tests such as comment(). But this resemblance is superficial, and the distinction is very important. Node tests can be used in certain places in a pattern, and functions can be used in other places. Many mistakes made in attempting to create patterns arise from confusing these two concepts, and trying to use node tests and functions in inappropriate places. For example, while the Match attribute of a Template element in XSLT can contain the expression 'comment()', it cannot consist of just the expression 'position()'.

First step

A pattern must begin with an element name, an attribute name or a node type, a document root identifier, '/', a root and unknown-number-of-descendants identifier, '//', or an element identifier keyword, **id**() or **key**() (an XSLT extension):

```
match="para/..."

match="child::para/..."

match="*/..."

match="text()"

match="@level"

match="attribute::level"

match="/..."

match="//..."

match="id('link99')/..."

match="key('color', 'yellow')/..."
```

When a pattern begins with '/', an explicit location in the document is specified (as explained above). For example, '/book/chapter/para' applies to paragraphs in Chapter elements that are within a root Book element.

When a pattern begins with '//', this specifies that the first step needs to be tested against every node in the document tree. This is just an empty step, but placed before the first real step, and the root identifier '/' is omitted (it would otherwise be necessary to use three slashes '///' to indicate this meaning). But in the case of patterns, rather than location paths, it is not necessary to state this explicitly. It is implied, because patterns are applied to each node in the document as the XSLT processor works its way through the document tree. It is not necessary to match all paragraphs in a document using '//para' when 'para' will work just as well.

Subsequent steps

After the first step, each subsequent step in a pattern is usually an element name or an attribute name (prefixed with the axis specifier '@'), or an element or attribute name prefixed with the axis specifiers '**child::**' or '**attribute::**':

```
<template match=".../chapter/...">...</template>

<template match=".../child::chapter/...">
  ...
</template>

<template match=".../@author" ...>...</template>

<template match=".../attribute::author" ...>...</template>
```

The symbol '*' represents any element or any attribute, depending on whether or not it is preceded by '@':

```
match=".../*/..."

match=".../@*"
```

However, other node types can be included, and element names may have a namespace prefix:

```
match=".../acme:price/..."

match=".../comment()"

match=".../text()"

match=".../processing-instruction()"

match=".../node()/..."
```

Most of the step types above are only appropriate as the final step in a pattern, because they cannot include children. For example, it does not make sense to ask if a Paragraph element is within a comment, because XML rules do not allow this.

Predicate filters

One or more **predicate filters** are also allowed after each node test:

```
match=".../chapter[...]/..."
```

The possible content of a predicate filter cannot be covered here because a predicate filter opens-up the full power of the XPath expression language (as discussed in the next three chapters). Location paths (see the next chapter) and other expression language constructs may be used without any artificial limitations, even though they are being used in a pattern. However, it is not necessary to understand the full power of predicate filters to see how a couple of techniques make patterns more flexible. In the example below, the paragraph is only applicable in a secret chapter (a Chapter element that has a Level attribute value of 'secret'):

```
match="chapter[@level='secret']/para"
```

In the following example, the paragraph is only selected if it is in a chapter that also has a title, and is also a secret paragraph:

```
match="chapter[title]/para[@level='secret']"
```

```
<chapter>
  ...
</chapter>
<chapter>
  <title>...</title>
  <para>...</para>
  <para level="secret"><!-- SELECTED --></para>
  <para>...</para>
</chapter>
```

Predicate filters are discussed in more detail in Chapter 22.

21. Location paths

XPath expressions may be used to navigate into and around an XML document in order to select one or more nodes. A location path is used to perform this navigation process. Chapter 20 should be read before this chapter because the concepts discussed here build on those introduced there.

Introduction

Using a **location path** it is possible to take steps in directions other than downward into the structure of the document (unlike a simple pattern). It is also possible to begin a journey from any location in the document and arrive at a different destination to another, identical path, with a different starting location:

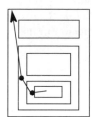 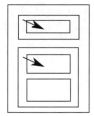

The real difference between a pattern and a location path is that a pattern can only be used to establish which node in the document structure is currently selected, whereas a location path is used to travel into and around the document.

Location paths are defined in the XPath standard (unlike patterns, which are defined in the XSLT standard), as a subset of the complete XPath expression language (discussed in the next chapter).

Context node and context list

The **context list** and **context node** concepts must be appreciated before location paths can be fully understood. Many mistakes made in formulating a location path are directly attributable to a hazy understanding of these concepts. In particular, XPath functions (described in Chapter 22) are in many cases dependent on these concepts.

Each step in a location path creates a new context list and context node. This concept is illustrated below. First, consider the following location path:

```
/book/chap/para
```

This path is an abbreviated version of the following location path, which makes it clear that the path steps down into the document structure, stopping at each child element along the way:

```
/child::book/child::chap/child::para
```

This path also begins with '/' indicating that the search for applicable nodes must begin at the root of the document tree. The first step in the path stipulates that only child element nodes of type 'book' are of interest. As usual when starting from the root of the tree, there is only one node that can possibly match this requirement. If this element node has the name 'book', it is selected for inclusion in the context list:

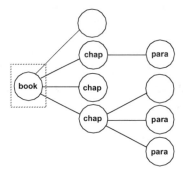

On completion of this step, the Book element node (if the root element is of this type) is the only node in the context list.

The next step in the path specifies that the child of each node in the context list that is an element node of type 'chap' should be selected. This step therefore selects the three Chapter element nodes that are children of the Book node, creating a new context list:

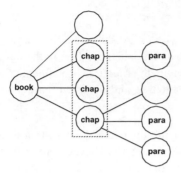

The new context list has three nodes within it. Each of these will be used in turn as the context node for the next step. The next step is to select the children of each context node that are element nodes, specifically of type 'para'. There will be successful matches in the first and third chapters in this example:

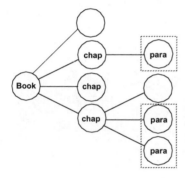

The location path has therefore ultimately selected the three Paragraph elements shown above.

Using XPath functions, it is always possible to make decisions based on how many nodes there are in the context list, and on which node in the list is the current node. For example, if the middle paragraph in the diagram above is the current node, then this is recognized to be the second node of three in the list. This is true even though the first node is in a previous chapter, so this concept must never be confused with simply counting previous sibling nodes.

Path directions

While simple patterns are only concerned with establishing the direct ancestry of an element, which is sufficient to establish a contextual location in the document structure, a location path can be used to navigate around the document, working up and down the branches of the document tree and across to earlier or later branches.

To facilitate this freedom, a number of additional **axis** keywords are needed beyond 'child::' and 'attribute::' (or '@'). A further 12 axis keywords allow navigation to parents and higher-level ancestors, descendants below the level of children, material that simply precedes or follows the current element, and even back to the starting point.

In addition to children and attributes, it is possible to reach all the following elements from the Start element:

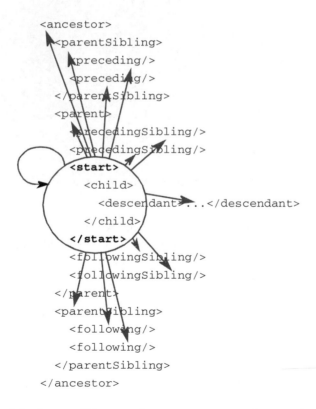

```
<ancestor>
  <parentSibling>
    <preceding/>
    <preceding/>
  </parentSibling>
  <parent>
    <precedingSibling/>
    <precedingSibling/>
    <start>
      <child>
        <descendant>...</descendant>
      </child>
    </start>
    <followingSibling/>
    <followingSibling/>
  </parent>
  <parentSibling>
    <following/>
    <following/>
  </parentSibling>
</ancestor>
```

It is also possible to reach text, comments and processing instructions in all these locations.

Parent axis

The 'parent::' axis specifier selects the **parent** of the current node. As this is usually done simply to step back out of the node, as a preliminary step to moving elsewhere in the document, it is commonly used along with the node() test ('parent::node()') in order to successfully match the parent, regardless of what node type it is (though it can only be either a parent element or the root node of the document tree). Indeed, this is such a common requirement that there is a shorthand equivalent, '..', which should be familiar to users of some command-line operating systems. The location path '../title' (or 'parent::node()/ child::title'), for example, selects a Title element that is a sibling of the current element.

A path that begins at the currently selected element is known as a **relative path** because the node actually selected by this expression depends on the location of the current node. For example, a different title would be selected by the expression above if the current element was in a different chapter.

Note: Those familiar with the use of '..' (and '.' which is described below) from experience with MS-DOS and UNIX operating systems should be aware that the obvious analogy with directory paths can be stretched too far. Operating systems always require that sibling directories have unique names, so that a path identifies a single target directory. XML documents have no such restriction; a location path will often match many target elements. For example, '../title' would select multiple titles if there were more than one present as siblings of the current element.

Self axis

The 'self::' axis specifier, followed by node(), identifies the current node regardless of what kind of node it is. This can be useful when specifying relative paths, particularly when the target node is a descendant of the current node but the number of intermediate levels is not known. In this scenario, the '//' empty step instruction is needed, but if this empty step instruction appears at the start of an expression it indicates a descendant of the root node rather than of the current node. Therefore, the current node needs to be the first step of the expression, as in 'self::node()//...'.

Because this is a common requirement, the single character '.' is used as an abbreviation for 'self::node()'. For example, the expression './/title' finds all descendant Title elements of the current node.

The XSLT current() function can also be used but sometimes differs in meaning from '.' (see Chapter 23).

Note that in this circumstance the node test node() can represent an attribute node. For example, in an XSLT template that matches any attribute node ('@*'), the Value Of element can be used to output the value of the attribute by placing 'self::node()' (or just '.') in its Select attribute.

Descendant or self axis

The **descendant-or-self::** axis specifier represents zero or more steps down into the fragment of the document structure that is contained within the branches of the source tree that lie beneath the current node. The 'or-self' part of the name is significant because it indicates that if the current node matches the node test, then no actual step needs to be taken at all. In the following example, the message in the If element is output even if the current node happens to be a Paragraph element node:

```
<template match="*">
  <if test="descendant-or-self::para">
    <text>THIS IS INSIDE A PARAGRAPH,
    OR ACTUALLY IS A PARAGRAPH</text>
  </if>
</template>
```

When used with the node() node test, this represents any number of intermediate objects (including none). If this concept sounds familiar, it is because this is the longhand equivalent of the empty step '//' which can be used in a pattern. As previously shown, the expression fragment '/descendant-or-self::node()/' means the same thing but is far more verbose, so is rarely used (and is not allowed in patterns at all). The following two Apply Template instructions both output the values of all Emphasis elements:

```
<apply-templates select="//em"/>
<apply-templates select="/descendant-or-self::node()/em"/>
```

This step only makes sense when it precedes another step that is more specific, such as '//para', because the actual number of steps taken into the document structure varies, depending on how many are needed to reach the node specified in the next step. An expression should therefore never end with the empty step (this is not even legal). If all descendant nodes in a specific element (except for attribute nodes) are to be selected, then '//node()' should appear at the end of the expression.

Other axis directions

Steps can be taken in various directions, other than those discussed above, including down into the tree structure (without including the current node as a possible destination), up into the ancestors of the current node, forward and backward to sibling nodes, or to any preceding or following node.

Descendant nodes

The **descendant::** axis specifier is similar to the descendant-or-self:: axis specifier, but does not include the current node (the 'self') as a possible match. If the expression is 'descendant::para' and the current node is a Paragraph element, this particular node will not be considered a match. A single step specifier may select several descendants (some perhaps the descendants of others) if more than one matches the step requirements:

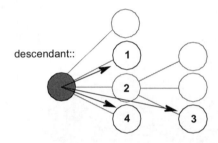

Note that a count is maintained of the elements encountered in the direction taken. The significance of this is explained later (in the next chapter) but for now it is only necessary to know that this enables a specific instance of the matching nodes to be individually identified and selected.

Ancestor nodes

The **ancestor::** and **ancestor-or-self::** axis specifiers work in the same way as the those described above, but outwards from the current element instead of into its contents. For example, the expression 'ancestor::chapter' selects the chapter containing the current element. Again, a single step could select multiple ancestor nodes:

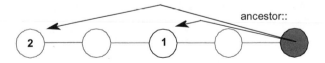

The only difference with the second axis type is that the first node selected could be the current node:

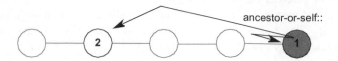

Sibling nodes

The **following-sibling::** and **preceding-sibling::** axis specifiers represent elements that follow or precede the current element within the parent element that they all share. To select paragraphs that follow the current element, within the same parent, the expression 'following-sibling::para' is used:

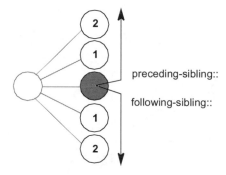

Preceding and following nodes

The **preceding::** and **following::** axis specifiers are variants of the sibling-specific axis specifiers described above.

Preceding elements are all elements that occur in the document before the current element, and end before the current element begins (their end-tags occurring before this element's start-tag). Preceding siblings are included, but ancestors are therefore not included (because they are still open).

Following elements are all of the following elements that do not begin before the end of the current element, and so ancestors are again not included, but following siblings are:

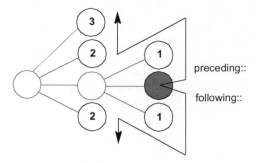

Combined example

The real power of location paths to select material from anywhere in the source document is revealed when paths include a combination of the axis specifiers described above. Also note that **predicate filters** can be used in any step of the location path (just as they can be used in pattern steps). In the following example, all elements that precede the title of each non-secret chapter are selected:

```
//chapter[not(@type="secret")]/title/preceding-sibling::*
```

```
<book>
  <chapter>
    <author>J Smith</author>
    <title>Chapter One Title</title>
    ...
  </chapter>

  <chapter>
    <version>1.3</version>
    <date>12/4/2000</date>
    <title>Chapter Two Title</title>
    ...
  </chapter>

  <chapter type="secret">
    <author>J Jones</author> <!-- NOT SELECTED -->
    <title>Secret Chapter Three</title>
    ..
  </chapter>
</book>
```

22. Complete XPath expressions

The complete XPath expression language includes values, operations and functions that allow values to be calculated and decisions to be made depending on a value or comparison of values. The values created, analysed and manipulated by these functions and operators must conform to one of four defined data types.

Introduction

The complete XPath expression language contains patterns and location paths, as described previously, but also includes a wider set of features built around the use of **functions** to manipulate and analyse **values** of various types, and **operators** to compare values and perform calculations. Readers familiar with programming languages will have little difficulty with these routine concepts. The following example of a complete XPath expression includes a function (containing a location path), an operator and a value. The function counts the number of Author elements in a book, and the operator compares the result with the fixed value '5':

```
<if test="count(/book/author) > 5">
  <!-- MORE THAN 5 AUTHORS -->
</if>
```

All these features are also allowed in predicate filters, which can be employed by patterns and locations paths to 'filter-out' unwanted nodes at each step.

Values

The XPath expression language handles **values** of various kinds. The following data types are supported:

- boolean
- numeric
- string
- node-set.

A **boolean** value must be either '**true**' or '**false**'. It can have no other value.

A **numeric** value can be any positive or negative real number, such as '3', '+55.5' or '-9999'. Numbers are stored as binary values in eight bytes (64 bits), and so there is a (very high) limit on the size of a numeric value.

A **string** value is a sequence of characters, enclosed by quotation marks, that can be compared with text in a container element, or the value of an attribute.

A **node-set** value is the string value of the nodes selected using a location path.

An expression may consist of nothing more than a value of one of these types. For example, an expression could consist of a single numeric value, as in the expression '19'.

Variable values

A **variable** may be used to represent a value of any type. Wherever a value may appear in an expression, a variable reference may appear instead.

Variables are names, prefixed with a '$' symbol. An expression can even consist solely of a variable reference. For example, '$age' is a possible expression (and this reference may refer to a variable with the value '19').

When an expression is being used in an XSLT stylesheet, any variables referenced within it will have been defined using Variable or Param elements (XSLT variables are described in Chapter 13).

Operators

Values really come to life when mixed with **operators**. In particular, fixed values can be compared with values held in variables, in this case to test whether the age variable holds the value '19' (by asking if it is equal to this value):

```
$age = 19
```

Other operators include:

- '+', '-', '*', 'div' and 'mod' (used to perform simple calculations)
- '<', '>', '<=', '>=' and '!=' (used to compare values)
- 'and' and 'or' (used to combine expressions).

Functions

A number of **functions** are supplied to transform values from one data type to another, and to compare, manipulate and analyse values. XPath functions perform a specific operation and return the value that results from this. The returned value effectively replaces the function at its position in the expression. Functions have names that represent their purpose, such as 'round' and 'string-length', followed by brackets:

```
function()
```

In many cases, functions operate on supplied information passed to them as parameters placed within the brackets:

```
function(parameter1, parameter2)
```

For example, a location path can be passed to the count() function, which returns the number of occurrences of matching nodes in the tree:

```
count( /book/author )
```

When there is more than one parameter to pass, the comma character ',' is used as a separator.

A parameter can even be another function. The inner function is processed first, and the returned value then acts as a normal parameter value to the outer function:

```
function(parameter1, another_function(...))
```

There are a number of functions available to support specific data types.

The values returned by functions can be compared with other values, and included in calculations. For example, the result of counting several numeric variables can be compared with a fixed value, and the expression only succeeds if the sum of the variables matches this value (in this case, if no money needs to be paid):

```
sum($fee, $expenses, $tax) = 0
```

Expressions in XSLT

XSLT allows the complete XPath expression language to be used in a number of places, including the Select attribute of the Copy Of element, Parameter element, Sort element (so long as it returns a string), Variable element, Value Of element (so long as it returns a string), and the With Parameter element:

```
<copy-of select="expression">...</copy-of>
```

```
<param select="expression">...</param>

<sort select="expression">...</sort>

<variable select="expression">...</variable>

<value-of select="expression"/>

<with-param select="expression">...</with-param>
```

Complete expressions can also be used with the Test attribute of the If element (so long as it returns a boolean value) and the Value attribute of the Number element (so long as it returns a numeric value):

```
<if test="expression">...</if>

<number value="expression" />
```

Complete expressions may also be used in predicate filters within patterns and location paths:

```
<template match=".../test[expression]/...">...</template>
```

Finally, complete expressions may be used in attribute value templates:

```
<IMG SRC="{expression}.gif" />
```

When an XPath expression is used elsewhere in XSLT, such as in the Match attribute of the Template element, it must conform to the constraints of either the location path or pattern subsets of this language.

Operators

The XPath expression language includes a number of **operators** that are used to perform calculations and comparisons. Operators give purpose to the functions described later, allowing the returned values to be compared with each other, and compared with fixed values. Comparisons for equality, for inequality and for comparative size can be made.

Equality test

The '=' operator compares two items for equality. If they are equal, the boolean value 'true' is the result; otherwise, the value 'false' is the result. Boolean values, numeric values and strings can all be compared using this operator (the true() function is discussed later):

```
<if test="true() = true()"><!-- BOOLEAN COMPARE --></if>

<if test="3 = 3"><!-- NUMERIC COMPARE --></if>
```

```
<if test="'Hi' = 'Hi'"><!-- STRING COMPARE --></if>
```

Two strings are compared in the following example, Some action is taken if the text content of the current element contains '345' at position three:

```
test="self::node()[substring(text(),3,3) = '345']"
```

Before making the comparison, however, the two sides must be made to be of the same object type if they are not already. This is done automatically. If one side is a boolean value, the other side is converted into a boolean value. Otherwise, if one side is a number, the other side is converted into a number. Otherwise, if one side is a string, and the other is not, it is made into a string. In the following example, a string is to be compared with a number. Because one of the items is a number, the other (string) item is converted into a number. The two numbers are then compared:

```
<if test="'3' = 3"><!-- ENABLED --></if>

<if test="7 = '3'"><!-- NOT ENABLED --></if>
```

Nodes can also be compared, but in this case it is the string values of each node that are compared. This test is *not* used to see if two node references actually refer to the same node.

Inequality test

The opposite of equality is inequality. Placing an exclamation mark before the equals symbol, '!=', indicates the need for the compared items to be different rather than the same. This test can be made wherever a test for equality can be made. The result is 'true' if the compared items differ:

```
<if test="'3' != 3"><!-- NOT ENABLED --></if>

<if test="'3' != 7"><!-- ENABLED --></if>
```

Larger than and smaller than tests

When two values are different, it is sometimes useful to know which of the two values is smaller. Placing the '<' symbol between two values tests whether or not the first value is smaller than the second, returning 'true' if it is. However, the rules of XML mean that this symbol must be replaced by the sequence **<** (less than):

```
<if test="9 &lt; 3"><!-- NOT ENABLED --></if>

<if test="3 &lt; 9"><!-- ENABLED --></if>
```

Similarly, placing the '>' symbol between two values tests whether or not the first value is larger than the second. In this case, the equivalent entity reference can be used (> (greater than)) but it is not obligatory:

```
<if test="9 > 3"><!-- ENABLED --></if>

<if test="3 &gt; 9"><!-- NOT ENABLED --></if>
```

Numerical comparisons are ultimately made, provided that neither value is a node or set of nodes. Strings and booleans are converted to numbers ('0' or '1' in the latter case) prior to making the comparison.

At least and at most tests

A variation of 'less than' and 'greater than' comparisons allows a slightly different question to be asked. It is sometimes useful to know whether a value is at least as big as another, or at most as big as another. This is done by combining the '<', '>' and '=' symbols.

The combination '>=' means 'greater than or equal to'. It is important that the symbols appear in this order because '=>' will not be recognised as valid:

```
<if test="4 >= 3"><!-- ENABLED (greater) --></if>

<if test="3 >= 3"><!-- ENABLED (identical) --></if>
```

The combination '<=' (which must actually be '<=') means 'less than or equal to'. Again, the order of the two symbols is important:

```
<if test="3 &lt;= 4"><!-- ENABLED (smaller) --></if>

<if test="3 &lt;= 3"><!-- ENABLED (identical) --></if>
```

Additions and subtractions

Addition and **subtraction** operations are both supported. Numeric values can be added together using the '+' operator, and subtracted using '-':

```
<value-of select="0 + 1"/>, <value-of Select="1 - 1"/>.
```

    1, 0.

Note that, to avoid confusion with hyphens in names, the '-' symbol is recognized as a minus by adding whitespace before it:

```
test="first-node - second-node"
```

Multiplications and divisions

There is also support for **multiplication** and **division**. Values can be multiplied using the '*' symbol in the same way that many programming languages use this symbol:

```
One times one is one: <value-of select="1 * 1"/>.
```

One times one is one: **1**.

Division does *not* use the '/' symbol in the way that many programming languages use this symbol. This is because of its important role as a step separator in location paths. Instead, the '**div**' operator returns the quotient. For example, '9 div 4' returns '2' because four goes into nine twice.

The '**mod**' operator supplies the remainder of a truncated division. For example, '9 mod 4' returns the value '1' because there is a remainder of one after dividing nine by four. This feature is useful for selecting alternate items, such as even numbered paragraphs:

```
para[ position() mod 2 = 0 ]
```

Multiple conditions

An expression can be split into pieces that are evaluated individually and then compared. The whole expression can be made to succeed when any one of the separate conditions is 'true', or only when all of the conditions are 'true'.

Combined expressions

The **and** operator can be used to connect two or more expressions. All of the sub-expressions return a boolean value, and all must be 'true' for the complete expression to succeed. If the first part of such an expression is 'false', the processor does not need to bother evaluating the remaining parts because the whole expression must be 'false':

```
<if test="99 > 5 and 5 > 0"><!-- both OK --></if>

<if test="99 > 5 and 0 > 5"><!-- NOT ENABLED --></if>

<if test="5 > 99 and 5 > 0"><!-- NOT ENABLED --></if>

<if test="5 > 99 and 0 > 5"><!-- NOT ENABLED --></if>
```

Each of the tests above can be seen to be equivalent to two separate XSLT If elements, with one embedded in the other. For example, the first test can be formulated as follows:

```
<if test="99 > 5">
  <if test="5 > 0"><!-- both OK --></if>
</if>
```

Alternative expressions

The **or** operator can be used to connect two or more expressions. If any of the sub-expressions is 'true', the complete expression succeeds. The four examples below are identical to those above except that the 'or' operator replaces the 'and' operator. In this case, three of the tests are successful instead of just one:

```
<if test="99 > 5 or 5 > 0"><!-- both OK --></if>

<if test="99 > 5 or 0 > 5"><!-- left OK --></if>

<if test="5 > 99 or 5 > 0"><!-- right OK --></if>

<if test="5 > 99 or 0 > 5"><!-- NOT ENABLED --></if>
```

Each of the tests above can be seen to be equivalent to two separate XSLT If elements, with one following the other, both with identical content. However, simulating this behaviour using multiple If elements would be complicated by the need to avoid repeated outputting of the content in the event that both conditions happen to be 'true'. For example, the first test could be formulated as follows (the not() function is discussed later in this chapter):

```
<if test="99 > 5"><!-- left OK --></if>
<if test="5 > 0">
  <if test="not(99 > 5)"><!-- right (ONLY) OK --></if>
</if>
```

Operator precedence

An expression that contains a number of operators of the same type is evaluated from left to right. For example, the expression '2 + 3 + 4' is interpreted as 2 plus 3 (giving 5), added to 4 (giving 9). However, expressions are not read in this order when they contain operators of *different* types. The expression '3 + 4 * 2' is not interpreted as 3 plus 4 (giving 7), multiplied by 2 (giving 14). Instead, this expression gives the answer 11, because the multiplication is done first.

Just how an expression is interpreted depends on the precedence level assigned to each operator type. For example the '*' operator has a higher precedence than the '+' operator. A high precedence means that the operator is dealt with before other operators of lower precedence.

Note that the following discussion on sub-expressions shows how these precedence rules can be overriden as needed.

Multiplication and division operations

The '*' and 'div' operators have the highest precedence. They are always calculated first. When an expression contains multiple operators of these types, they are interpreted from left to right:

```
<value-of select="1 * 10"/>,
<value-of select="1 * 10 div 2"/>,
<value-of select="1 div 2 * 10 "/>.
```

10, 5, 5.

Addition and subtraction operations

The '+' and '-' operators are next in precedence. When an expression contains multiple operators of these types, they are interpreted from left to right:

```
<value-of select="1 + 2"/>,
<value-of select="1 + 2 - 3"/>,
<value-of select="1 - 3 + 2"/>,
<value-of select="1 + 1 * 10"/>.
```

3, 0, 0, 11.

Greater than and smaller than tests

The '<', '>', '<=' and '>=' comparison operators are next in precedence. The following example succeeds because the left half is smaller than the right half:

```
<if test="1+1 < 4-1"><!-- ENABLED (2 < 3) --></if>
```

Equal and not equal tests

The '=' and '!=' comparison operators are next in precedence. All the following examples succeed because both halves of the expression evaluate to 'true', or both halves evaluate to 'false', or both halves have the same numeric value:

```
<if test="1+1 = 3-1"><!-- ENABLED (2 = 2) --></if>

<if test="1<2 = 3<4"><!-- ENABLED (both true) --></if>

<if test="1>2 = 3>4"><!-- ENABLED (both false) --></if>
```

Multiple tests

The 'and' operator is the next in precedence. The following expression will succeed:

```
<if test="1=1 and 2=2"><!-- ENABLED (both true) --></if>
```

Alternative sub-expressions

The 'or' operator has the lowest precedence of all (and is therefore the most significant operator of all). It is used to break up a large expression into a series of smaller expressions, and the whole expression succeeds if any one (or more) of these sub-expressions succeeds.

In the following example, 2 does equal 2, but 3 does not equal 4. However, the 'or' operator is evaluated last and so the final part of the expression (5 does equal 5) is sufficient for the whole expression to succeed:

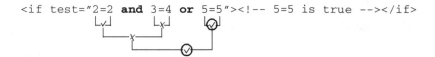

```
<if test="2=2 and 3=4 or 5=5"><!-- 5=5 is true --></if>
```

Sub-expressions

The operator precedence rules described above may not always be convenient. For example, consider the following calculation:

```
$dayRate * $daysWorked + $completionBonus
```

This would be interpreted as adding a completion bonus to the total pay for the work done. This may well be what is intended, but consider the following similar calculation:

```
$dayRate * $daysWorked + $dailyBonus
```

In this case, it is clear that the bonus should be added to each day's salary. Yet this will not be the interpretation made by XPath. Simply reordering the expression as follows will not help either because precedence rules are more significant than ordering:

```
$dailyBonus + $dayRate * $daysWorked
```

Bracketed sub-expressions

The solution is to use sub-expressions. Rounded brackets are used to isolate part of an expression that must be evaluated first. The expression above can be made to work as required by adding brackets around the addition part of the expression:

```
($dailyBonus + $dayRate) * $daysWorked
```

Ordering remains unimportant. The following alternative expression will work equally well:

```
$daysWorked * ($dayRate + $dailyBonus)
```

Embedded brackets

Brackets can be nested to any number of levels. The inner-most sub-expressions are evaluated first. The following illustration shows the order in which expressions are evaluated when many levels are used:

```
6 ( 5 ( 4 ((( 1 ) 2 ) 3 )) 5 ) 6
```

Axis ordering overrides

Brackets can be used in places that are counter-intuitive. For example, the two expressions below have different meanings:

```
preceding::item[1]

(preceding::item)[1]
```

The first example selects the nearest previous sibling Item element that is encountered when searching backwards up the document structure. The second example first selects all of the preceding Item elements, then filters the list of selected nodes by selecting only the first one in document order (the Item element furthest away).

Boolean functions

A **boolean** value can be created and given a '**true**' value using the **true**() function:

```
<if test="true()"><!-- ENABLED --></if>
```

The **false**() function always returns the value '**false**'. The following test is never successful:

```
<if test="false()"><!-- NOT ENABLED --></if>
```

Reversing a value

The **not**() function reverses a boolean value, from 'true' to 'false' or from 'false' to 'true':

```
<if test="not(true())"><!-- NOT ENABLED --></if>
<if test="not(false())"><!-- ENABLED --></if>
```

Converting values to boolean

When a boolean test is needed but the expression does not return a value of this kind, the value is automatically converted to boolean as if it were enclosed within the **boolean**() function, which converts values to 'true' or 'false' according to the following rules.

A number is considered to be 'true' if it is not zero (and is definitely a valid number). The value zero is therefore 'false', as is negative zero, '-0', and **NaN**:

```
<if test="1"><!-- ENABLED --></if>

<if test="0"><!-- NOT ENABLED --></if>

<if test="1bad"><!-- NOT ENABLED (NaN) --></if>
```

A string is considered to be 'true' if it contains at least one character. An empty string is 'false':

```
<if test="'x'"><!-- ENABLED --></if>

<if test="''"><!-- NOT ENABLED (empty string) --></if>
```

A set of nodes is 'true' if there is at least one node in the set. An empty set is 'false'. This is demonstrated by the simple XSLT test for the presence of elements of a specific type. In this example, if at least one Title element is present as a child of the current element, then 'true' is returned:

```
<if test="title">
  <!-- ENABLED (if embedded child title(s) present) -->
</if>
```

Numeric functions

Functions are available that allow **numeric** values to be rounded up, rounded down, and added together. Other data types can also be converted into numeric values.

Converting to number

A number of functions are included for manipulating numeric values. First, other data items can be converted to numbers using the **number**() function. Boolean values are converted to '1' when 'true', and '0' when 'false'.

Recall that the XSLT If element test converts the resulting numbers back to boolean values and that the value '0' is interpreted as 'false':

```
<if test="number(true())"><!-- ENABLED ('1') --></if>

<if test="number(false())"><!-- NOT ENABLED ('0') --></if>
```

Strings are converted to numbers if their contents are pure numbers, optionally surrounded by whitespace. If a string does not conform to these constraints, it is converted to **NaN** (**Not a Number**) (which is then considered 'false' as a boolean value):

```
<if test="number('1')"><!-- ENABLED --></if>

<if test="number(' -1 ')"><!-- ENABLED --></if>

<if test="number('-0')"><!-- NOT ENABLED (zero) --></if>

<if test="number('99 bad')"><!-- NOT ENABLED (NaN) --></if>
```

Nodes are converted to numeric values by first converting them to strings (as described later), then converting the strings to numbers (as described above).

When no parameter is given to the function, then the current node is taken to be the implied parameter.

Many functions that are described below take parameters that need to be numeric values. But it is possible to pass other data types to these functions without having to use the number() function described above. This function can be omitted in these cases because its presence can be implied. The two examples below are functionally identical, but the latter is preferable because it is more legible:

```
<if test="numeric-function(number('0.5'))">...</if>

<if test="numeric-function('0.5')">...</if>
```

Rounding values up and down

The **floor**() function returns the nearest positive integer that is smaller than the value passed to it. For example, the floor of both '3.9' and '3.2' is '3'. The **ceiling**() function rounds real numbers up to the nearest higher integer value, so '3.2' becomes '4'. The **round**() function rounds real numbers up or down to the nearest integer, with '0.5' rounded up to '1', and '0.4' rounded down to '0':

```
<if test="ceiling(0.5)"><!-- ENABLED (1) --></if>

<if test="floor(0.5)"><!-- NOT ENABLED (0) --></if>

<if test="round(0.5)"><!-- ENABLED (1) --></if>

<if test="round(0.4)"><!-- NOT ENABLED (0) --></if>
```

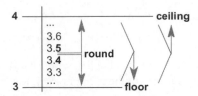

Adding values

The **sum()** function is passed a single node-set. The values to sum are the values extracted from each node. These values are first converted to strings (as described below), then the strings are converted to numbers. Finally, the numbers are added together.

```
<quantity>123</quantity>
<quantity>200</quantity>
<quantity>1</quantity>
```

Total quantity: <value-of select="**sum(**//quantity**)**"/>.

Total quantity: **324**.

String functions

Functions are available that allow strings to be analysed, and for new strings to be created from manipulated versions of existing strings. Other data types can also be converted into string values.

Converting to string

Other data types can be converted into strings using the **string()** function.

When a boolean value is converted into a string value, the string holds either the word 'true' or the word 'false'.

When a number is converted into a string value, the string consists of characters that represent each digit of the number, plus any decimal point or leading '-' symbol (though minus zero becomes just '0'). An invalid number becomes the string '**NaN**'.

When a node set is converted into a string, only the first node (in document order) is used, and the string value of this node is extracted. When no parameter is given, the current context node is adopted as an implied parameter.

String analysis

Strings can be analysed using the **string-length()**, **starts-with()** and **contains()** functions. The first of these returns a numeric value representing the number of characters in the string. The second and third functions return a boolean value indicating whether or not the string starts with, or contains, the given series of characters:

```
<if test="string-length('a')"><!-- ENABLED (1) --></if>

<if test="string-length('')"><!-- NOT ENABLED (0) --></if>

<if test="starts-with('the boat', 'the' )">
  <!-- ENABLED (true) -->
</if>

<if test="starts-with('a boat', 'the' )">
  <!-- NOT ENABLED (false) -->
</if>

<if test="contains('the boat is yellow', 'boat' )">
  <!-- ENABLED (true) -->
</if>

<if test="contains('the car is yellow', 'boat' )">
  <!-- NOT ENABLED (false) -->
</if>
```

String conversions

Strings cannot be edited directly, but a new string can be created from a manipulated copy of an existing string. Functions are used to return altered versions of the strings passed to them as parameters:

```
new-string = string-function( original-string )
```

The **substring-before()** function and the **substring-after()** function extract initial or trailing characters from a string, with the cut-off point being the character in the second parameter to the function:

```
substring-before('abc-123', '-')

substring-after('abc-123', '-')
```

Of course, the string may contain multiple occurrences of the character specified, but this does not matter because only the first occurrence is deemed to be significant:

```
substring-before('abc-def-123', '-')

substring-after('abc-def-123', '-')
```

The **substring**() function specifies an offset and a range to isolate the series of characters to be extracted. In the following example, four characters are selected starting from the fifth character in the string:

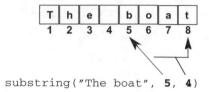

```
substring("The boat", 5, 4)
```

Characters in strings can be replaced using the **translate**() function, which takes three parameters. The first parameter is the string containing characters to be replaced. The function returns a modified version of this string. The second parameter is a list of the characters that must be converted to some other character, wherever these characters happen to occur in the first parameter string. Finally, the third parameter is the list of replacement characters. A single character replacement requirement is specified by pairing a character in the second string with the character at the same position in the third string. For example, values of 'abc' and 'xyz' for these two parameters specify that 'a' is to become 'x', 'b' is to become 'y', and 'c' is to become 'z'. Each occurrence of any of these characters in the first string is replaced using these rules. For example, 'translate('bad day', 'abc', 'xyz')' returns the string 'yxd dxy'. The following example of this function returns an upper-case representation of any string of alphabetic characters passed to it:

```
translate('Convert This To All Upper-Case',
          'abcdefghijklmnopqrstuvwxyz',
          'ABCDEFGHIJKLMNOPQRSTUVWXYZ')
```

CONVERT THIS TO ALL UPPER-CASE

Note that characters that are not given replacement values are not affected. The hyphen in the example above is unaffected.

The **normalize-space**() function returns a string that removes unnecessary whitespace characters from the parameter string. For example, ' the   boat ' becomes 'the boat'.

A number of strings can be concatenated into a single string using the **concat**() function, which takes two or more string parameters:

```
concat("Original string.", " Append this", " and this.")
```

Original string. Append this and this

Node-set values

Every node has a value, which is represented by a string. But the string value of a node is determined in different ways, depending on the node type.

The value of the root node of the document is the concatenation of all the text nodes in the document.

The value of an element node is the concatenation of all the text nodes in that element and all descendant elements. For example, the value of the following Paragraph element includes the text in the embedded highlighted section:

```
<para>All the <emph>text</emph> here is the value</para>
```

Note that, for this reason, the Value Of instruction can be useful for extracting the text from an element for reuse as an attribute value (which cannot contain element tags).

The string value of an attribute node is its normalized value (tabs and line-feeds are converted to spaces first).

The string value of a comment node is the entire content of the comment, not including the surrounding markup delimiters ('`<!--`' and '`-->`').

The string value of a processing instruction node is the instruction part of the code and so does not include the target name. It is not possible to retrieve the target name. However, processing instructions can be selected on a target-specific basis by including the target name in the node test:

```
processing-instruction('ACME')

    <?XYZ columnBreak?> <?ACME column-break?>
    ...
    <?XYZ pageBreak?>   <?ACME page-break?>
```

The string value of a text node is all the characters in that node. A text node cannot be empty because it only exists in order to hold one or more characters.

Unlike the simpler data types described earlier, a node always exists already, outside of the expression, at a specific location in the document tree. Therefore, in order to use a node in an expression, it must first be found. A location path is used for this purpose. But the issue this raises is that location paths often target multiple nodes. For example, '`//title`' returns a list of all Title element nodes. Some functions work on a single node. Therefore, when a list of nodes is passed to any of these functions, only the first node in the list is considered to be relevant and the others are ignored.

Identity and context functions

The current node is always part of a current node list, though it is possible for the list to contain only this one node. The length of the current node list, and the position of the current node within this list, can provide useful additional context information.

Node position function

The **position**() function returns a numeric value that indicates the position of the current node among the current list of nodes. In the simplest case, this may be the position of the node among its sibling nodes:

```
<template match="/">
  <apply-templates select="child::*"/>
</template>

<template match="*">
  <if test="position() = 1">
    <!-- ENABLED IF FIRST CHILD OF PARENT -->
  </if>
  <apply-templates select="child::*"/>
</template>
```

The position value is not always calculated in the same direction. In a location path, it depends on the direction of the step to be taken. The simple rule underlying the various directions illustrated below is that when the direction is forward, searching for nodes that follow the current node, then counting is in document order. Otherwise, it is in reverse order.

The position value is typically restricted to the presence of elements of a given type, and 'item[position()=3]' only counts Item elements. It is valid when the Item element is the third one selected by the node test. However, '*[position()=3]' counts all elements.

Last node function

The **last**() function returns the number of nodes in the current context list. The current position will always be a value between '1' and this maximum. When compared with the value returned by the position() function, it helps to recognize when the current node is the last node:

```
<if test="position() = last()">
  <!-- ENABLED FOR LAST NODE ONLY -->
</if>
```

Node count function

The **count**() function returns the total number of nodes passed to it. For example, 'count(child::para)' returns the number of paragraph children of the current element, and 'count(*)' counts all of the child elements:

```
<if test="count(child::para)">
  <!-- ENABLED (if any child paragraphs present) -->
</if>
<if test="count(*)">
  <!-- ENABLED (if any child elements present) -->
</if>
```

Node identifier function

The **id**() function returns the element node with the given unique identifier, if such an element node exists. The function 'id('xyz')' returns the element node with the unique identifier 'xyz'. Unique identifiers are only recognized if a DTD (or schema) is used, and this DTD assigns one or more attributes to the ID attribute type. This is typically used to apply formatting or to reuse the content of a specific element:

```
<xsl:template match="id('JSmith')">
  <P>J. Smith details:</P>
  <P><xsl:apply-templates/></P>
  <P>J. Smith works for company -
    <xsl:value-of select="id('company19')"/>
  </P>
</xsl:template>
```

Node name function

The **name**() function returns the string value of the name of the given node. In the case of element nodes, the name returned is the name of the element, with a namespace prefix where appropriate.

For example, 'name(.)' returns the name of the current node. This could be used in a named template to debug a stylesheet:

```
<xsl:template name="debug">
  <P>ELEMENT NAME = <xsl:value-of select="name(.)"/></P>
</xsl:template>
```

If no parameter is supplied, then the current node is assumed, so 'name()' and 'name(.)' have the same meaning.

Predicate filters

A location path may select several elements. For example, consider the expression '/book/chapter/para'. When used in a Match pattern, all paragraphs directly inside all chapters match this pattern. When used in a Select expression, all chapter paragraphs are selected. Often, especially in the latter scenario, the actual requirement is to locate a single element, or at least to take into consideration factors beyond simple contextual location that will eliminate some of the matching nodes.

A **predicate filter** can be added to 'filter out' unwanted nodes. For example, a simple filter may eliminate a node based on its position in the context list. In the example below, the third Chapter element node is filtered out. This means that the paragraphs it holds will not be selected in the next step:

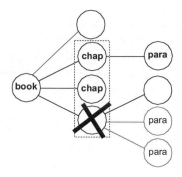

Filters are expressions enclosed in square brackets, '[' and ']', and they return a boolean value. When the value returned is 'true', the node is accepted; when the value returned is 'false', it is rejected. Only accepted nodes are retained and form the basis of the next step in the path.

The filter always immediately follows a node test, such as 'para[...]' or 'node()[...]'.

Numerical filter

The simplest kind of predicate filter holds a numeric value. This value represents a specific sequential location in the list of matching nodes. For example, the expression '//chapter/para' may, in one particular chapter, identify 23 paragraphs. Paragraph '1' will be the first paragraph in the chapter, and paragraph '23' will be the last. By entering a value in the predicate filter, only the paragraph at that position is valid. All others are discarded. The following example therefore selects the fifth paragraph in the third chapter of the book:

```
/book/chapter[3]/para[5]
```

The expression 'following-sibling::*[2]' likewise selects the element following the element that follows the current element. However, the direction of the count is important, and not always immediately obvious. When taking a direction outward or backward ('ancestor::', 'ancestor-or-self::', 'preceding::' and 'preceding-sibling::') the count is in reverse order. For example, 'preceding-sibling::*[1]' selects the element immediately before the current one (not the first element in their shared parent). An easy way to remember this is to appreciate that the value '1' will always be the node nearest to the starting point:

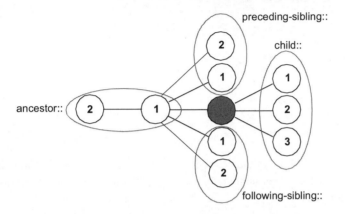

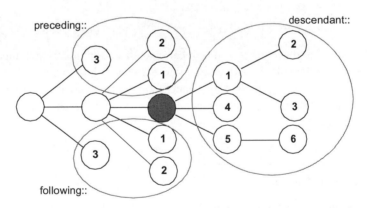

Note that the earlier section covering sub-expressions includes a technique that can be employed to override the backwards-counting technique so that, for example, it is possible to find the second preceding sibling in document order, rather than the one that is two places away from the context node.

Expressions in filters

Filters can contain any expression. This is an important point because filters are used in patterns, which are otherwise constrained to a limited subset of the expression language. Patterns are therefore much more flexible when they include filters. In the following example, paragraphs are only selected if they are in chapters that have no title:

```
/book/chapter[not(title)]/para
```

```
<book>
  <chapter>
    <para>No title in this chapter.</para>
  </chapter>
  <chapter>
    <title>Chapter With Title</title>
    <para>There is a title in this chapter.</para>
  </chapter>
</book>
```

It should also be understood that the placing of simple numeric values in filters is a shorthand version of a comparison that uses the **position**() function. The examples below are equivalent:

```
/book/chapter[3]/para[5]
/book/chapter[position() = 3]/para[position() = 5]
```

The shorthand version is provided because it is a common requirement to target a specific element by its sequential location (when it has no unique identifier), such as the fourth paragraph of the seventh section of the second chapter of a book. The following example would be much more verbose if this shorthand technique was not available:

```
match="/book/chapter[2]/section[7]/para[4]"
```

Multiple filters

More than one filter can be used to qualify a single step in the expression:

```
node[...][...]
```

Normally, this is not an essential feature because multiple expressions can be combined into a single expression using the 'and' operator. However, it is not possible to use numeric values for node positions in a filter that also contains other tests. For example, while '[position() = 3 and not(title)]' is legal (the element is the third one, and does not contain a Title element), the shorthand version '[3 and not(title)]' is not allowed. Using separate filters overcomes this limitation:

```
[3][not(title)]
```

There is another reason for using multiple filters concerning the possible need to test the results of a previous filtering process. Each filter is applied in sequence to create a new, shorter list of nodes. The order in which multiple filters are presented is therefore very important. The examples below are *not* the same:

```
chapter[3][not(title)]
```

```
chapter[not(title)][3]
```

The first example selects the third chapter, then selects or eliminates this chapter depending on whether or not it contains a title. But the second example selects all chapters that do not have a title, then selects the third of the remaining chapters (which may perhaps still be the third chapter of the book, depending on whether or not the three initial chapters all contain a title).

When no position information is included, the ordering of filters becomes irrelevant, and indeed so does the need for multiple filters. The following three examples have identical meanings, but the last is the easiest to read (and probably more efficient to process):

```
chapter[not(title)][author]
```

```
chapter[author][not(title)]
```

```
chapter[not(title) and author]
```

Namespaces

When using namespaces (see Chapter 17), element names are separated into two parts: a local part, such as 'h1', and a namespace prefix part, such as 'html', giving a complete name of 'html:h1'. The prefix is mapped to a URL reference, such as 'http://www.w3.org/Profiles/xhtml1-strict'. The **namespace-uri**() function returns the URL of the first node in the list that forms its parameter. The **local-name**() function returns the local part of the name:

```
*[namespace-uri(.) =
        "http://www.w3.org/Profiles/xhtml1-strict"]

    <html:h1>An HTML Header One</html:h1>
    <html:p>An HTML paragraph.</html:p>

*[local-name(.) = "score"]
```

```
<music:score>Ferde Grofé</music:score>
<competition:score>57</competition:score>
```

It is not necessary in either case to supply a parameter value. When no parameter is given, this implies the current context node, so 'local-name(.)' and 'local-name()' mean the same thing.

23. Added XSLT functions

XSLT adds some functions to those defined in the XPath standard. These functions are therefore relevant only to the use of XPath in the XSLT application. They are used to access other documents, find indexed elements, generate unique element identifiers, format numbers, refer to the current node, retrieve URLs from unparsed entities, and locate information about the XSLT processor and the vendor of the software.

Functions covered elsewhere

Some of the XSLT functions added to XPath are discussed in detail in earlier chapters.

Document function

The document() function is fully described in Chapter 12. It is used to gain access to material in other XML documents.

Key function

The key() function is fully described in Chapter 16. It is used to access elements that have been indexed using unique identifiers.

Generate id function

This id() function is fully described in Chapter 16. It is used to access elements that have been given unique identifier values by a DTD.

Format number function

Numeric values can be reformatted using the **format-number()** function. For example, the number '12345.6' may be formatted as '12,345.60'.

This function takes at least two parameters and returns a string representation of the number that contains appropriate symbols and padding. First, the number to be formatted is given and then a formatting template, which uses conventions copied from a Java class (the DecimalFormat class, which is part of the 'java.text' package). For example, to reformat a number to ensure that the decimal point appears and that there are at least two digits after the point, the pattern '0.00' can be used:

```
format-number(123.4, '0.00')
```

```
123.40
```

To pass an attribute value as the first parameter, it is only necessary to enter the attribute name because it is automatically converted to a number before it is passed to the function:

```
<price val="123.4"/>
```

```
<xsl:template match="price">
  <P>Price:
    <xsl:value-of select="format-number(@val, '0.00')"/>
  </P>
</xsl:template>
```

```
<P>Price: 123.40</P>
```

The characters '0', '#', '-', '%', ',' and '.' have special meanings in the template. All of these characters are discussed below.

The character '0' indicates a placeholder for a digit that must be present. If the number to be formatted has no digit at this position, '0' is output. This is demonstrated in the example above. The minimum template pattern is a single '0' character, indicating that the formatted number must be at least a single digit value (anything less is certainly not a number).

Most templates are divided into two major parts: a required integer part and an optional fractional part. The '.' symbol is a placeholder for the decimal point, which indicates the division between these two parts. The number to format is aligned on this point. For example, '123.4' becomes '123.40' when using the template '0.00', as shown above, but remains '123.4' using the template '00.0'. It is an error for a pattern to include two '.' symbols.

The '#' symbol is also a placeholder for a digit, but in this case is not replaced by '0' if the digit is absent. It can be used before zeros in the integer part of the number (there must be at least one '0' here), and after any zeros in the fraction part of the number, as in the following example:

```
###00.0##
```

The '#' symbols in this example appear to be superfluous. But the '0' and '#' characters in the fraction part of the number indicate how many digits are allowed. So '.0#' indicates two digits only, and a longer fraction is reduced to this length by rounding the last valid digit. Using the example pattern, the value '1.12111' becomes '1.12', while '1.12999' becomes '1.13'. This rule does not apply to the integer part of the number, so '##0.' does *not* truncate the number '123456' to three digits. They are useful in the integer part of the number as place-holders for grouping separators, which are indicated using a comma ','. For example, '###,##0' indicates that the comma appears for numbers greater than '999'. Particular attention should be paid to the highlighted digits in each of the values below:

```
        12
       123.4
       123.45678
       876.54321
      1234.56
 123456789.12
```

Using the pattern '###,###,000.00#', the above numbers appear, respectively, as:

```
       012.00
       123.40
       123.457
       876.543
     1,234.56
 123,456,789.12
```

A different pattern can be specified for negative values and is separated from the first pattern using a semi-colon ';'. In the following example, negative numbers are padded to six digits, preceded by a minus sign:

```
###,##0.00;-000000
```

The percent symbol '%' is used to indicate a percentage. The value is automatically multiplied by 100. A fraction is thereby converted to a percentage:

```
0.1
0.99
```

```
%0
```

```
10%
99%
```

Similarly, the '?' symbol represents 'per mille' (per thousand). The value is multiplied by 1000. Also, the '¤' symbol (currency symbol) represent the current currency symbol, such as '$' or '£'.

It is important to recognize that the '0', ',', '%', '¤' and '-' symbols are only the default characters used in patterns in English. An optional third parameter to the function identifies a **Decimal Format** element that is used to control formatting and override the default settings. This element is identified by the value of its **Name** attribute:

```
<decimal-format name="England" ... />

... format-number(123.4, '###,##0.00', England) ...
```

A number of other attributes on this element specify characters for each role. The **Decimal Separator** attribute and **Grouping Separator** attributes indicate which characters take these specific roles (defaulting to '.' and ',' respectively). For example, in France the full-point character is the grouping character, and the comma is the decimal point:

```
<decimal-format name="France"
                decimal-separator=","
                grouping-separator="." />
```

Note that the redefined character roles apply to the pattern, as well as to a number formatted according to the rules in this pattern. In this example, the roles for the command and full-point characters have been reversed, so must also take reversed roles in the pattern itself:

```
'###.##0,00'
```

When a number is formatted, it may be an infinite number, an illegal number or a negative number. The symbol for infinity is given in the **Infinity** attribute, and this attribute may contain a string of characters. Likewise, the **NaN** attribute holds the string that should be presented when the supplied number is not valid. Remaining attributes must have a single character value. The minus symbol for negative numbers is specified using the **Minus Sign** attribute (default '-'):

```
<decimal-format name="England" ...
                infinity="INFINITY AND BEYOND!"
                NaN="NOT A NUMBER"
                minus-sign="M" />
```

Within the pattern template, reserved symbols are used to indicate digits ('#') and the separator when there are two templates (';'). The **Digit** attribute specifies the symbol used to represent a digit, and the **Pattern Separator** attribute provides the separator character:

```
<decimal-format name="England" ...
                digit="D"
                pattern-separator="+" />
```

Finally, a number of attributes are used both to define special characters in the template and, at the same time, to define the output characters for the percent symbol, the per-mille symbol and the zero digit. The **Percent**, **Per Mille** amd **Zero Digit** attributes are used:

```
<decimal-format name="England" ...
                percent="P"
                per-mille="?"
                zero-digit="Z" />
```

Current node function

While the **current node** is normally represented by the full-point symbol '.', it can also be represented by the **current()** function. The following tests are directly equivalent because they both test for the occurrence of at least one paragraph somewhere in the current element:

```
<if test=".//para">...</if>
```

```
<if test="current()//para">...</if>
```

However, their meanings differ considerably in other circumstances. The concept of a 'current' element becomes ambiguous, because there are two possible interpretations of this term. In one sense, the current element could be considered to be the element selected for processing by the template, regardless of where it is referenced from within an expression in the template. In another sense, the current element could be the one selected by a previous step in an expression, as each step identifies new current elements from which the remaining steps take their context. It is sometimes useful to be able to distinguish between these two meanings.

The '.' symbol refers to different nodes, depending on where it is used in the expression. The current() function, however, always refers to the element selected by the template, so that the node it represents does not change, regardless of where it is used within an expression. In the following example, the first test matches any directly embedded paragraphs that include (directly or indirectly) a Secret element. But the second test selects the paragraph if there is a Secret element anywhere in the book:

```
<template match="book">
  <if test="para[.//secret]">PARA WITH SECRET</if>
  <if test="para[current()//secret]">PARA IN BOOK WITH
  SECRET</if>
</template>
```

Another example of the need for this function is to compare attribute values. The following example compares the revision number of all embedded paragraphs with the revision number of the book itself, and only the latest paragraphs are processed:

```
<book rev="3">
  <para rev="1">Old paragraph.</para>
  <para rev="2">Still an old paragraph.</para>
  <para rev="3">New paragraph.</para>
</book>
```

```
<template match="book">
  <DIV>
    <apply-templates
        select="para[./@rev = current()/@rev]" />
  </DIV>
</template>
```

```
<DIV>
  <P>New paragraph.</P>
</DIV>
```

Note that this function cannot be used in a pattern and so it must not be used in the Match attribute of the Template element or Key element, or on the attributes of the Number element.

Unparsed entity URI function

XML DTDs may contain entities that refer to external non-XML data, such as image files. The **unparsed-entity-uri**() function obtains the system identifier when an attribute value contains a reference to an entity name.

Consider the following example, where the DTD defines an Image element that uses a Name attribute to hold the entity name:

```
<!DOCTYPE book [
  <!NOTATION GIF SYSTEM "GIFviewer.EXE">
  <!ENTITY Boat SYSTEM "/images/boat.GIF" NDATA GIF>
  ...
  <!ELEMENT image EMPTY>
  <!ATTLIST image name ENTITY #REQUIRED>
]>
<book>
  ...
  <image name="Boat" />
  ...
</book>
```

When converting such an example to HTML, the Src attribute must hold the path to the image instead of the entity name (so '`/images/boat.GIF`' must replace '`Boat`'). When the name of an unparsed entity is passed to the function, it returns the URL for that entity:

```
<image name="Boat" />
```

```
<xsl:template match="image">
  <IMG SRC="{unparsed-entity-uri(@name)}" />
</xsl:template>
```

```
<IMG SRC="/images/boat.GIF">
```

System property function

Information about the version of XSLT in use and the vendor of the XSLT processor currently processing the stylesheet can be obtained using the **system-property()** function. A string parameter passed to this function determines what item of information is wanted. For the core items, the parameters needed are **xsl:version**, **xsl:vendor** and **xsl:vendor-uri**. For example, a comment could be constructed that records the technology and tool used to create the document:

```
<template match="book">
  <comment>
    <text>XSLT version: </text>
    <value-of select="system-property(xsl:version)" />
    <text>XSLT Processor vendor: </text>
    <value-of select="system-property(xsl:vendor)" />
    <text>XSLT Processor vendor Web site: </text>
    <value-of select="system-property(xsl:vendor-uri)" />
  </comment>
  ...
</template>
```

```
<!-- XSLT version: 1
XSLT Vendor: Apache Software Foundation
XSLT Vendor Web site: http://xml.apache.org/xalan
-->
```

A specific XSLT processor may provide access to a large number of additional information items.

24. XSL

At the heart of the original XSL proposal was a method for styling XML documents. Most of the discussion up to this point has focussed on the now separate XSLT standard for manipulating content. While this capability can be used to format a document using other formatting languages (such as HTML) and for non-formatting tasks, it was originally intended to prepare material for styling using XSL. However, XSL is independent of XSLT, because XML documents can be converted into XSL documents using other tools, and XSL documents can be created from non-XML sources. For example, a database management system could have an 'export as XSL' reporting feature.

Note that XSL is a large and complex standard. While all XSL elements are introduced in this part of the book, a few of their attributes that are both obscure and complex are only mentioned in passing.

Background

XSL is a markup language that is suitable for formatting material for presentation on screen or paper.

XSL is a powerful, complex language with 57 formatting object types, including simple items such as blocks and in-line areas, as well as lists, tables, dynamic features and links. The formatting objects are configured using the 248 properties that are also specified.

New products have been developed around this standard. While it is expected that XSL support will be added to many existing formatting products, including DTP applications, typesetting engines and document browsers, it is unlikely that any of these products will have features that exactly match those defined in the XSL standard. However, competing products will be pressured to reveal which features are supported, and product comparisons will therefore be easier to make than ever before.

Many of the formatting options are similar or identical to CSS formatting proper-ties. In such cases, CSS property names have been adopted by XSL in order to sim-plify transition between languages and reduce the effort needed to learn both. In general, a CSS property name is simply translated into an XML attribute name.

Note that an unofficial forum for discussing the implementation, use and future direction of XSL can be accessed by registering with the newsgroup governed by majordomo@mulberrytech.com, including 'subscribe xsl-list' in the body of the message.

An archive of past correspondence can be accessed at www.mulberrytech.com/xsl/ xsl-list.

XSL instructions

XSL formatting instructions are XML elements that contain the text needing to be formatted according to these instructions. Attributes are frequently used to specify each style to be applied to the text. Those familiar with CSS and other stylesheet languages will find that this is an unfamiliar concept. With these languages, the content is always separate from the styling instructions. The XSL approach more closely resembles traditional typesetting languages, where formatting instructions are embedded in the text.

XSL documents are therefore XML documents. Although no DTD is specified for XSL elements, one could be derived from the definitions in the XSL standard, and this DTD could be used to validate an XSL document. One possible reason why a DTD has not been defined could be to discourage the idea that XSL documents may be created directly by document authors. This would certainly be a bad idea because XSL documents break the cardinal rule for XML documents; that they be self-describing. Instead, XSL documents should almost always be created from information in other formats, including other XML documents (but not excluding others forms, such as data stored in relational databases), and discarded after being used by an XSL formatting engine to create formatted output. Of course, one way to convert arbitrary XML documents into XSL documents would be to use an XSLT stylesheet.

The following example demonstrates the use of two of the most common instruc-tions. It emulates the HTML fragment below:

```
<block>A <inline font-weight="bold">bold</inline>
statement.</block>

<P>A <B>bold</B> statement.</P>
```

XSL formatting instructions are known as **formatting object** elements, or **FO** elements for short. In the event that these elements are mixed with elements from other document types, there is a namespace defined for them. The FO namespace is http://www.w3.org/1999/XSL/Format, which is commonly mapped to a prefix of 'fo':

```
<fo:block>A
<fo:wrapper font-weight="bold">bold</fo:wrapper>
statement.</fo:block>
```

This namespace is referenced from XSLT stylesheets:

```
<stylesheet ...
            xmlns:fo="http://www.w3.org/1999/XSL/Format" >

<template match="para">
  <fo:block><apply-templates/></fo:block>
</template>
```

Examples in this chapter dispense with the prefix because they do not include elements from other namespaces and their absence improves legibility. But it should not be forgotten that such prefixes are often necessary.

Document structure

Though not very imaginative, perhaps, the root element of an XSL document is actually called **Root**. All XSL documents are then divided into two major parts, surrounding one small optional part. The final part is the actual content of the document to be formatted. But before this, it is necessary to construct a document template consisting of one or more page designs (or 'blueprints'), possibly also specifying how these page templates are to be arranged. Between these two parts, global (colour) definitions may be defined:

```
<root>
  <!-- TEMPLATES -->
  <!-- DECLARATIONS (only colours at the moment) -->
  <!-- CONTENT -->
</root>
```

It is recommended that the Root element should contain information on the source XML document, so that this document can be accessed if the formatter, for some reason, finds that the XSL rendition of it is not appropriate. The **Source Document** attribute is used for this purpose, and contains at least one URL reference. The **Media Usage** attribute should also be used to control how page sequences are presented. The default value **'auto'** indicates that the formatter can make its own decision, based on other information and the medium it is presenting the material on. The value **'paginate'** is appropriate for print publishing, where the page sequences really do represent a sequence of pages, each having a fixed height and width. The value '**unbounded**' creates a single, usually scrollable, page area from a page sequence specification (the area is as wide as the longest single line of text). Finally, the value '**bounded-in-one-direction**' specifies that the width or height must be fixed (but not both, and not neither) and that when the page is not rotated left or right, and the text flows from left-to-right (or right-to-left), then the page width must be fixed (otherwise, the page height must be):

```
<root source-document="source.XML"
      media-usage="unbounded" >
  ...
</root>
```

Templates

First, templates are defined that specify the characteristics of the pages to display or print, including the size of these pages. More than one page template may be defined (for example, this book requires a different template for the preliminary pages than for the chapters, the first page of each chapter differs from the remainder, and left-hand pages differ from right-hand pages). The **Layout Master Set** element contains these templates:

```
<root>
  <layout-master-set>
    <!-- TEMPLATES -->
  </layout-master-set>
  <!-- CONTENT -->
</root>
```

Some templates may have header and footer regions, and the even-numbered pages may differ from the odd-numbered pages (as they do in this book). The **Simple Page Master** element is used to define each template, and may therefore occur several times within the Layout Master Set element:

```
<root>
  <layout-master-set>
    <simple-page-master ...>
    <!-- TEMPLATE 1 -->
    </simple-page-master>
    <simple-page-master ...>
    <!-- TEMPLATE 2 -->
    </simple-page-master>
  </layout-master-set>
  <!-- CONTENT -->
</root>
```

The individual page templates are described in the next chapter.

Declarations

The **Declarations** element is optional and can only occur immediately after the layouts described above. It is used to hold any non-XSL declarations that could be supported by XSL processors that have additional capabilities, and may also define colour profiles.

The **Color Profile** element may occur any number of times. It is used to refer to an ICC colour profile and to give the colour a name that can be referenced later (see Chapter 27 for more details).

Content

After the templates (and optional declarations), the actual information to present is stored, including embedded formatting tags. This information may be divided into sections that will use different templates, or combinations of templates (there would be a separate section for each chapter of this book), and each section must therefore be linked to a specific template or template combination. The **Page Sequence** element is repeatable, and each instance holds the content to be associated with a particular template. It has a **Master Reference** attribute to identify the template it is associated with. The Simple Page Master element has a Master Name attribute, and the two are linked when they have identical values in these attributes:

```
<root>
  <layout-master-set>
    <simple-page-master master-name="Prelims">
    <!-- TEMPLATE 1 -->
    </simple-page-master>
    <simple-page-master master-name="MainContent">
    <!-- TEMPLATE 2 -->
    </simple-page-master>
  </layout-master-set>

  <page-sequence master-reference="Prelims">
    <!-- CONTENT 1 -->
  </page-sequence>
  <page-sequence master-reference="MainContent">
    <!-- CONTENT 2 -->
  </page-sequence>
</root>
```

Pages are created by selecting an appropriate template and 'flowing' the content into areas that follow the page template rules. If there is too much content to fit the page, another page may then be generated that conforms to the same template design and the content then continues to flow into this new page. For example, in this book the number of actual pages produced varies for each chapter, depending on how much there is to say on each topic. But this behaviour can be prevented. For example, the first page of every chapter uses a distinct template. This is used for the content placed on the first page, but not for subsequent content:

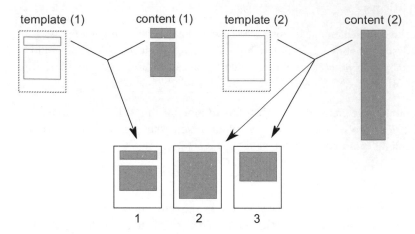

The way that content is arranged and formatted within a flow is discussed in the next chapter.

25. Page templates

A page template is used to specify the height, width, margins, and the number of columns of all pages that comply with this blueprint. Several page templates may be needed, and it is then necessary to specify the circumstances under which each is to be used.

Page properties

Simple page master

The dimensions of the page itself, and the margins that surround the area of the page that can be written to, are both specified using attributes on the **Simple Page Master** element.

Height and width

The height and width of the page are supplied by the **Page Height** and **Page Width** attributes (an A4 page has a height of 29.7 cm and a width of 21 cm):

```
<simple-page-master master-name="Prelims"
                    page-height="29.7cm"
                    page-width="21cm">
  ...
</simple-page-master>
```

The default value '**auto**' is used when the page size is not known and can be set by the formatting engine. The value '**indefinite**' specifies that the size of the page should be driven by the content. This is appropriate for the height dimension when the information is presented as an electronic page in a browser window:

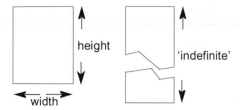

Note that when creating a stylesheet for presentation of material in an electronic product that creates a simple, scrollable interface (such as a Web browser), this can be considered to be a single (possibly very long) page and the following discussion on page sequences is not relevant. In this very simple case, a single page master template is created and is referenced from a single page sequence object.

The width and height can also be specified using a single **Size** attribute. A single value sets both sizes (creates a square page). Two values may be used instead, in which case the first sets the width and the second sets the height. The default value '**auto**' allows the XSL formatter to decide on the size. The values '**landscape**' or '**portrait**' can be used, in which case the page size is set to the maximum possible, and page orientation is set at the same time.

Orientation

Most printers are able to print to a page in both **portrait** and **landscape** orientation. In XSL, the **Reference Orientation** attribute can be used to specify what is to be considered the top and bottom of the page, irrespective of how the page is fed into the printer. Degree angles are entered in this attribute. The values '0' (the default), '90' (counter-clockwise), '180' (upside-down), and '270' (a 90 degree clockwise turn) are all allowed (and it is also possible to use a '-' prefix to change the direction, so '-90' is a clockwise rotation):

```
<simple-page-master reference-orientation="90" ... >
```

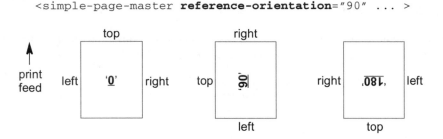

Writing direction

Text can be written left-to-right and top-to-bottom (as in English documents), or in any other combination, such as right-to-left and bottom-to-top. The possible values of the **Writing Mode** attribute are abbreviations of these settings, using 'l' for left, 'r' for right, 't' for top and 'b' for bottom. The value 'lr' stands for left-to-right, 'rl' stands for right-to-left, 'tb' stands for top-to-bottom and 'bt' stands for bottom-to-top, so '**lr-tb**' (the default) is appropriate for an English book:

```
<simple-page-master writing-mode="lr-tb" ... >
```

The other values allowed are 'rl-tb', 'tb-rl', 'lr', 'rl' and 'tb'.

Note that the 'top' of a page is the side of the page defined to be at the top according to the page orientation described above. When the value is 'lr-tb', writing follows the paths shown below:

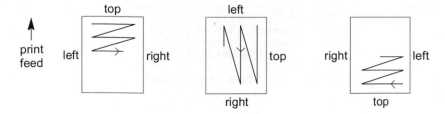

In English, when discussing objects that need to appear over a block of text, the term 'above' can be safely used. Likewise, when discussing objects that need to appear to the left of a line of text, the term 'left of' is unambiguous. But when lines can be written in either direction, and from bottom-to-top, these terms will often be misleading. Instead, the terms '**before**' and '**after**' are used to indicate position relative to blocks of text ('above' and 'below' in English), and '**start**' and '**end**' are used to indicate position relative to in-line objects ('left' and 'right' in English).

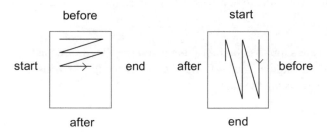

These terms are used frequently in the XSL standard. They often appear as part of an element or attribute name that is targetted at one of these positions (such as the attribute named 'border-start-style' and the element named 'region-after').

Margins

Most printing devices are unable to print text right up to the edge of a page, and even when this is possible it is usually undesirable. The area between the edge of the printable region and the edge of the paper is known as the margin, and widths of the margins for each edge are defined using the **Margin Top**, **Margin Right**, **Margin Bottom** and **Margin Left** attributes.

Each of these attributes takes a value that specifies the distance between the edge of the paper and the edge of the printable area. When printing double-sided for binding into a document or book, the left-side and right-side pages often have different margin widths (to cater for the space lost in the centre of the book due to the binding):

```
<simple-page-master master-name="left-page"
                    margin-left="1cm"
                    margin-right="1.5cm"
                    margin-top="1.5cm"
                    margin-bottom="2cm" >
```

Again, the definition of 'top' is taken from the page orientation:

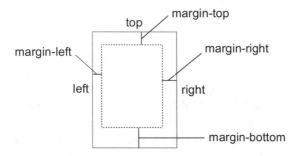

The **Margin** attribute holds the four values in the order top, right, bottom, left:

```
margin="3pt 2pt 2pt 3pt"
```

If only three values are supplied, the first sets the top margin, the second sets the bottom margin, and the middle value sets the left and right edges (so this is appropriate when these margins are the same):

```
margin="3pt 2pt 3pt"
```

Similarly, if the top and bottom margins are the same then only two values are needed. The first sets the top and bottom margins and the second sets the left and right margins:

```
margin="3pt 2pt"
```

Finally, a single value applies to all four sides:

```
margin="3pt"
```

Page sequences

When a number of different templates are defined (using Simple Page Master elements), the way in which these templates are selected for the content flow needs to be specified. One way to do this is to directly assign each section of the content to a different master (as described in the previous chapter). But this technique is very limited. In this book, for example, the text from each chapter would need to be flowed into at least three different templates. As much text as will fit on the first page needs to use a template exclusive to that page. Following this, as much text as will fit on the next page needs to occupy a page that uses the template for left-sided pages. After an alternating sequence of right and left pages, there may also be a final blank page (defined by yet another template). It is not possible for the document author to determine in advance what text will appear on each page, and then place this text in sections that refer to the relevant templates because this depends on many factors, such as font size, column width and rules for hyphenation all of which are determined by the templates and the pagination engine.

It is therefore possible to create a definition for a sequence of templates, including rules on which template to select in a given circumstance, using the **Page Sequence Master** element, which appears in the Layout Master Set element (by convention, below the page master templates but not restricted to this position). The content then links to this sequence, instead of to an individual template:

```
<root>
  <layout-master-set>
    <simple-page-master master-name="first-page">
      <!-- TEMPLATE 1 -->
    </simple-page-master>
    <simple-page-master master-name="left-page">
      <!-- TEMPLATE 2 -->
    </simple-page-master>
    <simple-page-master master-name="right-page">
      <!-- TEMPLATE 3 -->
    </simple-page-master>
    <simple-page-master master-name="blank-page">
      <!-- TEMPLATE 4 -->
    </simple-page-master>
    <page-sequence-master master-name="ChapterSequence">
      <!-- CHAPTER SEQUENCE DEFINITIONS -->
    </page-sequence-master>
  </layout-master-set>
  ...
</root>
```

The Page Sequence Master element then contains references to the master templates in the order that they are to be used. Finally, the **Page Sequence** elements refer to this sequence definition, instead of directly to a master page definition:

```
<root>
  ...
  <page-sequence master-reference="ChapterSequence">
    <!-- CHAPTER 1 CONTENT -->
  </page-sequence>
  <page-sequence master-reference="ChapterSequence">
    <!-- CHAPTER 2 CONTENT -->
  </page-sequence>
  <page-sequence master-reference="ChapterSequence">
    <!-- CHAPTER 3 CONTENT -->
  </page-sequence>
</root>
```

Page numbering

The pages in a page sequence can be numbered. The **Initial Page Number** attribute provides the number of the first page in the sequence, if a numeric value is entered in this attribute. Alternatively, the value '**auto**' (the default) implies that the number should be automatically calculated as the next page number after the last page of the previous sequence (for instance, the chapters in this book are separate page sequences, but they do not restart page numbering). When the new sequence must begin on an odd or even page, the values '**auto-odd**' or '**auto-even**' may be used instead. If 'auto-odd' is selected, and the previous sequence ended on '27', then the new sequence would begin with '29' rather than '28' (like the chapters in this book, all of which begin on odd-numbered pages):

```
<page-sequence master-reference="Prelims"
               initial-page-number="1">
  ...
</page-sequence>
<page-sequence master-reference="Chapter"
               initial-page-number="auto-odd">
  ...
</page-sequence>
<page-sequence master-reference="Chapter"
               initial-page-number="auto-odd">
  ...
</page-sequence>
```

Sequences often need to occupy an even number of pages (such as the chapters in this book) regardless of how many pages are actually needed to hold the text. The **Force Page Count** attribute can be given the value '**even**' to achieve this. Though generally less useful, the number of pages can also be forced to be an '**odd**' number. Later in this chapter it is shown how a special template can be selected for the last page if it has no content:

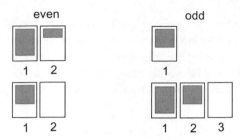

The default value '**auto**' forces the last page to be even if the first page of the next sequence is odd, and odd if the first page of the next sequence is even. It has no effect when the initial page number of the next sequence is 'auto' (or when there is no next sequence), when it does not force any additional pages:

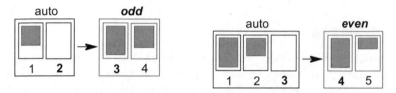

Other possible values are '**no-force**', which does not generate any pages beyond those needed to hold the content under any circumstances, and '**end-on-even**' and '**end-on-odd**', which force the last page to be an even or odd number respectively, regardless of what the initial page number is:

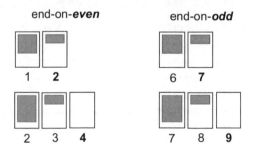

Page numbers may be referred in text, such as 'see Page 5', in which case it may need to be formatted in some way. The attributes **Format** (default value '1'), **Letter Value** (default value 'auto'), **Grouping Separator** (no separator by default), **Grouping Size** (no size by default), **Country** and **Language** (both defaulting to 'none') are used for this. They work as described in Chapter 15. These default values indicate that normal numbering takes the form of Arabic numbers without separators, such as page '1' and page '1234'.

Single pages

The **Single Page Master Reference** element is used to refer to a master page template, while indicating that this template should be used only to generate a single page of output. This is ideal for referencing the 'first-page' template in the example above (each chapter in this book would use this template only once). This element has the **Master Reference** attribute, which is used to reference the template needed:

```
<simple-page-master master-name="first-page">
  ...
</simple-page-master>
  ...
<page-sequence-master master-name="ChapterSequence">
  <single-page-master-reference
                    master-reference="first-page"/>
</page-sequence-master>
```

Repeatable pages

The **Repeatable Page Master Reference** element is used to refer to a master page template, while indicating that this template should be used repeatedly. By default, the template is used as many times as necessary to hold the content that uses it (this could, for instance, be used for the body pages of the chapters in this book, immediately following the simple reference described above that is needed for the first page of each chapter) because each chapter has an unknown number of pages to fill. But this would only be satisfactory if the headers and footers on each page were the same.

The **Maximum Repeats** attribute may be used to specify a limit on the number of pages generated using this template. A value of '0' means that the template will not be used at all. Other possible values are integers, such as '16' (meaning that it cannot repeat more than sixteen times). If more material is present than will fit the pages the next template is used, but if there are no further templates then this material will be omitted from the document. The default value is '**no-limit**', meaning that repetitions are not restricted.

This element has the **Master Reference** attribute, which is used to reference the template needed:

```
<simple-page-master master-name="body-page">
  ...
</simple-page-master>
  ...
<page-sequence-master master-name="ChapterSequence">
  ...
  <repeatable-page-master-reference
                    master-reference="body-page"/>
</page-sequence-master>
```

Alternative pages

The **Repeatable Page Master Alternatives** element is far more complex than the options described above and can perform sophisticated page master handling (of the kind needed to format this chapter):

```
<root>
  <layout-master-set>
    ...
    <page-sequence-master master-name="ChapterSequence">
      <repeatable-page-master-alternatives>
        ...
      </repeatable-page-master-alternatives>
    </page-sequence-master>
  </layout-master-set>
</root>
```

Each of these elements contains a number of **Conditional Page Master Reference** elements:

```
<page-sequence-master master-name="ChapterSequence">
  <repeatable-page-master-alternatives>
    <conditional-page-master-reference .../>
    <conditional-page-master-reference .../>
    <conditional-page-master-reference .../>
  </repeatable-page-master-alternatives>
</page-sequence-master>
```

Only one of the conditional references is selected for a particular page, and the order in which they appear in the Repeatable Page Master Alternatives element is significant because it is the first appropriate reference that is chosen.

This element references a template that is to be used under the conditions specified in a number of attributes. These conditions all relate to the location of the page to be formatted next. The first, last, even, odd and blank pages of a page sequence can all be recognized using these attributes.

The **Page Position** attribute can be used to activate a specified template when the page to be generated is the '**first**', '**last**', '**rest**' (any page except for the first or last) or '**any**' (the default) of the pages in a sequence. This is ideal for selecting the correct template for the first page of each chapter:

```
<conditional-page-master-reference
                page-position="first"
                master-reference="first-page" />
```

The **Odd Or Even** attribute can be used to activate a specified template when the page to be generated is an odd-numbered page, such as '1', '3' or '5', or an even-numbered page, such as '2', '4' or '6'. The values '**odd**', '**even**' or '**any**' (the default) are allowed.

This is ideal for selecting pages that have different headers or footers for left and right pages. Every chapter in this book begins on a right-hand page, and because the first page is a right-hand page and is page number '1', then all right-hand pages must be odd-numbered:

```
<conditional-page-master-reference
               odd-or-even="odd"
               master-reference="right-page" />

<conditional-page-master-reference
               odd-or-even="even"
               master-reference="left-page" />
```

These references should follow a reference to the first page because the first page is a special case of an odd page and therefore needs to be selected in preference for the first page of the sequence.

The **Blank Or Not Blank** attribute can be used to activate a specified template when a page needs to be generated, even though there is no text to place on it (such as the left-hand pages at the end of many of the chapters in this book). The values '**blank**', '**not-blank**' or '**any**' (the default) are allowed:

```
<conditional-page-master-reference
               blank-or-not-blank="blank"
               master-reference="blank-page" />
```

Although described last, this reference would typically be placed before the odd-or-even references because a blank page will also be an odd page or an even page but needs to be treated as a special case (recall that the first valid conditional reference is selected from the list of options). Note that the **Force Page Count** attribute needs to be used to create the blank page (typically with the value 'even'), because it would not otherwise be generated and the blank template would then never be needed.

Five conditional elements would be used to reference the five templates needed for the chapters in this book. The order in which they appear is significant, and the example below demonstrates the most suitable ordering:

```
<conditional-page-master-reference
               page-position="first"
               master-reference="first-page" />
<conditional-page-master-reference
               blank-page="blank"
               master-reference="blank-page" />
<conditional-page-master-reference
               odd-or-even="odd"
               master-reference="right-page" />
<conditional-page-master-reference
               odd-or-even="even"
               master-reference="left-page" />
```

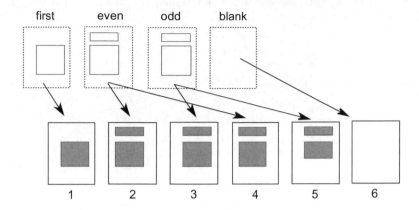

Page regions

A simple page master is able to contain one or more regions to hold the document text. A region is a rectangular area in the template into which text can be placed. This can be static text that needs to be repeated each time the template is used, or part of a text 'flow' that continues onto other pages.

Body region

One region, called the 'body region', must always be specified. It is placed centrally within the page and is generally used for the main text flow:

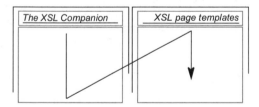

When some or all of the other, optional regions are also needed, they occupy space around the region body (but within the page margins). The margin attributes can also be used on the **Region Body** element (borders and padding are not relevant in this version of XSL, and if used they must be set to '0pt'):

```
<simple-page-master ...>
  <region-body margin-left="2cm"
               margin-right="2cm"
               margin-top="4cm"
               margin-bottom="3cm" />
</simple-page-master>
```

In effect, the body region margins are added to the page margins to position this region on the page:

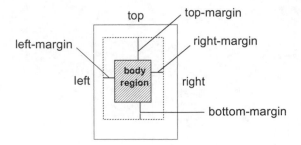

The width of the body region is calculated by taking the page width, subtracting the left and right page margin widths, and then subtracting the body region left and right margin widths.

Body region columns

The body region can have multiple columns (other regions discussed below cannot). The **Column Count** attribute has a default value of '1' but this may be changed to a greater number. The document content flows from one column to the next. In an English document, the columns are ordered from left to right. In a language that uses right-to-left writing, the column order is reversed. The **Column Gap** attribute indicates how much space to place between columns, and has a default value of '12pt'. The width of the columns is determined by taking the body region width, subtracting the sum of the intercolumn gaps, then dividing the remaining horizontal space by the number of columns:

```
<region-body column-count="3" column-gap="5mm" ... />
```

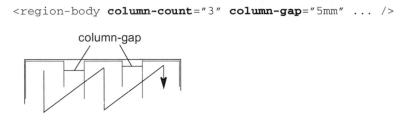

Region names

The **Region Name** attribute identifies a region for later use. If not specified, the default name for the body region is '**xsl-region-body**'. Specific names are needed if the text flowing into the body region of an odd page is different from the text flowing into the body region of an even page (a typical example being a legal document that contains the same text in two languages).

The reference orientation for the body region may be changed relative to the page orientation. For example, all pages may be aligned vertically (as portrait pages), and all header and footer regions (see below) may inherit this setting, but in some cases the body text may need the additional horizontal space that landscape orientation provides. Tables with many columns, for example, typically need this additional space.

Overflows

A region, or other area type, may be too small to contain the information placed in it. This may not appear to be an issue from the description above; the text cannot be too wide because new lines are created as needed, and the text cannot be too long because new pages are generated as needed. Nevertheless, this issue does arise even here.

When the content of an element is too large to fit in its containing box, some of the content will overflow. The extra material can be displayed as normal, removed, or (when presented electronically) can be accessed by scrolling down or across. The **Overflow** attribute controls this behaviour with the values '**visible**', '**hidden**' and '**scroll**' respectively:

The '**error-if-overflow**' value has the same effect as 'hidden', but the XSL formatter is expected to raise an error as well. The value '**auto**' is also available but will often be interpreted as being the same as 'scroll'.

The **Clip** attribute may be used to remove the edge of the content (when the Overflow attribute value is not set to 'visible'), but has a default value of '**auto**'. Clipping regions may in future take many different shapes, but for now it must take the form of a rectangle, 'rect(...)'. This shape takes four space-separated parameters that give the size of the clipped region above, to the right, below and to the left, in each case being the depth of the region from the relevant edge:

Viewports

As well as the region itself, a **viewport** is created. The viewport concept is only relevant to electronic displays where the user can view the content through an area smaller than the content and use scroll-bars (or other means) to bring other information into view. For those familiar with HTML frames, each viewport can be seen as a single frame. The viewport for the body region is simply the area of the region itself. When creating a single large page, it will contain a scroll-bar to provide access to all the content. To work in this way, the **Overflow** attribute must be set to '**scroll**' (note that it is not possible to have both multiple columns and scrolling).

Optional regions

Within the margins of the body region, other regions can be defined to hold headers, footers and margin notes. Only one region can be placed within each margin of the body region, and distinct elements are used to define each one. These elements have the names **Region Before**, **Region After**, **Region Start** and **Region End**.

They all have the same basic form as the Region Body element, and their names reflect their positions relative to the body region, depending on the writing direction used (for English documents, 'before' is above, 'after' is below, 'start' is to the left and 'end' is to the right). The 'before' and 'after' regions will be the most commonly needed because they are used to create headers and footers:

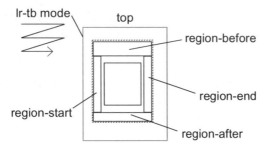

These regions cannot have multiple columns and so do not have the Column Count and Column Gap attributes described above.

Each of these areas has both a viewport and a region. The viewport area is calculated by taking the **Extent** attribute value to give it depth, and stretches to the edges of the page area. If the **Precedence** attribute of the Region Before or Region After elements have the value '**true**', the area then takes precedence over other overlapping areas. If the value is '**false**', the region is overlapped by adjacent regions. The

Region Start and Region End elements do not have this attribute (because it would otherwise be possible to create conflicting rules):

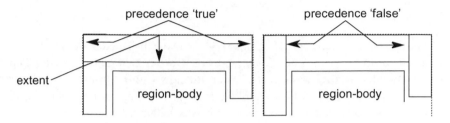

The region area lies beneath the viewport and has the same size, except when the Overflow attribute has the value 'scroll' (just as for the body region).

Each region can use the margin attributes, and so the headers and footers can be reduced in size and more carefully positioned than the explanation above implies.

Borders

By default, the content placed in a region appears within the region defined by the inner edge of each margin. However, it is possible to make room for a border line. The **Border Left Width**, **Border Top Width**, **Border Right Width** and **Border Bottom Width** attributes set the thickness of each side and are CSS-compatible. The writing-direction-based equivalents are **Border Start Width**, **Border Before Width**, **Border End Width** and **Border After Width**:

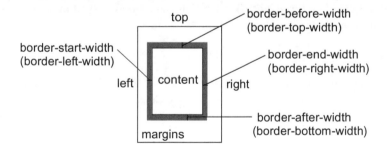

The **Border Width** attribute provides a shorthand method for specifying a simple width for all borders, or to define separate widths for top and bottom, followed by left and right, or to define separate widths for the top, the sides and the bottom, or to define separate widths for all four sides:

```
<!-- all sides 2pt -->
<block border-width="2pt">

<!-- 4pt sides -->
<block border-width="2pt 4pt">
```

```
<!-- 2pt top, 4pt sides, 3pt bottom -->
<block border-width="2pt 4pt 3pt">

<!-- top, right, bottom, left -->
<block border-width="1pt 2pt 3pt 4pt">
```

The border can have a colour. The colour is given using the **Border Color** attribute when all borders have the same colour, or by the **Border Left Color**, **Border Top Color**, **Border Right Color** and **Border Bottom Color** attributes when the colours differ. The Border Color attribute may thus take up to four values (with meanings the same as described above for border widths). Finally, the direction-sensitive variants **Border Start Color**, **Border Before Color**, **Border End Color** and **Border After Color** may also be used.

The border line can itself take a number of forms. The options are 'none', 'hidden', 'dotted', 'dashed', 'solid', 'double', 'groove', 'ridge', 'inset' and 'outset'. The **Border Style** attribute defines a style to use for the border, and takes up to four values (with placement meanings the same as described above for border widths). To give each side a different style, the **Border Left Style**, **Border Top Style**, **Border Right Style** and **Border Bottom Style** attributes may be used. As before, direction-sensitive variants **Border Start Style**, **Border Before Style**, **Border End Style** and **Border After Style** may also be used:

```
<block border-width="1pt 2pt 1pt 2pt"
       border-style="dashed"
       border-color="red" >
```

The **Border Left**, **Border Right**, **Border Top** and **Border Bottom** attributes simultaneously set the border width, style and colour:

```
<block border-left="1pt dashed red">...</block>
```

Finally, the **Border** attribute can be used to specify a single thickness, style and colour for all sides:

```
<block border="1pt dashed red" >...</block>
```

Padding

When a border line is present, some 'padding' space between the text and the border line is normally desirable. The **Padding** attribute specifies how much space to insert. Different amounts of padding can be added to each side if desired. This attribute can take up to four values (as described for borders widths), or be replaced by the **Padding Left**, **Padding Top**, **Padding Right** and **Padding Bottom** attributes, or by the writing-direction-sensitive variants **Padding Start**, **Padding Before**, **Padding End** and **Padding After**:

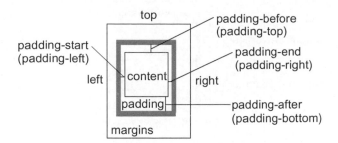

Background

Documents are not always printed or displayed on a white background. It is possible to specify a colour for the background using the **Background Color** attribute. The value '**transparent**' may be used to allow the background colours of enclosing objects to be seen behind the current object, and this is the default value:

```
<block background-color="red">
  <block background-color="transparent">
   ...<!-- RED BACKGROUND -->
  </block>
  <block> <!-- ALSO TRANSPARENT -->
   ...<!-- RED BACKGROUND -->
  </block>
  ...
</block>
```

An image can be displayed behind the text, using the **Background Image** attribute, which uses a URL reference to identify the image file. A colour may be specified as well, using the Background Color attribute, and this colour appears around the image and through any transparent parts of the image. By default, the image appears in the top-left corner of the object that contains it (occupying the padding area, so appears immediately within any border lines) but can be offset horizontally and vertically using the **Background Position Horizontal** and **Background Position Vertical** attributes. Either a fixed distance or a percentage can be given, and the default value is '0%' in both cases. Alternatively, the values 'left', 'center' or 'right' apply in the first case, and 'top', 'center' or 'bottom' in the second case. When displaying electronic documents, the image may '**scroll**' with the document, and this is the default value of the **Background Attachment** attribute, or it may be '**fixed**' so that text scrolls over the image:

```
<block background-image="boat.gif"
       background-position-horizontal="1cm"
       background-position-vertical="3cm"
       background-attachment="fixed">...</block>
```

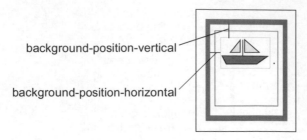

The **Background Position** attribute combines horizontal and vertical settings in a single value.

A small image can be repeated to fill the available area, and by default is repeated both across and down the area. The **Background Repeat** attribute has the default value '**repeat**', but can be given the value '**repeat-x**' to repeat only across the page, '**repeat-y**' to repeat only down the page, and repeat can be switched-off with the value '**no-repeat**':

```
<block background-image="boat.gif"
       background-repeat="repeat-x">...</block>
```

The **Background** attribute combines all of these characteristics:

```
<block background="blue repeat-x">...</block>
```

26. Flow objects

Wherever text may appear within a region defined by the page template, this text may be composed of blocks of paragraphs, lists and tables, and in-line objects such as small images and styled phrases. Text may also be hyphenated and aligned in various ways.

Content

The **Page Sequence** element first contains an optional Title element, which is used to give the page sequence a name that can be referenced by display software, for such purposes as to create a hypertext linked table of contents, or to show as the user browses through the document. It then contains any number of **Static Content** elements followed by a single **Flow** element. For the examples below, it will be assumed that there is a page sequence for each chapter of this book:

```
<root>
  <layout-master-set>
    <simple-page-master master-name="MainContent">
    <!-- TEMPLATE 2 -->
    </simple-page-master>
  </layout-master-set>

  <page-sequence master-reference="MainContent">
    <title>...</title>
    <static-content...>...</static-content>
    <static-content...>...</static-content>
    <flow...>...</flow>
  </page-sequence>
</root>
```

Static content

The **Static Content** elements hold the items that are repeated across a number of pages (such as the text 'The XSL Companion' on every even-numbered page in this book, and the text 'Flow objects' on every odd-numbered page of this chapter). Each element is mapped to a flow name in order to identify which region of the master page selected is to receive the text held in this element. The value of the **Flow Name** attribute must match the value of a Region Name attribute of the region-defining element. When no explicit name is given in the definition element, the appropriate default name can be referenced instead. The default names are the names of the region-defining elements but with an 'xsl-' prefix, such as 'xsl-region-body' and 'xsl-region-before':

```
<root>
  <layout-master-set>
    <simple-page-master master-name="MainContent">
      <region-body ... />  <!-- xsl-region-body -->
      <region-before ... /> <!-- xsl-region-before -->
      <region-after ... /> <!-- xsl-region-after -->
      <region-start ... /> <!-- xsl-region-start -->
      <region-end ... /> <!-- xsl-region-end -->
    </simple-page-master>
  </layout-master-set>

  <page-sequence master-reference="MainContent">
    <static-content flow-name="xsl-region-before">
      <block>
        <xsl:text>Page </xsl:text> <page-number/>
      </block>
    </static-content>
  </page-sequence>
</root>
```

Default mappings are not adequate when wanting to place different text on odd pages to that which must appear on even pages. Two Static Content elements are needed (one for each piece of content) and they must map to different regions:

```
<root>
  <layout-master-set>
    <simple-page-master master-name="OddPage">
      ...
      <region-before region-name="BeforeOdd" />
    </simple-page-master>
    <simple-page-master master-name="EvenPage">
      ...
      <region-before region-name="BeforeEven" />
    </simple-page-master>
    <page-sequence-master master-name="Chapter">
      <repeatable-page-master-alternatives>
        <conditional-page-master-reference
                      odd-or-even="odd"
                      master-reference="OddPage" />
        <conditional-page-master-reference
                      odd-or-even="even"
                      master-reference="EvenPage" />
      </repeatable-page-master-alternatives>
    </page-sequence-master>
  </layout-master-set>
```

```
    <page-sequence master-reference="Chapter">
      <static-content flow-name="BeforeEven">
        <block><page-number/> The XSL Companion</block>
      </static-content>
      <static-content flow-name="BeforeOdd">
        <block>Flow objects <page-number/></block>
      </static-content>
      ...
    </page-sequence>
  </root>
```

The **Role** attribute can be added to any object, and is used to assign a meaningful name to that object. This could be the original element name that contained the text, or a URL reference to an RDF (Resource Description Framework) resource. The formatter may used this information in special cases, such as to provide information for aural rendering of image data.

Flow content

In most cases, the main content of a document will consist of large streams of information that need to be spread across many pages. As the information is formatted, it is said to 'flow' into pages generated from the master page templates. The **Flow** element holds this information. There can be only one Flow element in a Page Sequence element, and its content is usually flowed into the body region of the master template (or templates) referenced from the sequence. This element must appear after any static content definitions. The **Flow Name** attribute references the region into which the content should flow, and this will usually be the body region (by default named 'xsl-region-body'):

```
    <page-sequence master-reference="Chapter">
      <static-content ...>...</static-content>
      <static-content ...>...</static-content>
      <flow flow-name="xsl-region-body">
          <!-- FLOW CONTENT -->
      </flow>
    </page-sequence>
```

Blocks

Both static and flow content consists of one or more blocks of information. A small number of elements represent block-like information items, and these elements can be used in any order and quantity. They are used to create simple text blocks (such as headings and paragraphs), lists and tables. The content of these elements is assigned to block areas that are stacked on top of each other (in the top-to-bottom writing direction).

Text blocks

The **Block** element is used to create paragraphs, titles and other simple text block objects. It can contain text, in-line objects, and even embedded blocks. Some blocks may contain all three:

In the following example, a block contains the title of a book ('The XSL Companion'), which is to be placed in the page header:

```
<page-sequence master-reference="Chapter">
  <static-content flow-name="BeforeEven">
    <block>The XSL Companion</block>
  </static-content>
  ...
</page-sequence>
```

When the body region is split into columns, blocks are normally placed in a single column at the next available position in the flow. The default value of the **Span** attribute is therefore '**none**' (do not span across columns). However, it is possible for a block to span across all columns by setting the value to '**all**'. Spanning occurs even if the block is placed in the final column, as the second example below illustrates (in this case, the XSL processor must then make room for the spanning block in the previous columns, which in turn affects the starting position of this block – perhaps moving it on to the next page, where it would then occupy the first column after all):

The formatting and style of text in a block is specified using attributes. There is a large number to choose from. It is possible to specify borders, padding within the borders, background colours, font characteristics, hyphenation rules, text colour, first-line and last-line indentation, the height of text lines, strategies for dealing with page-breaks within blocks, column spanning (as shown above), text alignment within lines, and writing direction.

Blocks can be separated from each other using the margin attributes as used for page margins (described in the previous chapter):

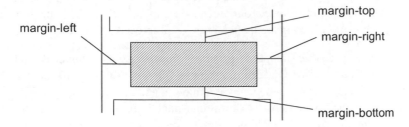

However, margins are quite limited (and are only included for compatibility with CSS), especially when deciding how much space to place between two blocks. For example, a value can be specified for the space needed above each paragraph, but if a paragraph begins a new chapter this space should not appear. Also, a larger space would be specified after a title. While the after-title space could simply be added to the before-paragraph space, this is rarely desired. As the next example demonstrates, typically only the after-title space should be preserved. The 'space-before.*xxx*' and 'space-after.*xxx*' attributes are used for this purpose. Each is given a set value using the **Space Before** and **Space After** attributes (note that Space Start and Space End are for in-line objects only). Spaces for adjacent blocks overlap if neither of the **Space Before Precedence** attributes are set to '**force**' (which ensures the space given is preserved in all circumstances), and by default would have equal precedence levels of '0'. When one has a higher precedence than the other, then the block with the lower precedence loses its space setting in favour of the other. In the following example, the title is given precedence (because the following paragraph has the default precedence level of '0'), so the '12pt' of paragraph space is ignored:

```
<block space-after="16pt"
       space-after.precedence="1">The Title</block>
<block space-before="12pt">A paragraph.</block>
```

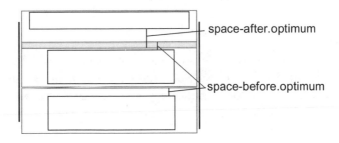

Note that if either element was given a '**force**' precedence, then this space is used in preference to the other, no matter what its precedence value is and regardless of its size. Also, if both spaces have the same precedence value, then the larger space may be chosen (which would be appropriate in the example above, where the title-following space is more significant than the paragraph-preceding space).

Instead of a fixed space size, an optimum value can be set using the **Space Before Optimum** and **Space After Optimum** attributes (the default value for both is '0pt'). It is then appropriate to also include minimum and maximum values. This can be done using the **Space Before Minimum**, **Space Before Maximum**, **Space After Minimum** and **Space After Maximum** attributes (all default to '0pt'). This approach gives the XSL formatter more freedom to juggle what material appears on each page, while not breaking reasonable constraints on the size of gaps between blocks of various types:

```
<block space-before.optimum="14pt"
       space-before.minimum="12pt"
       space-before.maximum="16pt"
       space-after.optimum="5pt"
       space-after.minimum="3pt"
       space-after.maximum="8pt">...</block>
```

The **Space Before Conditionality** and **Space After Conditionality** attributes determine whether the space is preserved ('**retain**') or discarded ('**discard**') (the default) if the block is the first or last in its containing block (or page). If a paragraph has a space-before value, but happens to be the first item in a chapter that begins a new page, then usually the paragraph space will be unwanted:

```
<block space-before.conditionality="discard">...</block>
```

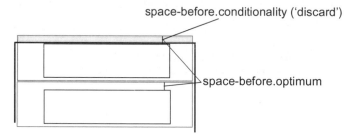

Similarly, blocks are indented within their surrounding areas (enclosing blocks or the whole page area) using the **Start Indent** and **End Indent** attributes (which have default values of '0pt'), or the relevant margin attributes (but not Space Start or Space End, which are used for in-line objects):

```
<block start-indent="5mm"
       end-indent="15mm">...</block>
```

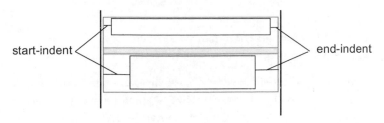

A block may be split into two or more separate blocks by the XSL formatting engine when it does not fit into the containing area (such as the current page):

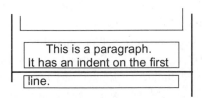

It is possible to prevent this happening by setting the value of the **Page Break Inside** attribute to '**avoid**' breaks in the block (in place of the default value of '**auto**'). A more advanced version of this feature uses the **Keep Together** attribute to specify whether or not the entire block must be kept on one page (or column of the page) by giving it a value of '**always**' (the default value is '**auto**'). Yet more specific variants of this variable can be used to indicate whether or not the block can span columns, but not whole pages. The **Keep Together Within Page** and **Keep Together Within Column** attributes are used:

```
<block keep-together.within-page="always">...</block>
<block keep-together.within-column="always">...</block>
```

Furthermore, it is possible to ensure that the current block is always kept on the same page as the previous block using the **Keep With Previous** property. Given the value '**always**', the **Keep With Previous Within Page** attribute ensures that the two blocks are not separated by a page break, and the **Keep With Previous Within Column** attribute ensures that the two blocks are not separated by a column break.

The **Keep With Next Within Page** and **Keep With Next Within Column** attributes work in the same way to keep the current block with the next one (for example, in this book a heading is always kept with the first following paragraph):

```
<block keep-with-previous.within-page="always">...</block>
<block keep-with-previous.within-column="always">
...
</block>
<block keep-with-next.within-page="always">...</block>
<block keep-with-next.within-column="always">...</block>
```

Another way to do this in the case of page breaks is to use the **Page Break Before** attribute giving it the value '**avoid**'. The value '**always**', on the other hand, ensures that there is always a page break before the block. The value '**left**' ensures that the page the block is placed on is a left-hand page, even if two page breaks are needed to achieve this. Likewise, the value '**right**' can be entered. The default value '**auto**' neither forces nor forbids a page break, but allows one to happen if the formatter wishes. The **Page Break After** attribute works in the same way for breaks after the block. A more advanced version of this capability is provided by the **Break Before** and **Break After** attributes, which take the values '**auto**' (the default), '**column**' (start a new column, and if necessary start the first column of the next page), '**page**' (starts a new page), '**even-page**' (start the next even numbered page, even if this means also creating an intermediate, blank odd-numbered page) and '**odd-page**' (start the next odd-numbered page, even if this means also creating an intermediate even-numbered page).

Even when a block is allowed to span page boundaries, some control can be provided over how much text appears in each part. It is a common convention to avoid the situation of having a single line of text in either part. The second illustration on the previous page shows what typographers call a **widow** line. With this in mind, it should not be surprising that when a single line appears at the end of a page, this is termed an **orphan**. The **Widows** and **Orphans** attributes specify the minimum number of lines that must occur in each of these situations, using the '**widow**' and '**orphan**' values. The default value is '2' in both cases, indicating that there must be at least two lines at each location (a paragraph with three lines or less is not broken over pages). This value can be raised, or lowered to '1'. Lowering the value gives the XSL formatting engine more freedom to balance the objects on the page.

Block container

Blocks may be grouped within a container that specifies settings for all the enclosed blocks. The **Block Container** element performs this role. This element is usually used to define settings shared by a number of consecutive blocks. Typical changes made at this level include border and margin widths, background colours and the orientation of text. The container can even have a fixed height or width, and be forced to override natural page breaks:

```
<flow flow-name="xsl-region-body">
  <block-container margin-left="2cm" >
    <block>Related to next block</block>
    <block>Related to previous block</block>
  </block-container>
</flow>
```

This element may use the Overflow attribute to control how overflowing text is to be handled when the container is given a specific width or height.

Lists

Lists are more complex structures than simple title, headers and paragraphs. They are composed of a number of items, each divided into prefix and content portions. The **List Block** element contains one or more **List Item** block elements:

```
<flow flow-name="xsl-region-body">
  <list-block>
    <list-item>...</list-item>
    <list-item>...</list-item>
    <list-item>...</list-item>
  </list-block>
</flow>
```

Each item is split into label and body parts using the **List Item Label** and **List Item Body** elements. Both must be present in every item, in the order shown below:

```
<list-item>
  <list-item-label><block>A)</block></list-item-label>
  <list-item-body>
    <block>first item, labelled A)</block>
  </list-item-body>
</list-item>
```

These two parts occupy adjacent areas on the page. The width of each part can be specified directly, using indentation attributes, but there will usually be ideal widths for each. This is specified on the List Block element using two attributes. The **Provisional Label Separation** attribute specifies the ideal gap between the item label and the item content (default '6pt'), and the **Provisional Distance Between Starts** attribute specifies the ideal spacing beween the start of the label and the start of the content (default '24pt'):

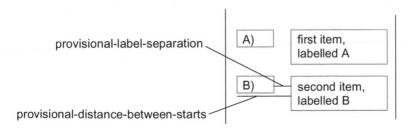

But the label is usually indented from the left edge and the body is often indented from the right edge, and both areas are actually given horizontal space by providing values using the **Start Indent** and **End Indent** attributes. However, while the user can easily decide where to start the label and where to end the body, the other two settings need to take account of the desired distances described above. Fortunately, the indents affected can be given values that are calculated by the XSL formatter and returned by the **label-end**() and **body-start**() functions. For example:

```
<list-block provisional-distance-between-starts="20mm"
            provisional-label-separation="5mm" ...>
  <list-item>
    <list-item-label start-indent="5mm"
                      end-indent="label-end()">
      ...
    </list-item-label>
    <list-item-body start-indent="body-start()"
                     end-indent="5mm">
      ...
    </list-item-body>
  </list-item>
</list-block>
```

It is also possible to indent the label from the left edge, and the body from the right edge, using other indentation attributes. (Note that the labels are indented in the illustration on the previous page.)

Tables

Tables are constructed from grids of areas, arranged primarily into rows, and then into columns within the rows, thus creating individual cells. A table is identified using the **Table** element. However, the **Table And Caption** element may be used as a simple wrapper for the main Table element, which is then preceded by a **Table Caption** element. By default the caption is placed '**before**' the table but, using the **Caption Side** attribute, it can be placed '**after**' or at one side ('**start**' or '**end**') or at any edge ('**top**', '**bottom**', '**left**' or '**right**'):

```
<table>...</table>

<table-and-caption>
  <table-caption caption-side="after">
    <block>The Table</block>
  </table-caption>
  <table>...</table>
</table-and-caption>
```

The grid is composed of cells within rows within body, header and footer blocks using the **Table Header**, **Table Body**, **Table Footer**, **Table Row** and **Table Cell** elements:

```
<table>
  <table-header>...</table-header>
  <table-footer>...</table-footer>
  <table-body>...</table-body>
</table>


  <table-body>
    <table-row>...</table-row>
    <table-row>...</table-row>
  </table-body>


  <table-row>
    <table-cell>...</table-cell>
    <table-cell>...</table-cell>
    <table-cell>...</table-cell>
  </table-row>
```

An individual cell can be made to occupy space that would otherwise be occupied by adjacent cells. A cell can stretch across into cells further along the row, or down into cells below it. It can also do both simultaneously. The **Number Rows Spanned** attribute specifies the number of rows encompassed and has a default value of '1' (no horizontal spanning). Likewise, the **Number Columns Spanned** attribute specifies the number of columns spanned and has a default value of '1' (no vertical spanning).

The Table Row element is optional. When cells are not embedded in row elements, some of the Table Cell elements need to use **Starts Row** and **Ends Row** attributes in order to identify the start and end of each row. The value '**true**' overrides the default value of '**false**' in both cases:

```
<table-body>
  <table-cell starts-row="yes">
    <block>1,1</block>
  </table-cell>
  <table-cell ends-row="yes">
    <block>1,2</block>
  </table-cell>
  <table-cell starts-row="yes">
    <block>2,1</block>
  </table-cell>
  <table-cell ends-row="yes">
    <block>2,2</block>
  </table-cell>
</table-body>
```

1,1	1,2
2,1	2,2

The Table Row element includes the **Height** attribute, and the means to control page breaks before and after the row using the **Keep Together** attribute:

```
<table>

  <table-header>
    <table-row height="24pt">
      <table-cell number-columns-spanned="2">
        <block>Headings</block>
      </table-cell>
    </table-row>
    <table-row height="24pt">
      <table-cell><block>Head 1</block></table-cell>
      <table-cell><block>Head 2</block></table-cell>
    </table-row>
  </table-header>

  <table-body>
    <table-row height="16pt">
      <table-cell><block>cell 1</block></table-cell>
      <table-cell number-rows-spanned="2"
                  keep-together="always">
        <block>span down</block>
      </table-cell>
    </table-row>
    <table-row height="16pt">
      <table-cell><block>cell 2</block></table-cell>
    </table-row>
  </table-body>
</table>
```

Often, table header rows are repeated at the top of each column or page that the table spans. This happens by default, but the **Table Omit Header At Break** attribute can be set to '**true**' to suppress this feature (default '**false**'). The heading is suppressed at the top of the second page in the example above. Likewise, footer sections can be placed at the bottom of each page, or omitted, using the **Table Omit Footer At Break** attribute.

Borders and padding can be applied at all levels in the table structure. A border is drawn around an empty cell if the **Empty Cells** attribute is set to the default '**show**' value; but if it is set to '**hide**' then these borders are not drawn. Separate borders can be drawn around each cell, or the borders of adjacent cells can be shared (as in the diagram above). The **Border Collapse** attribute has a default value of '**collapse**', but this can be changed to '**separate**' (or '**collapse-with-precedence**'). When borders for each cell are separate, the space between adjacent border lines is governed by the **Border Separation** attribute, when the vertical and horizontal spacing is the same, or by the **Border Separation Block Progression Direction** attribute and the **Border Separation Inline Progression Direction** attribute when they differ (both default to '0pt'). The **Border Spacing** attribute can be used instead, which takes two space-separated values for horizontal then vertical settings:

```
<table empty-cells="hide" border-collapse="separate"
   border-separation.block-progression-direction="2pt"
   border-separation.inline-progression-direction="3pt" >
...</table>
```

Another complication with borders is that all components of a table can have them, and in some cases there is a possible conflict. For example, the left edge of a bordered row may occupy the same space as the left edge of the first cell in that row, and when one of these items has a border specified, but the other does not, it is not immediately obvious whether to draw the border line or not. This conflict is resolved by specifying a precedence level. The object with the higher precedence wins the argument. The **Border After Precedence**, **Border Before Precedence**, **Border End Precedence** and **Border Start Precedence** attributes are used to make the precedence of a specific object explicit. The value '**force**' can be used to set the highest possible value to an object. By default, the whole table has the highest precedence level value of '6' (a line around the table will not be broken by different settings on rows, columns or cells). An individual cell is next, with a value of '5'. Below this comes the table columns ('4'), then the table rows ('3'), the whole table body ('2'), the whole table header ('1') and finally the whole table footer area ('0'):

The **Table Column** element is used to define, in advance, shared properties for cells in the same column of the table. For example, if all the cells in a column are right justified, it is time consuming to set this alignment value on every cell. But perhaps the most significant use of this element is to set the width of each column, using the **Column Width** attribute, either as a fixed length or as a percentage of the table width. The **Column Number** attribute identifies the column to apply the formatting settings to. It can be omitted for the first instance of this element, if it specifies formatting characteristics for the first column of the table. It can also be omitted for any instance that assigns formats to the next column in the sequence:

```
<table>
  <table-column column-number="1" column-width="3cm" />
  <table-column column-number="2" column-width="2cm" />
  <table-column column-width="1cm" /><!-- COLUMN 3 -->

  <table-header>
    ...
  </table-header>
  <table-body>
    ...
  </table-body>
</table>
```

Individual cells refer to the settings in the Column element using the **from-table-column**() function. Therefore, not every cell in a column needs to adopt these settings (and for this reason, it is a good idea to include the Number Columns Spanned attribute in the Column element when most of the cells in the column span):

```
<table>
  ...
  <table-column
          column-number="2" text-align="right" />
  ...
  <table-body>
    <table-row>
      <table-cell>...</table-cell>
      <table-cell
        text-align="from-table-column(text-align)">
        ...
      </table-cell>
    </table-row>
  </table-body>
</table>
```

In tables with many columns, there may be occasions when a series of columns have the same settings. Instead of simply repeating the Table Column element for each one, a single Table Column element may be used. The number of columns affected by the settings in this single element is given in the **Number Columns Repeated** attribute (the default value of '1' indicates a single column, so there is no repetition).

It is not necessary to specify column widths if the table is formatted automatically to fit the available space. This is the default '**auto**' mode as specified in the **Table Layout** attribute, which can also take the value '**fixed**'.

Lines

When text is flowed into a block, it may occupy more than one line in that block. Blocks may therefore contain line areas that are adjacent to each other in the line-progression direction (vertically, working down the block in English documents).

The number of line areas needed depends on how much text can be placed on each line. This will depend on the font chosen and the size chosen to display characters in this font (such as 9pt Times Roman, or 12pt Helvetica). A major task of the XSL formatting engine is deciding how to arrange text over multiple lines (as well as how much material to place on each page). There is no element to represent a single line because the document author would not know how much text to place in each one:

```
<block>This is a paragraph. It may be spread over a number
of lines.</block>
```

By default, line areas are simply stacked on top of each other (in English documents), with each line set to be the height of the font size chosen (or slightly greater). The **Line Height** attribute can be used to override the default value of '**normal**', with a specific point size or other value.

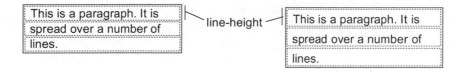

First line style

The first line of text can be given a different style to the remaining text using the **Initial Property Set** element. Again, this element cannot surround the text it affects because the document author will not know how much text to include. It is therefore an empty element that must appear as the first item in a block:

```
<block font-size="12pt">
<initial-property-set font-size="14pt"
                      font-weight="bold" />This is a
paragraph. It is spread over a number of lines.</block>
```

```
This is a paragraph.           ⟩  initial-property-set
It is spread over a number
of lines.
```

It is common practice to begin a new paragaph with an indent. The **Text Indent** attribute is used to indent the first line of text in a block, and the **Last Line End Indent** attribute similarly indents the last line of text, though a negative value is typically used here to create an 'outdent' for such items as page numbers in content lists:

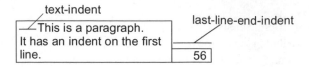

Text alignment

Text occupying a number of lines may be vertically aligned on one side or on both sides. The **Text Align** attribute takes the values '**start**' (or '**left**' in left-to-right mode), '**end**' (or '**right**' in left-to-right mode), '**center**' or '**justify**' (align to both edges). The default value is 'start':

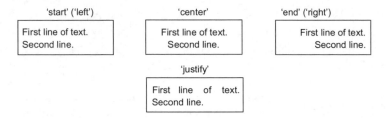

The **Text Align Last** attribute deals with the last line of text. Possible values are as described above for general text alignment, but an additional default option of '**relative**' operates as shown in the examples above (with '**start**' being the default value for the last line of justified text). Note that the last line of justified text is often aligned only on one side because it is too short to pad with spaces without looking ridiculous.

Both of these attributes can also take values of '**inside**' and '**outside**', which align text left or right depending on which edge of the page is being bound within a physical document. Typically, a left-hand, even-numbered page is bound at its right edge, so has an 'inside' right edge and an 'outside' left edge; while a right-hand, odd-numbered page is bound at its left edge, so has an 'inside' left edge and an 'outside' right edge.

Hyphenation

More care is usually taken over splitting words across lines on paper than on screen, and hyphenation is a common way of balancing the need to put as many words on each line as possible, while not reducing the space between words to such a degree that it is not possible to read the text. Moving a long word down to the next line because it will not fit on the current line leaves behind a large space which looks particularly bad when the lines are justified (even though this space is then divided into smaller gaps that are added to the inter-word spaces). The **Hyphenate** attribute defaults to '**false**', but can be set to '**true**' so enabling the splitting of words across lines.

The character to be inserted by the formatter at the end of the line when hyphenating words can be specified using the **Hyphenation Character** attribute. Normally, the Unicode hyphen character, value '2010' in that character set, is specified (which may look slightly different to a normal keyboard-generated dash character '-').

Many typesetting systems and DTP packages have access to a hyphenation dictionary showing acceptable break points in each word. When such a dictionary is not available, the system must follow some simple rules instead. One criterion that could be used involves placing a minimum number of characters on each side of the break. The **Hyphenation Push Character Count** attribute specifies the minimum number of characters that need to be pushed onto the next line, and the **Hyphenation Remain Character Count** attribute specifies the minimum number of characters to be retained on the original line. Typically, these values would both be set to '2' (words shorter than four letters are then never split across lines):

```
<block hyphenate="true"
       hyphenation-character="-"
       hyphenation-push-character-count="2"
       hyphenation-remain-character-count="2">...</block>
```

The **Hyphenation Keep** attribute can be used to prevent the use of hyphens in words at the end of any line at the end of a column or a page. If set to '**column**', a hyphen is not allowed at the end of a column. If set to '**page**', a hyphen is not allowed at the end of a page. The default value '**auto**' implies no restrictions.

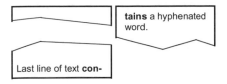

Text can be difficult to read if a number of consecutive lines have hyphenated words. By default, the **Hyphenation Ladder Count** attribute allows any number of consecutive hyphens, using the default value '**no-limit**', but this can be changed to a number indicating the maximum number of hyphenated lines:

```
┌─────────────────────┐
│ First lines of text con-│
│ tain some  hyphen-  │
│ ation, as these fur-│
│ ther lines show.    │
└─────────────────────┘
```

The use of hyphens, and the general rules for deciding where to sensibly place a hyphen when splitting a word, depends on the script and language in use and possibly the country of the readership. The **Script** attribute can hold the default value '**auto**' (the script is determined by comparing the characters against ranges in the Unicode character set), or the value '**none**', or the name of a script (as defined in ISO 15924). The **Language** attribute has a default value of '**none**' (the language is not known, or is not significant), or the name of a language (as defined in RFC 3066). Finally, the **Country** attribute has a default value of '**none**' but can be set to a country code (also defined in RFC 3066).

In-line objects

It is often not sufficient simply to break a block down into lines. Sometimes, a word or phrase within a line needs to be formatted in a different manner (such as the bold terms below), or a picture or page number (both current and referenced pages) needs to be inserted into the text at a specific point. These are all examples of **in-line** objects. An in-line object may apply styles to a range of text within a line, or one starting on one line and ending on another (such objects are ignorant of line breaks). In-line objects are also used to format individual characters, and to insert leader dots ('....'), commonly used in indexes.

In-line areas are stacked within a line area in the in-line progression direction. For English documents this is left to right. When a formatted in-line element spans lines, additional in-line areas are created (one for each line occupied):

```
inline-progression direction
    ──────────▶
┌─────────────────────────┐
│    This is a paragraph.  │      ...<emph>first line</emph>...
│ It has an indent on the first│
│ line.                    │
└─────────────────────────┘
```

The **Space Start** and **Space End** attributes are used on in-line objects to separate them from surrounding objects (recall that Space Above and Space After are used on block-level elements):

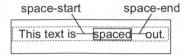

The length may be specified as a percentage rather than a fixed value, in which case the percentage given relates to the width of the block containing the line. It is also possible to set optimum, minimum and maximum widths, using the **Space Start Optimum**, **Space End Optimum**, **Space Start Minimum**, **Space End Minimum**, **Space Start Maximum** and **Space End Maximum** attributes. These attributes work in the same way and have the same default values as the block-level equivalents discussed earlier. The **Space Start Precedence**, **Space End Precedence**, **Space Start Conditionality** and **Space End Conditionality** attributes also work in the same way.

The **Keep Together Within Line** attribute can be used to prevent line-wrapping of the contents by changing the default value of '**auto**' to '**always**':

```
<block>The following text
<inline keep-together.within-line="always">must be kept
together</inline> at all times.</block>
```

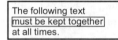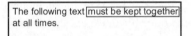

In-line text

The **Inline** element is the in-line equivalent to the Block element; a general purpose container for a consecutive range of characters that need to share some formatting characteristic such as border, padding and background settings, or a change of font, font style or size. All the characteristics shown below can be used in the Block element to set default styles for the entire block. The Inline element then acts as an override for the specific range of text it encloses. For example, the text it contains can be emphasized:

```
<block>A <inline font-weight="bold">bold</inline> word.
</block>
```

A **bold** word.

The baseline can be shifted up or down, the line height altered, and characters within the element can be forced to stay together within a single line (overriding any line breaks that the formatter would otherwise apply). The text can even be made invisible.

Basic character appearance can be specified. This includes the font family (such as '**sans-serif**' or 'Arial'), the font size (such as '12pt'), the style ('**normal**', '**back-slash**', '**oblique**' or '**italic**'), the weight ('**normal**', '**bold**', '**bolder**' or '**lighter**'; or '100', '200', '300', '400', '500', '600', '700', '800' or '900'), stretch ('**normal**', '**wider**', '**narrower**' and others), and variant ('**normal**' or '**small-caps**'). The **Font Family**, **Font Size**, **Font Size Adjust**, **Font Style**, **Font Variant** and **Font Weight** attributes perform these functions. The default font size is 'medium', the adjust value 'none', and the style, variant and weight are all 'normal':

```
Some <inline font-family="Helvetica"
             font-size="12pt"
             font-size-adjust="none"
             font-style="italic"
             font-variant="small-caps"
             font-weight="bold" >Very Special
</inline>formatting.
```

Some *VERY SPECIAL* formatting.

The **Font Stretch** attribute allows characters to be stretched horizontally. The default value is '**normal**' but it can be changed to '**narrower**' or '**wider**' (and a number of other subtle variations).

The single **Font** attribute can replace many of the attributes shown above providing the style, variant, weight, size, line height and name. The following example is equivalent to the one above, except that the line height is also given ('14pt') and the stretch value is missing (because it cannot be provided in this form):

```
Some
<inline font="italic small-caps bold 12pt/14pt Helvetica">
Very Special</inline>formatting.
```

Note that, despite appearances, the font-handling attributes above do not actually specify a font to be used. An XSL formatter uses this information to help decide which font to use, and the final factor in the decision may be the actual character that is about to be rendered. Occasionally, the formatter may have a choice of fonts that it can use and at this point a strategy is needed to decide which is most suitable. The most obvious decision would be to choose the best font. But another major factor in this decision could be whether or not the same font can be used for other characters in the sequence because font switching may be detrimental to the general quality of the text. Therefore, it is possible to state whether the selection must be made on a '**character-by-character**' basis, or possibly take into account the wider context in which case the '**auto**' value (the default) should be assigned to the **Font Selection Strategy** attribute.

The **Text Decoration** attribute can be used to place a line under the text (an '**underline**') but can also be used to place the line elsewhere (taking the value '**overline**' or '**line-through**') but has a default value of '**none**'. The **Score Spaces** attribute is used to decide whether or not to draw the line where spaces appear, taking the value '**true**' (the default) or '**false**':

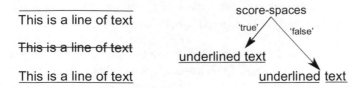

The **Vertical Align** attribute moves text up or down and takes the values '**base-line**' (the default), '**middle**', '**sub**' (subscript), '**super**' (superscript), and a number of other subtle variations. The **Letter Spacing** attribute can take a value of '**normal**', or any specific length of whitespace to insert between characters. The **Word Spacing** attribute does the same for the spaces between words (but is ignored when the line is justified because spaces are then adjusted to make the right-hand edge of the last word reach the border of the content area). The **Text Transform** attribute is used to transform letters to all upper-case ('**uppercase**') or all lower-case ('**lowercase**'), or to convert the first letter in each word to upper-case and the rest to lower-case ('**capitalize**'). The **Text Shadow** attribute enables shadows to appear around individual characters. It has a default value of 'none', but may take a multiple parameter value giving the horizontal then vertical length of the shadow, the blur angle and then the colour:

```
Some <inline text-decoration="underline"
             vertical-align="super"
             letter-spacing="1pt"
             word-spacing="9pt"
             text-transform="lowercase"
             text-shadow="normal">Very Special</inline>
formatting.
```

some <u>very special</u> formatting.

Note that the Text Transform attribute is not generally recommended because it does not apply to many languages. However, it can safely be used in languages such as English.

The **Color** attribute assigns a colour to the text (see Chapter 27 for details on the colours allowed). This attribute can be added to any element, and it would typically be used in the Block element or the Page Sequence element to set the default colour. For example:

```
<block color="red">DANGER: This is dangerous.</block>
```

In-line containers

The **Inline Container** element is the in-line equivalent to the Block Container element, but in this case it is a container for a consecutive range of in-line objects that need to refer to an in-line reference area. It can be usefully employed to change the direction of writing, using the **Writing Mode** attribute.

This element may use the **Overflow** attribute to control how overflowing text is to be handled when the container is given a specific width that is too small, and to change the reference orientation (using the **Reference Orientation** attribute). The **Clip** and **Display Align** attributes are also relevant.

Characters

The **Character** element represents a single character that requires special formatting to be applied to it. The XSL processor treats all normal characters as if they were represented by the Character element, with the **Character** attribute set to the actual character. The two examples below are therefore equivalent:

```
<block>abc</block>

<block><character character="a"/>
<character character="b"/>
<character character="c"/></block>
```

This element is relevant when special formatting is required (though the Inline, Inline Container or Wrapper elements can also be used in many circumstances). The **Vertical Align** attribute can be used to create superscript and subscript characters:

```
H<character character="2" vertical-align="sub"/>O is
water.
```

> H_2O is water.

The **Treat As Word Space** attribute specifies whether or not the character is considered to be a space between words. When the default value 'auto' is applied, the normal space character and the non-breaking space character are considered to be word separators, and so have an implied value of '**true**', and all other characters have an implied value of '**false**' (including fixed space characters). But it is possible to explicitly apply one of these values to any character.

Text characters can be rotated using the **Glyph Orientation Horizontal** attribute, which takes a degree value, with '90' indicating a rotation of 90 degrees clockwise (and '-90' indicating an anticlockwise rotation):

```
<block>ABC<character glyph-orientation-horizontal="90"
```

```
character="D">EFG</block>
```

The **Glyph Orientation Vertical** attribute works in the same way for vertically written text.

External graphics

The **External Graphic** element represents graphic data stored in a binary data file elsewhere. The graphic data is inserted at the location of this element. The **Src** attribute identifies the file to insert:

```
<block>Here is a picture of a boat:
<external-graphic src="boat.gif"/>.</block>
```

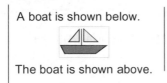

While this element is described as an in-line element, the image can be separated from surrounding text simply by placing it in a dedicated block element:

```
<block>A boat is shown below.</block>
<block text-align="center">
<external-graphic href="boat.gif"/>
</block>
<block>The boat is shown above.</block>
```

A boat is shown below.

The boat is shown above.

The **Height** and **Width** attributes define a fixed area into which the graphic must be placed:

```
<external-graphic href="boat.gif" width="5cm"
                                  height="7cm" />
```

Because the image may not be this precise size, it may need to be scaled to fit. If the **Scaling** attribute has the value '**non-uniform**', the image is scaled in both directions to fit the given region. This means that the image may appear stretched in one direction or the other. As an alternative, the default value '**uniform**' may be used, which maintains the aspect ratio (and so avoids distorting the image) by scaling both dimensions equally until one dimension of the image reaches the given limit:

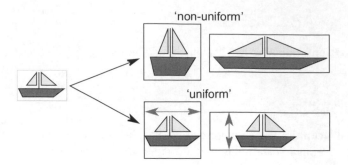

Alternatively, the scale can be given as a numeric value, such as '0.5' (reduce to half) and '2' (double in size). If two values are given, the first indicates the horizontal scaling and the second indicates the vertical. The values '1.5 3' increase the size of the image by half horizontally, and by three times vertically. The default value for this attribute is simply '1.0', meaning that no scaling is to be performed in either direction.

The **Scaling Method** attribute specifies how to handle bitmapped images that are being scaled, and takes the values '**auto**' (the default, which allows the formatter to decide the best way of handling the image), '**integer-pixels**' (which maintains image quality by treating every source pixel as of equal worth by mapping them all to the same number of new pixels, even at the cost of not sizing the image to the exact boundaries given), or '**resample-any-method**' (which ensures that the image is scaled to the precise size desired, at the possible cost of distortion due to resampling and treating some source pixels as more important than others).

The **Minimum Width**, **Maximum Width**, **Minimum Height** and **Maximum Height** attributes can be used to specify limits to the size of the image. The box is sized to fit the image (or the image scaled as described above) provided that it lies within these limits:

```
<external-graphic href="boat.gif" min-width="3cm"
                                  max-width="7cm"
                                  min-height="5cm"
                                  max-height="6cm" />
```

The **Instream Foreign Object** element represents graphic data that is part of the XML document (using a different namespace). It can also be used for other embedded data. One popular use is expected to be to embed SVG (Standard Vector Graphics) fragments.

External graphics and internal objects conform to a data format (such as SVG or GIF) that can be identified using a mime type or a namespace. The **Content Type** attribute has a default value of '**auto**' but this can be changed to the relevant mime type of namespace. This can be useful if there is any doubt that the formatter can accurately determine the data format in some other way.

Leaders

It is common practice to put a row of dots between an item and its page number in the index of a book. This is done to ensure that the correct page number is seen when glancing across the page (though this book does not use this convention because the two-column approach used reduces the space between the item and the page number sufficiently to minimize the possibility of error). The **Leader** element is used to insert a given character, repeating it as many times as necessary, to fill the gap.

The **Leader Pattern** attribute dictates the content of the leader area: the '**space**' option is the default and implies no visible leader marks. The '**rule**' option draws a simple line. The '**dots**' option inserts dots (which is common in indexes); the '**use-content**' option indicates that the text content of this element is to be used and repeated as many times as necessary to fill the space:

```
<leader leader-pattern="dots" />
```

```
XSL ............................. 92
XSLT ........................... 155
```

```
<leader leader-pattern="use-content" >x</leader>
```

```
XSL xxxxxxxxxxxxxx  192
```

Every leader occupies horizontal space. The **Leader Length** attribute holds a width value. However, as the first example above demonstrates, leaders are often used to justify the entire line. In this example, the leader dots repeat enough times to ensure that the page numbers are right-justified. The Leader element can therefore be given minimum and maximum widths, as well as an optimum width, using the **Leader Length Optimum**, **Leader Length Minimum** and **Leader Length Maximum** attributes:

```
<leader... leader-length.optimum="5cm"
           leader-length.minimum="4cm"
           leader-length.maximum="7cm" />
```

When the Leader Pattern attribute has a value of 'dot' (or 'use-content'), by default the dots or other characters are spaced as they would normally be in text ('.........'). But it is possible to widen the spacing using the **Leader Pattern Width** attribute, giving it a value such as '1mm' ('. . . . . . .'), or the default value of '**use-font-metrics**' (use the width of the leader pattern, as specified by the font).

Finally, when the Leader Pattern attribute has the value '**rule**', the rule style can be specified using the **Rule Style** (defaulting to '**solid**') and **Rule Thickness** (defaulting to '1.0pt') attributes:

```
<leader leader-pattern="rule"
        rule-style="double"
        rule-thickness="2pt" />
```

The **Leader Alignment** attribute takes the value '**none**' (the default), '**page**' or '**reference-area**'. The last two values are used to vertically align leaders that have the same settings so that they look better on the page:

```
item one   .  .  .  .  .  .  . 56
item 2   .  .  .  .  .  .  . . 97
item three  .  .  .  .  .  . 103
```

Page numbers

Page numbers are used to give a unique label to each page, and to reference another page from the current page. But actual page numbers cannot be known until the formatter has paginated the source text. Instead, the position where the current page number must appear can be specified using the **Page Number** element:

```
This text is on page <page-number font-weight="bold" />.
```

This text is on page **300**.

Typically, this element is used in a static flow area, such as a header section (as at the top of this page).

The **Page Number Citation** element is used to reference an object that is (or may be) placed on another page. It is replaced by the page number of the page that contains that object. The **Reference Identifier** attribute provides the unique identifier of the object in question. Note that most objects can have **Id** attributes to facilitate the use of this feature:

```
Please refer to the summary on page
<page-number-citation ref-id="sum" font-weight="bold" />.

<block id="sum">To summarize, ...</block>
```

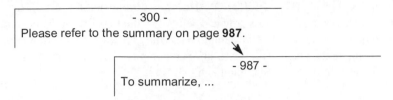

This element is particularly useful for creating content lists and indexes.

Hypertext links

Electronic documents are able to contain 'hot text' that acts as a link to other items in the same document, or to items in another document. Web browsers commonly highlight such 'hypertext' links using underlined, coloured styles. The **Basic Link** element is used to create such a link:

```
See <basic-link...>Chapter 9</basic-link> for details.
```

See **<u>Chapter 9</u>** for details.

The link must be either internal (to an object in the same document), or external (to an object in another document), using the **Internal Destination** attribute or the **External Destination** attribute respectively.

An internal destination is identified by the Id attribute on the other object:

```
See <basic-link internal-destination="CH9">Chapter 9</ba-
sic-link> for details.

<block id="CH9">Chapter 9</block>
```

An external destination is identified by its URL:

```
See <basic-link external-destination="ch9.xml">Chapter 9</
basic-link> for details.
```

ch9.xml

The **Show Destination** attribute specifies how the link is to be followed. The value '**replace**' indicates that the source text should be replaced by the destination text, by scrolling when the destination is in the same document and by document replacement when it is not. The value '**new**' indicates that a new window should be opened for the destination text, leaving the source still visible.

When the destination text is presented it may need to be highlighted, possibly by colouring the background. The **Indicate Destination** attribute has a value of '**true**' or '**false**' (the default). Also, most browsers will show the first line of the destination text at the top of the window by default, but it may be desirable to show some of the preceding text as well. The **Destination Placement Offset** attribute can be given a size value to do this (the default is '0pt').

The **Target Presentation Context** attribute can be used to specify by URL a fragment of the resource that is of interest. This information might be used to call-in only this fragment. This approach only works for data types such as XML and HTML, and only when the External Destination attribute is used (it is not appropriate for internally stored data). The default value is '**use-target-processing-context**'. The **Target Processing Context** attribute is used to identify a new root element in an XML or XHTML document. Only this fragment is of interest, so the rest can be ignored and not styled. It has a default value of '**document-root**'. A stylesheet needed to render the external resource can also be specified directly, by using a URL in the **Target Stylesheet** attribute, which has a default value of '**use-normal-stylesheet**'.

Wrappers

Sometimes, it is useful to be able to specify a style to be applied to a sequence of characters without creating an enclosing area. Although the **Inline** element can be used to specify character styles (which the characters inherit), it creates an in-line object as well. The styles specified in an Inline element are actually applied to the in-line object, and then inherited by embedded Character elements (which are implied when characters are entered directly). The Inline element is necessary when the intent is to add a border round the text, because the border is actually placed around the in-line object created by this instruction. But when the intent is only to apply individual styles to each of the embedded characters, the **Wrapper** element is preferable. This element does not create an object on the page but is used simply as a convenient 'wrapper' with inheritable properties:

```
<block>A <wrapper font-weight="bold">bold</wrapper>
word.</block>
```

This element can also be employed around block elements:

```
<wrapper margin-left="2cm">
  <block>...</block>
  <block>...</block>
  <block>...</block>
</wrapper>
```

Whitespace and line feeds

Most characters are simply rendered by formatting engines, but whitespace characters, including spaces, tabs and line-feed characters can be treated in different
ways. A number of attributes are available to control how they are handled.

Whitespace collapse

Consecutive whitespace characters may be due to the formatting of the source
XML document rather than any intended document content. The popular Web
browsers reduce sequences of whitespace down to a single space character, but
allow this behaviour to be overridden in special cases (such as in the PRE (preformatted) element in an HTML document). By default, XSLT normalizes
whitespace in this way but the **Whitespace Collapse** attribute may take the value
'**false**' (instead of '**true**') to prevent this action:

```
<block white-space-collapse="false">This    text    is
widely         spaced.</block>
```

This   text   is widely   spaced.

```
<block white-space-collapse="true">This    text    is
widely         spaced.</block>
```

This text is widely spaced.

Space and line-feed treatment

The **White Space Treatment** attribute can be used to remove all whitespace characters, other than line-feed characters (which are described below). This attribute
therefore affects the space character and the tab character. When its value is set to
'**preserve**', all whitespace is retained (though non-space characters, such as the tab
character, are converted to space characters). It can also be set to '**ignore**', in order
to remove all whitespace characters, or to '**ignore-if-before-linefeed**' (only discard the whitespace character if it immediately precedes a line-feed character), or
to '**ignore-if-after-linefeed**' (only discard the whitespace character if it immediately follows a line-feed character):

```
<block white-space-treatment="ignore">This text contains
spaces and    tabs.</block>
```

Thistextcontainsspacesandtabs.

However, the default value is '**ignore-if-surrounding-linefeed**', which removes
all whitespace characters immediately surrounding a line-feed character:

```
<block>
This text
   contains
spaces and tabs.</block>
```

>   This text contains spaces and tabs.

Similarly, the **Linefeed Treatment** attribute is used to '**preserve**' or '**ignore**' line-feed characters, but adds the default '**treat-as-space**' option. The 'preserve' option instructs the formatter to treat line-feeds as line-ending instructions (to place the next character on the following line). The 'treat-as-space' option treats the line-feed as a normal space character:

```
<block linefeed-treatment="ignore">Line one.
Line two.
Line three.</block>
```

>   Line one.Line two.Line three.

```
<block linefeed-treatment="preserve">Line one.
Line two.
Line three.</block>
```

>   Line one.
>   Line two.
>   Line three.

```
<block linefeed-treatment="treat-as-space">Line one.
Line two.
Line three.</block>
```

>   Line one. Line two. Line three.

The 'treat-as-space' option is the default because it is used to format normal text in documents or books. The 'preserve' option is reserved for special cases, such as lines of poetry or lines of computer code that happen to be not held in separate elements in the source document:

```
<block linefeed-treatment="preserve">
10 PRINT "Hello world."
20 GOTO 10
</block>
```

Wrap options

Normally, the formatter will wrap text onto the following line when the right edge of the content area is reached. The **Wrap Option** attribute has a default option of '**wrap**', but changing this to '**no-wrap**' overrides this behaviour. This means that the text may occupy space outside the content area. When this happens, the appearance of this text is governed by the value of the **Overflow** attribute (where it may be '**visible**' or '**hidden**', or in electronic documents it may be possible to '**scroll**' in order to see it). It may also hold the value '**error-if-overflow**', which the formatter should treat in the same way as 'hidden', while also raising an error. The default value is '**auto**' (undefined behaviour, but probably creating a scrolling area):

Whitespace short-cut

XSL has inherited the **White Space** attribute from the CSS property of the same name. XSL treats this attribute as a short-cut for setting a number of the properties described above to achieve a commonly required effect. This attribute has three possible values: '**normal**' (the default), '**pre**' and '**nowrap**'. Note that in all three cases the equivalent White Space Treatment attribute value is 'preserve'. Therefore, none of the options remove all spaces from the text (although some remove extraneous spaces).

A '**normal**' item has line-feed characters treated as spaces, whitespace normalized to single spaces, and text wrapped onto following lines by the formatter. This is the default behaviour. The two examples below are equivalent:

```
<block white-space="normal">...</block>

<block linefeed-treatment="treat-as-space"
       white-space-collapse="true"
       white-space-treatment="preserve"
       wrap-option="wrap" >...</block>
```

A '**pre**' (preformatted) item has line-feed characters preserved and whitespace preserved, but text is *not* wrapped onto following lines by the formatter. The two examples below are therefore equivalent:

```
<block white-space="pre">...</block>

<block linefeed-treatment="preserve"
       white-space-collapse="false"
       white-space-treatment="preserve"
       wrap-option="no-wrap" >...</block>
```

A '**nowrap**' item has line-feed characters treated as spaces and whitespace normalized to single spaces, as for the 'normal' option, but text is *not* wrapped onto following lines by the formatter. The two examples below are therefore equivalent:

```
<block white-space="nowrap">...</block>

<block linefeed-treatment="treat-as-space"
       white-space-collapse="true"
       white-space-treatment="preserve"
       wrap-option="no-wrap" >...</block>
```

27. Advanced XSL features

There are a number of miscellaneous features of the XSL language that are either irrelevant to its primary task of producing print-ready document formatting, or provide object positioning facilities that are too complex to be supported by some XSL processor implementations.

Colours

Adding colours to an XSL document can be simple matter of naming a colour, such as 'red' in an appropriate attribute. However, advanced use allows colours to be specified as RGB (Red, Green Blue) values and ICC (International Color Consortium) profiles.

Colour keywords

A colour can be a keyword. The keywords must be one of the following values: 'aqua', 'black', 'blue', 'fuchsia', 'gray', 'green', 'lime', 'maroon', 'navy', 'olive', 'purple', 'red', 'silver', 'teal', 'white' or 'yellow'. For example:

```
<block background-color="red">...</block>
```

RGB Values

Any attribute that can contain a colour keyword can instead contain a function that is used to return a colour. The **rgb()** function is passed three values, representing the amount of red, green and blue to add to form the mixed colour (just as a TV set uses combinations of red, green and blue phosphor dots to build a full-colour picture):

```
<block background-color="rgb(128,0,56)">...</block>
```

ICC profiles

A colour management system (CMS) is needed to ensure accuracy of colours in data files that are created and read by different software applications and devices (such as scanners and printers). The ICC is responsible for defining ICC profiles (a standard and well-supported CMS). This format can be used to maintain accurate colour definitions through the typical stages of print production, from scanning and designing to proofing and final printing. Any device, such as an image scanner, can embed its characteristics as an ICC profile. Another device can accurately interpret the colours embedded in the file by taking account of this contextual information. Note that TIFF image files can contain ICC profiles, that the most popular illustration and painting software applications support them, and that it is a simple matter to convert between PDF colour space resources and ICC profiles.

The **Color Profile** element is the only element allowed in the optional Declarations element (that occurs between the page layout definitions and the document content) and may occur any number of times at this location. It is used to refer to an ICC colour profile and to give the colour a name that can be referenced later:

```
<declarations>
  <color-profile src="http://MyProfiles/Profile1.dat"
                 color-profile-name="MyColours"
                 rendering-intent="auto" />
  <color-profile src="http://MyProfiles/Profile2.dat"
                 color-profile-name="OtherColours"
                 rendering-intent="saturation" />
</declarations>
```

The colour profile is identified by the URL specified in the **Src** attribute. This URL may identify an internally recognized colour profile or it may point to ICC colour profile encoding that should be loaded and interpreted (for details see www.color.org/ICC-1_1998-09.PDF). The colour profile is used in the document content by reference to the name given in the **Color Profile Name** attribute. The **Rendering Intent** attribute has a default value '**auto**' (the XSL processor decides what to do, based on the content type), but can be given the value '**perceptual**', which preserves the relationship between colours and is often the preferred choice for images, or '**relative-colorimetric**', which leaves colours that fall inside the range unchanged but usually converts out-of-range colours to in-range colours of the same *lightness*, or '**saturation**', which preserves the relative saturation (strength or dilution by white) values of the original pixels, but converts out-of-range colours to in-range colours of the same *saturation*, or '**absolute-colorimetric**', which disables white-point matching when converting colours.

In the document content, the profile can be referenced using the **rgb-icc()** function. This function returns a specific colour from the ICC colour profile. The color profile is specified by the name parameter (the fourth parameter). The first three parameters are RGB values, which are used as a fallback when the named colour cannot be found (is not defined). The actual colour required from the colour space is specified by a sequence of one or more colour values specified after the name:

```
<block background-color="rgb-icc(128, 0, 56, MyColour, 1,
                         22 )">...</block>
```

Markers

Some published documents benefit from repeating the text of a header in the header region, so that it will repeat at the top of each page until the next header is encountered. Many reference books (though not this one) repeat section titles in the header; dictionaries often include in the header the first term that occurs on each page. In fact, these two examples are subtly different. In the first case, the previous header is required, no matter how many pages back it occurs. In the second, the first occurrence on the current page is required. XSLT includes a feature that not only allows a range of text to be identified, or 'marked', for possible reuse in the header, but also for the two scenarios above, as well as many others. Two elements are used to support this feature; one is used to set a marker, and the other is used to retrieve the content of a marker and reuse its content.

Marked text

The first element, **Marker**, is used to isolate and identify the text that may need to be repeated in a header. This element is allowed in the Flow element content, but not in a static header. However, it may only occur as the first child of its parent element (or immediately following another marker):

```
<block>
  <marker ...>...</marker>
  <marker ...>...</marker>
  but <marker ...>ILLEGAL</marker> after other content.
</block>
```

This element can contain any block-level or in-line-level formatting elements that the Flow element may include, or text, or a combination of text and formatting objects:

```
<marker ...>Some Marked Text!</marker>

<marker ...>Some
<wrapper font-weight="bold">Marked</wrapper>
Text!</marker>

<marker ...><block>Some Marked Text!</block></marker>
```

The only constraint is that the formatting objects used must also be allowed at the location of the references to the markers.

The content of a Marker element is not presented. If this content needs to be shown, then it must be repeated after the marker. The reason for this is to allow the running header to differ from the content it is associated with (in this case by using all capitals and omitting punctuation):

```
<block><marker>HEADER TWO</marker>Header Two.</block>
```

Individual markers do not have identifiers because they will never be referenced directly. However, every marker must belong to a group of related markers, creating a marker 'class'. This allows markers of a particular type to be targetted later, which means that this feature can be used multiple times in the same document. The **Marker Class Name** attribute performs this role. In the following example, two classes called 'titles' and 'entries' are used to identify both the sections of a dictionary, and the entries in each section:

```
<block text-size="12pt"><marker
      marker-class-name="titles">A</marker></block>
...
<block text-size="9pt"><marker
      marker-class-name="entries">a</marker></block>
<block text-size="9pt"><marker
      marker-class-name="entries">Aardvark</marker>
</block>
...
<block text-size="12pt"><marker
      marker-class-name="titles">B</marker></block>
...
<block text-size="9pt"><marker
      marker-class-name="entries">bus</marker></block>
...
```

It is then possible to construct headers that include both (or either) the current title and the current entry (using multiple marker references):

| B - bat | 132 | 133 | bus - B |

Retrieving marked text

The **Retrieve Marker** element is an empty element that identifies the location where previously marked text is to be replicated, and is only allowed in static header content (in the Static Content element but not the Flow element). However, this element can occur at any position within the content of its parent element:

```
<block>Marker content = "<retrieve-marker .../>"</block>
```

The **Retrieve Class Name** attribute is used to reference the unique identifier of the marker. The example headers for the left-hand page shown above would be constructed as follows:

```
<block>
  <retrieve-marker retrieve-class-name="titles"/> -
  <retrieve-marker retrieve-class-name="entries"/> ...
</block>
```

Formatting

Usually, it is not desirable for text inserted into a header to be formatted in the same way as the original text. For this reason, when text is copied the original formatting is not brought with it. Instead, locally defined formatting is applied to the copied text. Although the titles and entries in the example on the previous page are presented in the main flow at 12pt and 9pt respectively, a smaller point is likely to be more appropriate in the header. The point size set in a surrounding Block element, for example, will be applied to the inserted text:

```
<block font-size="12pt"><marker ...>...</marker></block>

<block font-size="7pt">
   ... <retrieve-marker .../> ...
</block>
```

Marker selection

The dictionary example above highlights the need for at least two different methods of marker selection. When the header of a particular page contains a marker, it must select just one of the possibly many markers in the document that are assigned to the required class type. Markers that will occupy subsequent pages are ignored first. But it is less obvious which marker to select when the current page has two or more markers of the given type, or when previous pages contain many instances, or when both the current page and previous pages have markers of this type. The default selection is the first marker on the current page, if there is one, or the closest preceding marker in the page sequence. But this can be overriden.

When the **Retrieve Boundary** attribute is given the value '**page-sequence**' (the default value), this indicates that only pages in the current page sequence should be considered. Valid markers in previous page sequences are ignored. The value '**page**' specifies that only the current page is relevant. At the other extreme, the value '**document**' extends the range to the entire document (there is no limit to how far back the search can reach). When there is at least one matching object on the page, then the **Retrieve Position** attribute is used to select one. It has the default value '**first-starting-within-page**', but can also take the values '**first-including-carryover**', '**last-starting-within-page**' or '**last-ending-within-page**':

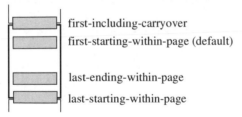

first-including-carryover
first-starting-within-page (default)

last-ending-within-page
last-starting-within-page

Object positioning

By default, block and in-line objects are positioned on the page, or within containing blocks, as described previously. Each object is simply placed after the preceding object, either in the block-progression direction or in the line-progression direction. However, the **Absolute Position** attribute allows for other options. Apart from the default value '**auto**', it can also take the values 'fixed' and 'absolute'. The **Top**, **Right**, **Bottom** and **Left** attributes position the object, though their relevance depends on which position option is chosen (they all default to 'auto').

A '**fixed**' object is placed in a location that is fixed relative to the page edges or, when viewing through electronic media, relative to the viewport (which means that fixed objects never move, even if the viewport contains a scrollbar).

The '**absolute**' value indicates that the positioning attributes are to be used to position the object relative to the containing block. Such objects are removed from the flow, in the sense that they leave behind a space to be occupied by following objects. The Left attribute value indicates the distance inwards from the left edge of the containing box to the right edge of the current box (and the other attributes have equivalent meanings).

The **Relative Position** attribute has a default value of '**static**'. If set to '**relative**' this indicates that the positioning attributes are to be used to place the object relative to the position it would normally occupy if it were a 'static' object. The positions of following static objects remains the same as if this had not happened (a gap is not left behind):

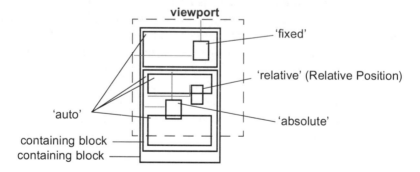

A positioned box can also be stacked on top of other boxes. The **Z Index** attribute has a default value of '**auto**' but this can be changed to an integer value that identifies a stacking level. The higher the number, the higher the priority of the box over other boxes that might occupy the same space on the page. A background property is needed to avoid overlaid boxes from showing through.

Out-of-line objects

There are times when it is convenient to remove an item from the normal text flow and place it at a new location on the page, or even on the next page. For example, a large picture may not fit on the current page and may therefore need to be moved to the next page, but this would leave a lot of whitespace at the end of the current page. As another example, footnotes must be moved to the bottom of the current page (where they can be either read or ignored by the reader).

The major page regions can contain 'conditional' sub-regions at the top or bottom. These regions only appear if there is information to place within them because a conditional sub-region grabs space from the region it is in. For example, the main body region may sometimes have footnote content. The body region has conditional areas at the starting edge and ending edge (top and bottom):

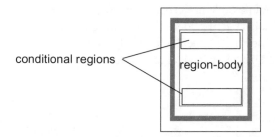

Floating objects

Large tables and figures are often moved to a location where they create the least possible disruption to the flow of text and the page balance, such as to the top of the next page or column. The **Float** element is used to contain such items, indicating to the formatting engine that it may move the content as appropriate. Only block-level elements can be used in the Float element:

```
<block>INLINE ITEM</block>
<float><block>FLOATING TEXT HERE</block></float>
<block>NEXT INLINE ITEM</block>
```

The formatting engine may move the enclosed items to the top of the current page, or to the top of a following page.

The **Float** attribute may be used to place the floating items to the '**left**' or '**right**' of the page (or the 'start', 'end' or 'before'). The default value is '**none**', which the standard indicates as 'not floating':

```
<float float="left"><block>LEFT TEXT</block></float>
<float float="right"><block>RIGHT TEXT</block></float>
```

Block-level elements, and the Float element itself, may contain the **Clear** attribute. This is used to move objects down beneath any previous floating objects. The value '**left**' means that it must be moved below any floating objects on the left-hand side. The value '**right**' means that it must be moved below any floating objects on the right-hand side. The value '**both**' means that it must be moved beneath all previous floating objects (the default value is '**none**'). The values '**start**' and '**end**' may also be used.

The **Span** attribute may be used, and given the value '**all**' to span the object across multiple columns.

Footnotes

A footnote is usually placed at the bottom of the first page that contains a reference to it, and it is of course not possible to determine in advance where a page break may occur. The **Footnote** element first contains an **Inline** element, which holds the text to remain the flow, such as '*', then contains the actual footnote text in the **Footnote Body** element. This text will float to the base of the page:

```
<block>Here is a footnote reference
<footnote>
<inline>*</inline>
<footnote-body>
  <block>* A reference to a footnote is
  usually a '*'</block>
</footnote-body>
</footnote>.</block>
<block>More text.</block>
...
```

```
Here is a footnote reference*.
More text.
...

* A reference to a footnote is
usually a '*'
```

Dynamic content

When publishing electronically, parts of the document can be 'switched-in' and 'switched-out', formatting can be changed and reapplied in response to user actions, and objects can be made invisible.

Switchable fragments

It is possible to hide and reveal portions of a document at any time, depending on user actions. For example, the opening and collapsing of portions of a contents list can be supported using such a feature. The **Multi Switch** element contains a number of **Multi Case** elements. Each of these elements holds an alternative document fragment, and each alternative must be given a unique name, so that it can be referred to and activated later. The **Case Name** attribute holds this value (there is no default value, a specific value must be supplied):

```
<multi-switch>
  <multi-case case-name="first">...</multi-case>
  <multi-case case-name="second">...</multi-case>
  <multi-case case-name="third">...</multi-case>
</multi-switch>
```

Only one of these fragments is active when the page is initially presented to the user. The content of the first Multi Case element with a **Starting State** attribute value of '**show**' (instead of the default value '**hide**') is presented first. The others can be revealed later:

```
<multi-case case-name="first">...</multi-case>
<multi-case case-name="second" starting-state="show">
  <block>THIS PORTION IS SHOWN FIRST</block>
</multi-case>
```

Within each document fragment, there may be any number of **Multi Toggle** elements that are used to switch-in one of the other fragments. The text contained in these elements becomes 'hot' text that the user can select. When selected, the associated case fragment replaces the current fragment. The **Switch To** attribute refers to the name of the fragment to swap in (the Case Name attribute of the relevant Multi Case element):

```
<multi-case case-name="closed" starting-state="show">
  <block>Heading
    <multi-toggle switch-to="opened" >
      [+]
    </multi-toggle>
  </block>
</multi-case>

<multi-case case-name="opened">
  <block>Heading
    <multi-toggle switch-to="closed" >
      [-]
    </multi-toggle>
  </block>
  <block>- item 1</block>
  <block>- item 2</block>
</multi-case>
```

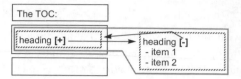

The Switch To attribute can be given the reserved value '**xsl-any**' (the default), which indicates that the formatter can make its own decision regarding which item to display next. There are also reserved values that represent the item immediately above and immediately below the current item; '**xsl-preceding**' and '**xsl-following**' respectively. Finally, it is also possible to include several names in the attribute, specifying that several items should be presented to the user to select from. The **Case Title** attribute is used to hold the diplayable title.

It is possible for a set of multiple cases to be embedded in each item in an outer set, creating a hierarchy of selectable items that the user can open and collapse while navigating through the structure. But this concept raises an interesting question. Imagine that the user selects the first of the outer items and sees the inner set of that item, and the inner item that is selected by default. The user then selects one of the inner items (not the default). The user then moves to another of the outer items, but later moves back to the first one. It is not clear if the inner item selected should now be the default item (as before), or the one the user selected earlier. The **Auto Restore** attribute can be added to the Multi Switch element. It takes a value of '**true**' or '**false**' (the default). If set to 'true', this attribute states that the default should be restored. Otherwise, the one selected previously is restored instead.

Changing styles

The style of a range of blocks, or range of text, can be changed depending on the current state of the environment. An example given in the XSL standard refers to the way that the colour of a hypertext link source may vary, depending on whether the link has been visited recently or is currently selected.

The **Multi Properties** element contains a number of initial, empty **Multi Property Set** elements, each providing the style to apply under a given circumstance, identified using the **Active State** attribute (there is no default value, a specific value must be supplied).

These elements are followed by the document fragment to be styled, which must be contained in a Wrapper element:

```
<multi-properties>
  <multi-property-set active-state="visited"
                      color="red" />
  <multi-property-set active-state="active"
                      color="green" />
  <multi-property-set active-state="link"
                      color="blue" />
  <wrapper>The colour of this text depends on
  the current state.</wrapper>
</multi-properties>
```

The Active Stage attribute can take the value '**link**' (specifying the style to apply to a hypertext link that has not yet been activated), '**visited**' (specifying the style to apply to a hypertext link that has been followed by the user), '**active**' (an area is currently being selected by the user), '**hover**' (the user might be about to select the area) and '**focus**' (the area has the current focus, and therefore accepts keystroke events).

Only style changes that do *not* affect the placement of the text in the page should be included, because support for reflowing of the text may not be present in some systems, or may be an undesirable side effect in any case.

Visibility

Block and in-line objects are normally '**visible**', as specified in the **Visibility** attribute. These objects can be rendered invisible by setting this attribute value to '**hidden**'. The objects then still exist, and still occupy the same amount of space as normal, but their contents are not presented. One reason to do this is to achieve unusual spacing effects. Another reason would be to add further interactive features, with software changing the value between 'visible' and 'hidden' as appropriate. In a table, a cell that is set to 'hidden', when the Empty Cells attribute is also set to 'hide', will have no border lines (assuming separate border lines for each cell).

A third option is '**collapse**'. In the circumstances above, this value is equivalent to 'hidden', but in table rows and columns it has a different effect. Unfortunately, the draft standard is not clear on what this difference is.

Aural styles

XSL includes a large number of properties that assist with the audible presentation of material (taken directly from the CSS Version 2 specification). Speech presentation is important, not just to those who are visually disabled but also to anyone who cannot switch visual attention from some other task, such as vehicle drivers.

The **Speak** attribute is used to render text audibly when given one of the values 'normal' (the default) or 'spell-out'. The 'spell-out' option is used to pronounce text such as 'XSL' by spelling out each letter; 'X', 'S', 'L'. A value of 'none' suppresses audible presentation of the content.

One of the most important properties of speech is volume. The **Volume** attribute can take a number of different types of value. A simple numeric value in the range 0–100 denotes a volume from barely audible to barely comfortable. A percentage value is used for volumes that are relative to inherited values:

```
<block speak="normal" volume="60">you should
<wrapper volume="150%">shout</wrapper> this and
<wrapper volume="50%">whisper</wrapper> this.</block>
```

The value 'silent' switches off sound (recall that a volume of '0' does not indicate silence, just very quiet speech), and there are several named volume values that represent common requirements, including 'x-soft' (the same as a volume of 0), 'soft' (25), 'medium' (50) (the default), 'loud' (75) and 'x-loud' (100). Whatever value is specified, this is simply an initial value that the listener should be able to adjust (using a volume knob or equivalent).

Rate of speech can be defined with the **Speech Rate** attribute. This attribute takes a numeric value that represents words per minute, though some conveniently named values are also available, including 'x-slow' (80 words per minute), 'slow' (120), 'medium' (180–200) (the default), 'fast' (300) and 'x-fast' (500). The values 'slower' and 'faster' adjust an inherited speech rate by 40 words per minute. As for volume, the listener should be able to override the initial setting.

Voices are also distinguished by type. The most obvious categories are 'male', 'female' and 'child', but it is also possible to refer to more specific categories (though the standard does not contain such a list of options), or even name an individual. Voice characteristics use an override system that is similar to the font specification so that generic types can be chosen when specific types are not available on the local system. The **Voice Family** attribute is used. For example, a play may comprise a number of blocks with alternating voices:

```
<block voice-family="male-cockney, male">...</block>
<block voice-family="female-scottish, female">...</block>
<block voice-family="child">...</block>
<block voice-family="churchill, male">...</block>
```

When generic voice types are used, it is possible to add some variety by using the **Pitch** attribute. This attribute takes a value of 'x-low', 'low', 'medium' (the default), 'high', 'x-high' or a numeric value giving the pitch (frequency) in hertz. The named values do not have a predefined hertz equivalent as it depends on the main voice characteristic chosen, such as 'male' or 'female' (the average pitch for a male voice is around 120 Hz, but for a female voice it is around 210 Hz):

```
<block voice-family="male" pitch="90Hz">...</block>
```

Some people speak with a steady pitch, others varying the pitch even in normal conversation. The **Pitch Range** attribute specifies the degree to which the pitch can change during speech, from '0' (no change, a monotonous voice) to '100' (a wildly animated voice), with '50' representing a default normal variance:

```
<block pitch="90Hz" pitch-range="20">...</block>
```

The voice can be further refined using **Stress** and **Richness** attributes ('50' is the default in both cases) that affect the inflection and the prominence or brightness of the voice.

Pauses are very important in speech. The ends of sentences, paragraphs and larger divisions of the text are marked by pauses of different lengths. The **Pause Before** attribute creates a pause before the content of the element is presented. A set duration can be given, such as '20ms' (20 milliseconds), or a time span relative to the speed of the speech can be specified instead, such as '50%' ('100%' represents the time it takes to speak one word, on average, at the current speech rate). The **Pause After** attribute works in the same way but creates a gap *after* the content. When specifying a pause both before and after, a more convenient **Pause** attribute is available that takes two parameters with the first providing the before value, and the second parameter providing the after value. It can also take a single value to represent both when they are of the same duration. The following two examples are equivalent:

```
<block... pause="30ms 20ms">...</block>

<block... pause-before="30ms"
          pause-after="20ms">...</block>
```

In some cases, the pauses they produce may not be sufficient to identify punctuation, and it may be necessary to ensure that punctuation is clearly identified. The **Speak Punctuation** attribute takes a value of '**code**' to specify that punctuation is to be read out. For example, 'this, and that' would be read out as 'this comma ...(*pause*)... and that'. The value '**none**' (the default) disables this feature.

The **Speak Header** attribute has the value '**once**' (the default) or '**always**'. It is used to control whether table headers repeated at the top of each page should be respoken on each repetition.

Similarly, while numerals are normally spoken as '**continuous**' digits, so that '237' is pronounced 'two hundred and thirty seven', the **Speak Numeral** attribute makes it possible to specify that digits are to be read out separately. The value '**digits**' ensures that the first example below is pronounced 'one two five four', whereas the second would be heard as 'thirty nine':

```
<block...>The alarm code is
<wrapper speak-numeral="digits">1254</wrapper>.</block>

<block...>My age is
<wrapper speak-numeral="continuous">39</wrapper>.</block>
```

Sound effects can be played before or after the spoken content. The **Cue Before** attribute specifies a sound to be played before the speech and **Cue After** plays a sound afterward. The **Cue** attribute is more convenient if surrounding sounds are required because it takes two values – one for before and one for after. A single value in the Cue attribute specifies that the given sound should be played both before and after the speech. Sounds can be inherited from parent elements, but existing sounds can be overridden using the default value '**none**' (to avoid playing a sound). A sound is identified by URL reference:

```
<block... cue-before="SOUNDS/BELL.WAV">...</block>
```

The **Play During** attribute allows a sound to be played throughout the speech. A value of '**auto**' means that an existing sound, activated by an ancestor element, should continue to play throughout this fragment of the speech. If there is a possibility (or even a certainty) that the sound will end before the speech ends, it is possible to repeat the sound using the '**repeat**' parameter. It is also possible to mix a new sound with one that is already playing, by adding the '**mix**' parameter. These two parameters must follow the URL reference, and when both are present they must appear in the order described above:

```
<block... play-during="HUMM1.WAV repeat">...</block>
```

Advanced sound systems are able to provide stereo sound, and in some cases also surround-sound effects. When there are several people speaking, it can be useful to give each a distinct spatial location. Horizontal locations are specified using the **Azimuth** attribute which accepts a value between '0deg' (zero degrees) and '360deg' (the same position). Values increase clockwise from the front centre.

For convenience, some named values are available that correspond to different degree settings, including '**center**' (zero degrees, the default), '**center-right**' (20 degrees), '**right**' (40), '**far-right**' (60), '**right-side**' (90), '**left-side**' (270), '**far-left**' (300), '**left**' (320) and '**center-left**' (340). The values '**leftwards**' and '**right-wards**' take an inherited value and move the sound left (by subtracting 20 degrees) or right (by adding 20 degrees), though both appear to move sound in the wrong direction when it is behind the listener.

The parameter '**behind**' can be added to a value, moving the sound to the back:

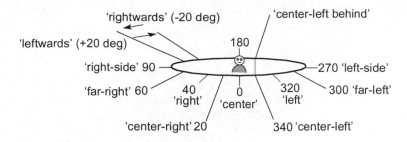

The following example places the judge at the centre front, with prosecution and defence on opposite sides:

```
<block... azimuth="center">JUDGE:...</block>
<block... azimuth="left-side">PROSECUTION:...</block>
<block... azimuth="right-side">DEFENCE:...</block>
```

Sound sources may also be located at different vertical locations. For example, a judge should perhaps be elevated above the other speakers. The **Elevation** attribute specifies a vertical location, from '0deg' to '90deg' (overhead) or '-90deg' (beneath), with '**level**' (the default), '**above**' and '**below**' also representing these extreme positions. The values '**higher**' and '**lower**' add and subtract 10 degrees respectively:

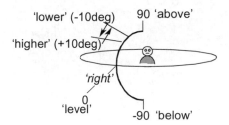

```
<block... elevation="75deg">JUDGE:...</block>
```

28. HTML 4.0

Although the primary impetus behind the development of XSLT has been to provide a mechanism for creating XSL documents, the reality is that most browsers in use today only understand HTML (along with CSS). Fortunately, XSLT is equally adept at converting XML documents into HTML documents (perhaps containing in-line CSS styles). This chapter explains HTML in sufficient detail to enable the formatting of XML documents for presentation in these browsers. HTML tags not used to format content are not discussed here. The most notable omission is the elements used to build interactive forms.

The mechanism for producing HTML documents using an XSLT stylesheet is described in Chapter 5.

Background

The concept of electronic links between text stored on computer systems is well established and many **hypertext** systems have been developed, though most have been confined to linking texts stored on the same system and have used proprietory technologies.

It was only a matter of time before the Internet became an obvious candidate to support a hypertext system that spans systems and countries. With the infrastructure in place, it was only necessary to define two additional protocols: first, a new access protocol that would allow hypertext documents to be requested from a server; second, a document markup language that would be used to both style the received document and locate and enable any embedded hypertext links. The **HTML** protocol devised in 1990 performs the second of these roles. HTML documents are transferred to the client browser.

The browser on the client system interprets the HTML document, removing the tags and presenting the content in an appropriate format. There are implied styles or behaviours associated with each tag.

The HTML markup language takes a position halfway between format and structure. It includes style tags, such as the Italic element, where the output format is stated explicitly, but it also includes generalized objects, such as the Emphasis element, where output format is left to the browser.

The core feature of HTML – the very reason for its existence – is its ability to let readers follow links to other HTML documents anywhere on the Internet. When a **URL** reference to another file is selected by the user, the browser extracts the reference and sends a further request to the server (or to another server) for another HTML document, usually to replace the original but possibly to be presented in a new browser window.

HTML documents are also known as **pages**. The first page made available to users is known as the **home page**, which usually has the default filename of 'index.html' (or 'index.htm').

Similarly, an HTML document may contain references to resources that conform to other data formats. In this way, image files and Java applets, amongst other objects, are downloaded to the browser and inserted into the presented version of the document.

HTML 4.0 is an application of SGML and is therefore defined by an SGML DTD. It is not possible for HTML to be considered as an application of XML because it cannot be accurately described by an XML DTD. It uses advanced features of SGML, such as element and attribute minimization, and adopts SGML conventions for representation of empty elements. However, XHTML has relatively recently (January 2000) been announced as the next, XML-compatible version of HTML (but in terms of features is still essentially HTML 4.0).

HTML versions

There have been five versions of HTML, known as **HTML Level One**, **HTML Level Two**, **HTML+**, **HTML Level Three** and now **HTML Level Four**, of which HTML+ was transitional to Level Three in that it included tables. The respective DTDs are named **HTML 2.0**, **HTML 3.2** and **HTML 4.0** accordingly (level one predating full compatibility with SGML).

HTML 2.0 was the first version of HTML that conformed to the formal structures defined in the SGML standard, and has been supported by all browsers for so long that it is no longer necessary to discuss version 1.0. Version 2.0 added an interactive 'forms' feature and still forms the core of all subsequent versions. The elements defined in this version are mostly still relevant. Nevertheless, some of the features of this (and the next) version of HTML have become deprecated or obsolete as more extensive or better-designed alternatives have emerged.

HTML 3.2, released in 1996, deprecated a few original elements but added numerous new elements for presenting tables, styling text, client-side image-based linking and document structuring. All popular browsers offer comprehensive support for this version.

HTML 4.0 is the current version and was released in December 1997 by **W3C**. Some of its features have long been available in at least one of the popular browsers. In particular, the **frame** concept is in widespread use. There is an SGML DTD for this standard (http://www.w3.org/TR/REC-html40/). As with earlier versions this DTD is not XML-compatible (though the next version probably will be). Once again, the opportunity was taken to make obsolete a number of elements and attributes that have been superseded. New elements in this version allow windows to be split into frames, extend the table model, extend the forms model, add changed-content highlighting and a generalized non-HTML object identifier, and introduce some general text descriptions. Styles and scripts are also supported, at last.

Basic document structure

An HTML-conforming document has a document element called **Html**. Unlike XML, element names are not case sensitive, so the element may actually be named 'html', 'HTML' or 'Html' and does not need to match either the document type declaration or the end-tag.

The Html element encloses a **Head** section and a main **Body** section. The header contains a **Title**, which is presented in the title bar of the browser. The Body element may contain any of a number of other elements but usually begins with the title repeated in a first-level-header element, **H1**. An **Address** element encloses details of the author of the document and is usually inserted at the end of the document, where it is displayed in italic, possibly indented or centred:

```
<HTML>
   <HEAD>
      <TITLE>A Description of HTML</TITLE>
   </HEAD>
   <BODY>
      <H1>This is HTML</H1>
      ......
      <ADDRESS>Neil Bradley
      (http://neil@bradley.co.uk)</ADDRESS>
   </BODY>
</HTML>
```

The document background colour and foreground text colour can be specified in the **Body** element (though the following techniques are now deprecated) using the

Bgcolor (background colour) attribute and the **Text** attribute. In both cases, the format of the attribute value comprises either the name of a colour, or a coded RGB (red, green, blue) mix. Available colour names are 'aqua', 'black', 'fuchsia', 'gray', 'green', 'lime', 'maroon', 'navy', 'olive', 'purple', 'red', 'silver', 'teal', 'white' and 'yellow'. The RGB scheme uses three hexadecimal (two-digit) values preceded by a hash symbol, for example '#FF2250'. The first two digits indicate the amount of Red, the next two indicate the amount of Green, and the final two indicates the amount of Blue to be mixed to create the desired colour. The example below produces a document with blue text on a yellow background:

```
<BODY BGCOLOR="#FFFF80" TEXT="blue">
```

As an alternative, the background can be composed from a picture, often in GIF format. The deprecated **Background** attribute provides a URL to the desired picture. When the picture is smaller than the display area, it is repeated across and down until it fills the display area:

```
<BODY BACKGROUND="images/background.gif">
```

A change to the document background or text colour may affect the visibility of **hypertext** links, so three additional attributes are available to set the colour of linking text (all now deprecated). The deprecated **Link** attribute sets the colour of a link that is not active and has not been visited. The deprecated **Vlink** (visited link) attribute sets the colour of all links that have been activated in the (recent) past. The deprecated **Alink** (active link) attribute sets the colour of the currently selected link. The format of the values is as described above for document foreground and background colours.

```
<BODY LINK="GREEN" ALINK="RED" VLINK="BLUE">
```

These attributes are deprecated because it is now possible to specify link styles using CSS:

```
A:link  { color:GREEN }
A:alink { color:RED }
A:vlink { color:BLUE }
```

The **Meta** element can appear in the header section, but is not used for document markup and is of most interest to those involved in browser/server communications. The Meta element is placed in the Head element to add meta information not covered by attributes of other elements. The content of a Meta element is not to be displayed in the document, but may be read by the browser or server. It has three attributes, HTTP-Equiv, Name and Content. The **Name** attribute provides the name of the meta information (almost an attribute name in itself). The **Content** attribute provides the current value for the named item. For example:

```
<META NAME="Index" CONTENT="cycle">
```

If more than one Meta element is present with the same Name attribute value, the various content values are accumulated into a comma-separated list; for example 'cycle, bus, car'. The third attribute, **HTTP-Equiv**, allows the content to be inserted into an HTTP header field (a topic not explored further in this book).

Differences from XML

HTML is currently an application of SGML, not XML, and unfortunately there are some minor differences in syntax. HTML takes advantage of a number of tag minimization techniques that SGML allows. In the early days of the Web, these were quite useful because Web page authors had to use standard text editors to create HTML documents and key every character in the tags. With the advent of WYSIWYG, HTML editors that generate the tags automatically (behind the scenes), the issue of minimization is no longer relevant (this also being the primary reason for omitting such features from the XML standard).

Element minimization

The most obvious and widely used technique in HTML 4.0 is the omission of end-tags. Very often, the end of an element can be implied by the start of another. For example, it is not necessary to include an end-head tag, '</HEAD>', because its presence can be implied by the following Body start-tag, and the end-tag for the Body element is likewise not needed because the end-tag for the Html element implies this:

```
<HTML>
    <HEAD>
        <TITLE>A Description of HTML</TITLE>
    <BODY>
        <H1>This is HTML</H1>
        ......
        <ADDRESS>Neil Bradley
        (http://neil@bradley.co.uk)</ADDRESS>
</HTML>
```

Attribute minimization

Attributes can also be simplified significantly. When the attribute value must be a single value or word, the quotes can be omitted:

```
<BODY LINK=GREEN ALINK=RED VLINK=BLUE>
```

In some special cases, when the attributes that may be applied are very limited and the values that they have cannot conflict, it is also possible to dispense with the attribute name and equals symbol, as the presence of the value is sufficient.

Empty elements

The ability to omit end-tags leads to a perhaps more significant difference between XML and HTML. Empty elements in HTML are simply start-tags with no matching end-tags:

```
<!-- NO END TAG AND NO '/>' IN START TAG -->
<META NAME="Index" CONTENT="cycle">
```

This can cause some difficulties when attempting to include HTML tags in an XSLT document. While minimization in general does not raise any issues because it is an optional feature of HTML, the differences in the way that empty elements are represented cannot be so easily avoided. Chapter 5 describes how the **Output** element can be used to overcome this problem.

Text blocks

Except in one special circumstance, a browser will not obey any line breaks in the ASCII text file that contains the HTML document, but it will instead reformat the text to break at the right-hand margin of the window (or sub-region of the window) into which it is being displayed. This makes sense because fonts differ in respect of the widths of each character, and because the viewable area is determined by the size of the user's monitor and the size of the area assigned by the user to the browser window. Yet it is usually not desirable for an entire document to be reformatted into a single large text block. HTML therefore includes tags that break the text up into meaningful blocks. The most essential of these is the **P** (paragraph) element, which defines a single paragraph in the text. The browser begins a new paragraph on a new line and creates gaps between paragraphs:

```
<P>This is a paragraph.</P>
<P>This is another paragraph.</P>
```

With the advent of CSS and some of the common attributes described later, it is possible to use this one tag for almost all block-level formatting, though a number of other tags were defined in early versions of HTML and are still widely used for identifying headings, lists and other block-like structures.

Basic hypertext links

The **Anchor** element, **A**, is used to locate both the source and target ends of a hypertext link.

When used as a target element, the Anchor element usually contains the title of the referenced text (in order that it may be highlighted on completion of a link to that item) within the **Name** attribute:

```
<P><A NAME="details">The Details</A> are
here. ...</P>
```

When used as a source element, the Anchor contains a **Hypertext Reference** attribute (**Href**) which contains a URL.

```
<P>See <A HREF="#details">the details</A> for
the details</P>
```

A single Anchor may be both the source of a link and the target of a link:

```
<A NAME="summary" HREF="#details">See details</A>
```

When inserting links to other documents, the target document does not require an Anchor element, because the entire file is the target. However, it is possible to link to an anchored item in the other file by appending the hash symbol and item name:

```
<A HREF="../myfiles/detail.htm#part3">See
details, part 3</A>
```

If the path ends with a forward slash, '/', the target Web server supplies the name of the default home page:

```
HREF="http://www.myserver.com/myfiles/"
```

To target a browser at a home page held on the user's own system, or another system visible over a local area network, the protocol becomes 'file:' (this is not officially a protocol name, and so should not be followed by the double slash):

```
<A HREF="file:/myserver/myfiles/me.html">
See My Server Home Page</A>
```

A **Title** attribute may be used to hold a brief description of the target resource, to be displayed by the browser when the mouse is over the link.

When relative paths are included in the URL, the starting point is normally the address of the page containing the link. The **Base** element can be used to provide a new fixed point in the directory structure from which relative links should be calculated. It uses an **Href** attribute to specify the replacement path.

The **Link** element identifies other resources that are connected to this Web page, such as a style sheet. To identify the resource, it has an **Href** attribute and the **Title** attribute holds a brief description of the resource:

```
<LINK TITLE="big print"
      HREF="bigprint.css"
      TYPE="text/css" >
```

The A and Link elements may contain a **Rel** (relationship) attribute, which identifies the relationship between the target object and the current page. The **Rev** attribute identifies the previous (reverse) relationship when the links form a chain. A browser could (in theory) style these links differently from others to indicate to the user that there is a preferred path to follow. These attributes are not widely used, but may be useful to Web search engines. The following is a Rel example:

```
<LINK REL="alternate stylesheet"
      TITLE="big print" HREF="bigprint.css"
      TYPE="text/css" >
```

Common attributes

Some useful attributes have now been added to almost every HTML element. The most ubiquitous are four core attributes: **Style**, **Class**, **Title** and **Id**. There are few elements that do not have them, the exceptions being structural tags (Html, Head, Title), background scripts (Script, Style and Area), applet tags (Applet and Param) and meta-data (Base, Basefont and Meta). In addition, many elements have new language attributes (Lang and Dir) and many others have attributes that allow scripts to be activated when the user interacts with the element in some way (Onclick, Ondblclick, Onmousedown, Onmouseup, Onmouseover, Onmouseout, Onkeypress, Onkeydown and Onkeyup).

In-line styles

The **Style** attribute allows **CSS** in-line styles to be applied. See Chapter 19 for general details on this standard. These in-line styles consist of CSS properties and values, separated by semi-colons (the curly brackets are not used):

```
<P STYLE="color: yellow ; background: black">This paragraph
will be styled in yellow on a black background.</P>
```

Element classes

The **Class** attribute introduces a measure of the generalized markup concept to HTML by allowing category names to be added to element instances. For example, some Paragraph elements may be more important than others:

```
P:{ color: black ; font-size: 10pt }
P:important{ color: red ; font-size: 14pt }

<P>This is a normal paragraph.</P>
<P CLASS="important">This is an IMPORTANT paragraph.</P>
<P>This is another normal paragraph.</P>
```

Note that the CSS style definitions in the example above may appear in the Head section of the document – this approach to including CSS in HTML documents is discussed later in this chapter.

Note also that it is the introduction of the two attributes described above that makes it possible to achieve so much with the Paragraph element.

Element identifiers

The **Id** attribute (identifier) gives the element a unique name that may be used for various purposes, such as to provide a target for a hypertext link, to allow a style defined in a separate style sheet to be applied specifically to this element, or to be manipulated in a specific way by an ECMAScript procedure. The following paragraph is given a red colour by the style sheet and is also the target of a link.

```
P:#Scarborough { color: red }
...
<P ID="Scarborough">This is a paragraph about
Scarborough, a seaside resort in the north of
England.</P>
...
... See <A HREF="#Scarborough">Scarborough</A>...
```

This technique is familiar to XML users and is certainly a less clumsy way to identify the target of a link than wrapping the paragraph text within an A element (using the Name attribute to identify it). However, some of the currently popular browsers do not yet support this feature.

Element titles

The **Title** attribute allows a brief description of the content of the element to be included. Normally not visible, this text would only be revealed on user request. It can be used to build a simple table of contents, and it may be presented in the status bar. Thus:

```
<P title="HTML document">This is a paragraph about
HTML documents.</P>
```

Language

The **Lang** attribute describes the human language used for the textual content of the element:

```
<P LANG="EN">This is an English paragraph.</P>
```

The **Dir** attribute (directory) describes the direction of writing conventional for the human language concerned. It takes a value of 'ltr' (left to right) or 'rtl' (right to left):

```
<P LANG="EN" DIR="ltr">This is an English
paragraph read left to right.</P>
```

Event triggers

The 'On...' attributes all specify an ECMAscript function that is to be activated when the user interacts with the element in some given way.

The **Onclick** attribute activates the named function when the user clicks the mouse button over the element:

```
<P ONCLICK="MyParaClickFunction()">Click here!</P>
```

Similarly, the **Ondblclick** attribute activates the named function when the user double-clicks the mouse button over the element, and **Onkeypress** activates when a key is pressed (and released). The **Onmousedown** and **Onmouseup** attributes detect the pressing and release of the mouse button while it is over an element. The **Onkeydown** and **Onkeyup** attributes work for key presses in the same way. Movement of the mouse pointer over the element is detected by the **Onmouseover** and **Onmouseout** attributes.

Alignments

Several elements have an **Align** attribute, with possible values of 'left', 'center' or 'right', including the Paragraph element. However, it is now deprecated because CSS can be used instead.

```
<P>Left!</P>
<P ALIGN="right">Right!</P>
<P>Left!</P>
```

Headings and divisions

Headings

Headers can be used to create crude section and sub-section divisions in the document, or to define outliner levels. The heading elements, **H1** to **H6**, hold title text with varying degrees of highlighting. H1 is the most important and is typically used only for the title of the document (perhaps in conjunction with the Center element described later). At the other extreme, H6 is the least important header and should only be used when six levels of heading are necessary. Each header element is a block, separated from preceding and following objects, including paragraphs and other headers. Although no specific formatting style is indicated, typically the header elements are all displayed in bold typeface and the point size of the text varies, increasing with the level of importance.

```
<H1>The Document Title</H1>
<H2>A Section Title</H2>
<H3>A sub-section title</H3>
```

Divisions

The problem with headers is that, although conceptually they give a title to the text that follows them, the tagging does not represent this relationship. For example, it would not be possible to give a unique style to all the paragraphs that 'belong' to a section given a title using an H3 element.

What is needed is a way to physically enclose a block of related elements, and then to apply styles to this new structure. The **Center** element can be used to enclose any other structure or group of structures, including the entire document.

```
<CENTER>
<H1>A centred heading</H1>
<P>A centred paragraph.</P>
</CENTER>
```

However, this tag has now been deprecated in favour of a more general mechanism. The **Div** (division) element extends the idea. It can be used to replicate the functionality of the Center element because it can take an **Align** attribute with a value of 'left', 'center' or 'right'.

```
<DIV ALIGN="center">
<H1>A centred heading</H1>
<P>A centred paragraph.</P>
</DIV>
```

But the real power of this element becomes apparent when the Style or Class attribute is applied to it.

```
<DIV STYLE="color: red">
<H1>A red heading</H1>
<P>A red paragraph.</P>
</DIV>
```

Horizontal rules

The **Horizontal Rule** element (**Hr**) draws a line across the screen. It is an empty element. It can be used to highlight divisions of a large document.

```
<P>The next para is in another section</P>
<HR>
<P>New section of the document</P>
```

It has additional attributes (all now deprecated) that specify: the thickness of the line (the **Size** attribute); the width of the line, measured in pixels or as a percentage of the screen width (the **Width** attribute); and the alignment of a line narrower than the screen width (the **Align** attribute). It also has attributes that dictate that the line must be solid (the **Noshade** attribute). The Noshade attribute has a single legal value of 'noshade', and the attribute name does not appear. In the example below, the line must be solid, occupy half the width of the window and be centred:

```
<HR NOSHADE SIZE="4" WIDTH="50%" ALIGN="center" >
```

Lists

HTML supports various types of list structures. In all cases, an element that expresses the type of list is used to enclose a number of others, each representing one item in the list.

The most basic type of list is the **Ul** (unordered list):

```
<UL>
. . .
</UL>
```

An unordered list is used when the items do not form a logical sequence or series of steps. It contains a number of **Li** (list item) elements. Each of these contains text, and is automatically preceded by a bullet, dash or other symbol:

```
<UL>
<LI>First Item</LI>
<LI>Second Item</LI>
<LI>Third Item</LI>
</UL>
```

- First Item
- Second Item
- Third Item

The deprecated **Dir** (directory list) element is intended to hold directory listings, which are very short items that may be formatted in columns (as in UNIX file listings):

```
<DIR>
<LI>MYBOOK.DTD</LI>
<LI>MYBOOK.XML</LI>
<LI>PARSER.EXE</LI>
<LI>REPORT.DAT</LI>
</DIR>
```

```
MYBOOK.DTD    PARSER.EXE
MYBOOK.XML    REPORT.DAT
```

The deprecated **Menu** list is intended to be used to represent software menu selections. The content of each item is assumed to be short, and the browser is likely to indent them and omit the bullet:

```
<MENU>
<LI>Activate</LI>
<LI>Options</LI>
<LI>Help</LI>
<LI>Exit</LI>
</MENU>


        Activate
        Options
        Help
        Exit
```

The **Ol** element (ordered list) is similar to the unordered list, but each item is preceded by a sequential, automatically generated number. It is used in preference to the Ul element when the items describe a series of steps, or are referred to individually elsewhere:

```
<OL>
<LI>Step 1</LI>
<LI>Step 2</LI>
<LI>Step 3 - Go To Step 1</LI>
</OL>


    1. Step 1
    2. Step 2
    3. Step 3 - Go To Step 1
```

A **Type** attribute is available on the **Ol**, **Ul** and **Li** elements (but is now deprecated in the first two cases). An ordered list can take Type values of 'A' (capital letters), 'a' (small letters), 'I' (large Roman letters), 'i' (small Roman letters) or '1' (digits), which is the default. An unordered list can take Type values of 'DISC' (bullet), 'CIRCLE' (hollow bullet) or 'SQUARE' (a square hollow bullet). The list item can take the same values, depending which list type it is within, and overrides the current setting for the list within all remaining items. In addition, the ordered list has a **Start** attribute, which indicates a start value for the first item when it is not '1' (or equivalent), and the list item has a **Value** attribute that can only be used within ordered lists to reset the current calculated value:

```
<OL TYPE="A" START="4">
   <LI>First Item
   <LI VALUE="G">Second Item
   <LI>Third Item
</OL>


   D  First Item
   G  Second Item
   H  Third Item
```

Some lists consist of a keyword or term, followed by an explanation of that keyword or term. The **Dl** (definition list) element contains a number of items (but *not* Item elements) each one consisting of two parts, a **Dt** (definition term) element and a (**Dd**) (definition details) element:

```
<DL>
<DT>HTML<dd>HyperText Markup Language
<DT>DTD<dd>Document Type Definition
<DT>XML<dd>Extensible Markup Language
</DL>
```

HTML   HyperText Markup Language
DTD   Document Type Definition
XML   Extensible Markup Language

All of the list types described above may be condensed by closing the gap between items using the **Compact** attribute (now deprecated in all but the Dl element). This implied attribute has a single value option of 'compact', and the attribute name does not appear:

```
<UL COMPACT>
```

HTML has inherited this minimization feature from SGML, and it is not available in XML (though the XSLT processor should be able to output this minimized structure).

In-line elements

A number of HTML elements are in-line elements, meaning that they do not break the flow of text onto a new line (except in one case). These elements modify the style of the text or identify the nature of a range of significant characters.

The **Tt** (teletype) element specifies a monospaced font such as Courier. The **B** (bold) element specifies a bold typeface. The **I** (italic) element specifies an italic typeface:

```
<P>This paragraph contains <B>bold</B>,
<I>italic</I> and <B><I>bold/italic</I></B> text.</P>
```

This paragraph contains **bold**, *italic* and ***bold/italic*** text.

Strong normally maps to bold typeface and **Em** (emphasis) to italic typeface. The computer sample elements **Code** and **Var**, as well as the **Kbd** (keyboard) element, normally map to a monospaced font. The **Samp** (sample) element and **Cite** (citation) element may both map to italic typeface:

```
<P><EM>Emphasized text</EM>.
<STRONG>Strong text</STRONG>.
<CODE>Computer text</CODE>.
<KBD>Keyboard text</KBD>.
<VAR>Variable text</VAR.
<SAMP>Sample text</SAMP>.
<CITE>Citation text</CITE>.</P>
```

> *Emphasized text.* **Strong text**. Computer text.
> Keyboard text. Variable text.
> *Sample text. Citation text.*

The **Dfn** (defining instance) element encloses the first occurrence or most significant occurrence of a term used in the text. Potentially, this element may be used by search engines to determine keywords, and by style sheets to highlight new terms as they are introduced:

```
... Although <DFN>XML</DFN> is related
to <DFN>SGML</DFN>, XML is also related
to <DFN>HTML</DFN> as HTML is an application
of SGML.
```

The font size may be varied using the **Font** element (now deprecated). The **Size** attribute dictates the new font size, either absolutely, as a value between '1' and '7' (the default being '3'), or relatively as a size change from the current value. A relative size is given by inserting a '+' or '-' character:

```
This text is <FONT SIZE="-1">smaller</FONT> than
normal.
```

An additional **Color** attribute uses the scheme described above for changing the document colour in the Body element. Font elements can also be embedded in each other.

The deprecated **Basefont** element is used to specify a new default font size for the whole document and should therefore be placed at the top of the Body segment. It also uses a **Size** attribute to set the font size:

```
<BASEFONT SIZE="2">Text size is smaller than normal but
<FONT SIZE="+1">is now as expected</FONT>.
```

The **Big** and **Small** elements are complementary and they specify larger and smaller text respectively, but the actual size is determined by the browser. The **U** (underline) element specifies a line under the enclosed text, and the **Strike** element specifies a line through the text (both elements are deprecated).

The **Sub** (subscript) and **Sup** (superscript) elements are complementary. The first encloses small text that appears below the baseline and the second encloses small text that appears above the baseline:

```
The W<SUP>3</SUP>C is responsible for HTML.
Water is H<SUB>2</SUB>O.
```

Formatted text

It is sometimes important to be able to control the way in which the browser formats a block of text into individual lines.

The **Br** (line break) element forces following text to be placed on a new line. This is very useful for semi-formatting text, such as lines of poetry. It is an empty element:

```
<P>Break this line here <BR>so this is line 2.</P>
```

The **Preformatted** element (**Pre**) composes the content in a monospaced font. All spaces and line-feed characters are retained, making it possible to use them to create simple character-based diagrams or columns of text. The **Width** attribute (now deprecated) can be used to give the browser a hint as to the maximum length of the lines of text, so that it can choose an appropriate font size to render it:

```
<PRE WIDTH="30">
Here is a face:    ---
                  /   \
                 [ o o ]
                  \ - /
                   ---
</PRE>
```

To use this element, the source XML data must already be in the necessary format. The Preserve Space attribute must be used, or each text line must be distinguished by separate elements (that can be removed during the transformation process). Also, if vertical alignment is important, the document author must have used a monospaced font.

The **Plaintext** and **Example** (**Xmp**) elements identify text that should be presented exactly as it is stored in the file, including preservation of line breaks. They are therefore indistinguishable from the Pre element (and are now deprecated or made obsolete).

Images

The **Img** (image) element identifies an image file, the content of which is to appear at the current location. This is an empty element; there is no end-tag. An **Src** (source) attribute specifies the name and location of the image file:

```
...there is a GIF file <IMG SRC="myimage.gif"> here.
```

The image name alone, as shown above, is sufficient when the image resides in the same directory as the HTML document. The rules for specifying an image file stored in another location are the same as for hypertext links (described later) so are not covered here. By default, the base of the image is likely to be aligned with the baseline of the text. Image alignment can be made specific using the **Align** attribute (now deprecated), which takes a value of 'top', 'middle' or 'bottom'. As some browsers are not able to display images, an **Alt** (alternative) attribute may be used to display alternative text. The second example below demonstrates its use:

```
...there is a GIF file
<IMG SRC="myimage.gif" ALIGN="top" ALT="no piccy"> here.

...there is a GIF file   --------   here.
                         |        |
                          --------

...there is a GIF file [no piccy] here.
```

This element takes additional alignment options using the **Align** attribute. In addition to the standard 'middle', 'top' and 'bottom' options, the new 'left' and 'right' options create floating images in the left or right margin. New attributes include **Border**, which specifies the thickness of the image border line, the **Vspace** (vertical space) attribute and the **Hspace** (horizontal space) attribute, which create extra space around the image, and **Width** and **Height**, which tell the browser the dimensions of the image to speed up downloading:

```
<IMG BORDER="2" VSPACE="3" HSPACE="4" ALIGN="left">
```

Due to the new floating images described above, the **Br** (line break) element has been extended to allow the break to force the next line to appear below large, horizontally adjacent floating images. Account can be taken of images that appear in just one of the margins. The **Clear** attribute (now deprecated) takes a value of 'all' (an image in either or both margins), 'left' (an image in the left margin only) or 'right' (an image in the right margin only):

```
<BR CLEAR="left">
```

A popular feature of HTML is its ability to attach links to parts of an image. This is called an image map. For example, a map of the world could be linked to other HTML documents that describe characteristics of each country. The source of the link is therefore an area of the image. In the well-supported concept of a 'server-sided' image map, the browser simply passes the coordinates of the mouse-click to the Web server, which calls a script that decides, depending on the coordinate values, which HTML document to return to the browser. The **Img** element takes an additional attribute, **Ismap**, to indicate that the coordinates of the mouse-click should be sent to the Web server. This implied attribute has a single legal value of 'ISMAP' (the attribute name never appears):

```
<IMG SRC="myimage.gif" ISMAP>
```

However, the Web server must also be told which script to activate when the mouse is clicked on this image. To do this, the Img element is enclosed in an **A** element, which uses a URL to locate the appropriate script:

```
<A HREF="/cgi-bin/imagemap/my.map">
<IMG SRC="myimage.gif" ISMAP>
</A>
```

This scheme relies on the use of the HTTP protocol, a Web server and CGI scripts, and so it is not particularly suitable for simple intranet solutions or for publishing HTML files on a CD-ROM. The concept of 'client-side' image maps overcomes this problem. The browser uses HTML tags to identify image areas and associated URLs to other documents or other parts of the same document. This approach provides the benefits of less interaction with the server (making the process more efficient) and independence from the HTTP protocol (making it suitable for simple intranet use, when a Web server may not be needed, and more efficient Internet use), as well as giving prior warning of the effect of clicking on any part of the image (the target URL is displayed as the pointer moves over the image). The **Usemap** attribute is added to the Img element and holds the name of a **Map** element that defines areas of the image:

```
<IMG SRC="/images/myimage.gif" USEMAP="#mymap">

<MAP NAME="mymap"> ..... </MAP>
```

Within the Map element, each area and associated URL is defined using an **Area** element. This element contains attributes to define the shape of the area, its coordinates and the URL associated with the area. The **Coords** attribute defines the coordinates of the area and the **Href** attribute provides the URL. The **Alt** attribute contains a textual equivalent to the area, to be used by applications that cannot support this feature. The **Nohref** attribute indicates that this area is not active, and it has a single possible value of 'nohref'. Consider an example of an image showing a new model of motor car. Each area of interest, such as the wheels or the engine, could be located and attached to an appropriate HTML document:

```
<MAP NAME="mymap">
    <AREA SHAPE="circle"
          COORDS="50, 150, 150, 250"
          HREF="wheels/back.html"
          ALT="Back Wheels">
    <AREA SHAPE="circle"
          COORDS="350, 200, 50"
          HREF="wheels/front.html"
          ALT="Front Wheels">
</MAP>
```

The default shape is assumed to be a rectangle, with four coordinates representing, in pixels, the left edge, top edge, right edge and bottom edge of the area. The first example above defines an area for the back wheel – '50' pixels in, '150' pixels down for the left and top edges, and (as the diameter of the wheel is 100 pixels), '150' in and '250' down for the right and bottom edges. The optional **Shape** attribute may be used to make this area type explicit, 'shape="rect"'. Another shape option is 'circle', which requires three values, namely the horizontal and vertical coordinates for the centre of the circle, followed by a radius value. The second example defines the area of the front wheel as a circle with a radius of '50' pixels, '350' pixels across and '200' down.

Backward compatibility can be provided for browsers not able to use this facility. Both schemes for creating image maps (client-side and server-side) can coexist by including both the Ismap attribute and the Usemap attribute in the same Img element. In the example below, a browser that does not support a client-side map scheme uses the Anchor to pass coordinates to 'myscript.cgi':

```
<A HREF="myscript.cgi">
    <IMG SRC="/images/myimage.gif"
         USEMAP="#mymap" ISMAP>
</A>

<MAP NAME="mymap">
<!-- image mapping commands -->
</MAP>
```

Tables

The **Table** element encloses a table grid. The cells may be separated by border lines, using the **Border** attribute. A number of pixels value may be applied, such as '3' – a value of '0' indicates no border and no space for a border (which is different from the effect of not including the attribute). Alternatively, the tag may simply include the word 'border', which can be considered the same as a border value of '1':

```
<TABLE>              no borders, space for them remains

<TABLE BORDER="0">  no borders, no space for them

<TABLE BORDER>      same as 'border=1' using 'dummy'

<TABLE BORDER="10"> very thick border lines
```

The space between cells can be adjusted. The **Cellspacing** attribute takes a numeric value that states how much space there is between cells (including their borders). If a value of '0' is used, the border lines overlap each other. It has a default value of '2':

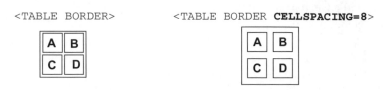

The space between the cell contents and the borders of the cell can also be adjusted using the **Cellpadding** attribute, which takes a numeric value. The default value is '1':

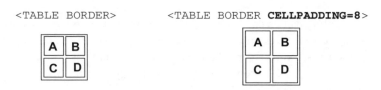

The width and height of the table are often left under the control of the browser, which composes the table within the restrictions of the available window area. The **Width** attribute may be used to 'encourage' the browser to take into account the wishes of the document author. This attribute takes a numeric value that dictates how many pixels wide the table should be, or what percentage of the available screen width it should occupy. A pure number is interpreted as a pixel value. A percentage symbol indicates a proportion of the screen dimensions:

```
<TABLE BORDER WIDTH=800>
```

The table may have a title, which is contained in a **Caption** element. This element is placed within the Table element but before the elements described later. The content is, by default, displayed above the main table grid, but it may be explicitly displayed below the table using the **Align** attribute, with a value of 'bottom':

```
<TABLE>
   <CAPTION ALIGN="bottom">Title Below</CAPTION> ...
</TABLE>
```

The table structure is row-oriented, which means that the grid is built by first defining each row and then separating each cell within a row. Each row of data is enclosed in a **Table Row** element (**Tr**), and each cell is enclosed in either a **Table Header** element (**Th**) or a **Table Data** element (**Td**), the only difference being one of emphasis – the Th element content is usually displayed in bold (and centred). Th and Td elements may be mixed in the same row, possibly to create side headings:

```
<TR><TH>Colour<TH>Status<TH>Level</TR>
<TR><TH>Red<TD>Danger<TD>1</TR>
<TR><TH>Green<TD>Normal<TD>3</TR>
```

Colour	Status	Level
Red	Danger	1
Green	Normal	3

As shown above, a cell may directly contain text. But it may also contain any document body elements, including a complete embedded table. The Line Break element is particularly useful for formatting text within cells. If a cell is empty, no border lines are drawn.

The width and height of a cell can be 'suggested' in the Td and Th elements, using the **Width** and **Height** attributes. The browser is not, however, required to obey these instructions.

The content of individual cells, or all the cells in a row, may be aligned horizontally and vertically in various ways. The default horizontal alignment is 'left' in Td elements, and 'center' in Th elements, as shown in the example above. The default vertical alignment is 'middle' for both types of cell. The **Align** attribute allows horizontal alignment to be set to 'left', 'right' or 'center'. The **Valign** attribute allows vertical alignment to be set to 'top', 'middle', 'bottom' or 'baseline' (where all cells in the row are horizontally aligned by last line, after the cell with the most lines is aligned to 'top'). An alignment set in the Tr element provides a default for all cells in the row, but individual cells may override this setting.

By default each cell occupies an area dissected by one column and one row, forming a simple position within the table grid, but may be expanded across or down using the **Colspan** and **Rowspan** attributes. These attributes take numeric values, and have implied values of '1' (zero is not a legal option). Higher values than '1' stretch the cell over adjoining areas:

```
<TR><TH>Colour<TH>Status<TH>Level</TR>
<TR><TH>Red<TD>Danger<TD>1</TR>
<TR><TH>Blue<TD COLSPAN=2>No Priority<TD>2</TR>
<TR><TH>Brown</TH><!-- NO CELL --><TD>3</TD></TR>
```

Colour	Status	Level
Red	Danger	1
Blue	No Priority	2
Brown		3

Note that the final row in the example above has only two cell elements, containing 'Brown' and '3', because the middle cell has effectively been replaced by the cell above it.

The content of a cell is normally formatted by the browser as it is composed to fit the available screen width. The **Nowrap** attribute may be used in the Th and Td elements to prevent lines being split. This is another example of a minimized attribute with a single possible value, in this case 'nowrap':

```
<TD NOWRAP>This line must not be broken</TD>
```

When presenting tables on paper, it is useful to be able to identify header rows so that the pagination engine can repeat the headings at the top of each page. Similarly, footer rows can be repeated at the base of each page containing a reference to a footnote. When presenting to a scrollable window, a large table body may be collapsed to just a few scrollable rows sandwiched between fixed, permanently visible headers and footers. The new elements **Table Head** (**Thead**), **Table Body** (**Tbody**) and **Table Footer** (**Tfoot**) enclose rows of each kind.

Only the Tbody element is required, and for backward compatibility both its start-tag and end-tag may be absent (its presence then being implied). The Thead and Tfoot elements are optional because not all tables have rows that fall into these categories. When present, the Thead element must occur first, as would be expected, but the Tfoot element must *also* precede the body. The reason for this unusual arrangement is that it allows the rendering package to collect the content of a footer and then place it at the base of each page, without needing to process the table twice:

```
<TABLE>
    <THEAD>...</THEAD>
    <TFOOT>...</TFOOT>
    <TBODY>...</TBODY>
</TABLE>
```

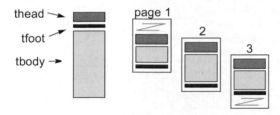

In addition to the usual array of core, event and language attributes, these three elements also contain the **Align** and **Valign** attributes, so introducing another level of cell content alignment overriding, above the row level. In a table containing mostly currency values, it may be appropriate to state that all header cells are centred, that all body cells are aligned on full-points and that all footer cells are left-aligned.

It is not uncommon to find tables where all the cells in a particular column are aligned in the same way. For example, a price table in a catalogue may have two columns, the first being a description of each product, with the text left-aligned, and the second being the price of that item aligned on a decimal point. Using the table model described in the previous section, each Td element would need to contain an Align attribute:

```
<TR>
<TD ALIGN="left">Red coat</TD>
<TD ALIGN="char" char=".">12.4</TD>
</TR>
<TR>
<TD ALIGN="left">Green coat</TD>
<TD ALIGN="char" CHAR=".">12.6</TD>
</TR>
```

Clearly, when many rows are involved, this is very time consuming to produce, and also wasteful of memory and bandwidth. It is now possible to define a style for all cells in a column using the **Column** element (**Col**). In the example below, the first Col element specifies an alignment of 'left' for the first column, and the second specifies an alignment on the decimal point for the second column, so removing the need to specify these alignments in individual entries:

```
<COL ALIGN="left">
<COL ALIGN="char" char=".">
<TR>
<TD>Red coat</TD>
<TD>12.4</TD>
</TR>
<TR>
<TD>Green coat</TD>
<TD>12.6</TD>
</TR>
...
```

For horizontal alignments, the Col element overrides the Tr element, though individual Entry element styles are still the most significant:

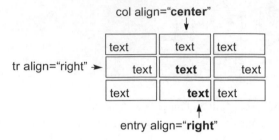

As indicated above, the first Col element is deemed to apply to the first column, the second applies to the next column, and so on. When several columns in a group have the same settings, only one Col element is required and the **Span** attribute is used to specify how many columns are affected. The total number of columns in a table can be calculated by adding together the span values (when not present, a value of '1' is assumed). In the following example, the table has six columns (and it is assumed that if a Col element is used at all, then all table columns must be covered by these elements):

```
<COL ALIGN="left">
<COL SPAN="3" ALIGN="right">
<COL SPAN="2" ALIGN="center">
```

This element can also be used to predefine the width of each column, using the **Width** attribute, so that Web browsers and pagination engines can start building the table presentation before reading the entire table. In the following example, the column widths are '30', '40', '40', '40', '50' and '50':

```
<COL WIDTH="30" ALIGN="left">
<COL WIDTH="40" SPAN="3" ALIGN="right">
<COL WIDTH="50" SPAN="2" ALIGN="center">
```

The Width values may also be proportional, so that the table width can expand to the area available, and each column is assigned a 'fair' proportion of that width based on the values in the Width attribute.

A value followed by an asterisk character denotes a proportional value. To make the column widths defined above keep their relative sizes but allow additional space to be exploited, it is only necessary to append the asterisk to the existing values, though the smaller values '3*', '4*', '4*', '4*', '5*' and '5*' would produce identical results. This approach is not yet universally supported.

When a large number of consecutive Col elements share some attribute values, but not others, a new and more efficient technique may be employed using the **Column Group** element (**Colgroup**). This element may enclose a number of Col elements and has exactly the same attributes, which when used are deemed to apply to each embedded Col element that does not itself contain an explicit definition. In this example, both columns in the group are given a width of 55 pixels:

```
<COLGROUP WIDTH="55">
   <COL ALIGN="left">
   <COL SPAN="3" ALIGN="right">
</COLGROUP>
<COLGROUP WIDTH="50" SPAN="2" ALIGN="center">
</COLGROUP>
```

The other major benefit of column groups is that they define an identifiable vertical component of a table, consisting of several columns and regardless of any degree of commonality in style between these columns. This defined object may be the target of a hypertext link, or the trigger for an event, such as Onclick. A Colgroup element does not even have to contain Col elements if their presence is not appropriate. In this case, it has its own **Span** attribute:

```
<COLGROUP SPAN="3" WIDTH="35"></COLGROUP>
<COLGROUP SPAN="2" WIDTH="20"></COLGROUP>
```

It is not possible to mix Colgroup and Col elements. If just one Colgroup is needed, then all definitions must be applied using it. Another way to look at this restriction is to imagine that Col elements must always be contained within a Colgroup element; but, when there are only Col elements present they are enclosed in an implied column group.

Descriptive markup

As stylistic elements are removed or deprecated, they are replaced by new descriptive elements. The following elements help stylesheet designers to develop more suitable formatting, and Web crawler search engines to perform more useful analysis of the document.

The **Abbreviation** element (**Abbr**) is used to identify an abbreviation in the text. It has a **Title** attribute, which is used to hold the full term:

```
...talk to <ABBR TITLE="Mister">Mr.</ABBR> Smith ...
```

Similarly, the **Acronym** element holds a form of abbreviation that substitutes each word in a name with one letter. The **Title** attribute is used in the same way:

```
... <ACRONYM TITLE="World Wide Web">WWW</ACRONYM> ...
```

The **Quote** element (**Q**) holds an in-line quotation:

```
... Shakespeare wrote <Q>To be or not to be...</Q> ...
```

The **Blockquote** element contains a block of text quoted from another source, which is typically indented by the browser.

The **Deletion** element (**Del**) identifies text that is to be considered as deleted, and is only present to bring attention to the fact that it no longer applies. Such text is typically presented with a line through it. Complementing this is the **Insertion** element (**Ins**), which identifies new text. Typically, new text is highlighted with a change bar in the margin. By convention, they should be used consistently as block-level elements, or as in-line elements, but not both as it may be difficult to apply a suitable style for both types. They both contain optional **Datetime** and **Citation** attributes (**Cite**), indicating respectively the time the document was changed, and pointing to another document that contains comments on why the change was made, though the Title attribute may also be used to contain a short note on the reason:

```
... there are <DEL>fifteen</DEL><INS>nine</INS> days left
to Christmas ...
```

Styles and scripts

The **Style** element encloses stylesheet instructions. The **Type** attribute is required and identifies the stylesheet language, such as 'text/css' or 'text/xsl'. The **Media** attribute identifies the type of media the stylesheet is aimed at, such as 'screen' (the default) or 'paper'. A **Title** attribute is also allowed to identify the stylesheet.

```
<STYLE TYPE="text/css" MEDIA="screen">
  p { color: green }
</STYLE>
```

A number of attributes have been added to the **Script** element, which is used to enclose script programs. The **Type** attribute describes the scripting language used, such as 'text/javascript'. The **Src** attribute identifies a remote file containing the scripts, using a URL. When Src is used, the **Charset** attribute may also be used to identify the character set used in the file that contains the scripts. The **Defer** attribute takes a boolean value of 'true' or 'false' to indicate whether or not the browser should defer executing the script. When set to 'true', this is a hint that the script does not alter the document in any way and so the browser can go ahead and render the document.

To prevent older browsers from simply displaying the scripts, it is necessary to surround them with a comment. Also, the **NoScript** element has been included to hold alternative information in the case that the browser is configured to prevent scripts from running, or it is not familiar with the scripting language used.

Frames

Using frames, the screen is divided into areas, with each area possibly displaying a different document, and each one scrolled independently. Among other uses, frames facilitate the use of table of contents and button bars that do not vanish as the user scrolls down the main document:

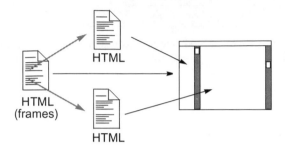

A frame-based document replaces the Body element with a **Frameset** element:

```
<HTML>
<HEAD>...</HEAD>
<FRAMESET>...</FRAMESET>
</HTML>
```

The Frameset element defines an area that generally fills the end user's screen. This area is divided into frames using the **Cols** or **Rows** attribute. These attributes take a value that specifies the width or height of the sub-areas. This value specifies the height or width using one of three methods, namely the number of pixels (not advised), proportion or percentage of the available space. Values are separated by commas, which also therefore implicitly specify the number of columns or rows in the set:

```
<FRAMESET ROWS="1500, 1000, 500">

<FRAMESET ROWS="3*, 2*, *">

<FRAMESET ROWS="50%, 33%, 16%">
```

The first example above specifies a height of 1,500 pixels for the first row, the second example reserves three proportional units for the first row (the asterisk character alone is equivalent to '1*'), and the third example specifies that the first row should occupy half the available height ('50%'). If the available height was 3,000 pixels, then all three examples above would be equivalent. These value types may be mixed:

```
<FRAMSET COLS="50%, 100, 2*, *">
```

When value types are mixed, fixed values have precedence, followed by percentage values and then proportional values. In the example above, the second column is assigned exactly 100 pixels of horizontal space, the first column is then assigned half the remaining space, and the remainder is divided among the proportional columns (the third column taking twice the space of the last column):

2nd (percentage) priority	1st priority	3rd (proportional) priority	
50% of remaining area	100 pixels	2*	1*

A Frame Set can contain further embedded Frame Sets. Each embedded Frame Set occupies the space reserved for it by the enclosing Frame Set. Taking the example above, a Frame Set embedded in the first column is restricted to the left half of the screen and will define subdivisions of this area:

```
<FRAMESET COLS="50%, 100, 2*, *">
   <FRAMESET COLS="60%, 40%">
   ...
   </FRAMESET>
   ...
</FRAMSET>
```

l-------- 60 % -------l--- 40 % ---l	100 pixels	2*	1*

A Frame Set may contain a **Noframes** element. This element is intended to hold information to be displayed by a browser that cannot interpret frames. Its function is therefore similar to the Alt attribute in the Image element. Its content, which may include normal blocks such as paragraphs and lists, is not displayed in frames-aware browsers:

```
<NOFRAMES>
<P>If you CAN see this, then you can NOT see the Frames!
</NOFRAMES>
```

A frames-aware browser ignores this tag and all its contents. A browser that does not understand frames will not be aware of the Noframes element, but is most likely to remove the tags, leaving the enclosed text intact for presentation to the user.

Finally, a Frameset element may contain a **Frame** element. This is an empty element so has no end-tag. It is used to identify the document to be displayed in the frame, to identify the frame itself (so that it can be made the target of links from other frames or documents), to determine if the width and height of the frame can be altered by the end user, to determine if scroll-bars are used, and to specify margin widths. The Frame element has a **Source** attribute (**Src**) which contains the URL of the HTML document to be displayed in the frame. If no URL is provided, the area is left blank. The Frame element also has a **Name** attribute, which contains the name of the frame, so that it can be the target of a link from another frame or from another document:

```
<FRAME NAME="main" SRC="../areas/myarea.html">
```

By referring to the Name value of another frame, a new document can be requested and displayed in that other area. This feature is ideal for changing the content of the main window as items are selected in a table of contents frame. The **A** (Anchor) element has a new **Target** attribute to refer to the actual frame in which the content should be displayed:

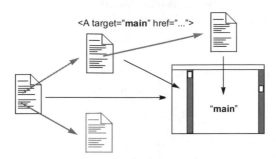

The Frame element also has a **Scrolling** attribute, which indicates whether horizontal and vertical scroll-bars are always present, present as required (when the height or width of the page exceeds the space provided on the screen), or never present. A value of 'yes' forces scroll-bars to appear even if not needed. A value of 'auto' displays scroll-bars when necessary and is the default value. A value of 'no' disables scroll-bars entirely.

The Frame element also has a **Noresize** attribute, which, if present, prevents the end user from changing the height or width of the frame. By default it is absent and resizing is allowed. In XML terms, this must be seen as an attribute called Noresize that has an optional, single value of 'NORESIZE', and that minimization is in use to avoid stating the attribute name:

```
<FRAME SRC="../areas/myarea.html" NORESIZE>
```

Finally, the Frame element has **Marginwidth** and **Marginheight** attributes, which specify the space to reserve between the borders of the frame and the enclosed text. Width settings affect the space between the left and right edges. Height settings affect the space above and below the content. Values are in pixels and, if present, must be at least '1' and not so large that content cannot be displayed; if absent, the browser provides default settings.

Elements and attributes list

The following table shows the elements and attributes defined in the currently most supported, and the latest, version of HTML. Items marked with an asterisk, '*', are not supported by the latest version of at least one of the most popular Web browsers and so should be used with caution.

There is a very large number of attributes first defined in HTML 4.0. Many of them are defined using entities. To keep this table to a reasonable size, these groups are described here and given the names 'Core' ('Id', 'Type', 'Class' and 'Style'), 'Events' ('Onclick', 'Ondblclick', 'Onmousedown', 'Onmouseup', 'Onmouseover', 'Onmouseout', 'Onkeypress', 'Onkeydown', 'Onkeyup') and 'Lang' ('Lang' and 'Dir') for reference under appropriate elements. However, note that when an attribute in one of these groups applies to the previous version of HTML, it is also included explicitly.

Elements and Attributes	HTML 3. 2	HTML 4.0
A	**YES**	**YES**
Core & Events & Lang		YES
accesskey *		YES
coords *		YES
charset *		YES
href	YES	YES
hreflang *		YES
methods	obsolete	
name	YES	YES
onblur *		YES
onfocus *		YES
rel	YES	YES
rev	YES	YES
shape *		YES
tabindex *		YES
target		YES
type *		YES

title	YES	YES
urn	obsolete	
ABBR		**YES**
Core & Events & Lang		YES
ACRONYM		**YES**
Core & Events & Lang		YES
ADDRESS	**YES**	**YES**
Core		YES
APPLET	**YES**	**deprecated** (use Object)
align	YES	
alt	YES	
archive		
code	YES	
codebase	YES	
height	YES	
hspace	YES	
name	YES	
object *		
title		
vspace	YES	
width	YES	
AREA	**YES**	**YES**
accesskey *		
alt	YES	
coords	YES	
href	YES	
nohref	YES	
onblur *		
onfocus *		
shape	YES	
tabindex *		
target		

B	YES	YES
Core & Events & Lang		YES
BASE	YES	YES
href	YES	YES
target		YES
BASEFONT	YES	deprecated
color *		
face *		
id *		
name *		
size	YES	
BDO		YES
Core		
dir *		
lang *		
BIG *	YES	YES
Core & Events & Lang		YES
BLOCKQUOTE	YES	YES
Core & Events & Lang		YES
cite *		YES
BODY	YES	YES
Core & Events & Lang		YES
alink	YES	deprecated
background	YES	deprecated
bgcolor	YES	deprecated
link	YES	deprecated
onload *		YES
onunload *		YES
text	YES	deprecated
vlink	YES	deprecated
BR	YES	YES
Core		YES

clear	YES	deprecated
BUTTON		**YES**
Core & Events & Lang		YES
accesskey *		YES
clear	YES	
disabled *		YES
name *		YES
onblur *		YES
onfocus *		YES
tabindex *		YES
type *		YES
value *		YES
CAPTION	**YES**	**YES**
Core & Events & Lang		YES
align	YES	deprecated
CENTER	**YES**	**deprecated**
Core & Events & Lang		
CITE	**YES**	**YES**
Core & Events & Lang		YES
CODE	**YES**	**YES**
Core & Events & Lang		YES
COL *		**YES**
Core & Events & Lang		
align		
char *		
charoff *		
span		
valign *		
width		

COLGROUP *		YES
Core & Events & Lang		
align *		
char *		
charoff *		
span *		
valign *		
width *		
DD	YES	YES
Core & Events & Lang		YES
DEL		YES
Core & Events & Lang		
cite *		
datetime *		
DFN *	YES	YES
Core & Events & Lang		YES
DIR	YES	deprecated (use UL)
Core & Events & Lang		YES
compact *	YES	YES
DIV	YES	YES
Core & Events & Lang		YES
align	YES	YES
DL	YES	YES
Core & Events & Lang		YES
compact	YES	YES
DT	YES	YES
Core & Events & Lang		YES
EM	YES	YES
Core & Events & Lang		YES
EMBED		YES
Core & Events & Lang		

FIELDSET		YES
Core & Events & Lang		
language *		
title *		
FONT	**YES**	**deprecated**
Core & Lang		
color	YES	
size	YES	
FORM	**YES**	**YES**
Core & Events & Lang		
action	YES	
accept-charset *		
enctype *	YES	
method	YES	
onreset		
onsubmit		
target		
FRAME		**YES**
Core		
frameborder		
langdesc *		
marginheight		
marginwidth		
name		
noresize		
scrolling		
src		

FRAMESET		YES
Core		
cols		
onload *		
onunload *		
rows		
H1	YES	YES
Core & Events & Lang		YES
align	YES	deprecated
H2	YES	YES
Core & Events & Lang		YES
align	YES	deprecated
H3	YES	YES
Core & Events & Lang		YES
align	YES	deprecated
H4	YES	YES
Core & Events & Lang		YES
align	YES	deprecated
H5	YES	YES
Core & Events & Lang		YES
align	YES	deprecated
H6	YES	YES
Core & Events & Lang		YES
align	YES	deprecated
HEAD	YES	YES
Lang		YES
profile *		YES
HR	YES	YES
Core & Events		YES
align	YES	deprecated
noshade	YES	deprecated
size	YES	deprecated

width	YES	deprecated
HTML	**YES**	**YES**
Lang		YES
version *		deprecated
I	**YES**	**YES**
Core & Events & Lang		YES
IFRAME		**YES**
Core		
align *		
frameborder *		
langdesc *		
marginheight *		
marginwidth *		
name *		
scrolling *		
src *		
width *		
IMG	**YES**	**YES**
Core & Events & Lang		YES
align	YES	deprecated
alt	YES	YES
border	YES	deprecated
height	YES	YES
hspace	YES	YES
ismap	YES	YES
langdesc *		YES
src	YES	YES
usemap	YES	YES
vspace	YES	YES
width	YES	YES

INPUT	YES	YES
Core & Events & Lang		
accept *		
accesskey *		
align	YES	
alt *		
checked *	YES	
disabled *		
langdesc *		
maxlength *	YES	
name *	YES	
onblur *		
onchange *		
onfocus *		
onselect *		
readonly *		
size	YES	
src	YES	
tabindex *		
type	YES	
usemap *		
value	YES	
INS		YES
Core & Events & Lang		
cite *		
datetime *		
ISINDEX	YES	**deprecated** (use INPUT)
Core & Lang		
prompt	YES	
KBD	YES	YES
Core & Events & Lang		YES

LABEL		YES
Core & Events & Lang		
accesskey *		
for *		
lang *		
language *		
onblur *		
onfocus *		
title *		
LEGEND *		**YES**
Core & Events & Lang		YES
accesskey *		YES
align *		deprecated
LI	**YES**	**YES**
Core & Events & Lang		YES
type	YES	YES
value	YES	deprecated
LINK	**YES**	**YES**
Core & Events & Lang		
charset *		
href	YES	
hreflang *		
media *		
rel	YES	
rev	YES	
title	YES	
LISTING	**deprecated**	**obsolete** (use PRE)
MAP	**YES**	**YES**
Core & Events & Lang		YES
name	YES	YES

MENU	YES	deprecated (use UL)
Core & Events & Lang		
compact	YES	
META	**YES**	**YES**
Lang		YES
content	YES	YES
http-equiv	YES	YES
name	YES	YES
scheme *		YES
NEXTID	**obsolete**	
N	obsolete	
NOFRAMES		**YES**
Core & Events & Lang		YES
NOSCRIPT		**YES**
Core & Events & Lang		YES
OBJECT *		**YES**
Core & Events & Lang		YES
align *		YES
archive *		YES
border *		deprecated
classid *		YES
codebase *		YES
codetype *		YES
declare *		YES
height *		YES
hspace *		YES
name *		YES
standby *		YES
tabindex *		YES
type *		YES
usemap *		YES
vspace *		YES

width *		YES
OL	**YES**	**YES**
Core & Events & Lang		YES
compact	YES	deprecated
start	YES	deprecated
type	YES	deprecated
OPTGROUP		**YES**
Core & Events & Lang		
disabled *		
label *		
OPTION	**YES**	**YES**
Core & Events & Lang		YES
selected	YES	YES
value	YES	YES
P	**YES**	**YES**
Core & Events & Lang		YES
align	YES	deprecated
disabled *		YES
label *		YES
PARAM	**YES**	**YES**
id *		YES
name	YES	YES
type *		YES
value	YES	YES
valuetype *		YES
PLAINTEXT	**deprecated**	**obsolete** (use PRE)
PRE	**YES**	**YES**
Core & Events & Lang		YES
width	YES	deprecated
Q		**YES**
Core & Events & Lang		YES
cite *		YES

SAMP	YES	YES
Core & Events & Lang		YES
SCRIPT	YES	YES
charset *		YES
defer *		YES
language		deprecated
src *		YES
type *		YES
SELECT	YES	YES
Core & Events & Lang		
disabled *		
multiple	YES	
name	YES	
onchange *		
onblur *		
onfocus *		
size	YES	
tabindex *		
SMALL *	YES	YES
Core & Events & Lang		YES
SPAN		YES
Core & Events & Lang		
align		
STRIKE	YES	**deprecated**
Core & Events & Lang		YES
STRONG	YES	YES
Core & Events & Lang		YES
STYLE	**YES**	YES
Lang		
media *		
title *		
type *		

SUB *	YES	YES
Core & Events & Lang		YES
SUP *	YES	YES
Core & Events & Lang		YES
TABLE	YES	YES
Core & Events & Lang		YES
align	YES	deprecated
bgcolor *		deprecated
border	YES	YES
cellpadding	YES	YES
cellspacing	YES	YES
frame *		YES
rules *		YES
summary *		YES
width	YES	YES
TBODY *		YES
Core & Events & Lang		
align *		
valign *		
TD	YES	YES
Core & Events & Lang		YES
abbr *		YES
align	YES	YES
axis *		YES
colspan	YES	YES
headers *		YES
height	YES	deprecated
nowrap	YES	deprecated
rowspan	YES	YES
scope *		YES
valign	YES	YES
width	YES	deprecated

TEXTAREA	YES	YES
Core & Events & Lang		
accesskey *		
cols	YES	
disabled *		
name	YES	
onblur *		
onchange *		
onfocus *		
onselect *		
readonly *		
rows	YES	
tabindex *		
TFOOT *		YES
Core & Events & Lang		
align *		
valign *		
TH	YES	YES
Core & Events & Lang		YES
abbr *		YES
align	YES	YES
axis *		YES
colspan	YES	YES
headers *		YES
height	YES	deprecated
nowrap	YES	deprecated
rowspan	YES	YES
valign	YES	YES
width	YES	YES

THEAD *		YES
Core & Events & Lang		
align *		
valign *		
TITLE	**YES**	**YES**
Lang		YES
TR	**YES**	**YES**
Core & Events & Lang		
align	YES	
bgcolor *		
valign	YES	
TT	**YES**	**YES**
Core & Events & Lang		YES
U	**YES**	**deprecated**
Core & Events & Lang		YES
UL	**YES**	**YES**
Core & Events & Lang		YES
compact	YES	deprecated
type	YES	deprecated
VAR	**YES**	**YES**
Core & Events & Lang		YES
XMP	**deprecated**	**obsolete** (use PRE)

29. CSS

CSS is a well established stylesheet technology that may be considered as a competitor to XSL, but not to XSLT. Indeed, there are a number of reasons why CSS could be of interest to XSLT stylesheet developers. When an XSLT stylesheet is used to convert XML documents into HTML Web pages, these pages can be enriched with CSS styles.

Background

CSS was developed for use with HTML and it has an important role in making Web documents more interesting. It is one of the core technologies that lie behind the marketing term DHTML (*Dynamic* HTML). With CSS, it is possible to control the appearance of most HTML elements: to define the font, size, style and colour to apply to the text content of a paragraph, table cell or list item.

CSS 1.0 was released in 1996 by W3C, and is reasonably well supported by current versions of the popular browsers. It is available from http://www.w3.org/pub/WWW/TR/REC-CSS1. A total of 53 properties are defined by this version of the standard, including properties used to define the style of the text (font, size, style), the colour of the text and background, layout information (line indents, alignments, spacing between letters and words), positioning (margins, borders, padding within borders), and generated constructs (lists and list items).

At the same time as early work began on XSL/XSLT, the same pressure for more control over the presentation of material in Web browsers also led to further work on the CSS standard. Version 2 adds 76 new properties. These new properties fall into two main categories. Many are simply additions to existing areas of functionality. Others are used to provide new features, such as support for tabular layouts, aural output and printed output. Unfortunately, CSS 2 is not yet well supported. The table at the end of this chapter lists all the properties, and makes clear which were introduced with version 2.

Format primer

CSS consists of properties that define formatting characteristics. Each property has two parts. First, the property name, such as 'color' or 'font-size'. Second, the property value, such as 'blue' or '14pt'. The name is separated from the value using a colon (and possibly also spaces):

```
color:blue


font-size : 14pt
```

When several properties are grouped together, the value of one property is separated from the name of the next property using a semi-colon (and possibly also spaces):

```
color: blue ; font-size: 14pt
```

These properties can be grouped into rules that assign the characteristics to an element. In the following example, the HTML H3 (header three) element is to be displayed as 14pt-in-blue style:

```
H3 { color:blue ; font-size:14pt }
```

Note that it does not matter if a semi-colon also follows the final property in a rule. Indeed, this character is often treated as if it was a terminating character for each property, rather than a separator of properties. This approach is considered by many to be good practice, as it makes adding properties to an existing rule less likely to cause errors (due to forgetting to insert a semi-colon before the first new property):

```
{ color:blue; font-size:14pt; }
```

A CSS document is an ASCII file that contains CSS rules. It is referenced from an HTML document using the LINK element:

```
<LINK HREF="CSS/MyStyles.CSS" TYPE="text/css">
```

However, a CSS stylesheet can also be embedded in an HTML document, using the STYLE element:

```
<STYLE>
H3  { color: blue ; font-size: 14pt }
</STYLE>
```

Finally, properties can be added directly to individual HTML elements, using the STYLE attribute:

```
<H3 STYLE="color:red;font-size:12pt">...</H3>
```

These in-line styles override general rules for the given element type, and styles defined at the top of the HTML file override those defined in an external stylesheet document.

CSS versus XSL/XSLT

As shown above, the syntax of CSS is more compact than XSL (which uses XML syntax). It is therefore easier to write (both faster and without errors) using standard text editing tools, and transfers over networks more quickly. CSS is already well supported by popular Web browsers and Web-page authoring tools. It has gained acceptance, and it would certainly be difficult for another, similar stylesheet language to compete with CSS at this stage.

However, CSS was designed to format text blocks that have already been arranged in the correct order in an HTML document. It therefore lacks the transformation capabilities of XSLT. This is one of its major weaknesses. CSS is also less powerful, especially when preparing content for presentation on paper rather than on-screen.

Although it is possible to think of CSS as a direct competitor to XSL/XSLT, many people who understand the strengths and weaknesses of each approach see that they can, and often do, complement each other. It is useful to know both when working on the Web and to know when to apply one or the other, or perhaps both, to a given problem.

Finally, in an encouraging spirit of cooperation, the latest drafts of the XSL specification borrow the names of properties defined in CSS. This has been done for two reasons. First, the learning curve of moving from one to the other is eased, making it more practical for both to continue to exist. Second, this agreement on the properties supported leads to a high degree of compatibility, which makes it easier for developers to create products that support both standards.

Relevance to XSL and XSLT

CSS has been one of the influences in the development of XSL. Indeed, as stated above, XSL has now adopted the names of properties defined in CSS. It is therefore possible to use experience of CSS, or a CSS textbook, to explain the behaviour and identify the attribute name needed in XSL to achieve a particular effect. For example, in CSS the property name 'font-size' defines the size of the text to present. This name has been adopted in XSL to achieve the same effect:

```
{ ... font-size: 12pt ... }

<inline font-size="12pt">...</inline>
```

When using XSLT to create HTML documents from XML documents, the HTML document can be enhanced by including in-line CSS properties. For example, the background colour of a note may depend on the importance of the note:

```
<xsl:template match="note[@type='danger']">
  <P STYLE="background-color:red">
    <xsl:apply-templates/>
  </P>
</xsl:template>
```

Rule constructions

It is useful to know how CSS stylesheet rules are constructed in order to create an XSLT stylesheet from an existing CSS stylesheet. The selector can be more than just a single element name, in the same way that the Match attribute value on the Template element can be more complex than a simple element name, though in CSS the options are not as extensive. There is no expression language in CSS, just a small number of specific features.

Merging rules

The first major difference is that there may be multiple rules in CSS for a given element. The properties in each rule are simply added together. When properties are duplicated across rules, the last rule has precedence. In the following example, the H3 element will be displayed in blue, 14pt text, with a word spacing of 3pt:

```
H3 { color: green ; word-spacing: 3pt }

H3 { color: blue ; font-size: 14pt }
```

There is no equivalent of this in XSLT. All properties must be collected together into a single template (though variables can be used to partially emulate the effect).

Shared rules

A single rule can apply to more than one element (so avoiding unnecessary repetition). Element names are separated by commas. In the following example, the highest three header levels will all appear in green text:

```
H1, H2, H3 { color:green }
```

The equivalent XSLT expression would be:

```
match="H1|H2|H3"
```

Context elements

It is possible for a rule to apply only to an element when that element occurs in another specified element. In the following example, only table titles adopt the given style:

```
table title { ... }
```

This construct can be deceptive. It actually represents a Title element that may occur within other structures inside the Table element. The equivalent XSLT expression would be:

```
match="table//title"
```

A number of variants of this have been added in CSS 2, making use of the '>', '*' and '+' symbols.

The '>' symbol is used to indicate direct descendants:

```
table > title { ... }
```

This is clearly equivalent to the following:

```
match="table/title"
```

Another option is to use the '*' as a wildcard that represents at least one level between the two elements:

```
book * title { ... }
```

The way to replicate this in XSLT is to use '*' *and* '//':

```
match="book/*//title"
```

Finally, it is possible to identify elements that immediately follow other elements, such as an initial paragraph after a title, using '+':

```
title + p { ... }
```

```
match="p[preceding-sibling::*[1][name() = 'title']]"
```

Attribute context

CSS 2 also allows context to depend on the presence, and possibly the value, of an attribute using square brackets to enclose the attribute name, or the name and value:

```
p[type] { ... }
```

```
p[type="secret"] { ... }
```

This is one case where XSLT requires little translation of syntax (though quotes may need to be changed, as shown below, depending on the quotes used for the Match attribute):

```
match="P[@type]"


match="P[@type='secret']"
```

However, apart from '=' to check that the attribute value matches a given value, it is also possible to use '!=' (not equals) and '~=' (given value must be present within the attribute value as a distinct word). The first of these is easily converted (unfortunately, the XPath expression language has no equivalent for the '~=' feature):

```
p[type!="secret"] { ... }
match="p[not(@type='secret')]"
```

Properties

The following table shows all CSS properties, including which version of CSS they first appear in. Note that, beyond the values shown below, CSS 2 also adds the Inherit value to all properties. See the explanation at the end of the table for values specified in italics.

Property	Ver	Example values	Values
Font properties			
font	1	italic small-caps bold 18pt/22pt Helvetica, sans-serif	combination of six properties – font-style, font-variant, font-weight, font-size, line-height and font-family, with '/' between size and line height
	2	caption	... caption, icon, menu, message, small-caption, status-bar
font-style	1	italic	normal (default), italic, oblique
font-variant	1	normal	normal (default), small-caps
font-weight	1	bold	normal (default), bold, bolder, lighter, 100, 200, 300, 400, 500, 600, 700, 800, 900
font-size	1	18pt larger	*Length*, xx-large, x-large, large, medium (default), small, x-small, xx-small, smaller, larger

font-family	1	Helvetica, sans-serif 'Times New Roman'	comma separated alternative font names, first has preference; can be generic name (serif, sans-serif, cursive, fantasy, monospace); quote name with spaces, "Times New Roman" (but use single quotes in Style attributes)
font-size-adjust	2	0.58	*Number*, none (default)
font-stretch	2	narrower	normal (default), wider, narrower, ultra-condensed, extra-condensed, condensed, semi-condensed, semi-expanded, expanded, extra-expanded, ultra-expanded
Colour and background			
color	1	blue #FF0	*Color*
background	1	red url(boat.gif) no-repeat scroll 10% 10%	combination (background-color, background-image, background-repeat, background-attachment, background-position)
background-color	1	green	*Color*, transparent (default)
background-image	1	url(boat.gif)	URL, none (default)
background-repeat	1	repeat-x	repeat (default), repeat-x, repeat-y, no-repeat
background-attachment	1	fixed	scroll (default), fixed
background-position	1	top 10mm 15mm	top, center, bottom, left, right, *Percent*, (*Length* – x, y)
Text properties			
text-decoration	1	underline	none (default), underline, overline, line-through, blink
vertical-align	1	sub	baseline (default), sub, super, top, text-top, middle, bottom, text-bottom, *Percent*
	2	2pt	... *Length*
text-align	1	center	left, right, center, justify
	2	"."	... *String*
text-indent	1	1cm	*Length* (default '0') (first line of text block, minus value gives hanging indent), *Percent*

letter-spacing	1	2pt	normal (default), *Length*
word-spacing	1	normal	normal (default), *Length*
text-transform	1	uppercase	capitalize, upper case, lower case, none (default)
line-height	1	22pt	none, (default), *Number, Length, Percent*
text-shadow	2	3px 3px red 2pt 4pt, -2pt -4pt 1pt blue	normal (default), *Length* (across) *Length* (down), and optional *Length* (blur angle) and optional *Color* (plus more optional shadows separate by commas)
Box properties			
margin	1	0.3cm	*Length, Percent*, auto – repeated ('x' = all margins, 'x x' = vertical and horizontal, and 'x x x x' = top/right/bottom/left)
margin-left	1	0.3cm	*Length* (default 0), *Percent*, auto
margin-right	1	0.3in	*Length* (default 0), *Percent*, auto
margin-top	1	9pt	*Length* (default 0), *Percent*, auto
margin-bottom	1	10%	*Length* (default 0), *Percent*, auto
padding	1	1pt	*Length* (default 0), percent*** – repeated ('x' = all edges, 'x x' = vertical and horizontal, and 'x x x x' = top/right/bottom/left)
padding-left	1	1pt	*Length* (default 0), *Percent*
padding-right	1	auto	*Length* (default 0), *Percent*
padding-top	1	1em	*Length* (default 0), *Percent*
padding-bottom	1	5pt	*Length* (default 0), *Percent*
border	1	1in	*Length* – repeated ('x' = all borders, 'x x' = vertical and horizontal, and 'x x x x' = top/right/bottom/left) or URL (or, from v2, also set width, color and style – see below)
border-left	1	0.3cm	*Length* or URL (or, from v2, also set width, color and style – see below)
border-right	1	0.3in	*Length* or URL (or, from v2, also set width, color and style – see below)
border-top	1	9pt	*Length* or URL (or, from v2, also set width, color and style – see below)

border-bottom	1	10%	*Length* or URL (or, from v2, also set width, color and style – see below)
border-width	1	thick, thin

2pt 4pt 2pt 4pt | thin, medium, thick, *Length* – repeated ('x' = all borders, 'x x' = vertical and horizontal, and 'x x x x' = top/right/bottom/left) |
border-left-width	1	thick	thin, medium (default), thick, *Length*
border-right-width	1	thin	thin, medium (default), thick, *Length*
border-top-width	1	medium	thin, medium (default), thick, *Length*
border-bottom-width	1	3pt	thin, medium (default), thick, *Length*
border-color	1	blue green	*Color* – repeated ('x' = all borders, 'x x' = vertical and horizontal, and 'x x x x' = top/right/bottom/left)
	2	transparent	as above, plus transparent
border-left-color	2	red	*Color*
border-right-color	2	black	*Color*
border-top-color	2	white	*Color*
border-bottom-color	2	red	*Color*
border-style	1	solid ridge solid ridge	none, hidden, dotted, dashed, solid, double, groove, ridge, inset, outset – repeated ('x' = all borders, 'x x' = vertical and horizontal, and 'x x x x' = top/right/bottom/left)
border-left-style	2	dotted	none, hidden, dotted, dashed, solid, double, groove, ridge, inset, outset
border-right-style	2	ridge	none, hidden, dotted, dashed, solid, double, groove, ridge, inset, outset
border-top-style	2	dashed	none, hidden, dotted, dashed, solid, double, groove, ridge, inset, outset
border-bottom-style	2	dotted	none, hidden, dotted, dashed, solid, double, groove, ridge, inset, outset
width	1	50px	*Length*, *Percent*, auto (default)
min-width	2	50px	*Length*, *Percent*
max-width	2	50px	*Length*, *Percent*, none (default)
height	1	auto	*Length*, auto (default)
	2	15%	as above, plus *Percent*
min-height	2	50px	*Length*, *Percent*

max-height	2	50px	*Length*, *Percent*, none (default)
float	1	left	left, right, none (default)
clear	1	left	left, right, both, none (default)
overflow	2	hidden	visible (default), hidden, scroll, auto
clip	2	auto	*Shape*, auto (default)
visiblity	2	visible	visible, hidden, collapse (default is 'inherit')
z-index	2	12	auto (default), *Integer*
Generated content			
content	2	open-quote "My prefix" close-quote	*String*, URL, *Counter*, attr(...), open-quote, close-quote, no-open-quote, no-close-quote (and any combination)
quotes	2	none "«" "»" "<" ">"	none, *String String* (repeating)
counter-reset	2	section -1 imagenum 99	none (default) or *Identifier*, then optional *Integer* (repeating)
counter-increment	2	section 10 item 1	none (default) or *Identifier*, then optional *Integer* (repeating)
list-style	1	decimal outside	combination of list-style-type, list-style-image, list-style-position
list-style-type	1	circle	disc, circle (default), square, decimal, lower-roman, upper-roman, lower-alpha, upper-alpha, none
	2	circle	as above, plus decimal-leading-zero, lower-greek, upper-greek, lower-latin, upper-latin, hebrew, armenian, georgian, cjk-ideographic, hiragana, katakana, hiragana-iroha, katakana-iroha
list-style-position	1	inside	inside, outside (default)
list-style-image	1	url(boat.gif)	URL, none (default)
Paged media			
size	2	8cm 12cm	auto (default), portrait, landscape, *Length* (one or twice)
marks	2	crop cross	none (default), crop cross
page-break-before	2	left	auto (default), always, avoid, left, right

page-break-after	2	always	auto (default), always, avoid, left, right
page-break-inside	2	avoid	auto (default), avoid
page	2	auto	auto (default), *Identifier*
orphans	2	3	*Integer* (default '2')
widows	2	3	*Integer* (default '2')
Tables			
caption-side	2	left	top (default), bottom, left, right
table-layout	2	fixed	auto (default), fixed
border-collapse	2	separate	collapse (default), separate
border-spacing	2	3pt 3pt 5pt	*Length* (default '0'), optional *Length*
empty-cells	2	hide	show (default), hide
speak-header	2	always	once (default) always
User interface			
cursor	2	crosshair, default url(eggtimer.gif), wait	auto (default), crosshair, default, pointer, move, e-resize, ne-resize, nw-resize, n-resize, se-resize, sw-resize, s-resize, w-resize, text, wait, help, or URL()
outline	2	red dashed 2pt	combination of outline-color, outline-style, outline-width
outline-width	2	2pt	thin, medium (default), thick, *Length* – repeated ('x' = all borders, 'x x' = vertical and horizontal, and 'x x x x' = top/right/bottom/left)
outline-style	2	dashed	none (default) , hidden, dotted, dashed, solid, double, groove, ridge, inset, outset – repeated ('x' = all borders, 'x x' = vertical and horizontal, and 'x x x x' = top/right/ bottom/left)
outline-color	2	red	invert (default), *Color*
Aural styles			
volume	2	medium	*Number*, *Percent*, silent, x-soft, soft, medium (default), loud, x-loud
speak	2	spell-out	normal (default), non, spell-out

pause	2	12ms 9ms	combination of pause-before and pause-after
pause-before	2	12ms	*Time*, *Percent*
pause-after	2	9ms	*Time*, *Percent*
cue	2	url(squeek.gif) url(go.gif) url(stop.gif)	combination of cue-before and cue-after
cue-after	2	url(squeek.gif)	url(...), none (default)
cue-before	2	url(squeek.gif)	url(...), none (default)
play-during	2	url(squeek.gif) repeat auto	auto (default), none, url(...) mix? repeat?
azimuth	2	far-right behind 240deg	*nnn* deg, leftwards, rightwards or left-side, far-side, left, center-left, center (default), center-right, right, far-right, right-side followed by behind
elevation	2	far-right behind 240deg	*nnn* deg, below, level (default), above, lower, higher
speech-rate	2	faster 120 *(words per minute)*	*nnn*, x-slow, slow, medium (default), fast, x-fast, faster, slower
voice-family	2	churchill female	male, female, child, (specific voice such as 'comedian')
pitch	2	low 200Hz	x-low, low, medium (default), high, x-high, *number*Hz
pitch-range	2	44	0–100 (default 50)
stress	2	53	0–100 (default 50)
richness	2	70	0–100 (default 50)
speak-punctuation	2	code	code, none (default)
speak-numerals	2	digits	digits, continuous (default)
Classifications			

display	1	inline	none, block (default), inline, list-item
	2	block compact table-row	none, block, inline (default), list-item ...*PLUS*... run-in, compact, marker, table, inline-table, table-row-group, table-header-group, table-footer-group, table-row, table-column-group, table-column, table-cell, table-caption
marker-offset	2	section 10 item 1	*Length*, auto (default)
position	2	relative	static (default), relative, absolute, fixed
top	2	2pt	*Length*, *Percent*, auto
bottom	2	2pt	*Length*, *Percent*, auto
left	2	2pt	*Length*, *Percent*, auto
right	2	2pt	*Length*, *Percent*, auto
direction	2	rtl	ltr (default), rtl (right-to-left)
unicode-bidi	2	embed	normal (default), embed, bidi-override
white-space	1	pre	normal (default), pre (pre-formatted), nowrap (single line)

Length – inches (in), centimetres (cm), millimetres (mm), points (pt), picas (pc), ems (em), x-height (ex), pixels (px). A '+' or '-' prefix is allowed.

Percent – '+' or '-', followed by a number, then '%', e.g. 200% = twice size.

Color – black, navy, blue, aqua, purple, maroon, green, red, gray, fuchsia, teal, lime, yellow, white, olive, silver, #rgb (hexadecimal), #rrggbb (hexadecimal), rgb(r,g,b) (each value decimal or percentage).

Number – digits, optionally prefix with '+' or '-', may include decimal point.

Integer – digits, optionally prefix with '+' or '-', not including decimal point.

Time – Number plus 'ms' (milliseconds) or 's' (seconds).

String – Quotes characters, single or double, no embedded quotes of same type, use '\"' or '\'' instead. Newline is '\A' and just '\' to split text over lines in style-sheet.

Shape – rect(*top*, *right*, *bottom*, *left*).

Counter – counter(*name*) or counter(*name*, *style*) or counters(*name*, *string*) or counters(*name*, *string*, *style*).

Identifier – word.

30. RTF

This chapter describes the general syntax of the RTF language, and some of its most commonly used and most complex features (the same features often appearing in both lists), while explaining how to use XSLT to create RTF documents.

Background

RTF is a popular interchange format for documentation, and is first and foremost a Microsoft Word export and import format. The ability to transform XML documents into Word documents can be very useful, either for subsequent editing in the Word environment, or simply for semi-professional formatting for print output, and it is much simpler to convert XML documents into RTF documents than it is to convert them into binary format Word documents.

Versions of RTF

The RTF standard has undergone a number of revisions. These updates have reflected the added capabilities of the Word application as this product has developed, thus ensuring that new document formatting features would not be lost when RTF is used as an interchange format.

RTF version 1.6 includes control words introduced in Word for Windows 95 version 7.0, Word 97 for Windows, Word 98 for Macintosh, and Word 2000 for Windows, as well as other Microsoft products (see msdn.microsoft.com/library/en-us/dnrtfspec/html/rtfspec.asp).

The latest release, 1.7, was created to support Word 2002, and can be found at www.microsoft.com/downloads/release.asp?ReleaseID=32443. But it is known to crash older versions of Word, so should not be used until the user-base of any documents converted to this standard is known to be using the later versions of Word.

HTML alternative

Recent versions of Microsoft Word can import HTML format data, which has the advantage of being able to handle images in a much simpler fashion than RTF. This can be considered a better and simpler alternative to RTF when there is a need for images to be handled, and when it can always be guaranteed that a recent version of this application will be available to open the file. Yet HTML does not have some of the more advanced features of RTF, for example stylesheet definitions, headers, footers and footnotes.

Syntax overview

RTF is a text-based language with a syntax reminiscent of many older typesetting languages.

RTF tags

RTF tags begin with a '\' symbol and end with a space character. For example, '\b ' switches-on bold styling:

```
Normal text followed by \b bold text ...
```

Normal text followed by **bold text ...**

There is no concept of an end-tag, but other tags may reverse the effect of earlier tags. For example, the tag '\b0 ' switches off bold styling:

```
Normal text followed by \b bold text \b0 and back to normal
...
```

Normal text followed by **bold text** and back to normal ...

A typical XSLT template would employ such tags as follows:

```
<template
    match="emphasis">\b <apply-templates/>\b0 </template>
```

Stacks

The concept of start-tag/end-tag pairs can be simulated using a stacking concept. Curly brackets enclose text that is processed in a given mode. When the right bracket is encountered, the format reverts to its state before the left bracket. A new formatting mode is specified using the normal formatting tag, immediately following the left bracket:

```
Normal text followed by {\b bold text} and back to normal
...
```

Normal text followed by **bold text** and back to normal ...

There can be any number of nested stacks, as in the following example, which uses the '\i ' tag for italic styling:

```
Some {\i italic text with embedded {\b bold text} and back
to} normal ...
```

Some *italic text with embedded **bold text** and back to* normal ...

One other distinct advantage of the stack method is that it makes no assumptions about prior settings. For example, the instruction '\b0 ' switches-off bold styling, regardless of whether or not the text was already in bold style before it was explicitly switched-on again:

```
\b Bold text followed by \b yet more bold text \b0 and back
to bold ...
```

Bold text followed by yet more bold text and back to bold ...

The following example will work as intended:

```
{\b Bold text followed by {\b yet more bold text} and back
to bold } ...
```

Bold text followed by yet more bold text and back to bold ...

Escape characters

Tag delimiter characters must be 'escaped' if they are needed as normal data characters. The '\' character is the escape character. For example, the sequence '\{' represents the character '{'. If a '\' character is needed in the text, it needs to be escaped by itself ('\\'):

```
There can be \\, \{ and \} characters in the text.
```

There can be \, { and } characters in the text.

Document structure

All RTF documents must be enclosed in the RTF stack:

```
{\rtf ...
...
}
```

Warning: the left curly bracket that opens this structure must be the *first* character in the file. If it is not, then the content of the file will simply not be recognized as an RTF document. Even a single preceding space will cause problems.

Before the content of the document, it is possible to define colours, an internal RTF stylesheet, and header and footer content (as described in detail below). The actual text then begins:

```
{\rtf
{\fonttbl ...}
{\colortbl;...;}
{\stylesheet ... }
\hdrftr {\header\ ... } {\footer\ ... }
...
}
```

Small measures (twips)

It is necessary to understand the unit of measure used in RTF in order to set measures such as the gap above a paragraph, or a column widths. RTF uses a measure called 'twip'. One twip is 20 times smaller than 1pt. This is therefore a very fine measure and typically there are more than 8,000 twips across the printable area of an A4 page.

XSLT issues

When XSLT is used to generate RTF there are some common requirements and issues. Specifying 'text' mode, removing unwanted spaces, and escaping significant RTF delimiter characters are all necessary.

Stylesheet output mode

Because RTF is a text-based format, the Output element should be used and the Method attribute should be given the value 'text':

```
<output method="text" />
```

Spaces

Many XML source files will contain spaces to format the tagging, as in the following example:

```
<book>
  <chapter>
    <title>First Chapter Title</title>
```

These spaces would be treated as document spaces if allowed to pass-through the styling process. It is therefore necessary to use the Strip Space element in an XSLT stylesheet, either to explicitly name the elements that do not directly contain text, or to name all elements (using '*'), and then allow the Preserve Space element to name the exceptions:

```
<strip-space elements="*" />
<preserve-space elements="title para cell" />
```

Unlike HTML-based browsers, a product that can read an RTF file will not interpret a line-feed character or a tab as a space, so all of these characters need to be converted into space characters as soon as they are read from the source XML:

```
<template match="text()">
  <!-- CONVERT LINE-FEED & TAB CHARACTERS INTO SPACES -->
  <variable name="string"
          select="normalize-space(
                    translate(., '&#10;&#13;&#09;', '   ')
                              )" />
  ...
</template>
```

Unlike HTML-based browsers, a product that can read an RTF file will not automatically remove leading, trailing and multiple space characters. The XML document should not contain superfluous spaces, as in the following example:

```
<para>  There are some improper spaces before the
text in this paragraph, and a less serious superfluous
line-feed (which will be converted into a space) at the
end.
</para>
```

The following paragraph is formatted properly:

```
<para>There are no improper spaces before the
text in this paragraph, and no superfluous
line-feeds at the end.</para>
```

Escape characters

The conversion from normal characters to escape sequences (for example, from '{' to '\{') is quite tricky using XSLT alone as it has no string replacement feature (beyond its simple character replacement function). Using a named template that performs a simple search/replace operation, all occurrences of '\' can be replaced with '\\', all occurrences of '{' can be replaced with '\{', and all occurrences of '}' can be replaced with '\}'. This template must be called from another template that processes all incoming text. This template must therefore match the 'text()' node. It first needs to replace line-feed (or carriage-return) characters with spaces (as shown above), then perform the three replacement operations described above, while preserving the results of each one to create the final string to be output. This is done using variables to capture the output of each of those templates (see Chapter 8, which includes a named string replacement template and also shows how it can be used to process text for RTF output).

Paragraphs

Individual paragraphs can be aligned and indented in various ways, can avoid page breaks, can be assigned tab stop positions, and can be shaded.

New paragraph

The paragraph tag, '\par', ends a paragraph, simultaneously creating a new one. It is directly equivalent to the interactive act of pressing the 'return' key to end a paragraph and start a new one. There is therefore no need to use this tag at the start of the document (or at the start of a table cell) because doing so would create an empty paragraph.

By default, a new paragraph will inherit all formatting characteristics from the previous paragraph. The default settings can be reasserted using the '\pard' (paragraph default) instruction.

Page breaks and paragraphs

The instruction '\keep' keeps the paragraph on the same page, even if this means having to break the page early. Similarly, the instruction '\keepn' keeps the paragraph on the same page as the next paragraph. This is useful when the paragraph is actually a heading (it is often considered bad practice to allow the last object on a page to be a heading).

The '\pagebb' instruction tells the formatter to break the page before the current paragraph. This is useful if the paragraph is actually a title that must start a new page.

Paragraph alignment

Paragraphs can be aligned left (the default), right or centred using the '\ql', '\qr' and '\qc' instructions. Alternatively, a paragraph can be aligned both left and right (justified) using the '\qj' instruction:

```
\par\ql Left aligned paragraph.
\par\qr Right aligned paragraph.
\par\qc Centered paragraph.
\par\qj Justified (aligned both left and right).
```

Spacing and indentation

The space between lines in a paragraph defaults to the height of the tallest character in the font, but can be made larger by setting the '\sl*nnn*' instruction to a value that is larger (it is ignored otherwise).

The space before and after a paragraph can be specified using the '\sb' and '\sa' instructions respectively. The values in these instruction are lengths in twips:

```
\par\sb600\sa300 Paragraph with space before and after.
```

The whole paragraph can be indented by specifying left and right indent values. The '\li' and '\ri' instructions perform these roles:

```
\par\li200\ri200 Paragraph indented both left and right.
```

However, the first line of a paragraph often has extra indentation. The '\fi' instruction specifies an extra indent for the first line only. Its value is calculated relative to the indentation of the whole paragraph:

```
\par\li400\fi200 The first line of this paragraph
is indented.
```

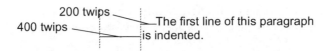

The indent value can take a leading minus sign, thus creating an 'outdent'. For example, the whole paragraph could be indented and the first line non-indented as follows:

```
\par\li400\fi-400 First line not indented.
```

This could be useful if a tab is set at the same indentation, so that prefix text can be inserted before the first line of text, creating a special form of list:

```
\par\li400\fi-400\... [X]\tab Special list item here,
with the prexif appearing in a 'margin'.
```

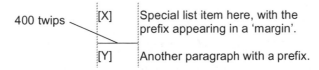

The negative value can be smaller than the indent value, so that the whole list is indented:

```
\par\li400\fi-200\... [X]\tab Special list item here,
with the prexif appearing in a 'margin'.
```

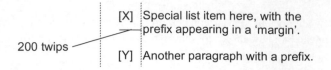

Borders

A border can be drawn around a paragraph using the '\box' instruction. This can be followed by an instruction to define the style of the border, with options such as '\brdrs' (single thin border line), '\brdrth' (single thick border line) and '\brdrdb (double line), though there are many other style options. Finally, the size of the gap between the text and the border line can be set using the '\brsp' instruction:

```
\par\box\brdrdb\brsp50 This paragraph has a thick
border around it, 50 twips from this text.
```

The border may be given a colour using '\brcf', which includes a colour number (and if present this instruction must follow the optional '\brsp' gap instruction).

It is also possible to place a line on one side only, using '\brdrl' (border left), '\brdrr' (border right), '\brdrt' (border top) or '\brdrb' (border bottom) in place of '\box'. If the colour or other details need to differ for each line, then the whole set of instructions is repeated with these changes (and a different edge identifier).

Finally, it is also possible to prevent adjacent paragraph borders of the same type merging, to switch off borders entirely, and draw a border line of a precise width (refer to the standard for these details).

Shading

A paragraph can be given a shaded background using the '\shaded' instruction. Large values are used to define very fine gradients of shading – a value of '\shaded1500' is typical.

Tab positions

The '\txnnn' instruction defines a tab position (in twips, from the left margin):

```
\par\tx2000\tx4000\tx6000 Three tabs in this paragraph.
```

By default a tab is left-handed, meaning that text placed after this tab position is left justified. A tab can be made right-handed by adding a prefix instruction of '\tqr', or centred using '\tqc', or decimal aligned (align on decimal point in the following text) using '\tqdec'.

```
\par\tqdec\tx6000 One decimal tab position\tab 123.456.
```

A tab can also include an instruction to fill the gap between preceding and following text with a 'leader' pattern. Again, a prefix instruction is used for this purpose. The '\tldot' instruction fills the gap with dots, '\tlmdot' with middle dots, '\tlhyph' with hyphens, '\tlul' with underline characters, '\tlth' with a thick line, and '\tleq' with equals symbols:

```
\par\tldot\tx6000 Dots between here\tab and here.
```

A single tab can have both a defined alignment and an applied style, but the alignment instruction must precede the style instruction:

```
\par\tqc\tldot\tx6000 Centred tab with preceding
dots\tab DOTS BEFORE THIS.
```

In-line styles

RTF includes instructions for specifying the font to use, for including unusual characters, and for styling the text in various ways.

Fonts

Fonts are defined in a font table (this topic is very complex, and is not covered here). The '\f*nnn*' command selects a font from the font table:

```
\f3
```

It is not necessary to define a font. If this is not done, then the default font is used.

The '\fs' command specifies a point size for the font to use, but its parameter value is in half-point units, thus allowing sizes such as 7.5 points to be set:

```
\fs15
```

Special characters

The following table shows instructions used to present characters not commonly found on computer keyboards:

\tab	tab position (move following text to the next defined tab stop position)
\bullet	bullet character (useful to prefix individual list items)
\lquote	left single quotation mark
\rquote	right single quotation mark
\ldblquote	left double quotation mark

\rdblquote	right double quotation mark
\-	optional hyphen (only show when breaking a word at this point at the end of a text line)
\endash	narrow dash (width of a capital 'N' character in the current font)
\enspace	narrow space (width of a capital 'N' character in the current font), not indicating a good line-break position
\emdash	wide dash (width of a capital 'M' character in the current font)
\emspace	wide space (width of a capital 'M' character in the current font), not indicating a good line-break position
\~	non-breaking space
_	non-breaking hyphen

Text styling

The most commonly used in-line text styling tags available are shown below (others are available and are described in the standard):

\plain	reset to normal font styling (and 12pt size)		
\b	bold	\b0	bold off
\i	italic	\i0	italic off
\ul	underline	\ul0	underline off
\caps	capitals	\caps0	capitals off
\scaps	small caps	\scaps0	small caps off
\shad	shadow style	\shad0	shadow style off
\outline	outline style	\outline0	outline style off
\strike	strikethrough	\strike0	strikethrough off
\sub	subscript	\nosupersub	subscript and superscript off
\super	superscript	\nosupersub	subscript and superscript off
\deleted	deleted text	\deleted0	deleted text off

Note that the tags that switch-off common styles include the zero character and not the capital letter 'O'.

Page control

It is possible to override default pagination by instructing the formatter to start a new line, column or page:

\line	start a new line
\column	start a new column
\page	start a new page

Variables

Word is able to supply information, such as the current date, that can be referenced from RTF instructions:

\chdate	current date (also \chdpl and \chdpa)
\chtime	current time
\chpgn	current page number
\sectnum	current section number

Colours

Text can be presented in various colours, rather than just black, and can be presented on a background other than the usual white.

Colour definitions

First, it is necessary to set-up some colour definitions, which is done almost immediately (certainly before the stylesheet discussed later). The colour definitions are grouped, and identified using the 'colortable' keyword:

```
{\rtf
{\colortbl;...}
...
}
```

Each colour defined is specified using three values representing red, green and blue intensities. To define the colour red, the maximum value of '255' is assigned to red and '0' to the others. A colour definition is completed by a semi-colon:

```
\red255\green0\blue0;
```

Definitions are inherently numbered according to their relative locations. In the following example, 'red' is colour one, because it is the first definition, 'green' is colour two, 'blue' is colour three, and 'yellow' (a mixture of red and green) is colour four:

```
{\colortbl;\red255\green0\blue0;\red0\green255\blue0;
\red0\green0\blue255;\red255\green255\blue0;}
```

References to colours

A reference to a colour makes the colour number explicit. Text can be coloured using the 'cf' (foreground colour) keyword, which is followed by the colour number:

```
Some {\cf1 red} {\cf2 green} {\cf3 blue} and
{\cf4 yellow} text.
```

The background of the text can be coloured using the 'chcbpat' keyword:

```
The background is {\chcbpat2 green}.
```

Tables

Tables are the most difficult object structures to handle. It is necessary to know in advance how many columns there will be in the table, and the width of each column (or, more precisely, the exact distance of the right edge of each column from the left edge of the page).

Note that placing another table in a table cell is very complex and is not dealt with here. For the same reason, spanning cells and borders are not discussed here.

Source XML table

While it should be possible, in theory, to convert any XML structure into an RTF table, in practice this can be quite difficult. For the purposes of this exercise, it is assumed that a model is being created that is particularly suited to conversion into RTF format. In this case, a typical source table will appear as follows:

```
<table cols="3" colRightEdge1="30" colRightEdge2="60"
      align1="left" align2="left" align3="right">
  <tr>
    <td><p>First cell across</p></td>
    <td><p>Second cell across</p></td>
    <td><p>Third cell across</p></td>
  </tr>
</table>
```

The Cols attribute of the Table element indicates how many columns there will be in the table. It will be assumed that there will always be as many cells in each row as indicated by this attribute.

The Col Right Edge attributes hold a percentage value of the page width. The first column therefore ends 30% of the way across the page, and the second and final column ends 60% of the way across the page.

The Align attributes specify the horizontal alignment of the text in each cell that belongs to the column indicated.

Width settings

Widths are defined using twips. Recall that there are more than 8,000 twips across a typical page. One idea is to use percentages in the source XML file, and simply multiply all values by 80 to get the twips equivalent.

```
<table cols="3" colRightEdge1="30" colRightEdge2="60">
  ...
</table>
```

In this example, the right edges of the first two columns are set at 30% and 60%, which are equivalent to 2,400 and 4,800 twips respectively. Because there is a third column, with no defined edge, the stylesheet may assume that the right edge of the final column is close to 100% (8,000 twips).

Rows and cells

Fortunately, just like most XML table models, RTF tables are row-oriented. This means that the structure comprises a number of rows, each consisting of a number of cells. The '\row' instruction ends a row, and the '\cell' instruction ends a cell:

```
...\cell...\cell...\cell\row
...\cell...\cell...\cell\row
```

Row definitions

At the start of each row it is necessary to specify the position of each cell (cell start and end positions can change between rows if necessary). This is done using the '\trowd' (table row definition) instruction, which includes '\cellx*nnn*' instructions to set the position of the right edge of each cell:

```
\trowd...\cellx2400...cellx4800...\cellx8000...
...\cell...\cell...\cell\row
\trowd...\cellx2400...cellx4800...\cellx8000...
...\cell...\cell...\cell\row
```

Warning: the number of actual cells in a row must match the number specified at the start of the row. If any are missing, Word may crash.

Warning: cell definitions starting before the left margin of the paper begins (that is, the parameter plus the left margin is negative) always generate an error.

Apart from specifying the cell edge location, there can be preceding instructions that specify half the space between the cells of a table row in twips ('\trgaph'), the height of a table row in twips ('\trrh*nnn*') (in which the height is guaranteed to be at least the given height, as well as possibly dictating that the content of the whole row must be kept together), on the same page ('\trkeep'), and an indentation of the left edge of the table ('\trleft*nnn*'):

```
\trowd\trgaph200\trrh400\trkeep\trleft400\cellx6000
```

Paragraphs in cells

Just as in the document as a whole, the first paragraph in a cell does not start with a '\par' command, but this code is used at the end of the paragraph if there are more paragraphs in the cell. However, the '\intbl' instruction is needed in each paragraph, including the first, in order to tell the RTF formatter that this paragraph belongs to the table:

```
\intbl...\cell
\intbl...\cell
\intbl...\par\intbl...\cell
\row
```

XSLT templates

A number of templates for handling tables of the type shown above are presented below. In all cases, there should (despite appearances) be no line-feed characters in the template. Wherever a line-feed is included in the sample templates, this should simply be removed in reality (not even replaced by spaces).

Table template

A template to handle the Table element might appear as follows:

```
<template match="table">\par\pard
\fs16 <apply-templates/> </template>
```

This template ends the previous paragraph, and sets the default style and an appropriate point size, before processing the contents of the source table.

Row templates

There could be a separate template for rows, depending on how many cells there will be in each row:

```
<template match="table[@cols='3']/tr">
\trowd\trgaph200\trrh400\trkeep\trleft400
\cellx
<value-of select="ancestor::table/@colRightEdge1 * 80"/>
\cellx
<value-of select="ancestor::table/@colRightEdge2 * 80"/>
\cellx8000\pard\plain\s12\fs16\sb100
\intbl <apply-templates/> \row\pard </template>
```

This template happens to handle three-column tables. It sets the position values of each cell, taking values from the Col Right Edge attributes of the ancestor Table element.

Cell template

The template for processing cell elements is very simple. It just appends the '\cell' instruction onto the end of the contents:

```
<template match="td"><apply-templates/>\cell </template>
```

Paragraphs in cells

The following template matches a paragraph in the second cell. The reason for being explicit about the cell is so that the appropriate alignment attribute in the Table element can be referenced. Although this template does not make it clear, it matches only the first paragraph in the cell (a later template overrides it for other paragraphs). In this example, paragraph style 12 is selected, and the font size is set to 8pt, with 100 twips of space above:

```
<template match="td[position() = 2]/p">
\s12\fs16\sb100\intbl
<if test="ancestor::table[@align2='left']">\ql </if>
<if test="ancestor::table[@align2='right']">\qr <if>
<if test="ancestor::table[@align2='centre']">\qc </if>
<apply-templates/></template>
```

The template for subsequent paragraphs is similar, but must include the '\par' instruction:

```
<template match="td[position() = 2]/p[position() > 1]"
          priority="2">\par\intbl\s12\fs16\sb100
<if test="ancestor::table[@align2='left']">\ql </if>
<if test="ancestor::table[@align2='right']">\qr <if>
<if test="ancestor::table[@align2='centre']">\qc </if>
<apply-templates/></template>
```

Some controls must be the same in all paragraphs in a row. In particular, all paragraphs in a row must have the same positioning controls, and all paragraphs in a row must have '\intbl' specified (or inherited).

Images

It is not impossible to have images in an RTF file, it is just very difficult to get existing images, associated with XML documents, into this form. First, RTF has its own image data format, and second the images are embedded in the RTF text.

When the need is only to have a single, identical image in each document, such as a company logo in the header area, then this can be achieved with a little effort. It is necessary to:

- create a blank Word document, then insert the image wanted (ensuring that it is an in-line image, not floating)
- save the document in RTF format
- open the RTF file in a text editor (something that does not interpret RTF and format accordingly)
- find and copy the image data, which starts with '{\pict', and ends '}}', or starts with '{{*\shppict' and ends with '}}}' (in between there should be many hexadecimal two-character codes, such as 'FF00880C0C0C')
- add this data to the output of an appropriate XSLT template:

```
<template match="CompanyLogo">{{\*\shppict{\pict{\*\pic-
prop\shplid1025{\sp{\sn ...
... 70101000000030000000000}}}</template>
```


Headers and footers

The '\hdrftr' instruction introduces the definition of header and footer text, each comprising a stacked section that begins with '\header' or '\footer' (in this order):

```
\hdrftr
{\header...}
{\footer...}
```

Within each of these segments, all the normal paragraph and in-line formatting codes can be used. For example, in the header it is possible to set a left-justified paragraph, with no indentation, in the default 9pt font, that includes two tabs (first, a centred tab halfway across the document, then a right-justified tab at the right margin). In this example, the text 'My Document' is placed at the left side, the text 'Page *nnn*' in the middle, and 'Version 2.2' at the right side:

```
{\header\pard\plain\ql\li0\ri0\fs18\tqc\tx4000\tqr\tx8000
My Document \tab Page \chpgn \tab Version 2.2\par}
```

Note that each section of a document can contain re-definitions of the header and footer:

```
\hdrftr{\header...}{\footer...} ...
\sect \hdrftr{\header...}{\footer...} ...
\sect \hdrftr{\header...}{\footer...} ...
```

Built-in formatting stylesheets

The term 'stylesheet' has meaning to most word processors, including Microsoft Word. In this case, the term refers to a set of paragraph or character formatting instructions that are given a name and can be accessed from a menu in order to apply several formatting characteristics in a single step.

One great strength of such stylesheets is that all the paragraphs or phrases that were styled using the same named style can be easily reformatted simply by changing the definition, or in Word by changing one instance and asking Word to change the definition to match the new style. Naturally, for this reason alone, it would be useful if an RTF document imported into Word could include a stylesheet that is used immediately to format the paragraphs and in-line objects, so that the user could easily modify the style of the document or create new, matching content. Fortunately, it is possible for a stylesheet to be defined within an RTF file and to assign paragraphs to the defined styles.

Stylesheet definitions

A style is defined in a group called 'stylesheet', which can follow the colour definitions (see above):

```
{\rtf
{\colortbl;...;}
{\stylesheet ... }
...
}
```

Each style definition is enclosed in a group that begins with '\s*n*', where '*n*' represents an identifier for the definition that will be referenced later (in the following case, style '2'). At the end of the group, following a space, is the name to assign to this format, which users will see and be able to select (in this case 'Header1'):

```
{\stylesheet {\s2\... Header1;} { ... } { ... } }
```

The definition first specifies another definition on which this one is based, by reference to the definition number of the other definition. Often, a new style will be based on 'Normal', which is predefined as definition '0', so 'sbasedon0' means that the new style is based on the normal style (the number '222' is reserved for default styling; based on nothing). It is then possible to specify which style definition should apply to the next paragraph when the user enters 'return' after creating a paragraph in the current style (commonly used in header definitions to state that when starting the next line it should not be another header but a normal paragraph instead). The instruction '\snext4' specifies that the next paragraph should adopt the style definition 's4':

```
{\s1\sbasedon222\snext1... Para;}
{\s2\sbasedon1\snext1... Header1;}
```

The remainder of the definition involves the same formatting instructions as used in the text. In the following example, the style 's1' specifies a point size of '22pt', some space above, bold and centred, with background shading, and gives the definition the name 'Header1':

```
{\s2\sbasedon1\snext1\fs44\sa200\b\qc\shading1500
Header1;}
```

Using defined styles

A defined style is used in the text by reference to its identifier number. Surprisingly, though, it is also necessary to include formatting instructions as well:

```
\par\pard\plain\s3\...\...
```

Microsoft Word allows paragraphs that belong to specific stylesheet formats to be modified, and therefore to 'override' the default style for that format. It is possible, though not wise, to do this in the RTF output, simply by referring to the defined style, but specifying different formatting requirements (such as changing the point size, or adding underlining):

```
\par\pard\plain\s3\fs12\b
```

However, once this is done the paragraph is no longer considered to be part of the defined style, and will not be affected by changes to the style definition made within Word. The real problem for the XSLT stylesheet author is to avoid accidentally doing this (there should rarely be a reason to do this on purpose). The solution is to use variables. The first variable below holds the RTF instructions common to both the definition and to every paragraph that uses this style. In this case, it specifies that the format will be 24pt text, with a large (240 twips) gap above:

```
<!-- HEADER ONE FORMAT -->

<!-- STYLE: 24pt, 240 twips space above -->
<variable name="Header1Style">\fs48\sb240</variable>

<!-- DEFINITION: Style 2, Based-on 1, Next Style 1 -->
<variable name="Header1Def">{\s2\sbasedon1\snext1
<value-of select="$Header1Style"/> Header1;}</variable>

<!-- PARAGRAPH USAGE: New paragraph, no override -->
<variable name="Header1Para">\par\pard\plain\s1
<value-of select="$Header1Style"/>
</variable>
```

The stylesheet section of the RTF file then includes the following:

```
{\stylesheet
<value-of select="..." />
<value-of select="$Header1Def" />
<value-of select="..." />
}
```

A specific paragraph is created as follows:

```
<template match="HeaderOne">
<value-of select="$Header1Para" /><apply-templates/>
</template>
```

If the format of the named style needs to be changed, the content of the first variable is changed and is automatically applied to both the definition and the templates that use it to create conforming paragraphs.

31. QuarkXPress tags

This chapter describes the syntax of the QuarkXPress tagging language (version 2.05) and explains how to use XSLT to create documents that conform to this format. It also discusses categories of products that convert between XML and QuarkXPress.

QuarkXPress

QuarkXPress is a DTP package that has dominated the professional publishing market for a number of years. It is used in most publishing companies, and in the internal publishing departments of other organizations, to produce designed and semi-designed print publications. At the time of writing it has attracted some competition but still deserves special attention because of the size of the existing user base.

XML export tools

Although it is possible to extract text from a QuarkXPress document, along with formatting tags conforming to the language described below, it is not then possible to convert this data into XML format using XSLT, because XSLT can only work with XML source documents. However, a number of software vendors have recently released products that convert QuarkXPress documents directly into XML documents. These products tend to work at one of three levels:

- flow-based
- document-based
- batched.

Some products are able to save all the text in the currently selected flow to XML format using an extension that adds a 'Save as XML' menu item, or similar.

Some products are able to work through all the text flows in a document, saving the text from each to a single XML document. This approach reduces the manual effort involved but requires a degree of artificial intelligence to select the text flows in the correct order (or at least in a sensible order). These products consequently tend to be priced at a higher level.

Finally, some products are able to process an entire document, as above, but also work on a number of documents consecutively without any human intervention (so called 'batch' processing). This category of product is almost essential for efficient conversion of legacy data, when perhaps thousands of QuarkXPress documents exist.

In all three cases, there is a possible role for XSLT in a post-processing operation. The problem with automatically converted XML output is that the resulting document hierarchy tends to be very shallow. There is a simple reason for this. Most QuarkXPress documents are created using stylesheets, with meaningful names assigned to each style needed. Source data is mapped to XML structures by matching paragraph styles to appropriate XML elements. But in most XML document models the elements that enclose text content are several levels deep in the structure. Automatic generation of the elements that wrap-around these elements can be a very complex task, especially when the same paragraph style is mapped to various elements that can occur in different contexts. Some of the software products discussed above will attempt to cope with this complexity, but they have only the document model itself to guide the work, which may not be sufficient. It is often better to attempt to solve this problem later, using an XSLT stylesheet that has been crafted to deal with a particular document type. In this scenario, a very shallow XML document structure is produced by the software tool, and XSLT analyses the arrangement of elements in order to try to establish appropriate surrounding structures (use of the preceding() and following() functions can be particularly useful here).

XML import extensions

A number of software vendors have released products that can convert XML documents into QuarkXPress documents. Typically, a QuarkXPress extension adds an 'Import XML' menu option, which allows an XML data file to be accessed, and each paragraph-level element to be mapped to a style that is defined in a document stylesheet. The role of XSLT in this operation is usually not very prominent, except when there is a need to reorder or duplicate content before flowing it into the document.

The following sections discuss another approach that does not require one of these products, but relies entirely on XSLT instead. This approach is practical because it is possible to convert XML documents into a text-based data format that can be interpreted by the QuarkXPress application.

Quark Tags importer extension

A free extension that adds a tagged text import filter to QuarkXPress is available from Quark (www.quark.com). This filter accepts data files that conform to the specification discussed below.

The QuarkXPress tagging language is similar in scope and functionality to RTF (see Chapter 30). Just as it is possible to convert an XML document into RTF format so that the text can be loaded into Microsoft Word and automatically styled, it is equally possible to convert an XML document into this tagging language so that the text can be styled and modified in QuarkXPress. The principle is the same, but the details are different. The **XPress Tags** language is syntactically closer to HTML than to RTF.

XSLT may play a significant role here. It can be used to convert an XML file into a QuarkXPress tagged document. The following discussion assumes the use of the import filter, and the possible use of XSLT to prepare an XML document for import in this form.

Tagged files and blank documents

It is not possible for a QuarkXPress document to be created simply by importing a tagged file (in the way that a Word document can be created by importing an RTF file). A QuarkXPress document must first be created in the application, and images and text boxes must be placed according to the need on each page. It is then possible to import the tagged text into a selected text box (or set of linked boxes). The QuarkXPress document may already include some text in the selected text box, in which case the imported text can be inserted before or within this text, or just be appended to it.

To avoid confusion, the terms 'tagged file' and 'blank document' are used in the following discussion to distinguish between the data file containing the tagged text that is ready to be imported, and the QuarkXPress document that this text is going to be imported into.

Importing tagged files

Before importing tagged text, the user must first place the text cursor in the text box that is to receive it. Once the filter described above has been installed, the 'Get Text' menu item under the 'File' menu can be used to import the text. It is necessary to select 'Include Style Sheets' in the dialog box to tell QuarkXPress to interpreted the tags embedded in the text (rather than just show the tags as part of the text).

Note that on a Microsoft Windows system, the text file to be imported must have an extension of '.xtg', or it will not be recognized and interpreted as a tagged document:

```
chapter3.xtg
```

Versions of Xpress Tags

As the QuarkXPress application has developed over time it has gained more features. The tagging language has also had to develop in order to keep up with the features it needs to support. The version numbers match-up as follows:

- XPress 3.1 - Filter 1.5
- XPress 3.2 - Filter 1.7
- XPress 3.3 - Filter 1.7
- XPress 4.0 - Filter 2.0
- XPress 4.01 - Filter 2.0
- XPress 4.02 - Filter 2.02
- XPress 4.03 - Filter 2.02
- XPress 4.04 - Filter 2.03
- XPress 4.1 - Filter 2.05.

Version 2.05 is discussed below.

Terminology conflicts

Quark uses terminology in a distinctive way that can cause confusion. Some terms may sound familiar, but have an unexpected meaning.

The term 'stylesheet' is used to describe what would normally be called a single 'stylesheet definition', and there is no term to describe the collection of all styles.

The term 'character level' is used to describe in-line formatting. Some stylesheet definitions are described as 'character stylesheets', which really means 'in-line stylesheet definitions'.

The term 'paragraph' is used to describe all block-level text content, including titles and headings. A title or heading is only distinguished from a true paragraph by having different stylesheet definitions applied to it. In this respect, a 'paragraph' is similar to the XSL Block element (and the HTML DIV element). Some stylesheet definitions are described as 'paragraph stylesheets', which can be interpreted as meaning 'block style definitions'.

Tagging language principles

As with any tagging language, there are rules and conventions that need to be understood before individual features can be discussed. There are some general syntax rules to consider, and line-end codes and other whitespace is also significant.

Syntax overview

Superficially, QuarkXPress tags resemble XML and HTML tags. However, this resemblance is very misleading. While '<B>' represents bold styling and '<I>' represents italic styling, these tags can also be merged into a single tag, such as '<BI>' or '<IB>'.

One way in which this tagging language resembles XML more than HTML is that all tags are case sensitive, so '<b>' will not work in place of '<B>'.

But another way in which QuarkXPress tags differ from XML tags is that there are no end-tags. Instead, the 'start-tag' is used as an on/off switch. In the following example, bold styling is applied to two words:

```
This paragraph has <B>two<B> bold <B>words<B> in it.
```

      This paragraph has **two** bold **words** in it.

Note that when using XSLT to create tagged documents, this fact implies that the 'text' output mode should be used (see Chapter 8):

```
<output method="text" />
```

Whitespace

Line-breaks in the text file are significant. Each line-break indicates the end of the current paragraph. Further text will be deemed to be in a subsequent paragraph:

```
This is a paragraph.
This is another paragraph.
```

This is a paragraph.

This is another paragraph.

For this reason, when using XSLT to create tagged documents, whitespace in the source document should be filtered very carefully to prevent accidental generation of blank paragraphs. It is a good idea to remove spaces from all but the contents of the elements that directly contain text to be transformed:

```
<strip-space elements="*" />
<preserve-space elements="Title Para Cell" />
```

Warning: Great care must be taken to use the correct end-of-line character, depending on the operating system in use. This is different for Windows, Macintosh OS 9 (and earlier) and Macintosh OS X (which is UNIX-based). For example, when working on a Macintosh system that uses an OS 9 version of QuarkXpress and an OS X text editor, such as SimpleText, there is a fatal discrepancy. New paragraphs created in the text editor would not be detected by the importing tool (and the markup text would be added, along with following document text, to the end of the previous paragraph).

All whitespace in the tagged file is deemed to be significant. If there are two consecutive spaces, then two spaces will be imported and presented on the page. For this reason, an XSLT stylesheet should include the following explicit template for text nodes (which first converts line-ending codes and tabs into spaces, then reduces a sequence of spaces down to one space):

```
<template match="text()">
<value-of
  select="normalize-space(
          string-replace(. ,'&#10;&#13;&#09;', '  ')
                        )"/>
</template>
```

Note that another template can be used for text nodes that occur in an element where such normalization is not wanted:

```
<template match="preformatted/text()">
  <value-of select="."/>
</template>
```

Block-level tagging

Block-level settings are distinguished from in-line settings by including the prefix '*'. For example, '<*R>' sets the paragraph justification to right-justified. It is possible to mix block-level and in-line settings within the same tag, such as '<*RB>' (right-justified paragraph with bold styling), though block-level settings must precede in-line settings, and when block-level settings are present the whole tag must be at the start of the paragraph:

```
<*LI>Left-justified italic paragraph.
<*RB>Right-justified bold paragraph.
```

Left-justified italic paragraph.

Right-justified bold paragraph.

Some other block-level tags must also be placed at the start of a new text line, and do not resemble XML tags at all.

Document structure

All tagged documents must start with the tagging language version number within chevrons and preceded by the letter 'v' (version):

```
<v2.05>...
...
```

One of three tags must be added at the top of the file to indicate which character set is in use. The '<e0>' tag specifies the Macintosh character set. The '<e1>' tag specifies the Windows ANSI character set. Finally, the '<e2>' tag specifies the ISO Latin 1 character set (see Chapter 34):

```
<v2.05><e0>
...
```

Following lines can include, first, any stylesheet definitions required, then any number of paragraphs (described next).

Escape characters

The '@', '<', '>' and '\' characters are significant markup characters. When the source text contains these characters as normal data characters, they must be converted into their 'escaped' forms, '<\@>', '<\<>', '<\>>' and '<\\>' respectively. (See Chapter 8 for an XSLT technique that can achieve this.)

Paragraph styles

It is not necessary to refer to stylesheet definitions, as described below, but it is highly desirable. It is very easy to refer to stylesheet definitions that may already be present in the blank QuarkXPress document, and also to define new stylesheet definitions in the tagged document itself. The benefits are also substantial. After importing a tagged document, the user can globally change the formatting by editing the stylesheet definitions (including those definitions, if any, that were created in the tagged file).

Paragraph stylesheet references

As already noted, paragraphs must begin on a new text line. When the next paragraph conforms to a different defined style, the first character on the line may be a '@' symbol. In the simplest case, the 'No Style' paragraph style is specified by placing a colon immediately after this symbol. The text then immediately follows this character:

```
@:New paragraph with 'No Style' assignments.
```

The settings assigned to the built-in 'Normal' stylesheet definition can be selected instead, by placing a '$' symbol in the middle of this tag. This style is always present in a new QuarkXPress document, and is always the default style for any new text box created in the document:

```
@$:New paragraph with 'Normal' style assignments.
```

But the real power of this tag is that it can refer to a user-defined stylesheet. The name assigned to the stylesheet (the name seen in the menu of paragraph styles) is copied into the middle of the tag. This name must be no longer than 63 characters and must not include the characters ' " ', ':', '=' and '@' (there is also a limit of 1,000 different names):

```
@MyTitle:Title of Document.
@MyPara:Normal paragraph in the document.
@MyNote:NOTE: A note paragraph.
```

A new line in the text file that does not include a reference to a default or named style is assumed to be a paragraph that conforms to the same style as the previous paragraph. If the first paragraph in a document does not reference an explicit style, it will be assumed to be a 'Normal' paragraph.

Paragraph styles can be defined in the tagged file (this is explained later), so there is no need to rely on the required stylesheet definitions being present in a blank QuarkXPress document. Note that when importing the tagged document, QuarkXPress first attempts to apply a style with the referenced name that is defined in the blank QuarkXPress document. If no such style is found, it then attempts to apply a style with this name that is defined in the tagged file instead, and if it finds this definition it also adds it to the QuarkXPress document (where it can then be modified by the user). Finally, if there is no such definition in the tagged file, it simply applies the 'Normal' style defined in the blank document (but still adds the new style name to the list of styles).

Paragraph style settings

Paragraphs can be aligned left, right, centred, justified (aligned both left and right), and forced justified. It is also possible to set tab stops, specify margins, refer to a hyphenation dictionary, draw lines above and below, use drop caps for initial letters, keep the paragraph with the previous paragraph, and ensure that the paragraph is not broken over two pages (by making the whole paragaph move to the next page when necessary):

Left-align	`<*L>`
Right-align	`<*R>`
Centre-align	`<*C>`
Justify	`<*J>`
Forced justify	`<*F>`
Set tab stops	`<*t(##.#,#,"..")>`
Set paragraph attributes	`<*p(##.#,##.#,##.#,##.# ,G or g)>`
Hyphenation and Justification	`<*h"specification name">`
Paragraph rule above	`<*ra(##,#,"color name",#,##,##,## or ##%)>`
Paragraph rule below	`<*rb(##,#,"color name",#,##,##,## or ##%)>`
Drop Cap	`<*d(character count,line count)>`
Keep with Next Paragraph	`<*kn1> or <*kn0>`
Keep together	`<*ktA> or <*kt(#,#)>`

The first parameter of the tab tag is the distance, in points, that the tab is set from the left edge of the paragraph, and the second is the alignment ('0' for left alignment, '1' for centre, '2' for right, '4' for decimal (centre on decimal point), '5' for comma, or any character within quotation marks for alignment on that character). The third parameter specifies the characters, if any, that are to fill the gap made by moving text to the next tab position. If a single character is to be used to fill the gap, then the value '1' is followed by that character, so that '1*' fills the gap with asterisks. If two characters are to be used repeatedly to fill the gap, then the value '2' is followed by both characters, so that '2\/' fills the gap with '\/\/\/\/'. For example, '`<*t(40,0,"1+")>`'. The tab stop tag can also be used to set multiple tab positions, by simply repeating the parameters, each set separated from the previous set by a comma ('`<*t(40,0,"1+",80,0,"1+")>`').

Paragraph attribute tag parameters are all, except for the last one, given as a point size. The following settings are defined in the order given here. First, the left indent is assigned, then the first line indent, then the right indent, then the leading (the line height), and then the space before (above) and after (below). The final parameter specifies whether to lock to the grid ('G') or not ('g'). For example '`<*p(16,16,16,14,8,8,g)>`'.

The two rule tags, rule above and rule below, have the same parameters; only the name of the tag differs. The 'ra' tag (rule above) and the 'rb' tag (rule below) take the form '`<*ra(...)>`' and '`<*rb(...)>`' respectively. The first parameter is the width of the rule in points. The second parameter is the style ('0' represents a solid line, '1' and '2' represent different kinds of dotted line, '3' represents a mixture of dashes and dots, '4' stands for all dots, '5' for a double line, '6' for a thin line and a thick line, '7' for a thick line and a thin line, '8' for three lines (the middle one thick), '9' also for three lines (the middle one thin), and '10' for three lines of the same thickness). The third parameter is the colour name, enclosed in quotation marks. The shade is given next, as a percentage; for example, the line could be 30% red (a light red). The next two parameters specify the offset location from the left edge and the right edge (but a prefix of 'T' on the left edge value specifies that the line length should be dictated by the length of the first or last line of the text in the paragraph, depending on whether it is the rule above or the rule below that is being defined). Finally, the offset from the top or bottom of the paragraph is given, possibly as a percentage instead of a number of points. For example '`<*ra(4,5,"Red",100,T12,12,50%)>`'.

The first paragraph of a chapter or article may begin with a letter, word or phrase that is larger than the rest of the text and descends into the space normally reserved for text on the following lines. The drop cap tag specifies how many characters or lines should be displayed in this way.

Some paragraphs, and in particular pararaphs that are actually headings, are often required to be kept on the same page or column as the first following paragraph. The keep with next tag acts a simple switch, with the value '0' meaning that the paragraph should be kept with the next one, and the value '1' indicating that it does not have to be.

The '`<*ktA>`' tag states that all lines of text in the paragaph must be kept together, on the same page or in the same column. The '`<*kt(#,#)>`' tag, however, specifies the start and end line numbers that must be kept together. For example, '`<*kt(3,7)>`' ensures that lines three to seven are kept on the same page or column.

Paragraph stylesheet definitions

A stylesheet definition begins with an '@' symbol (at the start of a new line in the text file), which is immediately followed by the name that is to be assigned to it (this name will appear in the QuarkXPress menu of styles), then an equals symbol, and then square brackets enclosing a number of parameters. Finally, the same tags that can be used to style paragraphs directly (and in-line formatting characteristics) are added, but merged into a single tag (delimited, as usual, by '<' and '>' characters:

```
@MyNewStyle=[...]<.......>
@AnotherNewStyle=[...]<........>
```

Within the square brackets, parameters are used to identify another stylesheet definition that this definition is based on (and overrides), specify the stylesheet definition to be used for the next paragraph (as soon as the user presses the 'return' key). The letter 'S' is always present as the first character:

```
@ParaDef=[S"","" ]<...>
@Header1Def=[S"","ParaDef"]<...>
@Header2Def=[S"Header1Def","ParaDef"]<...>
@Header3Def=[S"Header1Def","ParaDef"]<...>
```

It is possible for a paragraph stylesheet definition to include a reference to an in-line stylesheet definition. The in-line stylesheet is then automatically selected whenever the paragraph style is selected. The name of the in-line stylesheet definition is enclosed in quotation marks, and added as the final parameter in the square brackets:

```
@NoteDef=[S"","","NoteInlineDef"]<...>
```

It is also possible to include in-line formatting instructions directly in a paragraph-level stylesheet definition (without first defining and then referring to a separate in-line stylesheet definition). This is done by simply adding the in-line tags (described below) to the end of the definition.

In-line formatting options

It is possible to override the style of characters in a paragaph. Again, this can be done either by explicitly setting new type styles (as in the '<B>' tag to set the bold style), or by reference to an in-line stylesheet definition, and again this second approach is usually preferable. It is just as easy to create and reference an inline stylesheet definition as it is to create and reference a block-level definition, though it is less easy to manage complex combinations of styles when using XSLT to generate the tagged document.

In-line stylesheet references

An in-line stylesheet definition is referenced using the '<@...>' tag. The name of the style is inserted into this tag.

```
...  <@Emphasis>This text is in Emphasis style...
```

Just as there are tags that represent no paragraph style and the default 'Normal' paragraph style, there are equivalent in-line tags. The ' <@>' tag represents the 'No Style' in-line style definition, and the '<@$>' tag represents the 'Normal' in-line style definition.

In-line stylesheet references are not recommended if there is a possibility that one in-line style will be embedded in another, because there is no tag that simply ends the current style and reasserts the previous stylesheet settings. When the embedded style ends, it is necessary to know which other style was in effect before it started, and this is complicated when using XSLT. If this scenario is possible, then it is better to use direct styling tags (described below) instead of stylesheets (even at the expense of losing end-user ability to make global changes easily).

In-line style settings

All of the following styles act as switches. The tag is repeated to switch off the style concerned:

Bold	<B>	Strikethrough	</>
Italic	<I>	Caps	<K>
Outline	<O>	Smallcaps	<H>
Underline	<U>	Superscript	<+>
Word underline	<W>	Subscript	<->
Superior	<V>		

For example:

```
This is both <B>bold and <I>italic<I><B> text.
```

This is both **bold and *italic*** text.

However, note that the first <B> tag in a paragraph will turn-off bold styling (rather than turn it on) if the paragraph style includes bold styling. This is true of all other styles too.

It is also possible to switch off all current styling, and return to normal plain style (overriding the paragraph style too, if it does not define plain text styling) using the '<P>' (Plain) tag:

```
This is both <B>bold and <I>italic<P> text.
```

This is both **bold and *italic*** text.

Alternatively, it is possible to return to the default style of the paragraph (which often means the same thing), using the '<$>' tag:

```
This is both <B>bold and <I>italic<$> text.
```

This is both **bold and *italic*** text.

However, the technique of simply switching on and switching off individual styles is easier to use than either of these techniques when converting from XML using XSLT:

```
<xsl:template match="emph">
  &lt;B&gt;<xsl:apply-tempalates/>&lt;B&gt;
</xsl:template>
```

This approach is also safer, because in-line formatting is allowed to span across paragraphs that conform to the same stylesheet definition.

Fonts

The font used to render text can be changed using the '<f "font name">' tag:

```
This is <f "courier">markup<$> text.
```

This is `markup` text.

The tag '<f$>' resets the font to the original setting (as defined by the current character style sheet, if any, or by the 'Normal' character style if not).

The font size can be changed using the '<z###.##>' tag. For example, '<z12.5>' sets the text size to 12.5pt. The tag '<z$>' resets the size to the original setting (as defined by the current character style sheet, if any, or by the 'Normal' character style if not).

There are a number of other, less frequently used tags. The '<s###>' tag sets the shade, and the value is interpreted as a percentage. The '<h###>' tag sets the horizontal scale, and the '<v###>' tag sets the vertical scale, again in both cases as a percentage. The '<k###.##>' tag specifies that the next two characters should be kerned (should overlap or be very close together) by fractions of an em (the width of the capital 'M' character). The '<t###.##>' tag for tracking also uses fractions of an em. The baseline can be shifted by a given number of points using the '<b###.##>' tag.

Character stylesheet definitions

Character (in-line) level stylesheet definitions are created in almost exactly the same way as paragraph level stylesheet definitions. Indeed, the syntax of the command is identical when the stylesheet is based on another in-line stylesheet definition, with the only exception being that the command happens not to contain any paragraph level formatting tags. The following command creates a new style called 'Emphasis' that is based on Normal, but then sets the style to bold and italic:

```
@Emphasis=[S"","","Normal"]<bi>
```

However, the command is much simpler when the style definition is not based on another definition. In this case, the square brackets are not used at all:

```
@Emphasis=<bi>
```

Colours

Text can be presented in various colours. The four standard print colours are cyan, magenta, yellow and black traditionally represented by the letters C, M, Y and K. The tags '<cC>', '<cM>', '<cY>' and '<cK>' represent these colours. In addition, the tag '<cW>' represents the colour white.

When a colour name has been defined in the blank document, the tag '<C"colour name">' can be used instead. If the referenced name is not actually defined in the document, then black is selected by default.

The tag '<c$>' resets the colour to the original setting (as defined by the current character style sheet, if any, or by the 'Normal' character stylesheet otherwise).

Characters

A character can be included by referring to its ASCII character value, in the '<\#...>' tag. For example, '<\#183>' represents the bullet character (which is commonly used to mark each item in a list). The number must be exactly three digits in length, with leading zeros used as padding when necessary. For example, the value '064' represents the '@' character. Placing a '!' symbol before the '#' symbol makes the character non-breaking (the current line cannot be broken immediately after this character).

The actual character the number in the tag represents may depend on the character set in use, which in turn is based on the computer platform in use. Characters above the value 127 differ in meaning between platforms. The tag '<e0>' (at the top of the file) specifies the Macintosh character set, while '<e1>' specifies the Windows ANSI character set, and '<e2>' specifies the ISO Latin 1 character set (see Chapter 34).

If the source XML document has elements that represent any of the following concepts, then they can be converted to the tags shown in this table:

New line	`<\n>`	Breaking em dash	`<\m>`
Discretionary return	`<\d>`	Discretionary hyphen	`<\h>`
Hyphen	`<\->`	Previous text box number character	`<\2>`
Indent here	`<\i>`	Current text box number character	`<\3>`
Right indent tab	`<\t>`	Next page text box number character	`<\4>`
Standard space	`<\s>`	New column	`<\c>`
Figure space	`<\f>`	New box	`<\b>`
Punctuation space	`<\p>`		
Flex space	`<\q>`		

The hyphen, dash and space tags can be made non-breaking by inserting the '!' character into the tag, such as '<\!p>' (non-breaking punctuation space).

The new line code generates a soft carriage return (equivalent to pressing 'shift + return' on the keyboard, and is therefore similar to the HTML BR tag).

The discretionary return code has no effect on the text, unless it occurs near to the right edge of the box, in which case it indicates a convenient place to break the line.

The hyphen code seems to have no purpose, except perhaps when the hyphen character is not the same as the keyboard dash character '-'.

The indent here code and the right indent tab code break the paragraph at the respective indent positions.

There are several spacing codes, which represent space characters that may differ in width. Typically, spaces between groups of digits, and between punctuation characters, are narrower than the standard spaces placed between words.

The breaking em dash code represents a wide dash (the width of the capital 'M' character). If this character occurs near the right edge of the box, it may be used as a convenient place to split the line (after the dash, not before).

The discretionary hyphen code represents a hyphen character, but this character only appears if the code occurs near the right edge of the box, and indicates a place where the line can be split. Note that when the XML source text is generated by an application that has access to a hyphenation dictionary, then the application could insert these codes at all sensible hyphenation points in every word in the file.

Text box numbers can be generated. The number of the current, previous or next text box, representing its position in the chain of linked text boxes, replaces the respective code listed above.

The new column code forces the following text to be placed in the next column of the current text box.

The new box code forces the following text to be placed in the next text box in the linked sequence of text boxes.

Indexes

A tagged document can include markup that identifies words and phrases to be included in an index. This markup also specifies where this term should appear in a hierarchical index, specifies where the term starts and ends for the purposes of recording which page or pages it is on, and perhaps also references another term or overrides the natural sorting location of the term.

The '<XI...>' tag identifies a point-location for indexing:

```
The rest of this paragraph is <XI...>about XSL.
```

Alternatively, the '<XO>' and '<XC...>' tags are used as a pair to identify the start and end of a term:

```
An <XO>XSL<XC...> document is an <XO>XML<XC...> document.
```

The '<XI...>' tag and the '<XC...>' tag have the same possible parameters (as discussed below).

Levels

A term is assigned to a position in the index hierarchy by naming the terms above it. An empty parameter denotes the end of the list:

```
...  <XO>markup<XC,"markup",""  ...>  ...

...  <XO>XML<XC,"markup","XML",""  ...>  ...

...  <XO>XSL-FO<XC,"markup","XML","XSL-FO",""  ...>  ...

...  <XO>XSLT<XC,"markup","XML","XSLT",""  ...>  ...
```

This example creates the following structure:

```
markup
  XML
    XSL-FO
    XSLT
```

Sorting order

By default, entries at a given location in the hierarchical index are arranged by simply sorting them alphabetically. But it is possible to override this ordering for a specific term by supplying, as a parameter, another text string to sort it on. When no value is supplied, the original marked-up term is used as the sort term:

```
...  <XO>XSLT<XC,...,"",""  ...>  ...

...  <XO>8859<XC,...,"","ISO-8859"  ...>  ...
```

Style of index

It is possible that when the index is created, different text styles will be used for each level, and in some cases perhaps for individual entries. The style to use is specified in the next parameter:

```
...  <XO>XSLT<XC,...,"","","IndexStyle1"  ...>  ...
```

If this parameter is empty, then the default 'Entry' style is used.

Scope

The page or pages recorded against an indexed term is influenced by the scope of the index. A secondary parameter supplies additional information in some of the scenarios below.

The value '0' indicates that only the page containing the start of the term is to be referenced. If the term happens to cross page boundaries, then both page numbers are included in the index. The second parameter is not relevant, but should be set to '0':

```
...  <XO>XSLT<XC,...,0,0  ...>  ...
```

The value '1' indicates that the page or pages containing the term are to be referenced. The second parameter is not relevant, but should be set to '1':

```
... <XO>XSLT<XC,...,1,1 ...> ...
```

The value '2' indicates that the page or pages containing the term, plus all following text until a specified style is reached are to be referenced. The second parameter names the style:

```
... <XO>XSLT<XC,...,2,summaryStyle ...> ...
```

The value '3' indicates that the page or pages containing the term, plus the given number of following paragraphs, are to be referenced. The second parameter contains the number of paragraphs involved:

```
... <XO>XSLT<XC,...,3,2 ...> ...
```

The value '4' indicates that the page or pages containing the term, plus all remaining text up to the end of the story ('0') or the end of the document ('1') are to be referenced. The second parameter specifies end-of-story ('0') or end-of-document ('1'):

```
... <XO>XSLT<XC,...,4,0 ...> ...
```

The value '5' suppresses the page numbers. The second parameter is irrelevant, but should be set to '0':

```
... <XO>XSLT<XC,...,5,0 ...> ...
```

The value '6' specifies that the entry is simply a cross-reference to another entry. The second parameter specifies that the text shown in the index will be 'See' ('0'), 'See also' ('1') or 'See herein' ('2'). In this scenario, there is a final parameter that gives the name of the other term to see:

```
... <XO>XSL<XC,...,6,1,"XSL-FO"> ...
```

In the other scenarios above, the final parameter is an empty string.

32. DTD analysis for XSLT stylesheet design

There are many XML books that describe how to build a DTD or XML Schema model. This chapter covers these modelling languages only in sufficient detail to enable the analysis of existing models. Such analysis can provide important input to the development of appropriate stylesheets for documents that conform to these models.

Introduction

When a stylesheet needs to be created for the purpose of formatting or transforming a number of documents, it would be natural to think of these documents as comprising a specific 'class' of documents. After all, the templates in the stylesheet will need to be aware of the elements that these documents contain, and the contexts in which they might need to be transformed in a variety of different ways. Creation of a single stylesheet for these documents will only be practical if they have a similar, if not identical, element structure. This does not always mean that a formal model will have been created to describe this structure, but in many cases a DTD or XML Schema model will have been created. If such a model exists, it can be exploited during the stylesheet creation process.

The presence of a document model is an ideal source of information. It explicitly describes all the elements that may appear, and all the contexts in which they may appear. This knowledge can save a lot of effort. For example, it would be wasteful to create a template for a Title element that appears in a Note element, if the definition of the Note element in the model does not include the Title element as a possible child or descendant. Studying a model is also much faster than studying all the documents in the collection to determine what has been used (and this technique is not adequate in any case because allowed options that may be used in the future may not have been used up to the point of the investigation).

Ideally, each stylesheet created should be associated with a particular document model. It should be designed to transform documents that conform to this model. Of course, there may be more than one stylesheet for a given model, each designed to format or transform documents that conform to this model in a different way.

In order to study a model, it is necessary to know how to interpret the instructions it contains. In particular, the way that elements and attributes are defined must be understood.

Elements to style

To obtain a list of all the elements that may occur in a compliant document, it is simply necessary to read the names appearing after the ELEMENT declarations. In the following example, the DTD defines just four elements called 'Book', 'Title', 'Chapter' and 'Para':

```
<!ELEMENT Book      (Title, Chapter*)>
<!ELEMENT Title     (#PCDATA)>
<!ELEMENT Chapter   (Title, Para*)>
<!ELEMENT Para      (#PCDATA)>
```

The following is a conforming document instance:

```
<Book>
  <Title>The Book Title</Title>
  <Chapter>
    <Title>Chapter One Title</Title>
    <Para>First paragraph.</Para>
    <Para>Second paragraph.</Para>
  </Chapter>
  <Chapter>
    <Title>Chapter Two Title</Title>
    <Para>First paragraph.</Para>
    <Para>Second paragraph.</Para>
  </Chapter>
</Book>
```

A template could be created for each of these elements.

```
<template match="Book">...</template>


<template match="Title">...</template>


<template match="Chapter">...</template>


<template match="Para">...</template>
```

However, it is usually necessary to study the possible content of the elements to determine the role each element plays. Several templates may actually be necessary for a given element. In other cases, an element may not play any direct role in the styling of its content. In the example above, the Chapter element may not need to be processed explicitly (though its presence can be useful in creating context-sensitive styles for other elements). In the example above, the Title element may be used to give the whole book a name and to give each chapter a name, and it is not likely that these two classes of title are to be styled in the same way.

Hierarchical context

When the style of an element depends on its location in the document, it is necessary to understand what contexts are allowed by the model. The ELEMENT declarations in the DTD and the equivalent definitions in the XML Schema model provide this information.

In the example above, the Book element definition specifies that a book may contain a Title element, followed by any number of Chapter elements. One possible parent of the Title element is therefore the Book element. However, the Chapter element definition also names the Title element as its first child, and so a Title element may instead have a Chapter element parent. The Para element does not mention the Title element in its definition, and so a Title element cannot have a Para element parent. Assuming that book titles and chapters will need to be processed or formatted differently, the following two templates are needed:

```
<template match="Book/Title">...</template>

<template match="Chapter/Title">...</template>
```

Required and sequential context

An element may be optional, and may have a specific location in the document structure.

Optional elements

An element may be optional in some (or all) contexts. This can be a factor in stylesheet design. For example, it would not be a good idea to arrange for a chapter Title element to force a page break to start the new chapter, if the Title element happens to be optional (as defined in a DTD). If an element name is followed by a question mark, it is optional. In the following example, the title is optional within a Note element:

```
<!ELEMENT Note (Title? ...)>
```

The asterisk symbol is used to indicate that an element is repeatable but also optional. The Para element in the example below is therefore optional, and the note could be empty:

```
<!ELEMENT Note (Para*)>
```

Element ordering

An element model may include elements that can appear in any order, or elements that must appear in the order shown. Ordering is predefined when commas are used to separate element names in the model. In the following example, the Title element must appear first within any Note element. Because it is also required, it is possible to format the beginning of the note from the Title element template, and it may not be necessary to have a template for the Note element at all:

```
<!ELEMENT Note (Title, Para*)>


<template name="Note/Title">
  <html:H3>NOTE: <apply-templates/></html:H3>
</template>
```

Block and in-line elements

When formatting text, the concept of 'block' and 'in-line' elements is important. Block elements have content that is separated from neighbouring blocks, usually by starting a new line and by creating a gap above and below the block. Titles and paragraphs are typical examples. The XSL 'block' property is used to create a new block (and the DIV element can be used in an HTML document). In-line elements have content that is simply appended to previous text, without creating a new line. Bold and italic phrases are typical examples. The XSL 'inline' property is used to create a new in-line region (and the SPAN element can be used in an HTML document). It is possible to identify block and in-line elements from studying DTD content models.

It is important to discover which elements are block elements and which are in-line elements, not only to apply appropriate formatting to them but simply because they are the elements that are most likely to require templates to be defined.

Text content

Both block and in-line elements may directly contain text. Elements that directly contain text are in any case good candidates for requiring a template because this is the last chance to define a specific style for the embedded characters.

The **#PCDATA** keyword in the content model indicates this possibility. The Emph element defined below is allowed to contain only text:

```
<!ELEMENT Emph (#PCDATA)>


    <Emph>This is important text.</Emph>
```

When the definition includes other elements as well, further templates will probably be needed to cater for the text content of these other elements:

```
<!ELEMENT Emph (#PCDATA|Important)>


    <Emph>This is <Important>not</Important> very important
    text.</Emph>
```

This is **not** very important text.

In-line elements

In-line elements can be detected by studying the model of the parent element(s). If the parent element is allowed to contain text, as well as the given element, then it is almost certainly an in-line element. The Important element below is an in-line element:

```
<!ELEMENT Para (#PCDATA|Important)>
<!ELEMENT Important (#PCDATA)>
```

The case is strengthened further if the element may itself directly contain text, as in the example of the Important element above.

Some in-line elements may be present only for the purposes of allowing the enclosed text to be located (for searching purposes, for extraction and reuse, or for some other purpose), so it cannot automatically be assumed that the content needs to be styled in some distinctive way.

Block elements

Block elements are elements that can directly contain text but are not themselves used in other elements that can directly contain text. The Title and Para elements described above are good examples of this type. In the example above, they are used in the Chapter and Book elements, which cannot contain text.

```
<!ELEMENT Book    (Title, Chapter*)>

<!ELEMENT Chapter (Title, Para*)>

<!ELEMENT Title   (#PCDATA)>

<!ELEMENT Para    (#PCDATA | Important)>
```

Attributes

Attributes may play an important role in selecting elements by context. Attributes may also contain values that need to be presented, or be used to determine what is presented. In some cases it is necessary to know if an attribute is required to be present, or is optional, or to determine what possible values the attribute may hold. The ATTRIBUTE declaration defines one or more attributes for a given element. The element name follows the declaration keyword. In the example below, the Para element has four attributes assigned to it, namely an ID attribute, a Type attribute, an Author attribute and a Status attribute:

```
<!ATTLIST Para  ID      #REQUIRED
                Type    (Normal|Secret) "Normal"
                Author  #IMPLIED
                Status  "Draft">
```

If the attribute name is followed by the keyword #REQUIRED, then the element will always have this attribute present and it will always have a value. It is therefore not necessary to test for its presence in a template. However, if the attribute name is followed by the keyword #IMPLIED, then the attribute may be absent and it is appropriate to test for its existence:

```
<template name="Para[@Author]">...</template>
```

```
<template name="Para">
  <if test="@Author">...</if>
</template>
```

When a list of values is given between brackets, separated by vertical bar characters, this is the allowed list of values. The values 'Normal' and 'Secret' for the Type attribute above are typical. Again, these are case sensitive.

Sometimes, a following default value is given, as in 'Normal' and 'Draft' above, indicating that when a value is not present in the element tag, this value should be assumed. Depending on the parser used by the XSLT processor, the default may or may not be passed to the processor as an attribute value that is present. It is safer to test for its existence.

DTD construction features

Analysis of element and attribute declarations may be hindered if the way that a DTD can use entities and marked sections is not understood.

Entities

Just as XML document authors may use general entities to aid construction of a document, DTD authors may use parameter entities to assist with the construction of a DTD. Whenever a set of attributes or a particular element model is needed in more than one place, the DTD author may use an entity to store the information in a single place, and an entity reference at each point where the information is relevant.

For example, if the Title and Para elements have the same attributes, the following may appear (the four attributes appearing in both elements):

```
<!ENTITY % standardAttributes  'ID        #REQUIRED
                Type   (Normal|Secret)  "Normal"
                Author CDATA            #IMPLIED
                Status CDATA            "Draft"' >

<!ATTLIST Title  %standardAttributes;>

<!ATTLIST Para   %standardAttributes;>
```

A content model can be duplicated in the same way:

```
<!ENTITY % textBlock   '(#PCDATA|Emph)*'>

<!ELEMENT Title  %textBlock;>

<!ELEMENT Para   %textBlock;>
```

Marked sections

A DTD author may use marked sections to create multiple varieties of the DTD. Specifically, parts of a DTD can be switched off and switched on, perhaps to swap between alternative models. When creating a stylesheet that must cope with all the documents that comply with a given DTD, marked sections can often be ignored.

If the stylesheet does not need to cater for elements that are not part of the default application of the DTD, then all statements in marked sections that contain the IGNORE keyword (or an entity reference that is set to 'IGNORE') can be safely ignored:

```
<![IGNORE[
  ...
]]>

<!ENTITY % ignoreThis 'IGNORE'>

<![%ignoreThis;[
  ...
]]>
```

33. XSLT DTD

Introduction

An XML DTD exists to describe the elements and attributes allowed in an XSLT stylesheet. XML editing software can use this DTD to provide a guided environment for the authoring of stylesheets. It can also be used by XML parsers to validate a stylesheet received from elsewhere. The DTD is listed in Annex C of the standard. For those unfamiliar with XML DTDs, it is recommended that a book on XML be consulted before reading this chapter. Alternatively, Chapter 21 of this book provides a brief overview of DTD markup.

The default DTD includes the prefix 'xsl:' on all XSLT element names, such as 'xsl:template'. This can be changed to whatever is appropriate (including no prefix at all if XSLT elements are assigned to the default namespace).

Top-level elements

The **Top Level** entity defines the elements that can occur in the Stylesheet (or Transform) element. It forces all Import elements to appear first (if any occur at all), and then allows any mixture of other allowed elements:

```
<!ENTITY % top-level "
     (xsl:import*,
        (xsl:include | xsl:strip-space |
        xsl:preserve-space | xsl:output |
        xsl:key | xsl:decimal-format |
        xsl:attribute-set | xsl:variable |
        xsl:param | xsl:template |
        xsl:namespace-alias
        %non-xsl-top-level;)*) ">
```

Note that the Template and Variable elements shown in this list are described in the next section. The other elements are described below.

A mechanism for adding non-XSLT elements to this group is provided by the entity reference at the end. But the **Non-XSL Top Level** entity is initially empty:

```
<!ENTITY % non-xsl-top-level " " >
```

The Top Level entity is referenced from two places, namely the Stylesheet element definition and the **Transform** element definition:

```
<!ELEMENT xsl:stylesheet %top-level;>

<!ELEMENT xsl:transform %top-level;>
```

For example:

```
<xsl:stylesheet ...>
  <xsl:import .../>
  <xsl:import .../>
  <xsl:template ...>...</xsl:template>
  <xsl:template ...>...</xsl:template>
</xsl:stylesheet>
```

There are also a number of attributes that these two elements can take, and these are grouped within the **Top Level Attributes** entity:

```
<!ENTITY % top-level-atts "
      extension-element-prefixes CDATA      #IMPLIED
      exclude-result-prefixes    CDATA      #IMPLIED
      id                         ID         #IMPLIED
      version                    NMTOKEN    #REQUIRED
      xmlns:xsl                  CDATA
            #FIXED "http://www.w3.org/1999/XSL/Transform"
      %space-att;
```

```
<!ATTLIST xsl:stylesheet %top-level-atts;>

<!ATTLIST xsl:transform %top-level-atts;>
```

Import element

The **Import** element is defined as follows:

```
<!ELEMENT xsl:import EMPTY >
```

The attributes are as follows:

```
<!ATTLIST xsl:import href  %URI;   #REQUIRED >
```

With the entity replaced, the true model is as follows:

```
<!ATTLIST xsl:import href  CDATA   #REQUIRED >
```

For example:

```
<xsl:import href="./library/styleTables.xsl" />
```

Include element

The **Include** element is defined as follows:

```
<!ELEMENT xsl:include EMPTY >
```

The attributes are as follows:

```
<!ATTLIST xsl:include href   %URI;    #REQUIRED >
```

With the entity replaced, the true model is as follows:

```
<!ATTLIST xsl:include href   CDATA    #REQUIRED >
```

For example:

```
<xsl:include href="commonStyles.xsl" />
```

Strip Space element

The **Strip Space** element is defined as follows:

```
<!ELEMENT xsl:strip-space EMPTY >
```

The attributes are as follows:

```
<!ATTLIST xsl:strip-space   elements   CDATA    #REQUIRED >
```

For example:

```
<xsl:strip-space elements="book title para" />
```

Preserve Space element

The **Preserve Space** element is defined as follows:

```
<!ELEMENT xsl:preserve-space EMPTY >
```

The attributes are as follows:

```
<!ATTLIST xsl:preserve-space
                    elements   CDATA    #REQUIRED >
```

For example:

```
<xsl:preserve-space elements="example preformatted" />
```

Output element

The **Output** element is defined as follows:

```
<!ELEMENT xsl:output EMPTY >
```

The attributes are as follows:

```
<!ATTLIST xsl:output
          method                      %qname;      #IMPLIED
          version                     NMTOKEN      #IMPLIED
          encoding                    CDATA        #IMPLIED
          omit-xml-declaration        (yes|no)     #IMPLIED
          standalone                  (yes|no)     #IMPLIED
          doctype-public              CDATA        #IMPLIED
          doctype-system              CDATA        #IMPLIED
          cdata-section-elements %qnames;          #IMPLIED
          indent                      (yes|no)     #IMPLIED
          media-type                  CDATA        #IMPLIED >
```

With all the embedded entity references replaced, the true model is as follows:

```
<!ATTLIST xsl:output
          method                      NMTOKEN      #IMPLIED
          version                     NMTOKEN      #IMPLIED
          encoding                    CDATA        #IMPLIED
          omit-xml-declaration        (yes|no)     #IMPLIED
          standalone                  (yes|no)     #IMPLIED
          doctype-public              CDATA        #IMPLIED
          doctype-system              CDATA        #IMPLIED
          cdata-section-elements NMTOKENS          #IMPLIED
          indent                      (yes|no)     #IMPLIED
          media-type                  CDATA        #IMPLIED >
```

For example:

```
<xsl:output method="HTML" version="4.0" />
```

Key element

The **Key** element is defined as follows:

```
<!ELEMENT xsl:key EMPTY >
```

The attributes are as follows:

```
<!ATTLIST xsl:key
          name            %qname;            #IMPLIED
          match           %pattern;          #IMPLIED
          use             %expr;             #IMPLIED >
```

With all the embedded entity references replaced, the true model is as follows:

```
<!ATTLIST xsl:key
          name            NMTOKEN            #IMPLIED
          match           CDATA              #IMPLIED
          use             CDATA              #IMPLIED >
```

For example:

```
<xsl:key name="nameKey" match="name" use="name/first"/>
```

Decimal Format element

The **Decimal Format** element is defined as follows:

```
<!ELEMENT xsl:decimal-format EMPTY >
```

The attributes are as follows:

```
<!ATTLIST xsl:decimal-format
          name                  %qname;        #IMPLIED
          decimal-separator     %char;         "."
          grouping-separator    %char;         ","
          infinity              CDATA          "infinity"
          minus-sign            %char;         "-"
          NaN                   CDATA          "NaN"
          percent               %char;         "%"
          per-mille             %char;         "&#x2030;"
          zero-digit            %char;         "0"
          digit                 %char;         "#"
          pattern-separator     %char;         ";" >
```

With all the embedded entity references replaced, the true model is as follows:

```
<!ATTLIST xsl:decimal-format
          name                  NMTOKEN        #IMPLIED
          decimal-separator     CDATA          "."
          grouping-separator    CDATA          ","
          infinity              CDATA          "infinity"
          minus-sign            CDATA          "-"
          NaN                   CDATA          "NaN"
          percent               CDATA          "%"
          per-mille             CDATA          "&#x2030;"
          zero-digit            CDATA          "0"
          digit                 CDATA          "#"
          pattern-separator     CDATA          ";" >
```

Attribute Set element

The **Attribute Set** element is defined as follows:

```
<!ELEMENT xsl:attribute-set (xsl:attribute)* >
```

The attributes are as follows:

```
<!ATTLIST xsl:attribute-set
          name                  %qname;        #REQUIRED
          use-attribute-sets    %qnames;       #IMPLIED >
```

With all the embedded entity references replaced, the true model is as follows:

```
<!ATTLIST xsl:attribute-set
          name                  NMTOKEN        #REQUIRED
          use-attribute-sets    NMTOKENS       #IMPLIED >
```

For example:

```
<xsl:attribute-set name="standardSet" >
  <xsl:attribute...></xsl:attribute>
  <xsl:attribute...></xsl:attribute>
  <xsl:attribute...></xsl:attribute>
</xsl:attribute-set>
```

Parameter element

The **Parameter** element is defined as follows:

```
<!ELEMENT xsl:param        %template; >
```

This expands to the following:

```
<!ELEMENT xsl:param ( #PCDATA |
          xsl:apply-templates | xsl:call-template |
          xsl:apply-imports | xsl:for-each |
          xsl:value-of | xsl:copy-of |
          xsl:number | xsl:choose | xslif |
          xsl:text | xsl:copy | xsl:variable |
          xsl:message | xsl:fallback |
          xsl:processing-instruction | xsl:comment |
          xsl:element | xsl:attribute )* >
```

The attributes are as follows:

```
<!ATTLIST xsl:attribute-set
          name               %qname;       #REQUIRED
          select             %expr;        #IMPLIED >
```

With the embedded entity references replaced, the true model is as follows:

```
<!ATTLIST xsl:attribute-set
          name               NMTOKEN       #REQUIRED
          select             CDATA         #IMPLIED >
```

Namespace Alias element

The **Namespace Alias** element is defined as follows:

```
<!ELEMENT xsl:namespace-alias EMPTY >
```

The attributes are as follows:

```
<!ATTLIST xsl:namespace-alias
          stylesheet-prefix    CDATA       #REQUIRED
          result-prefix        CDATA       #REQUIRED >
```

Templates

Template element

Templates are defined by the **Template** element.

```
<!ELEMENT xsl:template (#PCDATA %instructions;
                         %result-elements; | xsl:param)* >
```

The keyword '#PCDATA' refers to text that can be inserted directly into the Template element:

```
<xsl:template ...>REPLACE WITH THIS</xsl:template>
```

A template can also contain various instruction elements. Apart from the Param element, and the content of the Result Elements entity (described later), the **Instructions** entity is used to group the instruction elements, because they are also allowed in other locations (the For Each element and the Template entity):

```
<!ENTITY % instructions " %char-instructions; |
                          xsl:processing-instruction |
                          xsl:comment |
                          xsl:element |
                          xsl:attribute ">
```

This entity encompasses all XSLT instructions. However, most of the instructions allowed are further referenced from another entity, called **Character Instructions**:

```
<!ENTITY % char-instructions " |
             xsl:apply-templates | xsl:call-template |
             xsl:apply-imports | xsl:for-each |
             xsl:value-of | xsl:copy-of |
             xsl:number | xsl:choose | xsl:if |
             xsl:text | xsl:copy | xsl:variable |
             xsl:message | xsl:fallback ">
```

This is done because these instructions are also referenced from another entity. The **Char Template** entity also uses this entity, and is in turn referenced from the Processing Instruction, Comment and Attribute element definitions:

```
<!ENTITY % char-template "
             ( #PCDATA  %char-instructions; ) ">

<!ELEMENT xsl:comment                 (%char-template;)>

<!ELEMENT xsl:processing-instruction (%char-template;)>

<!ELEMENT xsl:attribute               (%char-template;)>
```

The reason for splitting the instructions in this way is to avoid the possibility of some elements containing other elements, such as comments containing either comments or processing instructions (which would be illegal). Character instructions are therefore instructions that can contain characters *and* further instructions.

Attributes

The XSLT attributes specified for the Template elements are as follows:

```
<!ATTLIST xsl:template
                match      %pattern;     #IMPLIED
                name       %qname;       #IMPLIED
                priority   %priority;    #IMPLIED
                mode       %qname;       #IMPLIED
                %space-att;>
```

With all the embedded entity references replaced, the true model is as follows:

```
<!ELEMENT xsl:template
                match      CDATA                    #IMPLIED
                name       NMTOKEN                  #IMPLIED
                priority   NMTOKEN                  #IMPLIED
                mode       NMTOKEN                  #IMPLIED
                xml:space  (default|preserve)   #IMPLIED >
```

For example:

```
<xsl:template match="title" priority="2"
                mode="SpecialMode" >...</xsl:template>
```

Template instructions

A number of instructions may appear in a template, including comments, processing instructions, elements and attributes.

Template entity

The instructions allowed directly in a Template element are in some cases also allowed in the instructions themselves (with the exception of the Param element). For convenience, the Template entity is defined to group these elements:

```
<!ENTITY % template " (#PCDATA %instructions;
                %result-elements;)* " >
```

Elements that refer to this entity include the If, When, Otherwise, With Parameter, Variable, Parameter, Copy, Message and Fallback elements.

Comment element

A **Comment** element is defined as follows:

```
<!ELEMENT xsl:comment %char-template; >
```

With all entities replaced, the true model is as follows. The fact that all these elements can occur in a comment shows how the content of the comment does not have to be specified as a simple text string; its content can be determined using the full power of XSLT:

```
<!ELEMENT xsl:comment ( #PCDATA |
            xsl:apply-templates | xsl:call-template |
            xsl:apply-imports | xsl:for-each |
            xsl:value-of | xsl:copy-of |
            xsl:number | xsl:choose | xsl:if |
            xsl:text | xsl:copy | xsl:variable |
            xsl:message | xsl:fallback )* >
```

The attributes are as follows:

```
<!ATTLIST xsl:comment %space-att; >
```

With the entity replaced, the true model is as follows:

```
<!ATTLIST xsl:comment
          xml:space (default|preserve) #IMPLIED >
```

For example:

```
<xsl:comment xml:space="preserve">
This is a comment.
</xsl:comment>
```

Processing Instruction element

The **Processing Instruction** element is defined as follows:

```
<!ELEMENT xsl:processing-instruction %char-template; >
```

With all entities replaced, the true model is as follows. It is not clear why these elements are allowed to occur here as they can have no purpose in a processing instruction:

```
<!ELEMENT xsl:processing-instruction ( #PCDATA |
          xsl:apply-templates | xsl:call-template |
          xsl:apply-imports | xsl:for-each |
          xsl:value-of | xsl:copy-of |
          xsl:number | xsl:choose | xslif |
          xsl:text | xsl:copy | xsl:variable |
          xsl:message | xsl:fallback )* >
```

The attributes are as follows:

```
<!ATTLIST xsl:processing-instruction
                    name      %avt;     #REQUIRED
                    %space-att; >
```

With all entities replaced, the true model is as follows:

```
<!ATTLIST xsl:processing-instruction
            name      CDATA                #REQUIRED
            xml:space (default|preserve) #IMPLIED >
```

For example:

```
<xsl:processing-instruction name="ACME">
new_page
</xsl:processing-instruction>
```

Element element

The **Element** instruction is defined as follows:

```
<!ELEMENT xsl:element %template;>
```

With all entities replaced, the true model is as follows (with any output elements to be added). Note that an element can contain another element, which is necessary to build element hierarchies for output within a single template:

```
<!ELEMENT xsl:element ( #PCDATA |
        xsl:apply-templates | xsl:call-template |
        xsl:apply-imports | xsl:for-each |
        xsl:value-of | xsl:copy-of |
        xsl:number | xsl:choose | xslif |
        xsl:text | xsl:copy | xsl:variable |
        xsl:message | xsl:fallback |
        xsl:processing-instruction | xsl:comment |
        xsl:element | xsl:attribute )* >
```

The attributes are as follows:

```
<!ATTLIST xsl:element
            name                %avt;       #REQUIRED
            namespace           %avt;       #IMPLIED
            use-attribute-sets  %qnames;    #IMPLIED
            %space-att; >
```

With all entities replaced, the true model is as follows:

```
<!ATTLIST xsl:element
    name                CDATA                #REQUIRED
    namespace           CDATA                #IMPLIED
    use-attribute-sets  NMTOKENS             #IMPLIED
    xml:space           (default|preserve)   #IMPLIED >
```

For example:

```
<xsl:element name="TITLE">
  A <xsl:element name="EMPH">Title</xsl:element>
</xsl:element>
```

Attribute element

An **Attribute** instruction is defined as follows:

```
<!ELEMENT xsl:attribute %char-template;>
```

With all entities replaced, the true model is as follows (with any output elements to be added). Note that an element can contain another element, which is necessary to build element hierarchies for output within a single template:

```
<!ELEMENT xsl:attribute ( #PCDATA |
        xsl:apply-templates | xsl:call-template |
        xsl:apply-imports | xsl:for-each |
        xsl:value-of | xsl:copy-of |
        xsl:number | xsl:choose | xsl:if |
        xsl:text | xsl:copy | xsl:variable |
        xsl:message | xsl:fallback )* >
```

The attributes are as follows:

```
<!ATTLIST xsl:attribute
            name                %avt;       #REQUIRED
            namespace           %avt;       #IMPLIED
            use-attribute-sets  %qnames;    #IMPLIED
            %space-att; >
```

With all entities replaced, the true model is as follows:

```
<!ATTLIST xsl:attribute
    name               CDATA              #REQUIRED
    namespace          CDATA              #IMPLIED
    use-attribute-sets NMTOKENS           #IMPLIED
    xml:space          (default|preserve) #IMPLIED >
```

For example:

```
<xsl:attribute name="author">J. Smith</xsl:attribute>
```

Apply Templates element

An **Apply Templates** instruction is defined as follows:

```
<!ELEMENT xsl:apply-templates (xsl:sort|xsl:with-param)*>
```

The attributes are as follows:

```
<!ATTLIST xsl:apply-templates
            select              %expr;      "node"
            mode                %qname;     #IMPLIED >
```

With all entities replaced, the true model is as follows:

```
<!ATTLIST xsl:apply-templates
            select              CDATA           "node"
            mode                NMTOKEN         #IMPLIED >
```

Call Template element

A **Call Template** instruction is defined as follows:

```
<!ELEMENT xsl:call-template (xsl:with-param)* >
```

The attributes are as follows:

```
<!ATTLIST xsl:call-template
            name                %qname;         #IMPLIED >
```

With the entity replaced, the true model is as follows:

```
<!ATTLIST xsl:call-template
            name                NMTOKEN         #IMPLIED >
```

Apply Imports element

The **Apply Imports** instruction is defined as follows:

```
<!ELEMENT xsl:apply-imports EMPTY >
```

It has no attributes.

For example:

```
<xsl:apply-imports />
```

For Each element

A **For Each** instruction is defined as follows:

```
<!ELEMENT xsl:for-each (#PCDATA %instructions;
                        %result-elements; | xsl:sort )* >
```

With all entities replaced, the true model is as follows (with any output elements
to be added). Note that an element can contain another element, which is necessary
to build element hierarchies for output within a single template:

```
<!ELEMENT xsl:for-each ( #PCDATA |
        xsl:apply-templates | xsl:call-template |
        xsl:apply-imports | xsl:for-each |
        xsl:value-of | xsl:copy-of |
        xsl:number | xsl:choose | xsl:if |
        xsl:text | xsl:copy | xsl:variable |
        xsl:message | xsl:fallback |
        xsl:processing-instruction | xsl:comment |
        xsl:element | xsl:attribute | xsl:sort )* >
```

This model does not capture the precise requirement when the Sort element is used. If it occurs, it must precede all other elements and text.

The attributes are as follows:

```
<!ATTLIST xsl:for-each
            select                  %expr;        #REQUIRED
            %space-att; >
```

With all entities replaced, the true model is as follows:

```
<!ATTLIST xsl:for-each
     select               CDATA            #REQUIRED
     xml:space            (default|preserve)   #IMPLIED >
```

For example:

```
<xsl:for-each select="item">
  <xsl:comment>There was an item here.</xsl:comment>
</xsl:for-each>
```

Value Of element

The **Value Of** instruction is defined as follows:

```
<!ELEMENT xsl:value-of EMPTY >
```

The attributes are as follows:

```
<!ATTLIST xsl:value-of
            select                      %expr;    #REQUIRED
            disable-output-escaping  (yes|no)  "no">
```

With the entity replaced, the true model is as follows:

```
<!ATTLIST xsl:value-of
            select                   CDATA      #REQUIRED
            disable-output-escaping  (yes|no)   "no">
```

For example:

```
<xsl:value-of select="@price" />
```

Copy Of element

A **Copy Of** instruction is defined as follows:

```
<!ELEMENT xsl:copy-of EMPTY >
```

The attributes are as follows:

```
<!ATTLIST xsl:copy-of   select    %expr;     #REQUIRED >
```

With the entity replaced, the true model is as follows:

```
<!ATTLIST xsl:copy-of    select    CDATA       #REQUIRED >
```

For example:

```
<xsl:copy-of select="table" />
```

Number element

The **Number** instruction is defined as follows:

```
<!ELEMENT xsl:number EMPTY >
```

The attributes are as follows:

```
<!ATTLIST xsl:number
          level     (single|multiple|any)    "single"
          count     %pattern;                #IMPLIED
          from      %pattern;                #IMPLIED
          value     %expr;                   #IMPLIED
          format    %avt;                    "1"
          lang      %avt;                    #IMPLIED
          letter-value          %avt;        #IMPLIED
          grouping-separator %avt;           #IMPLIED
          grouping-size         %avt;        #IMPLIED >
```

With the entities replaced, the true model is as follows:

```
<!ATTLIST xsl:number
          level     (single|multiple|any)    "single"
          count     CDATA                    #IMPLIED
          from      CDATA                    #IMPLIED
          value     CDATA                    #IMPLIED
          format    CDATA                    "1"
          lang      CDATA                    #IMPLIED
          letter-value          CDATA        #IMPLIED
          grouping-separator CDATA           #IMPLIED
          grouping-size         CDATA        #IMPLIED >
```

For example:

```
<xsl:number level="multiple"
            count="chapter|section"
            from="part"
            format="1.a.i" />
```

Choose element

The **Choose** instruction is defined as follows:

```
<!ELEMENT xsl:choose (xsl:when+, xsl:otherwise?) >
```

The attributes are as follows:

```
<!ATTLIST xsl:choose %space-att; >
```

With all entities replaced, the true model is as follows:

```
<!ATTLIST xsl:choose
                xml:space   (default|preserve)    #IMPLIED >
```

See below for a description of the content of this element.

If element

The **If** instruction is defined as follows:

```
<!ELEMENT xsl:if %template; >
```

With the entity replaced, the true model is as follows:

```
<!ELEMENT xsl:if ( #PCDATA |
          xsl:apply-templates | xsl:call-template |
          xsl:apply-imports | xsl:for-each |
          xsl:value-of | xsl:copy-of |
          xsl:number | xsl:choose | xsl:if |
          xsl:text | xsl:copy | xsl:variable |
          xsl:message | xsl:fallback |
          xsl:processing-instruction | xsl:comment |
          xsl:element | xsl:attribute )* >
```

The attributes are as follows:

```
<!ATTLIST xsl:if
          test            %expr;           #REQUIRED
          %space-att; >
```

With all entities replaced, the true model is as follows:

```
<!ATTLIST xsl:if
     test                 CDATA            #REQUIRED
     xml:space            (default|preserve)  #IMPLIED >
```

For example:

```
<xsl:if test="@type='secret'">
  <xsl:message>Found secret paragraph</xsl:message>
</xsl:if>
```

Text element

The **Text** template instruction is defined as follows:

```
<!ELEMENT xsl:text (#PCDATA) >
```

The attributes are as follows:

```
<!ATTLIST xsl:text
          disable-output-escaping (yes|no) "no">
```

For example:

```
<xsl:text disable-output-escaping="yes">
create HTML &lt;P&gt; (paragraph) &lt;/P&gt;
</xsl:text>
```

Copy element

The **Copy** instruction is defined as follows:

```
<!ELEMENT xsl:copy %template; >
```

With the entity replaced, the true model is as follows:

```
<!ELEMENT xsl:copy ( #PCDATA |
          xsl:apply-templates | xsl:call-template |
          xsl:apply-imports | xsl:for-each |
          xsl:value-of | xsl:copy-of |
          xsl:number | xsl:choose | xsl:if |
          xsl:text | xsl:copy | xsl:variable |
          xsl:message | xsl:fallback |
          xsl:processing-instruction | xsl:comment |
          xsl:element | xsl:attribute )* >
```

The attributes are as follows:

```
<!ATTLIST xsl:copy
           use-attribute-sets    %qnames;    #REQUIRED
           %space-att; >
```

With all entities replaced, the true model is as follows:

```
<!ATTLIST xsl:copy
     use-attribute-sets NMTOKENS            #REQUIRED
     xml:space              (default|preserve)  #IMPLIED >
```

For example:

```
<xsl:copy>
  <xsl:message>Copied source element -
  but no attributes</xsl:message>
</xsl:copy>
```

Variable element

The **Variable** instruction is defined as follows:

```
<!ELEMENT xsl:variable %template; >
```

With the entity replaced, the true model is as follows:

```
<!ELEMENT xsl:variable ( #PCDATA |
          xsl:apply-templates | xsl:call-template |
          xsl:apply-imports | xsl:for-each |
          xsl:value-of | xsl:copy-of |
          xsl:number | xsl:choose | xsl:if |
          xsl:text | xsl:copy | xsl:variable |
          xsl:message | xsl:fallback |
          xsl:processing-instruction | xsl:comment |
          xsl:element | xsl:attribute )* >
```

The attributes are as follows:

```
<!ATTLIST xsl:variable
              name        %qname;         #REQUIRED
              select      %expr;          #IMPLIED >
```

With all entities replaced, the true model is as follows:

```
<!ATTLIST xsl:variable
              name        NMTOKEN         #REQUIRED
              select      CDATA           #IMPLIED >
```

For example:

```
<xsl:variable name="Copyright">
  <xsl:text>(c) ACME Productions</xsl:text>
</xsl:variable>

<xsl:variable name="BookTitle" select="/book/title" />
```

Message element

The **Message** instruction is defined as follows:

```
<!ELEMENT xsl:message %template; >
```

With the entity replaced, the true model is as follows:

```
<!ELEMENT xsl:message ( #PCDATA |
          xsl:apply-templates | xsl:call-template |
          xsl:apply-imports | xsl:for-each |
          xsl:value-of | xsl:copy-of |
          xsl:number | xsl:choose | xsl:if |
          xsl:text | xsl:copy | xsl:variable |
          xsl:message | xsl:fallback |
          xsl:processing-instruction | xsl:comment |
          xsl:element | xsl:attribute )* >
```

The attributes are as follows:

```
<!ATTLIST xsl:message
              terminate         (yes|no)         "no"
              %space-att; >
```

With the entity replaced, the true model is as follows:

```
<!ATTLIST xsl:message
     terminate             (yes|no)                "no"
     xml:space             (default|preserve)    #IMPLIED >
```

For example:

```
<xsl:message>Error in processing</xsl:message>
```

Fallback element

The **Fallback** instruction is defined as follows:

```
<!ELEMENT xsl:fallback %template; >
```

With the entity replaced, the true model is as follows:

```
<!ELEMENT xsl:fallback ( #PCDATA |
          xsl:apply-templates | xsl:call-template |
          xsl:apply-imports | xsl:for-each |
          xsl:value-of | xsl:copy-of |
          xsl:number | xsl:choose | xsl:if |
          xsl:text | xsl:copy | xsl:variable |
          xsl:message | xsl:fallback |
          xsl:processing-instruction | xsl:comment |
          xsl:element | xsl:attribute )* >
```

The attributes are as follows:

```
<!ATTLIST xsl:fallback          %space-att; >
```

With the entity replaced, the true model is as follows:

```
<!ATTLIST xsl:fallback
     xml:space             (default|preserve)    #IMPLIED >
```

Instruction constructs

Some of the instructions described above have a very specific internal structure, including references to elements not described above.

Apply Templates element

The **Apply Templates** element has the following content model:

```
<!ELEMENT xsl:apply-templates
                         (xsl:sort|xsl:with-param)*>
```

Note that the With Parameter element is discussed later (see *Call template*).

The **Sort** element is defined as follows:

```
<!ELEMENT xsl:sort EMPTY >
```

The attributes are as follows:

```
<!ATTLIST xsl:sort
          select        %expr;          "no"
          lang          %avt;           #IMPLIED
          data-type     %avt;           "text"
          order         %avt;           "ascending"
          case-order    %avt;           #IMPLIED >
```

With all entities replaced, the true model is as follows:

```
<!ATTLIST xsl:sort
          select        CDATA           "no"
          lang          CDATA           #IMPLIED
          data-type     CDATA           "text"
          order         CDATA           "ascending"
          case-order    CDATA           #IMPLIED >
```

For example:

```
<xsl:apply-templates>
  <xsl:sort select="firstname"/>
</xsl:apply-templates>
```

Call Template element

The **Call Template** element has the following content model:

```
<!ELEMENT xsl:call-template (xsl:with-param)* >
```

The **With Parameter** element has the following definition:

```
<!ELEMENT xsl:with-param %template; >
```

The expanded model for this element is as follows:

```
<!ELEMENT xsl:with-param ( #PCDATA |
          xsl:apply-templates | xsl:call-template |
          xsl:apply-imports | xsl:for-each |
          xsl:value-of | xsl:copy-of |
          xsl:number | xsl:choose | xsl:if |
          xsl:text | xsl:copy | xsl:variable |
          xsl:message | xsl:fallback |
          xsl:processing-instruction | xsl:comment |
          xsl:element | xsl:attribute )* >
```

The attributes are as follows:

```
<!ATTLIST xsl:with-param
            name      %qname;     #REQUIRED
            select    %expr;      #IMPLIED >
```

With all entities replaced, the true model is as follows:

```
<!ATTLIST xsl:with-param
                name        NMTOKEN        #REQUIRED
                select      CDATA          #IMPLIED >
```

Choose element

The **Choose** element has the following content model:

```
<!ELEMENT xsl:choose (xsl:when+, xsl:otherwise?) >
```

The When element must occur at least once, and may repeat any number of times. It is defined as follows:

```
<!ELEMENT xsl:when %template; >
```

The expanded model for this element is as follows:

```
<!ELEMENT xsl:when ( #PCDATA |
           xsl:apply-templates | xsl:call-template |
           xsl:apply-imports | xsl:for-each |
           xsl:value-of | xsl:copy-of |
           xsl:number | xsl:choose | xsl:if |
           xsl:text | xsl:copy | xsl:variable |
           xsl:message | xsl:fallback |
           xsl:processing-instruction | xsl:comment |
           xsl:element | xsl:attribute )* >
```

The attributes are as follows:

```
<!ATTLIST xsl:when
     test           %expr;                    #REQUIRED
     %space-att; >
```

With the entity replaced, the true model is as follows:

```
<!ATTLIST xsl:when
     test           CDATA                     #REQUIRED
     xml:space      (default|preserve)        #IMPLIED >
```

The **Otherwise** element is optional, but if present must occur at the end in the following format:

```
<!ELEMENT xsl:otherwise %template; >
```

The expanded model for this element is as follows:

```
<!ELEMENT xsl:otherwise ( #PCDATA |
          xsl:apply-templates | xsl:call-template |
          xsl:apply-imports | xsl:for-each |
          xsl:value-of | xsl:copy-of |
          xsl:number | xsl:choose | xsl:if |
          xsl:text | xsl:copy | xsl:variable |
          xsl:message | xsl:fallback |
          xsl:processing-instruction | xsl:comment |
          xsl:element | xsl:attribute )* >
```

The attributes are as follows:

```
<!ATTLIST xsl:otherwise      %space-att; >
```

With the entity replaced, the true model is as follows:

```
<!ATTLIST xsl:otherwise
     xml:space      (default|preserve)         #IMPLIED >
```

For example:

```
<xsl:choose>
  <xsl:when test="@colour='red'">...</xsl:when>
  <xsl:when test="@colour='green'">...</xsl:when>
  <xsl:when test="@colour='blue'">...</xsl:when>
  <xsl:otherwise>...</xsl:otherwise>
</xsl:choose>
```

Result elements

A template may also contain result elements, such as HTML or XSL FO elements. Because the nature of these elements is potentially infinite, it was not possible for the XSLT DTD creators to include them directly. Instead, a mechanism to make it easy to include them in variants of the XSLT DTD has been included.

The **Result Elements** entity is used to name output elements to be added to the XSLT elements. The value of this entity depends on the result elements needed. This could be the complete set of HTML elements, the FO elements from the XSL specification, or some other set of elements:

```
<!ENTITY % result-elements "...">
```
```
<!ENTITY % result-elements "html:P | html:H1 |
                            html:H2 | ..." >
```

As already shown above, this entity is referenced from the Template element definition. It is also referenced from the For Each element definition, and from the Template entity:

```
<!ELEMENT xsl:template  (...%result-elements;)*>

<!ELEMENT xsl:for-each  (...%result-elements;...)*>

<!ENTITY % template  "(...%result-elements;)*">
```

However, it is not sufficient to enter the element names in this entity. It is also necessary to add declarations for the elements in the result elements DTD. However, the original definitions should not be used. Instead, declarations that allow XSLT elements to be mixed in with these elements are needed. Reference to the Template entity is sufficient, as this entity in turn refers to the XSLT instruction elements as well as all the result elements.

```
<!ENTITY % template " (#PCDATA %instructions;
                %result-elements;)* " >
```

For example, if the HTML paragraph element is being added, as shown above, it is necessary to add the following declaration as well:

```
<!ELEMENT html:P (%template;)>
```

Note, however, that this approach removes any restrictions on the use of result elements in relation to each other that will typically be included in the original DTD.

At least four attributes also need to be added to an element. This is in addition to any attributes the element normally has. These are the **Use Attribute Sets**, **Extension Element Prefixes**, **Exclude Result Prefixes** and **Version** attributes:

```
<!ATTLIST html:P ...
        xsl:extension-element-prefixes CDATA    #IMPLIED
        xsl:exclude-result-prefixes    CDATA    #IMPLIED
        xsl:use-attribute-sets         %qnames; #IMPLIED
        xsl:version                    NMTOKEN  #IMPLIED>
```

To assist with adding these attributes to each result element, an entity called **Result Element Attributes** is included in the DTD:

```
<!ENTITY % result-element-atts  "
        xsl:extension-element-prefixes CDATA    #IMPLIED
        xsl:exclude-result-prefixes    CDATA    #IMPLIED
        xsl:use-attribute-sets         %qnames; #IMPLIED
        xsl:version                    NMTOKEN  #IMPLIED ">

<!ATTLIST html:P  ... %result-element-atts;>

<!ATTLIST html:H1  ... %result-element-atts;>
```

This entity can be empty in the case where no output elements are needed, and the Element element is used to declare output elements:

```
<!ENTITY % result-elements " ">
```

34. ISO 8859/1 character set

The character set most commonly used on the Web, and therefore by HTML and XSL, is ISO 8859/1. This character set is based on ASCII, and adds characters for common accented letters in latin-based languages.

Character set table

The **ISO 8859/1** character set is used by HTML and forms the basis of Microsoft Windows fonts (although reserved places are filled with extra characters in the Windows version) and UNIX fonts (for example, Open Windows). The first 128 characters are derived from the **ISO/IEC 646** version of **ASCII**. The remaining 128 characters cover European accented characters and further common symbols. The official ISO name for each character is placed in brackets, for example 'Solidus (slash)'.

Any XML document that uses this character set must include a reference to it in the XML declaration at the top of the document:

```
<?xml version="1.0" standalone="no" encoding="ISO-8859-1"?>
```

Any XML entity that uses this character set must include a reference to it in the encodin processing instruction at the top of the entity:

```
<?xml encoding="ISO-8859-1"?>
```

Any of these characters can be inserted into an XSLT or XSL document (or indeed any XML document) using an XML character entity reference, '&#...;'. For example, '&#233' represents the character 'é'.

Decimal and Hex	Char	Description
000 00		*NUL no effect*
001 01		*SOH – Start of Heading*
002 02		*STX – Start of Text*
003 03		*ETX – End of Text*
004 04		*EOT – End of Transmission*
005 05		*ENQ – Enquiry*

006	06		*ACK – Acknowledge*
007	07		*BEL – Bell*
008	08		*BS – Backspace*
009	09		HT – Horizontal Tab, HTML Tab
010	0A		LF – Line Feed, HTML new-line (with or without '013'), **record start (RS)**
011	0B		*VT – Vertical Tabulation*
012	0C		FF – Form Feed
013	0D		CR – Carriage return, HTML new-line (with or without '010'), **record end (RE)**
014	0E		*SO – Shift Out*
015	0F		*SI – Shift In*
016	10		*DLE – Data Link Escape*
017	11		*DC1 – Device Control (1)*
018	12		*DC2 – Device Control (2)*
019	13		*DC3 – Device Control (3)*
020	14		*DC4 – Device Control (4)*
021	15		*NAK – No Acknowledge*
022	16		*SYN – Synchronize*
023	17		*ETB – End of Transmission Block*
024	18		*CAN – Cancel*
025	19		*EM – End of Medium*
026	1A		*SUB – Substitute Character*
027	1B		*ESC – Escape*
028	1C		*FS – File Separator*
029	1D		*GS – Group Separator*
030	1E		*RS – Record Separator*
031	1F		*US – Unit Separator*
032	20		Space (space)
033	21	!	Exclamation (exclam)
034	22	"	Quotation (quotedbl), literal (use " in attributes with literal delimiters)
035	23	#	Number sign (numbersign), **reserved name indicator** ('#PCDATA')
036	24	$	Dollar sign (dollar)
037	25	%	Percent sign (percent), parameter entity reference open delimiter ('%ent;')
038	26	&	Ampersand (ampersand), entity reference open delimiter ('&ent;'), character reference open delimiter ('&#26;')
039	27	'	Apostrophe sign, literal alternative delimiter (use ' in attributes with literal alternative delimiters)
040	28	(	Left parenthesis (parenleft), group open delimiter ('(a, b)')
041	29	)	Right parenthesis (parenright), group close delimiter ('(a, b)')
042	2A	*	Asterisk (asterisk), optional and repeatable symbol ('a, b*')
043	2B	+	Plus sign (plus), required and repeatable symbol ('a, b+')
044	2C	,	Comma (comma), **sequence connector** ('a, b, c')
045	2D	-	Hyphen (hyphen), comment delimiter ('-- my comment --')
046	2E	.	Full point (period)
047	2F	/	Solidus (slash), end-tag open delimiter ('</tag>')
048	30	0	Zero (zero)
049	31	1	One (one)
050	32	2	Two (two)
051	33	3	Three (three)

052 34	4	Four (four)
053 35	5	Five (five)
054 36	6	Six (six)
055 37	7	Seven (seven)
056 38	8	Eight (eight)
057 39	9	Nine (nine)
058 3A	:	Colon (colon)
059 3B	;	Semicolon (semicolon), **reference close** ('&ent;')
060 3C	<	Less than (less), start tag open delimiter, end-tag open delimiter ('</'),
061 3D	=	Equals (equal), **value indicator** ('attrib=" value" ')
062 3E	>	Greater than (greater), **markup declaration close** ('<!.......>'), **processing instruction close** ('<?proc>'), **tag-close** ('<tag>')
063 3F	?	Question mark (question), **optional occurrence indicator** ('a|b'), **processing instruction open** ('<?')
064 40	@	Commercial at (at)
065 41	A	A
066 42	B	B
067 43	C	C
068 44	D	D
069 45	E	E
070 46	F	F
071 47	G	G
072 48	H	H
073 49	I	I
074 4A	J	J
075 4B	K	K
076 4C	L	L
077 4D	M	M
078 4E	N	N
079 4F	O	O
080 50	P	P
081 51	Q	Q
082 52	R	R
083 53	S	S
084 54	T	T
085 55	U	U
086 56	V	V
087 57	W	W
088 58	X	X
089 59	Y	Y
090 5A	Z	Z
091 5B	[	Left square bracket (bracketleft), **declaration subset open** ('<!DOCTYPE ... [...]>'), **data tag group open**
092 5C	\	Reverse solidus (backslash)
093 5D	]	Right square bracket (bracketright), **declaration subset close** ('<!DOCTYPE ... [...]>'), **data tag group close**, **marked section close** (']]')
094 5E	^	Caret (asciicircum)
095 5F	_	Underscore (underscore)
096 60	`	Grave accent
097 61	a	a
098 62	b	b

099	63	c	c
100	64	d	d
101	65	e	e
102	66	f	f
103	67	g	g
104	68	h	h
105	69	i	i
106	6A	j	j
107	6B	k	k
108	6C	l	l
109	6D	m	m
110	6E	n	n
111	6F	o	o
112	70	p	p
113	71	q	q
114	72	r	r
115	73	s	s
116	74	t	t
117	75	u	u
118	76	v	v
119	77	w	w
120	78	x	x
121	79	y	y
122	7A	z	z
123	7B	{	Left curly brace (braceleft)
124	7C	|	Vertical bar (bar), **or connector**
125	7D	}	Right curly brace (braceright)
126	7E	~	Tilde (asciitilde)
127	7F		Delete (del), Checkerboard effect
128	80		WINDOWS CHARS, delete (del)
....			...
....			...
....			...
159	9F		WINDOWS CHARS
160	A0		NBS – Non-break space
161	A1	¡	Inverted exclamation (exclamdown)
162	A2	¢	Cent sign (cent)
163	A3	£	Pound sterling (pound)
164	A4	¤	General currency symbol (currency)
165	A5	¥	Yen sign (yen)
166	A6	¦	Broken vertical bar (pipe)
167	A7	§	Section sign (section)
168	A8	¨	Umlaut (dieresis)
169	A9	©	Copyright (copyrightserif)
170	AA	ª	Feminine ordinal (ordfeminine)
171	AB	«	Left angle quote (guillemotleft)
172	AC	¬	Not sign (logicalnot)
173	AD	-	Soft hyphen (hyphen)
174	AE	®	Registered trademark (registerserif)
175	AF	¯	Macron accent (macron)
176	B0	°	Degree sign (ring)
177	B1	±	Plus or minus (plusminus)
178	B2	²	Superscript two (Reserved)

179 B3	³	Superscript three (Reserved)
180 B4	´	Acute accent (acute)
181 B5	µ	Micro sign (Reserved)
182 B6	¶	Paragraph sign (paragraph)
183 B7	·	Middle dot (periodcentered)
184 B8	¸	Cedilla (cedilla)
185 B9	¹	Superscript one (Reserved)
186 BA	º	Masculine ordinale (ordmasculine)
187 BB	»	Right angle quote (guillemotright)
188 BC	¼	Fraction one-fourth (Reserved)
189 BD	½	Fraction one-half (Reserved)
190 BE	¾	Fraction three-fourths (Reserved)
191 BF	¿	Inverted question mark (questiondown)
192 C0	À	Capital A grave (Agrave)
193 C1	Á	Capital A acute (Aacute)
194 C2	Â	Capital A circumflex (Acircumflex)
195 C3	Ã	Capital A tilde (Atilde)
196 C4	Ä	Capital A umlaut (Adieresis)
197 C5	Å	Capital A ring (Aring)
198 C6	Æ	Capital AE diphthong (AE)
199 C7	Ç	Capital C cedilla (Ccedilla)
200 C8	È	Capital E grave (Egrave)
201 C9	É	Capital E acute (Eacute)
202 CA	Ê	Capital E circumflex (Ecircumflex)
203 CB	Ë	Capital E umlaut (Edieresis)
204 CC	Ì	Capital I grave (Igrave)
205 CD	Í	Capital I acute (Iacute)
206 CE	Î	Capital I circumflex (Icircumflex)
207 CF	Ï	Capital I umlaut (Idieresis)
208 D0	Ð	Capital Eth Icelandic (Reserved)
209 D1	Ñ	Capital N tilde (Ntilde)
210 D2	Ò	Capital O grave (Ograve)
211 D3	Ó	Capital O acute (Oacute)
212 D4	Ô	Capital O circumflex (Ocircumflex)
213 D5	Õ	Capital O tilde (Otilde)
214 D6	Ö	Capital O umlaut (Odieresis)
215 D7	×	Multiply sign (Reserved)
216 D8	Ø	Capital O slash (Oslash)
217 D9	Ù	Capital U grave (Ugrave)
218 DA	Ú	Capital U acute (Uacute)
219 DB	Û	Capital U circumflex (circumflex)
220 DC	Ü	Capital U umlaut (Udieresis)
221 DD	Ý	Capital Y acute (Reserved)
222 DE	Þ	Capital THORN Icelandic (Reserved)
223 DF	ß	Small sharp s, sz ligature (germandbls)
224 E0	à	Small a grave (agrave)
225 E1	á	Small a acute (aacute)
226 E2	â	Small a circumflex (acircumflex)
227 E3	ã	Small a tilde (atilde)
228 E4	ä	Small a umlaut (adieresis)
229 E5	å	Small a ring (aring)
230 E6	æ	Small ae diphthong, ligature (ae)
231 E7	ç	Small c cedilla (ccedilla)

232	E8	è	Small e grave (egrave)
233	E9	é	Small e acute (eacute)
234	EA	ê	Small e circumflex (ecircumflex)
235	EB	ë	Small e umlaut (edieresis)
236	EC	ì	Small i grave (igrave)
237	ED	í	Small i acute (iacute)
238	EE	î	Small i circumflex (icircumflex)
239	EF	ï	Small i umlaut (idieresis)
240	F0	ð	Small eth Icelandic (Reserved)
241	F1	ñ	Small n tilde (ntilde)
242	F2	ò	Small o grave (ograve)
243	F3	ó	Small o acute (oacute)
244	F4	ô	Small o circumflex (ocircumflex)
245	F5	õ	Small o tilde (otilde)
246	F6	ö	Small o umlaut (odieresis)
247	F7	÷	Division sign (Reserved)
248	F8	ø	Small o slash (oslash)
249	F9	ù	Small u grave (ugrave)
250	FA	ú	Small u acute (uacute)
251	FB	û	Small u circumflex (ucircumflex)
252	FC	ü	Small u umlaut (udieresis)
253	FD	ý	Small y acute (Reserved)
254	FE	þ	Small thorn Icelandic (Reserved)
255	FF	ÿ	Small y umlaut (ydieresis)

Index

NOTES: This index identifies terms explained in the main text (where they are displayed in bold). If the first occurrence in the text does not explain the term, then it is not shown in bold there, and not included in this index. All entries are shown in the present tense, singular form (except where the term is a syntactic token name or keyword, or is always used in another form). Entries with an initial capital letter, such as 'Text,' are DTD-specific element or attribute names. HTML element and attribute names have the suffix '(HTML)' to distinguish them from XSLT and XSL element and attribute names. For example, there is an entry for 'Text' and another for 'Text (HTML)'.